Accounting, Finance, and Taxation

ACCOUNTING, FINANCE, AND TAXATION

A Basic Guide for Small Business

C. RICHARD BAKER

RICK STEPHAN HAYES

CBI

CBI Publishing Company, Inc.
51 Sleeper Street
Boston, Massachusetts 02210

Library of Congress Cataloging in Publication Data

Baker, C. Richard, 1946–
    Accounting, finance, and taxation.

    Bibliography: p.
    Includes index.
    1. Accounting.   2. Financial statements.
3. Small business—Finance. 4. Small business—
Taxation.   I. Hayes, Rick Stephan, 1946–   joint
author.   II. Title.
HF5635.B16   658.1'5904   79–16481
ISBN 0–8436–0784–X

Printed in the United States of America

Printing (last digit): 9 8 7 6 5 4 3 2

Contents

Introduction

Accounting is the language of business. But a knowledge of accounting alone is not enough, even for the accountant or CPA. Many other things in business run in courses parallel to accounting and affect it. Taxation affects accounting critically, as do government regulations and the regulations by accounting societies. Finance, too, is an extension of accounting in its use of ratios and ratio analysis. Furthermore, computer technology and international regulations expand and complicate the world of accounting.

In this book, we have taken a broad approach to the complexities of modern accounting, tracing its philosophical and historical beginnings that have culminated in present-day technological miracles of the computer. Our goal is to answer many of the questions of accounting without becoming mired in its intricacies. In short, we have tried to pique the imagination of the reader into realizing the worldwide ramifications of accounting.

Most accounting books read like tax statutes; but this does not have to be. If you believe that accounting is less than interesting, then read on, for this book is very different. It is different because of its use of simple examples and analogies, as well as its many drawings, graphs, tables, and sample forms that simplify many accounting complexities. It is different because the authors have placed accounting in context—in its own historical and philosophical niche, as it were. Indeed, the study of accounting can be stimulating.

Historically, accounting was conceived in 3500 B.C. in the plains of ancient Sumeria. It has grown and developed into, and coexists with, electronic computers, which have existed only since 1949. Accounting has come far, and is still developing. The authors are, however, primarily concerned that this book will be practical—attempting to deal pragmatically with the technical needs of the practitioner. The book touches, but does not dally in the theoretical.

Subjects covered include bookkeeping and basic journals and ledgers, including useful forms; the tax implications of expenses and income; and the tax and financial aspects of the balance-sheet items and accounts. In the areas of finance and management, there are chapters on cash management, debt and financing, leasing, pension and executive compensation, budgeting, and foreign operations. From the legal standpoint, we have a chapter on forms of business organizations. And, of course, there are financial and accounting review chapters on inventory, depreciation, and another chapter called "Computers and Accounting."

It is our hope that the readers will find our explanations both practical and enjoyable—and that they will sense the book's spirit.

1

Double-Entry Bookkeeping and Account Systems

The first part of this chapter is essentially a simple and straightforward review of bookkeeping fundamentals for the reader who has never been exposed to bookkeeping or for the reader who wishes to bring his or her knowledge of the subject up to date.

The fundamental basis of accounting is balance. Balance in accounting is represented by the equation:

assets = liabilities (creditors' rights) + capital (owners' rights)

Or, put another way:

property = financial interest

Or, when making or checking bookkeeping entries:

a debit = a credit

This principle is the fundamental accounting equation, the framework on which all business records are built.

The double-entry bookkeeping system, used universally by business, is an institutionalization of this equation. An entry in one account (a debit) requires an entry in another account (a credit). If a piece of equipment is purchased for the business, a check is written for the amount of the equipment cost and the business takes possession of the equipment. This transaction requires an entry in the cash account (a credit) and an entry in the equipment asset account (a debit) for an equal amount.

Balance, in the philosophical sense, was not invented by accountants. Science has similar laws of balance: there is gravitation and its opposite, centrifugal force. There are electrons (a negative charge) and protons (a positive charge). Night and day, male and female, earth and atmosphere — all are nature's balances. By achieving balance, understanding is possible. An accountant tries to balance numbers representing dollars in order that transactions of a business can be understood.

To comprehend the origins of accounting, let us go back about 5,000 years into a time the historians call prehistory. Archeologists have established that trade existed between tribes and also between villages during this era. Although there were no written records of this trade, excavations have uncovered pottery and other artifacts in one place that were manufactured in another place.

At some point, trade must have become so complex that no one man could remember it all. Therefore, in order to keep track of the trades of four sheep for twenty pounds of spices, or of building material for gold, the transactions had to be recorded. Records of business transactions in cuneiform characters from the Sumer region of ancient Iraq, which is located along the Tigris and Euphrates rivers, are the earliest known written records.

For thousands of years, trade transactions were recorded on clay, paper, and stone. The implementation of laws, such as the right to own property, required further records. If a businessperson had property without having a written record of ownership the law of the land could be used to take the property away and give it to the person who did have a written record, or deed, to that property. Business records thus became numerous and complex.

Organizing these records of business transactions became a necessity. The first step in organizing was to collect all the records (bills of sale and written receipts) and put their totals into one place — one book. Thus, a businessperson or merchant did not have to search all his stacks of records to determine how much lapis lazuli he had exchanged for twelve containers of bitumen the previous year, in Babylon. He consulted one book. Consequently, the present-day *journal* evolved. This procedure probably worked very well for a thousand years or so.

As time passed, recordkeeping became even more complex. During the Middle Ages (1300 AD to 1700 AD) taxes became important in supporting large towns and, incidentally, the luxuries of princes. Tax agencies became sophisticated enough to know when a merchant was underpaying his required taxes. Merchants, in many instances, were carrying out what amounted to worldwide trade. The single-entry journal was no longer sufficient to handle the many demands for information.

In order that businesspeople could keep track of what was spent or taken in from various areas, the idea of separating journal entries into categories of accounts was conceived. The advantage of keeping a book showing expenditures and income separated by subject (rent, salaries) was obvious. The use of only one journal necessitated consulting several different days' entries to discern the amount for salaries paid during the month. If all the salaries were kept separately under an independent account, one could look at a single page to find the salaries for several months, instead of searching through twenty or more journal pages. This kind of book of entries today is called a *ledger*.

With both a journal and a ledger, the businessperson could not only know at a glance what each day's transactions were, without looking at all the original sheets of paper (sales or refund slips, cash-register tapes), but he could also find out each category (account) total of expenditures or income.

Again, this journal and ledger, single-entry system worked for a few hundred years. However, another problem was developing. With books that were in fact symbolic representations, once or twice removed from the original transaction papers, control was lost. People make mistakes, and if three entries are made of the same item, or totals of items, there are three chances to make mistakes. The question became: "What can be done to minimize these mistakes, to check on each entry to assure accuracy?" It had to be a simple proces — one that required a minimum amount of time, and one easily checked by an outside person. At the time this problem arose, no one could conceive of the electronic computer in use today to insure accuracy. So how was this problem solved?

DEBITS AND CREDITS: THE ACCOUNTING BALANCING ACT

Most people believe that the double-entry bookkeeping system was devised within the last two centuries. This system is still the best way to check the accuracy of bookkeeping entries. The double-entry system does not tell where a mistake was made, but it does tell you that you have made a mistake. If all the entries do not balance, (if the debits do not equal the credits) then there is an error.

This discussion brings us back to balance. The person who invented the double-entry system probably thought: "If each entry is made in a negative way in one place and in a positive way in another, the negative and the positive should both add up to the same number since the negative and the positive added together results in zero. Balance." Perhaps he showed it in graphic form. (See Exhibit 1.1.)

EXHIBIT 1.1
The Accounts Circle: Balance in the Double-Entry System

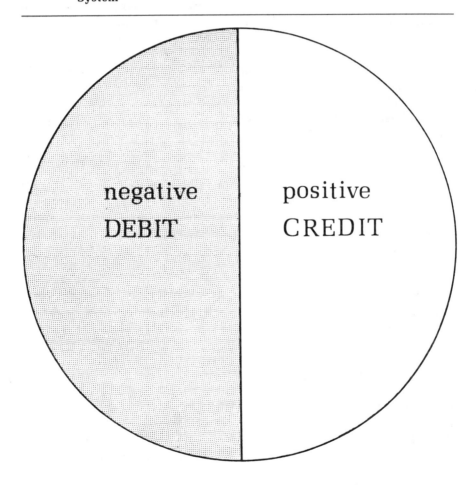

One side of this equation was called debit, from the Latin noun *debitum* (debt), and the other side credit, from the Latin noun *creditum* (trust, loan). Today, if you trust someone enough to loan this person money, you would credit your cash account for the amount of the money and debit the notes receivable account for the amount the person owes you. Put another way, if you give someone cash, you certainly want to take credit for it.

The double-entry system was balanced and orderly. In fact, it worked so well for lending transactions that people tried to apply this logic to all the business accounts. To accomplish this, the accounts were divided into negative and positive sides. This process was difficult because there had to be some logic between positive and negative accounts. It could not be purely arbitrary. Since *money*, especially money to "create a business with," usually carries positive connotations, the adapters made the creative money accounts (income) positive and made the others (expenses) negative. Creative money accounts will be called conductive accounts.

Conductive accounts represent money put into the system (business) from the outside. Conductive accounts cannot, by themselves, make a business productive. They represent money from outside the business that must be channeled through a cash account (checking account) before it can be used to pay for the equipment, services, and people, which in turn produce more money. *Income* is a conductive account. Income comes into the business through sales to companies and persons outside the business. Sales do not pay bills directly, but generate cash to pay expenses, buy equipment, and keep the business going. Income, therefore, is a conductive account.

Borrowed money is also conductive, for it is cash or goods received to go into your business to activate it. By itself the money represents an obligation to be paid in cash, but the money borrowed or paid back must recycle through another intermediary account, the cash account. The money you borrow, *liabilities*, by itself is not productive, but conductive. Liabilities transmit money into the system, but do not, by themselves, make the business productive. Liabilities are not tangible, as is equipment. Furthermore, the company does not receive services or goods directly from borrowed money (as is the case with expenses).

The money you put into the business or get out of the business, *owners equity*, is also conductive. It is similar to a liability in that it is an obligation of the company that by itself is neither productive nor tangible. *Owners' equity* represents the initial money put into the business by the owners (capital stock) and the amount that the business has retained for the owners (retained earnings). As with liabilities, this account does not pay the bills; but the money put into his account goes through the intermediary cash account. The equity account is conductive money,

money that comes into the business to create business activity, but that has to be channeled through the cash account to become productive.

These three accounts — income, liabilities, and equity — have their nonproductivity in common, in terms of income. They have nothing to do with paying for the services, material, and personnel required to run a business. Catalytic in effect, they function like a copper wire that conducts electricity to the doorbell. The wire conducts the energy to make the bell ring, but the wire does not produce the sound — the bell does. The wire is conductive. The bell is productive. Let us put these three accounts on the positive, right-hand (credit) side, graphically, of debit and credit. (See Exhibit 1.2.) Conductive accounts usually have a credit balance.

The remaining major account groups are *assets, expenses,* and *cost of sales.* Productive, tangible, and representative of money applied, these three groups fit into the left, or debit side, of the example, opposite the income, liabilities, and equity accounts.

Assets such as equipment, land, and property are easily recognized as productive. Inventory of materials, for instance, are visibly productive, for with no inventory to sell directly or to manufacture into a finished product, there are no sales. Since sales cannot be produced without inventory, it follows that inventory is required to produce sales. Accounts and notes receivable do not produce sales, but they do produce money. Directly convertible (by discounting through a bank) to money, accounts and notes receivable are money producers. By buying other assets, such as equipment and inventory, the cash account is the intermediary that takes money and makes it productive. This same account also pays for the services and people required to run the machinery and distribute the product. In essence, cash is the most productive of the asset accounts. Not only are there no sales, but also business effectively comes to a halt without cash.

It may be difficult, at first, to visualize how expenses (such as rent, office salaries, utilities) and cost of sales (material, factory labor, freight) can be productive. When it is recognized that the machines that produce solid-state mousetraps need people and electricity to make them run, it is apparent in what way expenses are productive. No solid-state mousetraps can be produced if you do not have material, people in the warehouse, supervisors, salesmen, telephones, paper clips, and a roof over your head.

Cost of sales, including material cost and freight, factory labor, factory overhead, and selling expense, is easily visible as a productive group of accounts. Literally, cost of sales encompasses the entire cost to you of selling your product. Possession of stock to sell implies that all costs of acquiring it have been met. Logically, you cannot market a solid-state mousetrap until you have one to sell. Therefore, money spent to pay cost

EXHIBIT 1.2
The Accounts Circle: The Positive Attributes of Credit

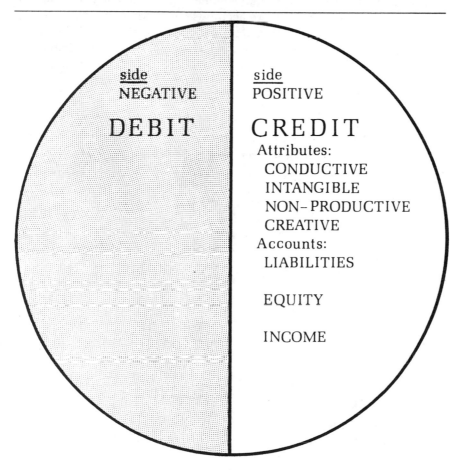

of sales can be considered money spent to make the business productive.

Even if you have the product to sell, other expenses are necessary to run the business. Telephones, people to type reports and letters, electricity to run your coffee machine, and business cards are operating expenses. They are the costs of operating the nonsales-related part of the business. These are the necessary costs of running the business; without services and people, the business would not be productive. Therefore, these accounts are productive.

These three groups of accounts — *Assets, Expenses, and Cost of*

Sales — have a common denominator. They are necessary in making a business productive, but are not, by themselves, sales producing. These accounts represent applied money, money that is applied to practical, productive uses. Since all of these accounts represent money that is being paid out, or in use, we might consider these accounts negative. They are to be subtracted from the money generated by income, equity, and liabilities. All of these accounts will typically have a debit, left-hand balance. (See Exhibit 1.3.)

EXHIBIT 1.3
The Accounts Circle: Negative and Positive Attributes
are in Balance

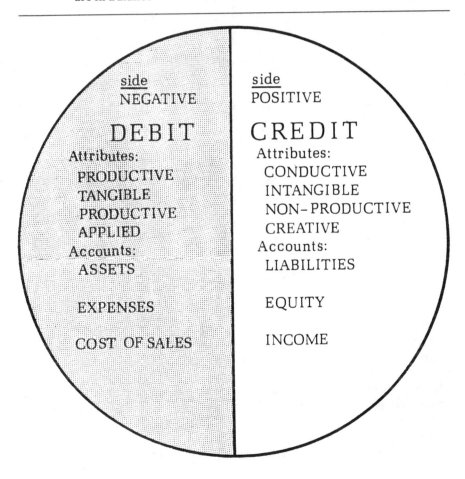

To increase one of the nonproductive, conductive accounts (income, liabilities, equity), the account must be credited. These accounts generally have a credit balance. In order to increase one of the productive, negative accounts (assets, expenses, and cost of sales), it is necessary to enter a debit in the account. In general, each account in the productive group of accounts has a debit balance. Conversely, everything that is increased must eventually be decreased. To decrease income, liabilities, and equity, the account is debited. To decrease assets, expenses, or cost of sales, the accounts must be credited. In other words, to decrease an account, an entry is made on the opposite side of the average balance, or increasing side. Since each account can be debited or credited, a further division to four sides is made, as shown graphically, in Exhibit 1.4.

Thus, the inventor of double-entry bookkeeping had a balanced system. The accounts are divided into two equal groups of accounts and can be increased or decreased by writing the figures on one side or the other (debit or credit). The system is also interreactive. Entries in one account cause opposite entries in another account. If liabilities are increased (credit) by borrowing money, that money increases the cash-asset account (debit). In other words, increases in the conductive group of accounts always cause increases in the productive group, and vice versa. Decreases in one group of accounts (debit for the conductive accounts) cause decreases in the opposite group of accounts (credit in the productive accounts). The opposite group of accounts work in tandem — increases or decreases in one cause increases or decreases in the other. Thus, the ideal of balance in business recordkeeping is achieved — all accounts are in equilibrium. When one account increases in value, in order to sustain equilibrium, an opposite account is increased in value. Since it is an opposite account, its increase is the opposite sign (debit or credit) of the first increase. By recording every transaction, double-entry bookkeeping shows this twofold effect twice. A debit entry in one account requires a credit entry in another. Either or both of the entries may be broken down into several items, but the total of the amounts entered as debits must equal the total of the amounts entered as credits.

Today, each account sheet in the ledger has a column for the date; one for the brief description of the entry; one for the posting reference; and two for dollar amounts. If the debit entries in an account total more than the credit entries, the account is said to have a debit balance (generally the case with assets, expenses, and cost of sales). If the credit entries total more than the debit entries, then the account has a credit balance (liabilities, equity, and income). The total of all the credit balances must equal the total of all the debit balances.

EXHIBIT 1.4
The Accounts Circle: The Interaction of Increase and
Decrease

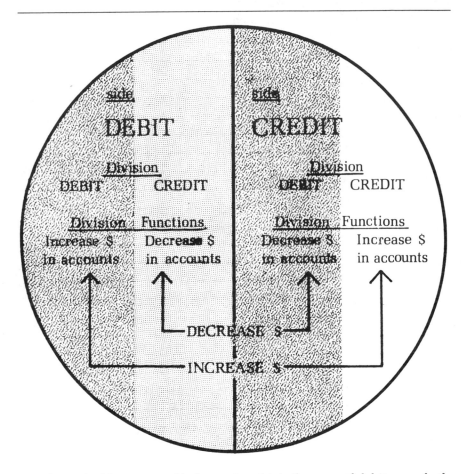

Through this system of balance, in which the sum of debits equals the sum of credits, the businessperson is able to verify all entries.

CHART OF ACCOUNTS

QUESTION: *What constitutes a business expense, asset, or liability?*
ANSWER:
The answer to this question is difficult to arrive at because it is subject to

legal interpretation. In most states and countries, the government defines expenses, assets, liabilities, and debts.

Before deciding what constitutes a legitimate expenditure or debt of a business, a definition of business is necessary. The Internal Revenue Service *Publication 583* states: "A business is a pursuit carried on for livelihood or for profit. For a pursuit to be recognized as a business, a profit motive must be present and some type of economic activity must be involved. Two characteristic elements of a business are regularity of activities and transactions and the production of income."

If a person makes payments, borrows money, or purchases assets that are used regularly in the activities and transactions of a business, or are used to produce income, then these transactions are related to the business. (See Exhibit 1.5.)

EXHIBIT 1.5
Some assets, liabilities, and expenses that are generally considered to be legitimate business-related accounts.

Assets

Cash
Inventory
Accounts receivable (sales that have not been collected)
Notes receivable (short-term money owed to your company)
Prepaid expenses (money advanced for services or goods not yet received)
Short-term investments
Equipment (for business use)
Land and building (for business use)
Leasehold improvements
Goodwill paid when the business was acquired
Long-term investments
Certain development costs

Liabilities
(money or goods not paid for but used for business purposes)

Accounts and notes payable
Provisions for pensions and taxes
Accrued items
Mortgages
Bonds and debentures
Long-term debt
Deferred taxes

EXHIBIT 1.5
continued

Expenses
(including cost of sales)

Rent or leases (for equipment or real property)
Outside services (accounting, consulting, janitorial, trash pick up, security)
Personnel salaries
Payroll taxes and benefit plans for employees
Entertainment required by the business
Travel required for business purposes
Material purchased
Supplies purchased
Inventory purchased
Freight
Utilities
Business license and local taxes
Equipment or tools with a life of one year or less
Repairs and maintenance
Certain clothing and laundry expenses

Equity accounts represent money put into or retained by the business. Equity includes stock in the company (preferred, common, or treasury), paid-in surplus, retained earnings, and interest in subsidiaries. When these accounts are arranged under the basic groups (assets, liabilities, equity, income, expenses, and cost of sales), the result is a *chart of accounts*.

Since there probably will be many different accounts in business records, it is necessary to establish a plan for identifying each account and locating it quickly. If, in addition to listing all the accounts under the above groups, numbers are assigned to them, identification becomes much easier. In developing an index, or chart of accounts, blocks of numbers are assigned to each group of accounts. For example, assets are assigned to the block of numbers from 100 to 199 (or 1000 to 1999 for large companies with many accounts); liabilities have the numbers 200 to 299 (2000 to 2999). (See Exhibit 1.6.)

EXHIBIT 1.6
Chart of Accounts

Account #	Account Name
100–199	*Assets*
101	Cash
110	Accounts Receivable
115	Notes Receivable
120	Prepaid Expense
120.1	Prepaid Rent
130	Equipment
130.18	1970 Dodge pick-up Truck
200–299	*Liabilities*
201	Accounts Payable
201.29	Accounts Payable—Associated Wagontongues
211	Notes Payable
211.2	Notes Payable Bank of Suez
221	Etc.
300–399	*Owners' Equity*
301	Capital Stock
310	Preferred Stock
330	Retained Earnings
. . . . .	Etc.
400–499	*Income*
401	Income from Operations
401.3	Income from Model B solid state Mousetrap
401.5	Income from Mousetrap accessories
410	Interest Income
450	Income from Extraordinary Items
. . . . .	Etc.
500–599	*Operating Expense*
501	Salary Expense

EXHIBIT 1.6
continued

501.7	Officer's Salary
505	Payroll Taxes
505.2	Administrative employees payroll Tax
508	Rent Expense
572	Small Tool Expense
. . . . .	Etc.
600–699	*Cost-of-Sales Expense*
601	Material Purchases
601.62	Purchases of steel hatchets
610	Factory Salaries
610.3	Factory Salaries, Plant #3
. . . . .	Etc.

The Basic Records and Books

The documents of business transactions fall into three groups: basic records (usually required by law), journals, and ledgers. The businessman of the eighteenth and nineteenth century had these same documents, but in a different format from that of today. The basic records of the business, such as summaries of cash receipts and of cash disbursements, date back to early history. The journals, ledgers, and double-entry bookkeeping system developed later.

In 3200 BC, summaries of business transactions for money or goods were written on clay tablets; at the present time, they are written on paper or printed by some mechanical device (cash register or computer). Not only has the method of writing these summaries changed, but what the summaries contain has changed as well. In the past, these summaries listed animals or objects bought, and their prices (3 sheep, 2 stacks of wood for 3 shekels of silver). Presently, the cash summaries show cash and collections from different departments, such as sales tax, miscellaneous receipts of money, cash in the register, and petty cash slips.

Basic Records

The *Daily Summary of Sales and Cash Receipts* records cash sales and

EXHIBIT 1.7
Daily Summary of Sales and Cash Receipts

DAILY SUMMARY OF SALES AND CASH RECEIPTS

Date March 23, 19—

CASH RECEIPTS

1. Cash sales		$435.00
2. Collections on account		100.00
3. Miscellaneous receipts [1]		15.00
4. TOTAL RECEIPTS TO BE ACCOUNTED FOR.		$550.00

CASH ON HAND

5. Cash in register or till:		
Coins	$ 25.00	
Bills	510.00	
Checks	95.00	
Total cash in register or till		$630.00
6. Petty-cash slips		14.00
7. TOTAL CASH ACCOUNTED FOR		$644.00
8. Less change and petty-cash fund:		
Petty-cash slips	$14.00	
Coins and bills	86.00	
Change and petty-cash fund (fixed amount)...		100.00
9. TOTAL CASH DEPOSIT		$544.00
10. CASH SHORT (Item 4 less item 9 if item 4 is larger).		$6.00
11. CASH OVER (Item 9 less item 4 if item 9 is larger).		——

TOTAL SALES

12. Cash sales		$435.00
13. Charge sales (sales checks #262 to #316)		225.00
14. TOTAL SALES		$660.00

By JOHN DOE

[1] Note to appear on back of summary: "Miscellaneous receipts: Refund on merchandise $15.00."

Source: *Financial Recordkeeping for Small Stores*, SBA Management Series No. 32.

collections for the day, in addition to accounts for the cash over and above the amounts in evidence (number of checks or dollars in the till) or, on paper (petty cash slips). Exhibit 1.7 shows such a summary.

Cash Receipts records all cash taken in during the day from all sources (see Exhibit 1.8). Cash Sales is determined from reading the cash register or computer print out, or by totaling the cash-sales slips. *Collections on Account* is the total of customers' cash or checks paid to your company as partial payment on an accounts receivable. Sales that cannot be classified as cash sales, or collections on account, are miscellaneous receipts. These receipts may include supplier refunds, allowances, collections on rent from subleases or concessions, and handling charges on coupons. Miscellaneous receipts are usually itemized on the back of the *Daily Summary* or printed out at the bottom (for computerized systems).

EXHIBIT 1.8
Daily Summary of Cash Receipts

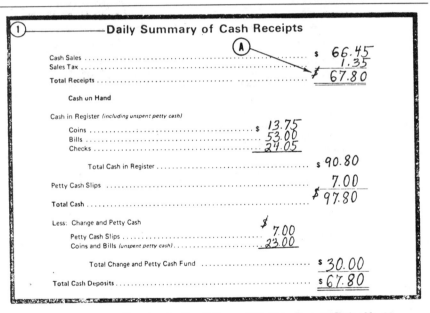

Source: *Financial Recordkeeping for Small Stores*, SBA Management Series No. 32.

Cash on Hand, represented by petty-cash slips is a count of the cash usually on hand. Cash in register or till is self-explanatory. It may be divided into bills, checks, coins, or denominations of bills and coins. Petty cash slips represent cash that has been paid out.

Some businesses also have printed weekly, monthly, or quarterly publications, *To Date Summaries of Cash Receipts*, consisting of summarized income activity for a given period, showing each item (receipts, sales, tax, and net sales) in separate columns. (See Exhibit 1.9.)

EXHIBIT 1.9
Monthly Summary of Cash Receipts

Date 1972	Daily Receipts	Sales Tax	Net Sales
Jan. 4	$67.80	$1.35	$66.45
5	59.70	1.19	58.51
6	75.20	1.50	73.70
7	68.40	1.39	67.01
8	57.40	1.15	56.25
Monthly Totals	$1,443.85	$28.92	$1,414.93

Source: *Financial Recordkeeping for Small Stores*, SBA Management Series No. 32.

The next basic record, the *Business Check Book*, is usually accompanied by a cash disbursements journal (discussed shortly). Before the advent of checking accounts and the modern banking system, businesses summarized their cash outlay much as they summarized their cash income.

Today all major payments made by a business are made by check. In many cases, a check can serve as a receipt, but usually every check has some sort of written document to support it — an invoice, bill, receipt slip, petty-cash voucher, or payroll record.

An *Employee Compensation Record* is kept for each full-time or part-time employee. It records the number of hours worked by the employee in a pay period and the individual's total pay. Withheld deductions (for state and federal taxes) are also recorded to show the computation of the employee's resulting net pay. Monthly gross payroll is also recorded. (See exhibit 1.10.)

Another separate basic record is a *Depreciation Record* (Exhibit 1.11). The sample depreciation record shows examples of items depreciated on the *straight line* and *declining balance* methods. The record is kept on a continuous basis over a period for which the item is depreciated. Deduction of depreciation for tax purposes is allowed only for property in use in a trade or business or held for production of income.

Journals

The journal is the daily summary of business transactions. Originally there was probably only one, the general journal, in which all transactions were recorded from the basic records. Because some types of transactions are continuous (such as cash disbursements) and others occur only at intervals (preparing a payroll), a series of special journals were developed. Today, there are about five types of journals: the sales and cash receipts journal, the cash disbursements journal, the purchases journal, the expense journal, and the general journal.

The *Sales and Cash Receipts Journal* records on one page the information from a number of Daily Summaries. Usually total sales, charge sales, collections on account, and the total cash deposit can be entered on the same line of the journal. (See Exhibit 1.12.) The amounts entered under Total Sales, Collections on Account, and Total Cash Deposit are taken from the Daily Summary items having the same identification as the journal columns. Items included in miscellaneous receipts on the Daily Summary and itemized on the summary sheet are generally identified in a description column and posted to the general ledger or expense journal. Miscellaneous receipts that represent either refunds on expense items or income not due to sales are entered in the credit column under Miscellaneous Income and Expense Items. This column includes receipts from rent collections, interest, refunds, and advertising rebates. Miscellaneous receipts that do not represent income or expense items are entered in the credit column under General Ledger Items, as are receipts for investment money or loan items. Proceeds from loans are entered directly in the journal rather than coming from the Daily Summary.

A company that sells primarily on credit, as do most large companies, maintains two separate journals — the *Sales Journal* and the *Cash Receipts Journal*. All sales on credit are recorded in the Sales Journal. All cash income on collections, or all cash sales, are recorded in the Cash Receipts Journal.

EXHIBIT 1.10
Employee Compensation Record

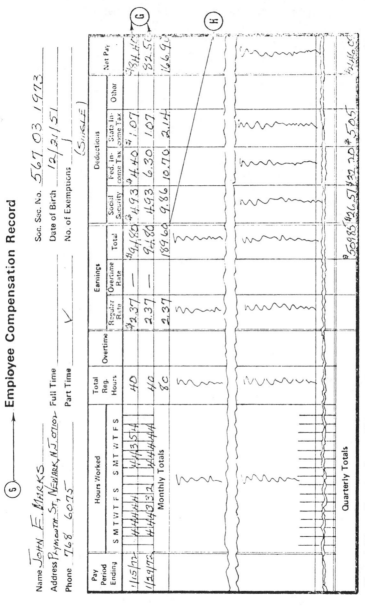

Source: *Financial Recordkeeping for Small Stores*, SBA Management Series No. 32.

EXHIBIT 1.11
Depreciation Record: Schedule C Entries

L I N E	Monthly Expenses						
	Rent	Interest	Taxes	Truck Exp (½ auto exp.)			Misc.
1	$ 150.00	$ 8.92	$ 69.51	$ 45.00			$ 3.00
2	150.00	8.92	—	28.50			2.80
3	150.00	8.92	—	32.80			2.65
4							
5							
6							
7							
8							
9							
10							
11							
12							
	$ 1,800.00	$ 107.04	$ 200.11	$ 540.00			$ 33.75

RECORD

19 70		19 71		19 72		19 73	
Depreciable Bal. Beginning of year	Depreciation This Year	Depreciable Bal. Beginning of year	Depreciation This Year	Depreciable Bal. Beginning of Year	Depreciation This Year	Depreciable Bal. Beginning of Year	Depreciation this year
1,840	460	1,380	460	920	460	460	
		3,418	967	1,451	530	871	
		300	50	250	105	150	
1,840	460	4,098	1,477	2,621	1,140	1,481	

(F)

Source: *Financial Recordkeeping for Small Stores*, SBA Management Series No. 32.

The Cash Disbursements Journal and Purchases Journal are sometimes combined in the *Cash Disbursements and Purchases Journal*, (shown in Exhibit 1.13). This combination journal is similar to a check register in the company checkbook. The standard journal has six columns, but more columns may be required. Columns may be added, for instance, for expenses (such as delivery and postage) that require several monthly payments. Expenses that normally have one or two payments a month (rent, for example) are entered in the debit column under Miscellaneous

EXHIBIT 1.12
Sales and Cash Receipts Journal

Date	Description and/or Account	PR	Total Sales (CR)	Charges to Customers (DR)	Collections on Account (CR)	Miscellaneous Income and Expense Items (DR)	Miscellaneous Income and Expense Items (CR)	General Ledger Items (DR)	General Ledger Items (CR)	Total Cash Deposit (DR)
19—	*Illustration I: Entries from exhibit 3*									
Mar 23	Daily Summary		660 00	225 00	100 00					544 00
	Refund on merchandise						15 00			
	Cash short					6 00				
	Illustration II: Entries from exhibit 16									
Mar 23	Daily Summary		660 00	225 00	100 00					562 00
	Refund on merchandise						15 00			
	Cash short					6 00				
	Exchange								18 00	

Source: *Financial Recordkeeping for Small Stores, SBA Management Series No. 32.*

EXHIBIT 1.13
Cash Disbursements, Purchases, and Expense Journal

Illustration 1: Miscellaneous entries—rent, merchandise purchase, asset purchase, spoiled check, payroll

Date 19—	Payee and/or Account	Ch. No.	Amount of Check (CR)	Merchandise Purchases (DR)	Gross Salaries (DR)	Income Tax (CR)	Soc. Sec. (CR)	Misc. Income and Expense (DR)	(CR)	General Ledger (DR)	(CR)
Jul 1	John Smith—Rent	92	200 00					200 00			
14	ABC Company	93	115 00	115 00							
19	Z Company—Furn. & Fix.	94	30 00							30 00	
	VOID	95									
20	Payroll	96	50 85		58 50	5 90	1 75				

Income and Expense Items. The General Ledger columns of the Cash Disbursements Journal are used only for entries that directly affect assets, liabilities, and capital of the business, which are recorded in the General Ledger.

Other companies, especially larger companies, separate the *Cash Disbursements Journal* from the *Purchases Journal.* The Cash Disbursements Journal is used to record every check written and has a sundry debits column that has the account numbers (from the chart of accounts, discussed earlier) and the dollar amounts of all the checks. It might also have a special column for accounts payable if many of the checks are to pay for trade credit. The *Purchases Journal* records all purchases on credit (not for cash). Included in the Purchases Journal are columns for invoice numbers, dates and terms, in addition to credits to accounts payable (increases in accounts payable brought about by purchases). If a trade account is paid off, the entry appears in the Cash Disbursements Journal.

The *General Journal*, a diary of business activities when used alone, is the book in which the analysis of each transaction is maintained. Before the development of the special journals, all entries went into a general journal. Today, however, when the special-purpose journals are in general use, the General Journal is used for all the transactions that do not fit into the other journals, such as complex payroll deductions and payments and acquisition of assets.

Ledgers

The ledger is the master reference book of the accounting system and provides a permanent and classified record of every element involved in the business operation. Weekly, monthly, or quarterly, all the journals are totaled and posted into ledgers. *Ledgers* are summaries of activities under each account in the chart of accounts. These ledgers are divided into two groups: a general ledger and a subsidiary ledger.

Originally, there was only the *General Ledger.* In it, all the accounts were posted after a given period from their respective journal or journals. Entries in the journal indicate what is to be debited and what is to be credited. With the journals as a guide, the accountant enters the information into the respective individual accounts. The accountant uses printed forms for account records. Each account is kept on a separate form, termed a *ledger sheet.* (See Exhibit 1.14.) All the accounts taken together comprise a ledger or book of final entry. Some accountants make up a balance sheet and profit-and-loss statement, posting from these statements into the ledger. Generally, however, the ledger is posted from the journals, and eventually a trial balance is made and put into the form of a balance sheet and income statement (profit-and-loss statement).

EXHIBIT 1.14
General Ledger Sheet

—General Ledger Sheet

Account:						No.	
			Items posted		**Balance**		
Date	**Description**	**PR**	**Debit**	**Credit**	**Debit**	**Credit**	

Source: *Financial Recordkeeping for Small Stores, SBA Management Series No. 32.*

The General Ledger is divided into separate accounts, (for example, Cash 101,) with a debit and credit column for each account. A look at the ledger account record will reveal a complete history of the increases and decreases of the items involved. Ledgers may be kept in book or card form in a ledger tray. These records may also be stored on computer records.

Subsidiary Ledgers are used for many similar items that require easy access. This is especially important in items involving much activity. Subsidiary ledgers are so termed because they are kept separate from, and subordinate to, the general ledger. The *Accounts Receivable Ledger* and the *Accounts Payable Ledger* are two examples of subsidiary ledgers. Both ledgers keep track of receivable or payables, respectively, under the name of the customer or creditor. For instance, if in the accounts receivable ledger there is a page for the customer, Afroflow Mfg., which contains a monthly (or some other period) summary of the sales to this company and the payments the company has made on account, the Accounts Receivable Ledger allows the businessperson to check at any given time on the status of one particular account by offering easy access for an active account. The Accounts Payable Ledger records period summaries of purchases and payments to a creditor under the creditor's name.

Other Bookkeeping Tools

Original transaction records, journals, and ledgers are as necessary in the past, as in the present, to keep accurate records of business transactions. Other tools are also needed to assure accuracy and thoroughness in bookkeeping. The trial balance, reconciliation of bank statements, and accounting for payroll and payroll taxes are the major ones to be discussed here.

The Trial Balance

The *Trial Balance* allows the accountant to test the balance of the books. If you remember the fundamental accounting equation that

$$\text{assets} = \text{liabilities} + \text{equity},$$

and that

$$\text{debits} = \text{credits}$$

then it follows that the sum of all the accounts with a debit balance should equal the sum of all the accounts with a credit balance. Since the books started with equality, and continued that equality in the recording process, it follows that the sum of debit balances should equal the sum of credit balances when all the transactions have been posted. If the books do not balance — the debits do not equal the credits — then the accountant knows that an error has been made.

The equality of debits and credits is tested in two ways:

Determining the balance in each account
Adding debit and credit balances separately to see if the totals are
    equal

The balance of each account is computed by adding the figures on the
debit side and the credit side and then subtracting the smaller total from
the larger to obtain the balance (which will be either a debit or a credit
balance). These totals, called *footings*, are usually put in small pencil
figures under the last item on each side. When the balance of each
account is known, the accountant lists the accounts in a trial balance to
see if the total of the debit balances equals the total of the credit balances.
Accounts are usually listed in numerical order. The balance of each
account is placed in the proper column — debit balances in the left column and credit balances in the right column, as in Exhibit 1.15.

When the trial balance is completed and balances, the accountant then
proceeds on a *worksheet* to put the various accounts into either an income
statement or balance-sheet format. The worksheet has a double-column
income statement and a double-column balance sheet. The income statement accounts, such as income, expenses, and cost of sales is put in the
double-column income statement form. Income is a credit account, and
the cost of sales and expense accounts will have a debit balance. Similarly,
for balance-sheet columns, the asset accounts will be put on the debit side
and equity and liability accounts on the credit side. (See Exhibit 1.16.)

Bank Reconciliation

A bank reconciliation is a way of verifying that the amount of the cash
account is the same as what the bank indicates remains in your checking
account. Since the cash account is the most active of all the accounts, this
verification process is necessary. Before reconciling your bank statement
with your account, make sure that your account is mathematically correct. Beginning with the bank balance shown in the cash account at the
end of the preceding period (usually one month), add the total cash
deposited to the bank during the past month and subtract the total cash
disbursements (from the cash disbursements journal). The result should
agree with your checkbook balance at the end of this month. If it does not,
an error has been made in entering or adding one or more of the items in
either the checkbook or the journals.

When the balance in your checkbook is mathematically correct, then

EXHIBIT 1.15
Trial Balance

Zap Mfg. Company
Trial Balance
May 31, 19x4

ACCT.	ACCOUNT NAME	DEBIT	CREDIT

EXHIBIT 1.16
Debit and Credit

	DEBIT *Productive*	**CREDIT** *Nonproductive*
INCOME STATEMENT	Cost of Sales Expenses	Income
BALANCE SHEET	Assets	Liabilities Equity

---

reconciliation between your account and the bank's account can begin through the following steps, as in Exhibit 1.17.

1. Arrange all the cancelled checks in numerical order.
2. Compare deposits listed on the bank statement with deposits entered in the business checkbook. List in the first section of the reconciliation any deposits recorded in the business checkbook during the month that do not appear on the bank statement.
3. Check off the cancelled checks from the previous month on the list of outstanding checks shown on the preceding month's reconciliation. List in the first section of the current reconciliation the checks still outstanding.
4. Check off, on the corresponding check stubs, all cancelled checks drawn during the month being reconciled. Add the checks recorded on the remaining stubs to the list of outstanding checks on the reconciliation.
5. If any errors in amounts are discovered in the preceding steps, list them in the second section of the reconciliation statement as adjustments added or deducted.
6. Examine the bank statement for service charges or other adjustments to your account and enter them in the second section of the reconciliation.
7. Carry out the additions and subtractions shown on the bank reconciliation. The adjusted balance for each bank statement should equal the adjusted balance for each business checkbook.

EXHIBIT 1.17
Bank Reconciliation

Bank Reconciliation November 30, 19—

Balance per bank statement......................		$793. 74
Add deposits not credited:		
November 29.......................	$247. 52	
November 30......................	302. 19	549. 71
		$1, 343. 45
Deduct outstanding checks:		
No. 913—10/20......................	$30. 18	
929—11/15....................	10. 14	
935—11/25.....................	142. 60	
939—11/30.....................	82. 60	
940—11/30.....................	95. 80	
941—11/30.....................	74. 50	435. 82
Adjusted balance per bank statement...............		$907. 63
Balance per checkbook...........................		$903. 38
Add:		
Check No. 920 entered as $58.30 should		
be $53.80........................	$4. 50	
Deposits of Nov. 1 recorded as $298.60		
should be $299.60.................	1. 00	5. 50
		$908. 88
Deduct bank service charge.......................		1. 25
Adjusted balance per checkbook...................		$907. 63

Source: *Financial Recordkeeping for Small Stores*, SBA Management Series No. 32.

Payroll Records and Payroll Taxes

If there are any employees in your business, the Federal government imposes certain obligations for paying payroll taxes and withholding income taxes in connection with any salaries paid to employees. There will probably be similar obligations for payroll and withholding taxes to State and perhaps to local jurisdictions.

Federal regulations do not prescribe the form in which payroll records must be kept, but the records should include the following information and documents:

1. The amounts and dates of all wage payments subject to withholding taxes and the amounts withheld
2. The names, addresses, and occupations of employees receiving payments
3. The periods of their employment
4. The periods for which they are paid by you while they are absent, because of sickness or personal injuries, and the amount and weekly rate of payments
5. Their Social Security account numbers if they are subject to Social Security tax
6. Their income-tax withholding exemption certificates
7. Your employ-identification number
8. Duplicate copies of returns filed
9. Dates and amounts of deposits made with government depositories

Usually, an employee earnings card is set up for each employee. Every wage payment to the employee is recorded on this card — all the information needed for meeting federal, state, and city requirements relating to payroll and withholding taxes, as well as all other amounts deducted from the employee's wages. A number of payroll-records systems are available commercially. Most of these are based on the pegboard or multiple-copy principle. A single writing of a check or payslip, to be given to the employee, makes a carbon entry on the employee's earnings card and on a payroll summary or journal for each pay period. If you have only one or two employees, it is usually not necessary to have a special payroll system. Paychecks may be entered directly in your cash disbursements journal or on an earnings card for each employee. (See Exhibit 1.10.)

There are three types of federal payroll taxes:

Income taxes withheld
Social Security taxes
Federal unemployment taxes

IRS *Publication 15* "Employer's Tax Guide" should be consulted for additional information about employer-employee relationships — what constitutes taxable wages, the treatment of special types of employment and payments, and similar matters.

Income taxes are withheld on all wages paid an employee above a certain minimum amount. The minimum is governed by the number of exemptions claimed by an employee. The Tax Reduction and Simplification Act of 1977 changed the old standard deduction to the zero bracket amount which is a flat rate of $2,200 for single individuals and $3,200 for married couples filing joint returns.

Social Security taxes apply to the first $22,900 (in 1979) of wages paid an employee during a year. A percentage deduction (presently 6.13 percent) from the employee's wages is matched by an equal amount in taxes paid by the employer.

Federal unemployment taxes (FUTA) are required only of employers who have:

1. Paid wages of $1,500 or more in any calendar quarter, or
2. Employed one or more persons for some portion of at least one day during each of twenty different calendar weeks. The twenty weeks do not have to be consecutive. Individuals on vacation or sick leave are counted as employees in determining the business status.

The FUTA tax is paid by you as the employer (no deduction is made from the employee's wages). For 1978 and 1979, the rate was 3.4 percent on the first $6,000 of wages. The Federal FUTA tax is reduced by any State unemployment tax which you pay.

If you are required to withhold income tax from wages or are liable for Social Security taxes in excess of $200 quarterly, you must file a quarterly return, Form 941. Form 941 combines the Social Security taxes (including hospital insurance) and income tax withholding. Form 941E is used for reporting income tax withheld from wages, tips, annuities, and supplemental unemployment compensation benefits when no FICA coverage is required.

Due dates for the Forms 941 or 941E and the full payment of tax are as follows:

Quarter	*Due Dates*
January – February – March	April 30
April – May – June	July 31
July – August – September	October 31
October – November – December	January 31, next year

If you are required to make deposits of taxes and you make timely deposits in full payment of the taxes due, you may file your quarterly return on or before the 10th day of the 2nd month following the period for which it is made. In this case, the due dates are as follows:

Quarter	Due Dates
January – February – March	May 10
April – May – June	August 10
July – August – September	November 10
October – November – December	February 10 next year

Deposits are made by sending a filled-in Form 501 "Federal Tax Deposit" together with a single remittance covering the taxes to be deposited to an authorized commercial bank or a federal reserve bank in accordance with instructions on the back of the Form 501. Names of authorized commercial bank depositories are available at your local bank.

ACCOUNTING AND THE TAX MAN

In modern times, as the mechanisms available to the government for investigating individual businesses became accurate, bookkeeping and accounting were no longer of concern only to the businessperson. Governments, through tax regulations, began to determine what accounting systems should look like, what comprised a legitimate expense, and vice versa. Furthermore, they were concerned about what comprised acceptable records, and what did not. Accounting began to be shaped by the type of organization businesses used (proprietorship, partnership, or corporation). The government stipulated what constituted effective records, what accounting periods and methods were acceptable, and issued ever-changing lists of ifs, ands, and exceptions.

Suddenly, what had been an effective method for keeping track of business transactions became the technique for evaluating whether or not a business was paying its proper taxes. What was once optional became codified into law. What was once simple became complex.

Accounting Periods

Every business must compute taxable income and file a tax return on the basis of a period of time called a *tax year*. A tax year is usually twelve consecutive months. It can be either a calendar year (from January 1 to December 31) or a fiscal year (any period of fifty-two to fifty-three weeks). The tax year under certain conditions can be shorter than twelve months, but never longer.

If a business chooses a fiscal (or fifty-two or fifty-three week) year, the period varies from fifty-two to fifty-three weeks, always ends on the same day of the week, and ends on the date that day last falls on in a particular calendar month, — a date nearest the end of the month. To use this type of tax year, a company attaches a special statement to its tax return.

A return is required for the period a business is in existence, even if this period is not for a full tax year. This provision is called a *short tax year*. The return in this case is considered to be for a full tax year and the income does not have to be annualized. This rule also applies to a subsidiary joining a consolidated group. Examples of short tax year returns are those filed by new companies at the end of the calendar year (December 31) after having been in existence for less than a full twelve months. (For example, they started business June 12.) Short tax year returns also would be filed when a company changes from a calendar tax year to a fiscal tax year.

QUESTION: *How do you go about changing from a calendar tax year to a fiscal tax year (or vice versa)?*

ANSWER:

A company must, with certain exceptions, obtain permission from the Commissioner of Internal Revenue to change its annual accounting period. The business submits a Form 1128 in triplicate to the IRS (addressed to the Commissioner of Internal Revenue, Washington, D.C. 20224, Attn: T.C.C.). The application must be filed before the 15th day of the 2nd month following the short tax year under your old method. This short year begins with the first day after the end of your present accounting period and ends the day preceding the opening date of your first twelve month accounting period.

Partnerships must get IRS approval of a tax year change *except* when the change is to the tax year of all the principle partners, or to the tax year to which all the principal partners are currently changing.

A corporation (other than Subchapter S) can change its accounting period without prior IRS approval under the following conditions:

1. The corporation has not changed its tax year any time within the ten-calendar years ending the calendar year in which the short period resulting from the change occurs

2. The short period is not a tax year in which the corporation has a net operating loss

3. The taxable income of the corporation for the short period is (when annualized) 80 percent or more of the taxable income of the corporation for the preceding tax year

4. If the corporation is not a personal holding company, foreign personal holding company, exempt organization, foreign corporation engaged in business within the United States, Western Hemisphere Trade corporation, or China Trade Act corporation, either for the short period or for the preceding tax year

5. If the corporation does not become a Subchapter S corporation within the first year of the new accounting period.

The Subchapter S corporation has changeover requirements like that of a partnership.

In other words, in almost all cases for a proprietorship or partnership, and in most cases for a corporation, permission is required from the Commissioner of Internal Revenue for a tax year change.

Accounting Methods

There are two basic accounting methods to choose from — the cash method and the accrual method. However, if inventories play an important part in accounting for your particular business income, the IRS requires the use of the accrual method for your purchases and sales. In addition to the cash and accrual methods there are special accounting methods such as the installment and deferred-payment methods. Furthermore, the IRS allows the use of any combination of these methods.

Under the *Cash Accounting Method*, the business reports income when the cash is actually or constructively received, and expenses are reported when they are actually paid (the check is signed). Constructive receipt of income occurs when an amount is deposited in your company checking account, credited to your account, or otherwise made available to you on demand.

In the *Accrual Method*, all items of income are included in gross income when they are earned, even though payment is received in another tax year. Income in this case includes all goods or services sold on credit, whether or not the customer had actually paid for those goods or services. A businessperson using the accrual method deducts business expenses when incurred in the same year, whether paid for or not. For example, if he or she is a calendar-year taxpayer and buys office supplies in December 1978, he or she is billed in January 1979 and makes payment in the same month. The expense is deductible in 1978 because the liability was incurred in that year.

Also under the accrual method, a dealer in personal property (such as home appliances or autos) who sells goods on the installment plan reports the full amount of the sale in the year in which it occurred (unless he or she uses the installment accounting method, discussed shortly). When a dealer repossesses merchandise sold on the installment plan — either through a voluntary or involuntary surrender by the buyer — the dealer may be entitled to a bad-debt deduction for the unpaid portion of the buyer's debt (which the dealer has previously declared as income). The amount deductible is the difference between the money still owed to the dealer and the market value (at the date of repossession of the property repossessed).

The *Installment Method of Accounting* allows the deferment of federal income tax on installment sales until the tax years that the payments are received. This method may be used both for sales under a traditional installment plan and, sometimes, under a revolving credit plan, regardless of whether you use the cash, accrual, or a combination method for the rest of your accounting needs.

The installment method can be used for three categories of sales:

1. Sales of real property
2. Casual sales of personal property (with a sales price exceeding $1,000)
3. Installment sales by dealers in personal property

The installment method of reporting income recognizes that each collection made from a customer on that customer's installment account contains two elements: a return of part of your cost and a part of your profit on the sale. It permits you to apportion your collections for that tax year between these two elements and to include in gross income only the part that represents profit. The profit declared on installment sales is determined by the use of a gross profit percentage. For example, if you sell merchandise at a contract price of $2,000 and there is a gross profit of $500, then your gross profit percentage is 25 percent ($500 divided by $2,000). Therefore, 25 percent of each payment collected on the sale (including the down payment) is profit and must be included in gross income for the tax year in which it was collected. This percentage remains the same throughout the period installment payments on the sale are received.

If your business chooses to use the installment method, only the gross profit on collections from installment is included as business income. The cost of goods sold reported on the installment method must not be deducted on your tax return in computing gross profit from other sales, since this cost is deducted in computing your gross profit percentage. Using a gross profit percentage of 25 percent, for instance, already takes into account a cost of goods of 75 percent. If you multiply your total income by 25 percent and declare that as your total income, you have already discounted the income for the 75 percent cost of sales.

Deductible expenses must be deducted in the tax year in which they are paid or incurred. They are not allocated to the years in which the profits from the sales of a particular year are to be returned as income. The personal property dealer is entitled to a bad-debt deduction because of uncollectible installments. To do so, either the specific charge-off method or the reserve method for bad debts (discussed in later chapters) can be used. The dealer may also be entitled to a bad-debt deduction for certain installment obligations of his customers for which he is contingently liable (anticipated losses because of liability as a guarantor, endorser, or indemnitor of guaranteed installment debt obligations).

Special *Long-term-contracts Accounting Methods* can be used for reporting income from long-term contracts. However, permission from the IRS is required for a change to or from these special methods.

A long-term contract means a building, installation, construction, or manufacturing contract that is not completed within the tax year in which work was begun. The manufacturing contract is usually for custom goods that take more than twelve months to complete. Income from a long-term contract may be included in gross income by either the percentage-of-completion method or the completed-contract method. Whatever method is used, it must be consistently applied to all long-term contracts within the same trade or business.

The *percentage-of-completion method* requires that the business report as income only that part of the contract price which represents the percentage of the entire contract completed during the current tax year. To determine the percentage of completion, one of the following methods is used:

1. Compare, as of the end of the tax year, the costs incurred under the contract with the estimated total contract costs, or

2.   Compare at the end of the year the work performed on the contract with the estimated work to be performed.

In either case, a certificate from an architect or engineer or other documentation showing the basis for the revision must be available at the company headquarters for inspection by the IRS.

The *completed contract method* requires that gross income be reported from a long-term contract and the deduction of all expenses (direct labor and material) be reported in the year the contract is finally completed and accepted. Guarantee, warranty, maintenance, or other service agreement expenses relating to the contracted item can be deducted either under the percentage-of-completion or completed-contract method. Expenses for office salaries, rent, taxes, and other related items not directly attributable to a long-term contract are deductible only in the year paid or incurred — depending on the method of accounting used. These expenses cannot be made part of the computations under the percentage-of-completion or completed-contract methods.

A *Combination of Methods* of the two foregoing methods is permitted by the IRS, if the combination clearly reflects income and is applied consistently. This combination of methods is sometimes called a *Hybrid Method*.

If you are engaged in a business using an accrual method for computing gross profit from purchases and sales, you can use the cash method in computing all other items of income and expense. If you use the cash method in computing gross income from your business, you must use the cash method for business expenses. Similarly, if you use an accrual method for business expenses, you must use an accrual method for all items affecting gross income. For example, insurance expense must be prorated over the life of the policy.

If you own more than one business, a different method of accounting for each separate and distinct business may be used, provided the method used for each clearly reflects income.

QUESTION: What is required to change your accounting method from one type to another?

ANSWER:
Any change in your method of accounting requires prior consent of the Commissioner of Internal Revenue. Some examples of changes requiring consent are:

1.   A change from the cash to the accrual method or vice versa

2.   A change in the method or basis used in the evaluation of inventories
3.   A change in the method of computing depreciation
4.   A change from the cash or accrual method to a long-term-contract method or vice versa.

The business seeking a change in their method should file Form 3115, "Application for Change in Accounting Method," with the commissioner.

A request to change from the cash method to the accrual method will almost always be granted. Simplified procedures now exist which allow a change in the method of computing depreciation without consent (Revenue procedure 74–11, 1974–1, C.B. 420). A similar simple procedure exists whereby a change can be made from the specific charge-off method to the reserve method in accounting for bad debts (revenue procedure 64–51, 1964–2 C.B. 1003). If you follow the steps outlined in the procedures and comply with all the provisions, you may assume consent has been granted.

As a dealer in personal property, you may change to the installment method for reporting income from sales on the installment plan, without permission from the IRS. If a dealer changes to the installment method, the dealer may not exclude any part of the installments collected in the year of the change, even though the entire profit on sales in years before the change had been reported on the accrual method.

Note, however, that a change to either of the methods of reporting income from long-term contracts is permissible only with the consent of the commissioner.

Other aspects of the tax code and accounting and finance will be discussed throughout this book.

THE ACCOUNTANT AND GENERALLY ACCEPTED ACCOUNTING PRINCIPLES

The tax consultant was the first person to bring some kind of conformity to accounting. Even today, the IRS does not require any particular kind of records, only that "every businessperson is required to maintain records that will enable them to prepare complete and accurate returns and insure that they pay only their proper tax" (IRS *Publication 583*).

What is reported on the income tax of a business and what is reported on its annual report are often different.

In the last one hundred years, increase in government control over industry has been worldwide. Control will probably increase before it decreases. Accounting, as the language of business, has also come under regulation in many ways.

Since the stock-market crash of 1929 and the resulting depression, a number of organizations, such as the Securities and Exchange Commission (SEC), the American Banking Association, and the American Institute of Certified Public Accountants (AICPA) have worked toward more consistency in accounting. Accounting principles advocated by these groups, in their effort to make accounting more consistent and informative, have created a complex job for accountants.

Accounting is essentially an art. Regulations and recommendations from the various government and nonprofit organizations, designed to make accounting more scientific, have only succeeded in making accounting a quasi-scientific art.

The Securities and Exchange Commission (SEC) has broad authority over the prospectuses issued to obtain capital in the public markets and over annual reports filed with the SEC by publicly held corporations. In seeking informative disclosures and assurances that the accounting meets with Generally Accepted Accounting Principles, the SEC has issued certain rules, regulations, and opinions.

The Accounting Principles Board (APB) of the American Institute of Certified Public Accountants developed a series of opinions on the accounting treatment that should be followed in meeting specific accounting problems. It was an AICPA rule that "departures from Board Opinions must be disclosed in footnotes to the financial statements or in independent auditors' reports when the effect of the departure on the financial statements is material." Although compliance with board opinions was not required, as a practical matter no financial officer or independent auditor would like to disclose any departures from a board opinion.

The Financial Accounting Standards Board (FASB) replaced the APB in 1973. This new board, comprised of seven full-time, salaried members, was created to replace the APB, which had eighteen members who received no compensation for their part-time work. (Please see the Appendix for a summary of of FASB Statements.)

Other national associations, such as the American Accounting Association, the National Association of Accountants, the Financial Executives Institute, and a number of national associations of bankers, credit officers, and financial analysts have also influenced the shape of modern accounting.

2

Financial Statements: The Income Statement

Financial statements — the balance sheet (statement of financial condition) and the income statement (profit and loss statement) — are the culmination of the accounting process and the beginning of finance. If accounting is the international language of business, then the balance sheet and income statement are its manifesto.

To illustrate the difference between the two statements, we can compare the balance sheet to a still picture of a business and the income statement to a moving picture. Consider a business as the Cannonball Express train rolling through the countryside. It approaches the Tahatchapi Bridge where a photographer near the bridge takes a snapshot. This is a picture of the Cannonball at a particular place in time, which can be compared to a balance sheet that shows a record (picture) of the company (assets, liabilities, and equity) on a given date. Suppose that a movie producer were making a documentary movie about the last ride of the Cannonball Express. The producer takes a moving picture of the train from the time it leaves the station until it arrives at its destination. If the decision is made to stop the movie footage when the Cannonball arrives at the Tahatchapi Bridge, then a moving picture results, which spans the time the train left the station until it arrived at the bridge. This moving picture is like an income statement that measures costs and expenses against sales revenues over a definite period of time (month, year) to show the net profit or loss of the business for the entire period. Whereas balance sheets are dated with one date only (for example, December 31, 19—) the income statement is dated over a longer time span, preceded by the words "year to date" or "year ended" (that is, year ended December 31 19—).

THE ACCOUNTS AND THE
FINANCIAL STATEMENT

In the first chapter, accounts of a business, which fell into the categories (account groups) of assets, expenses, cost of sales, liabilities, equity, and income were discussed. These are the basic account groups comprising the financial statements. Assets, liabilities, and equity are the three basic account groups in a balance sheet. Income, expense, and cost of sales are the basic account groups in an income statement (see Exhibit 2.1).

If you have a numbered chart of accounts, as discussed in the first chapter (refer to Exhibit 1.6), then the first three series of numbers goes on the balance sheet; the next three series goes on the profit-and-loss statement. Accounts designated assets (100–199), liabilities (200–299), and equity (300–399) are transferred to the balance sheet. Income (400–409), expenses (500–509), and cost of sales (600–609) are the accounts to be entered in the income statement. This procedure makes it easy to transform a trial balance into a balance sheet and income statement.

Income Statement

Basically, the income statement is divided into four parts: income (gross sales), cost of sales (cost of goods sold), operating expense, and net profit, which is the result of subtracting operating expense and cost of sales from income. Income statements may also include a provision for income taxes and the resulting net profit after tax. At times, selling expense is entered as an item separate from cost of sales and operating (or general and administrative) expense.

The income statements of retail, wholesale, service, and manufacturing

EXHIBIT 2.1
The Accounts Circle

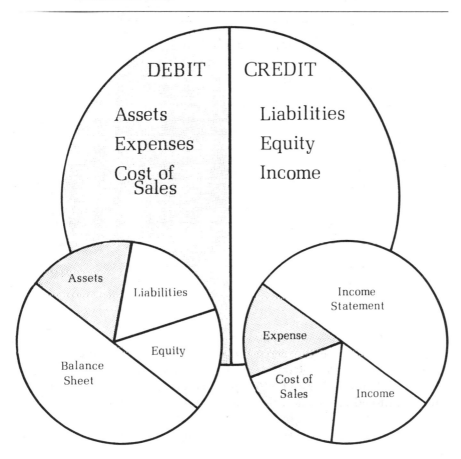

businesses differ to some extent. In wholesale and retail businesses, the cost of sales is generally the cost of the merchandise (and perhaps freight and shipping) alone. In a manufacturing business, the cost of sales includes more extensive costs including labor, factory overhead, and, occasionally, selling expense as well as the cost of the merchandise (raw materials). A service industry customarily has no cost of sales (except supplies). Cost of sales is not an important ingredient in calculating cost and resulting net profit. The following exhibits include a simplified one-step, profit-and-loss statement for Monar Company (Exhibit 2.2), a more comprehensive statement multistep for a wholesale company (Wald Wholesale Company) (Exhibit 2.3), and Hayes Manufacturing

EXHIBIT 2.2
A Simplified One-step Profit-and-Loss Statement

The MONAR Company

Profit–and–Loss Statement
For the Year Ended December 31, 19__

Sales		$120,000
Cost of goods sold		70,000
Gross margin		$50,000
Selling expenses:		
Salaries	$15,000	
Commission	5,000	
Advertising	5,000	
Total selling expenses		25,000
Selling margin		$25,000
Administrative expenses		10,000
Net profit		$15,000

Source: *Financial Recordkeeping for Small Stores*, SBA Management Series No. 32.

Company (Exhibit 2.4). Notice that in the instance of the manufacturing company the cost of goods sold includes not only finished-goods inventories, but also raw-materials inventories, goods-in-process inventories, and direct labor and factory overhead costs. To avoid a long and complicated profit-and-loss statement, the cost of goods manufactured is usually reported separately, as illustrated for Hayes Manufacturing Company (Exhibit 2.5). A more detailed discussion of inventories is covered in Chapter 6.

The item *sales* includes all sales of merchandise or services. The sales figures for Wald Wholesale and Hayes Manufacturing are reported as *net sales*. It is computed by subtracting sales discounts and sales returns and allowances from gross sales. If this were a report for public held corporation, then net sales would be explained in a footnote.

The *cost of goods sold* is the total price paid for the products sold during the accounting period. Most retail and wholesale businesses compute cost of goods sold by adding the value of the goods purchased during the accounting period to the beginning inventory, and then subtracting

EXHIBIT 2.3
A Multistep Profit-and-Loss Statement

Wald Wholesale Company

Profit–and–Loss Statement
For the Year Ended December 31, 19__

Net sales		$666,720
Cost of goods sold:		
Beginning inventory, January 1, 19___	$184,350	
Merchandise purchases	$454,920	
Freight and drayage	30,210	485,130
Cost of goods available for sale	$669,480	
Less ending inventory, December 31, 19___	193,710	
Cost of goods sold		475,770
Gross margin		$190,950
Selling, administrative, and general expenses:		
Salaries and wages	$88,170	
Rent	24,390	
Light, heat, and power	8,840	
Other expenses	21,300	
State and local taxes and licenses	5,130	
Depreciation and amortization on leasehold improvements	4,140	
Repairs	2,110	
Total selling, administrative, and general expenses		154,080
Profit from operations		$36,870
Other income	$7,550	
Other expense	1,740	5,810
Net profit before taxes		$42,680
Provision for income tax		15,120
Net profit after income tax		$27,560

Source: *Financial Recordkeeping for Small Stores*, SBA Management Series No. 32.

EXHIBIT 2.4
Statement of Cost of Goods Manufactured

Hayes Manufacturing Company

Statement of Cost of Goods Manufactured
For the Year Ended December 31, 19___

Work-in-process inventory, January 1, 19___			$18,800
Raw materials:			
Inventory, January 1, 19___		$154,300	
Purchases		263,520	
Freight In		9,400	
Cost of materials available for use		$427,220	
Less inventory, December 31, 19___		163,120	
Cost of materials used		$264,100	
Direct labor		150,650	
Manufacturing overhead:			
Indirect labor	$23,750		
Factory heat, light, and power	89,500		
Factory supplies used	22,100		
Insurance and taxes	8,100		
Depreciation of plant and equipment	35,300		
Total manufacturing overhead		178,750	
Total manufacturing costs			593,500
Total work in process during period			$612,300
Less work-in-process inventory, December 31, 19___			42,600
Cost of goods manufactured			$569,700

Source: *Financial Recordkeeping for Small Stores,* SBA Management Series No. 32.

EXHIBIT 2.5
Profit-and-Loss Statement of Cost of Goods Manufactured

Hayes Manufacturing Company

Profit-and-Loss Statement
For the Year Ended December 31, 19____

Net sales			$669,100
Cost of goods sold:			
Finished goods inventory, January 1, 19____		$69,200	
Cost of goods manufactured (exhibit 6)		569,700	
Total cost of goods available for sale		$638,900	
Less finished goods inventory, Dec. 31, 19____		66,400	
Cost of goods sold			572,500
Gross margin			$96,600
Selling and administrative expenses:			
Selling expenses:			
Sales salaries and commissions	$26,700		
Advertising expense	12,900		
Miscellaneous selling expense	2,100		
Total selling expenses		$41,700	
Administrative expenses:			
Salaries	$27,400		
Miscellaneous administrative expense	4,800		
Total administrative expenses		32,200	
Total selling and administrative expenses			73,900
Net operating profit			$22,700
Other revenue			15,300
Net profit before taxes			$38,000
Estimated income tax			12,640
Net profit after income tax			$25,360

Source: *Financial Recordkeeping for Small Stores*, SBA Management Series No. 32.

the value of the inventory on hand at the end of the accounting period. In addition, manufacturing concerns add factory overhead, direct labor, and certain other costs.

Selling expenses are expenses incurred directly or indirectly in producing sales. They usually include the salaries of the sales force, commissions, advertising expense, and freight-out if goods are sold F. O. B. destination. Also, shares of rent, heat, light, power, supplies, and other expenses that contribute to company sales activities may be charged to selling expenses. Sometimes these expenses are not shown separately, but are included in cost of sales or operating expense (general and administrative expense). Included in general and administrative expense (operating expense) are general salaries, supplies, and other operating costs necessary to the overall administration of the business.

Some businesses receive additional income from interest, dividends, miscellaneous sales, rents, royalties, and gains on sale of capital assets, to mention a few. In these cases, the net profit shown is really net operation profit and is referred to as such. Any other income will be added to the net operating profit, and the extraordinary costs, such as interest and loss from the sale of assets, will be subtracted from it.

Accounting Problems of Income Statements

The accounting problems relating to financial statements are the problems relating to the accountant's judgment. It is possible that two accountants, both using generally accepted accounting principles, could come up with two different net-profit figures. For example, if one accountant used straight-line depreciation and another used double-declining balance depreciation, but used the same inventory valuation, then each would come up with entirely different net-profit figures. Deciding which overdue accounts to write off or what inventory to write down could also cause a different reckoning on the bottom line.

Many of the difficult problems in accounting policy and practice stem not only from the custom of reporting periodically the condition of a business but also on its revenues, expenses, and net income for given periods of time. Problems in the periodic measurement of financial condition and results of operations occur because the purchase of labor, services, goods, and other properties, including legal claims, is not neatly matched by the date, exhaustion, or disposal of these same items in the same time period. Inventory bought in 1976 may not be sold until 1978. Prepaid interest is not an expense until the end of the contract period.

Stated another way, financial transaction involving costs are not always matched neatly in the same accounting period by financial transactions involving revenues. Under these conditions, problems arise in determining both what reasonably can be considered as a company's revenues for a given period and what are the costs to be charged against them.

Further, even when an accounting principle has become generally accepted, practice usually requires the exercise of judgment by the accountant. For example, consider the case of depreciation. Generally accepted accounting principles require that the cost of a machine be allocated to accounting periods over its expected life in a systematic and rational manner. Since there are several depreciation methods (straight-line, doubling-declining balance, sum-of-the-years-digits), the accountant must use not only his judgment in arriving at the best method, but also must determine the useful life of the machine and its salvage value. Problems of judgment in determining what the machine actually cost (freight and installation) also can arise. Furthermore, certain problems may arise if the machine is to be built by the company's own shop, instead of being purchased from an outside manufacturer.

REVENUE (SALES OR INCOME)

To a salesman, a sale takes place when he receives an order from a customer; but to the accountant, it is not a sale until the goods are shipped. A statistical record or order is kept for management purposes, but a sale is not a sale until the goods are out the door.

Thus, for most companies, the word sales in an income statement means goods shipped during the given accounting period. The monetary amount indicated for these sales is the amount recognized as the revenue realized on these shipments. Sales may be extended to cover fees for services performed, as well as other items of income, such as commissions, rents, and royalties.

In the case of sales involving the shipment of goods, there is normally a passing of legal title, which is evidence that a sale has in fact taken place. In other types of business transactions, however, revenue recognition does not depend on the passing of title. For example, service industries do not pass a legal title when they perform a service for their customer.

Other examples of revenue without passing legal title are situations involving long-term contracts. Legal title does not pass until the contract is completed. In the construction of a house, for example, revenue will be recognized each accounting period in accordance with the work performed during that period. This revenue is measured either by percentage of completion or completion of identifiable portions of work. (See "The Accountant and the Tax man," in Chapter 10.) As a precaution, something less than the full proportion of revenue will be recognized at such times (or a reserve will be established) to make good whatever parts of the work may fail to meet expectations. In the construction industry, a contractor may receive 10 percent of his money when the foundation is completed, 20 percent when the house is boarded in and the roof shingled, 20 percent when the rough wiring, plumbing, and heating have been installed and inspected and passed by the authorities.

Since companies are enthusiastic about recording inventory gains (through re-evaluation) and accounting for profit as goods are manufactured or as orders are received, it follows that they do not often carry their enthusiasm to the point of suggesting that such gains or profits be reported as taxable income. Similarly, companies that record income on long-term contracts in reports to stockholders as work progresses do not report the same thing to the tax man.

Companies selling on the installment-payment basis will commonly record in their accounts sales revenue from the time goods are delivered to the customers. However, they will defer reporting this income on sales for tax purposes until each of the installments are received. Where options are available that permit one report to the government and another to the stockholder, the natural tendency is for a company to be more conservative in computing net income for tax purposes than in their own accounting.

Sales Discounts and Returns

In many industries, catalog or list prices serve as a base point for pricing purposes. The real price charged to any given class of buyer is determined by the application of a discount to the list or catalog price. No buyer is foolish enough to pay full price when he may be able to get a discount. Under these conditions, sales reported for financial accounting purposes represent revenue net of trade discounts.

The question of whether cash discounts are a financial expense, a selling expense, or a reduction in sales revenue has been debated for many years. Treating the discount as a *financial expense* assumes that it is granted in order to receive payment earlier because it is a matter of either matching or bettering the offers of competitors. Treating the discount as a *reduction in sales revenue* also may be justified by competition. In any case, these costs are subtracted from gross sales to give a net sales figure.

The sales value of goods returned is another item subtracted from sales to arrive at net sales. The accounting problem caused by returns is that goods returned in the current accounting period may have been sold in the previous period. Theoretically, then, treating returned goods as a reduction from current sales is an incorrect matching of revenues and costs.

Unless the returns are unusually large, however, there is no serious distortion of results. The *distortion* of returns that lag behind sales in one period is matched by the same thing happening in the next period and in the previous period. In other words, these distortions will balance out over time.

Allowances for sales returns and adjustments are a set percentage of sales created to allow for adjustments, such as billing errors and other selling-price adjustments that occur after the fact. Some companies use an allowance for trade discounts as well.

Income and the Tax Man

According to the tax code, gross income includes, but is not limited to:

1. Income from trade or business
2. Compensation for services, including fees, commissions, and similar items
3. Gains derived from dealings in property
4. Interest
5. Dividends
6. Rents
7. Royalties
8. Income from discharge of indebtedness
9. Distributive share of partnership gross income

Business income arises from your business activity whenever there is a sale of your product or services in the ordinary course of business. Interest is business income to a lending institution; fees are business income to a professional person; rents are income to a person in the real estate business; and, dividends are generally business income to a dealer in securities.

Other items of income are bond premiums, capital gains from sale of assets, property received for services performed, promissory notes, recovery of damages, and recovery of items previously deducted for income tax purposes.

Bond premiums received by a corporation on issuance of its bonds is included in gross income. However, the entire amount is not included as gross income in the year the bonds are issued, but is included ratably over the life of the bonds.

Promissory notes and other evidences of indebtedness of responsible and solvent makers, received as part of a sales price, are included in gross income at their fair market value.

Recovery of damages received during the tax year as a result of patent infringement, breach of contract or of a fiduciary duty, or antitrust injury are included in gross income in the year received. Punitive damages are also taxable. (Ordinary damages are not taxable.)

The following items are not considered to be income: issuance of stock, contributions to capital, loans, appreciation in value of your property, improvements in your building by a leaseholder, exchange of property for comparable property, and consignments of merchandise (until the merchandise is sold).

QUESTION: *Is property received in lieu of cash taxable as income?*
ANSWER:

In most cases, yes. For instance, if you receive stock in a corporation for legal services you perform, this stock is taxable at its fair market value at the time it is received. You pay tax when the property is transferred. If, however, the stock or other property received is restricted in some way (stock cannot be sold for one year), then you are taxable in the year that those restrictions are lifted, that is, when your interest in the property becomes transferable or is not subject to a substantial risk of forfeiture. If you receive stock in exchange for property transferred to a corporation or partnership, there is usually no tax.

QUESTION: *In leasing property, how are advance payments, bonuses, lease cancellation payments, or other payments received from the lessee treated?*
ANSWER:

All of these payments are treated as taxable, ordinary income in the year they are received. Payments to third parties by your lessee are also taxable to you as income. This stipulation includes payments of real estate taxes that your tenant makes on your property.

QUESTION: *Is the cancellation of a debt by a stockholder considered income to the corporation?*

ANSWER:

No, it is considered a contribution to capital, and therefore not income. If a stockholder gratuitously cancels a debt owed to the stockholder by the corporation, the transaction is considered a contribution to capital.

COST OF GOODS SOLD

Cost of goods sold, sometimes listed as *cost of sales*, covers the cost of the goods themselves that are shipped. It does not cover the expenses of selling or shipping these goods or does it cover, ordinarily, any storing, office, or general administrative expenses involved in company operations. In professional and service businesses (service and professional type) there are usually no cost of sales. These kinds of companies receive income from fees, rents, commissions, and royalties and do not have inventories of goods.

In other businesses that have inventories, such as retail, wholesale, and manufacturing businesses, cost of sales and inventories are a major part of determining these costs. Since physical inventories are factors in determining the cost of goods sold, the IRS requires that this accounting be taken at the beginning and end of each tax year. Inventory amounts include goods held for sale in the normal course of business as well as raw materials and supplies that will physically become a part of the merchandise intended for sale. In addition, the IRS stipulates that companies with inventories must use the accrual method of accounting.

Cost of goods sold is established in one of several ways: directly, by using a gross margin approach, or indirectly, by a process of deduction. If detailed inventory records are maintained in both quantity and money, then the cost of goods sold can be established directly as sales take place. A good example of this procedure is the computer cash register system used by several large retailers. The clerk inputs the inventory number into the cash register as sales are added up. The computer keeps track of all the inventory as it is sold. Another direct method is to establish cost of sales by costing each line of a copy of each sales invoice, using data from a stock list of unit costs or file of standard unit costs. For large manufactured goods, the cost records maintained during production provide their total cost at the time of shipment.

A short cut in establishing the cost of goods sold directly, for monthly financial statement purposes, is to maintain classifications of sales by product groups that all have the same percentage of mark-up (gross margin) and to multiply the sales in each group by the appropriate percentage. For example, if the sales of a product group having a known gross margin of 30 percent are $100,000 for the period, then the cost of goods sold would be established as 70 percent of this, or $70,000.

Where it is not possible or practical to establish the cost of goods directly, or to establish it by the gross margin method, it is necessary to determine the cost by deduction. An inventory record has four elements:

1. What was on hand at the beginning of the period
2. What came in during the period
3. What went out during the period
4. What was left at the end of the period

If any three of these elements are known, then it is possible to find the fourth element by deduction. When using the method to determine cost of goods sold, we want to find what went out during the period. All companies are required to take inventory at the end of each year, in order that they know their ending inventory, and also, to be aware of their beginning inventory (taken at the end of last year). Incoming goods consist of the purchases of the company.

The following analysis illustrates the deductive method of determining cost of goods sold:

1.	Inventory at the beginning of the year	$30,700	
	Less: Merchandise contributed to charitable organizations	400	$ 30,300
ADD:			
2.	Merchandise (or raw materials) purchased during the year	60,000	
3.	Labor	20,000	
4.	Materials and supplies	4,000	
5.	Other costs	6,000	90,000
6.	Cost of goods available for sale		120,000
SUBTRACT:			
7.	Inventory at the end of the year		35,000
RESULT:			
8.	Cost of goods sold		$85,300

1. *Inventory at the beginning of the year* (opening inventory) for a manufacturer includes the total value of the raw material, work-in-process (goods not finished), finished goods, and materials and supplies used in manufacturing the goods. For retailers and wholesalers, inventory consists of merchandise held for sale. The ending inventory for one year is the beginning for the next tax year.

2. *Merchandise purchased during the year* includes the cost of all raw materials or parts purchased for manufacturing into a finished product for manufacturers. For merchants it includes all the merchandise bought for sale. Merchandise must be reported as net of trade discounts, purchase returns and allowances, merchandise withdrawn for stockholder or owner use, and sometimes cash discounts. Cash discounts can be accounted for in two ways: either credited to a separate discount account, or deducted from total purchases for the year. If you credit cash discounts to a separate account, then the credit balance in this account at the end of the tax year must be included in your business income. Whatever method you use, you must be consistent. Changing from one method of accounting for cash discounts to another may require IRS approval.

3. *Labor* costs are an element of cost of goods sold only in a manufacturing or mining business. Such costs include both direct and indirect labor used in fabricating the raw material into a finished product. *Direct labor costs are the wages paid to employees who spend all their time working directly on the product being manufactured. Indirect labor costs* are the wages paid to employees who perform a general factory function that does not have any immediate or direct connection with the fabrication of the product but is a necessary part of the manufacturing process. In a factory, the indirect laborer would be a janitor in the factory or a person in the boxing and shipping department.

   Generally, the only kinds of labor costs properly chargeable to cost of goods sold are direct or indirect labor costs. Certain other costs treated as overhead expenses are charged to the manufacturing process.

4. *Materials and supplies*, such as hardware and chemicals used in manufacturing goods, are charged to cost of goods sold. Materials and supplies that are not consumed in the manufacturing process are treated as deferred charges, deductible as a business expense when used.

5. *Other costs* are costs incurred in connection with a manufacturing or mining process, such as containers and packages; freight-in, express-in, and cartage-in costs; and certain overhead expenses.

    If containers and packages are an integral part of the product manufactured, then they are considered part of cost of goods sold. If they are not an integral part of the manufactured product, then their costs are charged to shipping or selling expenses. Overhead expenses include such expenses as rent, heat, light, power, insurance, depreciation, taxes, maintenance labor, and supervision. The overhead expenses incurred as direct and necessary expenses of the manufacturing operation are included in cost of goods sold.

6. *Cost of goods available for sale* is the total of items 1 through 5 representing the cost of goods available for sale during the year.

7. The *inventory at the end of the year* (closing inventory) should be subtracted from cost of goods available for sale (item 6).

8. *Cost of goods sold* is reached when the closing inventory is subtracted from the cost of goods available for sale. When you subtract your cost of goods sold from your adjusted total receipts or net sales for the tax year, you will have determined gross profit from sales.

Inventory Identification

Inventories will be discussed in greater detail in Chapter 4, but at least a cursory explanation is called for in this chapter. Since inventories are, for the most part, cost of goods sold, it is necessary to include physically all finished or partly finished goods, raw materials, and supplies that become part of the business's merchandise intended for sale.

Merchandise for which you have a title, can be included in your inventory, regardless of whether the merchandise is physically in your possession. Inventory should also include goods under contract for sale that you have not yet segregated and applied to the contract, such as goods on consignment.

If you sell merchandise by mail and intend that payment and delivery be concurrent (goods sent COD), the title passes when payment is made. Merchandise so shipped is excluded from sales and included in your closing inventory until paid for by the buyer.

Assets such as land, buildings, and equipment used in the business, notes and accounts receivable, and similar assets are not to be included in inventory. Real estate dealers are allowed to inventory real estate held for sale. (Typically, real estate is inventory in the hands of dealers in real estate.) Freight-out, express-out, and cartage out costs are shipping or selling expenses and are not part of the cost of goods sold.

GROSS PROFIT (GROSS MARGIN)

Once the cost of goods sold has been established, it is subtracted from net sales to arrive at a figure for the gross margin (gross profit). This figure is the amount of revenue over and above that necessary to cover the purchasing or manufacturing cost of goods sold. It represents the revenue available to cover selling and administrative expenses and also to provide an operating profit for the period.

In any business in which an inventory is not an income determining factor, gross sales (less returns and allowances) is equivalent to gross profit. Most professions and businesses that provide personal services determine gross profit as gross sales. Since gross profit is the money available to pay for all the selling and for general and administrative expenses of a corporation or business, it becomes a very important item in finance. The gross profit percentage (gross profit divided by net sales) is also important in determining how a particular company is doing in relation to the industry or historical averages.

Operating Expense and Selling Expense

Operating expense and selling expenses are listed in an income statement after the figure for gross margin. They are not included in inventory valuations. They are accounted for as period costs and not inventory costs (cost of goods sold). Both selling and operating expenses are sometimes listed simply under operating expense, general and administrative expense, or just expenses.

Selling Expenses

Practice varies among companies with respect to the specific types of cost that are included under the title of selling expenses. But in general, selling expenses consist of two major types: order getting (sales) and order handling (shipping). *Order-getting expenses* are those such as advertising, salesmen's salaries and commissions, and sales office costs. *Order-handling costs* are those such as order editing and filing expense, warehouse-ing, and shipping.

The majority of expenses included under the title of selling expenses does not necessarily bear any direct relationship to the sales figure. The shorter the period covered by the statement, the less likely is there any relationship between these figures. This is particularly true of order-getting expenses, since realization of sales is more than the sum total of the efforts expended to achieve it and sales figures represent only the goods shipped.

Operating Expense (General and Administrative Expense)

General and administrative expenses (operating expense) are costs to be deducted from gross profit to arrive at operating income. They are not cost of goods purchased or produced, and if the company has a separate cost group for selling expense, they are not sales related. From a budgeting and control standpoint, these are managed costs and in the short run they will be fixed costs. They are regulated over time by management decisions and do not necessarily bear any direct relationship to production or sales volume.

Items Included in Operating and Selling Expense

Certain expenses are deductible; others are not. For the purposes of this chapter, items can be grouped into: wages and salaries; rental expense; repairs; replacements; improvements; depreciation; bad debts; travel and transportation; business entertainment; interest; insurance; taxes; and other business expense. Each of these groups will be discussed in turn.

Wages and Salaries

Salaries, wages, and other forms of compensation paid to employees are deductible business expenses for tax purposes if they meet the following four tests:

Test 1: You must be able to show that salaries, wages, and other compensation are "ordinary and necessary expenditures directly connected with carrying on (your) business or trade" (IRS Regulation 1.162-1). The fact that you pay your employees reasonable compensation for legitimate business purposes is not enough, by itself, for the expense to qualify as a deductible expense. Remunerations of services can be deducted only if the payment is an ordinary and necessary expense of carrying on your trade or business. Expenses (including salaries) incurred in completing mergers, recapitalizations, consolidations, and other reorganizations are not expenses of carrying on a business, unless the reorganization, or merger, falls through. If the merger or reorganization is abandoned, the expenses of that reorganization are deducted in that year.

Test 2: Reasonable compensation is determined by the amount that "ordinarily would be paid for like services, by like enterprises, under like circumstances" (IRS Regulation 1.162-7). The following factors are considered in determining reasonableness of compensation:

1. Duties performed by the employee
2. Volume of business handled
3. Character and amount of responsibility
4. Complexities of the business
5. Amount of time required
6. General cost of living in the locality
7. Ability and achievements of the individual performing the service
8. Comparison of the compensation with the amount of gross and net income of the business.

As a practical matter, however, most compensation deducted never gets questioned. If the amount of compensation is questioned, the foregoing serve as a basis for determining reasonableness.

Test 3: It is necessary to be able to prove that the payments were made for services actually rendered. It also should be expected that your business will benefit reasonably from the service performed.

Test 4: Compensation must have been paid or the expense incurred during the tax year. Using the cash accounting method, only the salaries actually paid during the year are deductible. If the accrual method of accounting is used, then the deduction for salaries and wages is allowable when the obligation to pay the compensation is established.

Employee bonuses are allowable deductions if they are intended as additional compensation, not as gifts, and are paid for services actually rendered. If, to promote employee goodwill, you distribute turkeys, hams, or other merchandise of nominal value at Christmas time, and on these special occasions the value of these gifts is not considered salary or wages to your employees. You can deduct the cost of these gifts as a business expense, however, under the gift category. These gifts are limited to a $25 value for each person. If, however, you distribute cash, gift certificates, or similar items of readily convertible cash value, then the value of such gifts is considered additional wages or salary, regardless of amount.

Loans and advances to an employee for which you do not expect repayment generally are deductible as compensation, if they are for personal services actually rendered and the total is reasonable when added to the employee's other compensation. Interview expense allowances or reimbursements made to a job candidate and moving expenses paid to employees are not wages subject to federal payroll taxes, but they are deductible expenses for the business.

Compensation need not be paid in cash. It may be in the form of meals, lodging, inventoriable items, capital assets, and shares of stock in the business.

If you give stock in your company to your employees as compensation, then you are entitled to deduct the fair market value of that stock as of the date given. If you transfer a capital asset or an asset used in your business to one of your employees in payment for services, then its fair market value, on the date of the transfer, is deductible. Both of these forms of compensation are taxable income of the employee.

The cost of meals, lodging, and inventoriable items, furnished to the employees as part of their compensation is deductible by the employer. In some cases, meals and lodging are not taxable to the employee as income. To enable the employees to exclude from their gross income the value of meals and lodging furnished to them without charge by the employer the following tests must be met:

1. The meals or lodging must be furnished on the employer's business premises.
2. The meals or lodging must be furnished for the employer's convenience.
3. In the case of lodging (but not meals), the employees must be required to accept it as a condition of their employment. This means that acceptance of the lodging is required to enable them to perform properly the duties of their employment, as being available for duty at all times.

Fringe benefits such as premiums on insurance, hospitalization, and medical care for employees are deductible by the employer. These benefits do not include life insurance premiums, except under special circumstances.

Contributions made for deferred compensation, such as a security benefit plan, supplemental unemployment benefits, pension plans, annuity plans, profit-sharing plans, bond-purchase plans, and stock bonus plans, are deductible if made by the employer.

QUESTION: *Are payments of salaries to employee-stockholders restricted in their deductibility?*

ANSWER:

The salaries of employee-stockholders are subject to the same requirements for deductibility as those of any other executives. However, the burden of proving that the payments to employee-stockholders are both reasonable and for personal services actually rendered is somewhat greater than in the case of payments to employees, who have little or no stockholdings. In other words, although salaries of employee-stockholders have to meet the same requirements as any other employee, there is a greater chance of IRS scrutiny. Payments to employee-stockholders that are in the form of compensation and are not, in fact, for services rendered, are not deductible. These payments are considered to represent the distribution of a dividend on stock.

QUESTION: *How are stock options treated in regards to taxation?*

ANSWER:

If your business grants an employee or an independent contractor an option to buy stock, or any other property, as payment for services, then your company is generally considered to have paid compensation to the recipient. This compensation is treated as a deduction if it is a currently deductible expense, or as a capital expenditure if it is attributable to a capital asset. The amount of deduction is equal to the fair market value of the option at the time of the grant. If the exercise price of the option is equal to the market value of the stock the fair value of the option is zero.

Rental Expenses

Ordinarily a person may deduct, as current expenses, rent paid or accrued for property used in your trade or business. If he or she allocates rental expenses to the cost of goods sold, of course these expenses cannot again be included as an operating expense.

Rent paid in property, other than money or services, is deductible as rent to the extent of the fair market value of that property or service. Rent paid in advance, sums paid to acquire a lease, and commissions, bonuses, fees, or other expenses paid to obtain possession of property under a lease covering a period of more than one year must generally be deductible, ratably, over the term of the lease, or the period covered by the advance.

For example, in May of 1978 you leased a building for five years, beginning July 1 1978 and ending June 30 1983. Under the terms of the lease, you are to pay a yearly rental of $1,200. You paid the first year's rent on June 2 1978. In your income tax return for calendar year 1978, you may deduct only 6/12 of $1,200, or $600, for the rent applicable to 1978.

Costs for acquiring a lease must be deducted ratably over the term of the lease. Any renewal period in the lease must be included in determining the period over which amortization of cost is allowed, but only if less than 75 percent of the cost is for the remaining term of the lease, excluding renewal period. For example, in 1978 you paid $10,000 to acquire a lease for twenty years with options to renew for five years each (ten years total renewal). Seven thousand dollars ($7,000) of your cost was paid for the original lease and $3,000 was applied to the renewal options. Since less than 75 percent of $10,000 is attributable to the twenty-year remaining life of your present lease, you must amortize the $10,000 over 30 years, the remaining life of your present lease plus the period for renewal. However, if the term of the lease plus renewal options exceeds the economic life as determined by depreciation guidelines, then depreciation guidelines may be used.

Improvements by a lessee are generally treated as capital expenditures (to acquire the asset *leasehold improvements*) and not as deductible current expenses. These improvements are to be amortized over the period of their useful life or the term of the lease, whichever is shorter. Taxes that you, as lessee, are required to pay to or for the lessor of business property are deductible as additional rent. If you lease equipment, you should determine whether the agreement is a lease or a conditional sales contract. If the agreement is a lease, you may deduct rental payments for the use of the equipment. If the agreement is a conditional sales contract and you have acquired, or will acquire, title to or equity in the equipment, the payments under the agreement (excluding interest) are considered as payments for the purchase of the equipment. Payments for the purchase of equipment are not deductible as rent or lease expense. The fair market value of the leased asset must be capitalized as an equipment asset and depreciated over the life of the asset. In addition, the portion of the lease payment that is attributable to interest may be deducted from taxable income.

Ordinarily, an agreement is considered a conditional sales contract, rather than a lease, if any of the following conditions are present:

1. Portions of the periodic payments are specifically applicable to an equity to be acquired by you (as lessee).
2. Title will be acquired, on payment of a stated amount of rentals, that you are required to make under the contract.
3. The total payment required for a relatively short period of use constitutes an excessively large proportion of the total sum required to be paid to secure transfer of title.
4. The agreed rental payments exceed materially the current fair rental value. This may indicate that the payments include an element other than compensation for the use of the property.
5. The property may be acquired under a purchase option at a price that is nominal, in relation to the value of the property at the time when you may exercise the option, determined at the time of entering into the original agreement, or, if the option price is a relatively small amount when compared with the total payments you are required to make.
6. Some portion of the periodic payments is specifically designated as interest, or is otherwise readily recognizable as the equivalent of interest.
7. Title will be acquired upon payment of an aggregate amount (the total of rental payments plus the option price, if any) that approximates the price, plus interest, at which you could have purchased the equipment when you entered into the agreement.

QUESTION: What tax treatment is required for money received or spent for cancellation of a lease?

ANSWER:

Gain or loss from the cancellation of a business lease may be ordinary gain or loss or capital gain or loss. Gain or loss resulting from cancellation of a lease held for more than twelve months is subject to the special treatment provided for gains and losses from the sale or exchange of such property (capital gains or losses). Gains or losses from leases held for less than twelve months are subject to ordinary gains or loss tax treatment.

Repairs, Replacements, and Improvements

Any expenditure for property or equipment may be deductible as an expense, or not, depending on whether it just maintains the property or actually adds to the value and life of the property.

Repairs, including labor, supplies, and certain other items are deductible expenses. This is because repairs, for the most part, merely maintain property. The value of your own labor expended in this repair, however, is not deductible as an expense. Examples of repairs include: patching and repairing floors, repainting the inside and outside of a building, repairing roofs and gutters, and mending leaks.

Replacements that arrest deterioration and appreciably prolong the life of the property are *not* deductible as expense. They should be capitalized and depreciated. Expenditures for replacement parts of a machine to maintain it in operable condition *are* deductible business expense. Major overhauls of machinery require capitalization and depreciation.

Since improvements increase the value of property, prolong its life, or adapt it to different uses, it follows that improvements are considered a capital expenditure (creation of an asset) and *cannot* be deducted as an expense. Examples of improvements include: new electric wiring, a new roof, new floor, new plumbing, structural changes, and lighting improvements.

The cost of repairs to business vehicles is deductible. However, amounts paid for reconditioning and general overhauling of business vehicles are capital expenditures. The cost of tires and tubes for business vehicles is deductible as an expense. Amounts spent for tools or short-lived parts of a machine are deductible as a business expense, if they wear out or have to be replaced in less than one year.

Depreciation

Depreciation is the deductible allowance for the exhaustion, wear and tear, and obsolescence of property used in your trade or business, or "held for the production of income" (IRS Regulation 167 (a)-1). Depreciation is not a real expense in the sense that you have to write out a check to depreciation each year. Depreciation is a noncash, artificial expense that is allowed as a deduction for tax purposes, but, in fact, does not cause you to make a cash outlay. If income-producing property or property used in a trade or business has a limited useful life (including all fixed assets except land) that can be determined or estimated, then a deduction for its cost over the period of its useful life can be made. This deduction is called depreciation. The cost of property with a useful life of more than one year, such as buildings, furniture, machinery, copyrights, patents, and oil wells, may not be deducted entirely in one year. Since land and goodwill have an indefinite life, it follows that they are not depreciable.

Bad Debt

Worthless debts arising from sales, professional services rendered, unpaid rents, interest, and similar items of taxable income, will not be allowed as bad-debt deductions unless these items have been included in gross income on the return for the year for which the deduction is claimed or for a previous year. In other words, if you do not, or did not, declare the income, you cannot declare the bad debt. A taxpayer using the cash accounting method, for instance, is not entitled to deduct business bad debts because the taxpayer has never included in gross income the sales that created the bad debt. However, if a cash method taxpayer declares the sales as income (from the cash register tape, for instance) and later the check taken is found to be bad, he may deduct the bad debt because he has declared the sales.

The business using the accrual method of accounting (sales counted when shipped or billed) is the most likely to encounter deductible bad debts. If accounts receivable, notes receivable, or both are created or acquired in connection with a trade or business, and become partially or totally worthless, they are business bad debts. They may be deducted from business income in one of two ways: (1) the specific charge-off method or (2) the reserve-for-bad-debts method. (For additional information on this subject, see Chapter 5.)

Travel and Transportation Expenses

Travel expenses are the expenses incurred while traveling away from home overnight in pursuit of your trade or business. *Transportation expenses*, on the other hand, include only the costs of travel (not meals and lodging) directly attributable to the actual conduct of your business while you are not away from home overnight.

Travel expenses include: meals and lodging (both en route and at your destination); air, rail, and bus fares; baggage charges; the cost of transporting sample cases or display materials; the cost of maintaining and operating your automobile; the cost of operating and maintaining your house trailer; reasonable cleaning and laundry expenses; telephone and telegraph expenses; and the cost of a public stenographer. Travel expenses also include:

1. The cost of transportation from the airport or station to your hotel, from your hotel to the airport or station, from one customer or place of work to another
2. Reasonable transportation costs from where you obtain meals and lodging to where you are working while away from home overnight
3. Other similar expenses incidental to qualifying travel
4. Reasonable tips incidental to any of the expenses

You can deduct travel expenses incurred for yourself, but not for your family, in attending a convention. Incidental, personal expenses incurred for your entertainment, such as sight-seeing and social visiting, are not deductible.

If the trip were in the United States, primarily for business, and while at your business destination you extended your stay for nonbusiness reasons, made a nonbusiness side trip, or engaged in other nonbusiness activities, the travel expenses to and from your destination are deductible. If the trip is outside the United States, undertaken primarily for business, but some nonbusiness activities occurred, you *cannot* deduct all of your travel costs from your home to your business destination and return.

Transportation expenses (sometimes referred to as local travel expenses) include such items as air, train, bus, and cab fares, and the cost of operating and maintaining your business vehicle. Commuting expenses between your residence and usual place of business are not deductible, regardless of the distance involved. However, if you use your automobile entirely for business purposes, you can deduct all of your actual expenses for its operation, including depreciation. Nevertheless, if your automobile is used partly for business, you must apportion its expense between a reasonable allowance for depreciation of business and personal usage.

If a leased car is used in your business, you can deduct the lease payments to the extent that they are directly attributable to your business. No portion of the lease payments are deductible if the car is used for commuting or personal reasons.

Instead of using actual expenses and depreciation to determine deductible costs of operating an automobile (including pickup or panel truck) for business purposes, you can use a *standard mileage rate* of 17 cents a mile for the first 15,000 miles of business usage per year, and 10 cents a mile for each additional business mile in that year. To use the standard mileage rate, you must:

1. Own the car
2. Not use more than one car simultaneously in your business or profession
3. Not use the car for hire, such as a taxi
4. Not operate a fleet of cars of which two or more are used simultaneously
5. Not have claimed depreciation using any method other than the straight-line method and
6. Not have claimed additional first-year depreciation on the car.

If the car is fully depreciated, you can only deduct 10 cents a mile for all miles of business usage.

Parking fees and tolls incurred during business use are deductible in addition to the standard mileage rate.

QUESTION: *What substantiation of travel expenses is required by the IRS?*

ANSWER:

You must prove the following for all travel expenses claimed:

1.   The amount of each separate expenditure for traveling away from home, such as the cost of your transportation and lodging; (the daily cost of your breakfast, lunch, dinner, and other incidental elements of such travel may be aggregated if they are set forth in reasonable categories such as: meals, gas and oil, taxi fares).
2.   The dates of your departure and return home for each trip in addition to the number of days spent on business away from home.
3.   The destination or locality of your travel.
4.   The business reason for your travel or the nature of the business benefit derived or expected to be derived as a result of your travel.

QUESTION: *If I buy a new business car during the year and I am taking a depreciation deduction, how do I change the deduction from the old car to the new one?*

ANSWER:

If you replace your car during the year and both cars qualify, you compute your deduction by taking into account the total business mileage of both cars during the year. Remember, you have to maintain adequate records to establish the actual business miles you have driven. Approximations and estimations are unacceptable. This is true whether you replace your car or not.

Business Entertainment Expenses

Entertainment includes any activity generally considered entertainment, amusement, or recreation. Customarily, this covers entertainment of guests at restaurants, theaters, sporting events, on yachts, or on hunting, fishing, vacation, or similar trips. It may also include satisfying the personal or family needs of any individuals, the cost of which would otherwise be a business expense to you. These include furnishing food and beverages; providing a hotel suite or automobile to business customers or their families.

Items are considered business entertainment expenses and are deductible only if they are ordinary and necessary expenses "directly related to or associated with the active conduct of your trade or business" (IRS Regulation 1.167–1).

For an entertainment expense to meet the test of being *directly related* to the active conduct of business, you must show:

1. You had more than a *general expectation* of deriving income or some other specific benefit at some future time from the people entertained.
2. You did engage in business during the entertainment period with the person being entertained.
3. The principal characteristic of the combined business and entertainment was the transaction of your business.

You are required to show that business income or other business benefits actually resulted from each and every entertainment expenditure. If entertainment takes place on hunting or fishing trips or on yachts or pleasure boats, the conduct of business is not considered to be the principal character or aspect of the combined business and entertainment unless you are able to establish otherwise. These types of costs will not be deductible unless you can show that they are directly related to the active conduct of your business.

Entertainment expenses in a *clear business setting* are generally considered to be deductible. Examples of clear business settings are:

1. Entertainment in a hospitality room at a convention where business goodwill is created through the display or discussion of business products.
2. Entertainment that has the principal effect of price rebates in the sale of your products usually will be considered directly related to your business. One example of this would be free meals furnished by a restaurant owner to regular customers.
3. Entertainment of a clear business nature occurring under circumstances in which there is no meaningful personal or social relationship between you and the persons entertained. An exam-

ple would be entertainment of business and civic leaders at the opening of a new hotel or theatrical production to obtain business publicity rather than to create or maintain goodwill of the persons entertained.

Entertainment expenses that do not meet the directly related tests mentioned above, but are associated with the active conduct of your trade or business, are allowable if the entertainment directly precedes or follows a substantial and bona fide business discussion. If it can be shown there was a clear business purpose in incurring the expenditure, such as to develop new business or to encourage the continuation of an existing business relationship, then the expense is deductible. A substantial and bona fide business discussion is generally considered to be a discussion, meeting, or negotiation held to obtain income or some other specific business benefit. You must show that the business discussion was substantial in relation to the entertainment, but this does not mean that more time must be devoted to business than to entertainment.

If the business entertainment expenses are not in a clear business setting, then proving they are directly related to the conduct of the business becomes more difficult and depends on the facts and circumstances of each case. Basically, this requires documentation. The better the documentation of every entertainment expense, the better your chances are of proving that the expenses are legitimate. For expenses relating to entertainment, amusement, or recreation, for a facility used in connection with such activities, as well as expenses for gifts, the following elements must be substantiated:

1. The amount of the expense or other item
2. The time and place of entertainment, amusement, recreation, and use of the facility, or the date and description of the gift
3. The business purpose of the expense
4. The business relationship between the business filing the claim of the persons entertained or receiving a gift

For entertainment expenses specifically, the following must be proven:

1. The amount of each separate expenditure for entertaining (exception: such incidental items as cab fares and telephone calls can be aggregated as are travel expenses)
2. The date the entertainment took place

3. The name, address, or location, and the type of entertainment, such as dinner or theater, if it is not apparent from the name or designation of the place
4. The reason you entertained or the nature of the business benefit derived, or expected to be derived, as a result of entertaining; the nature of any business discussion or activity that took place
5. The occupation or other information relative to the person or persons entertained including title, name, or other designation sufficient to establish such person's business relationship to you.

Your records of travel, entertainment, and business gifts should be maintained in an account book or similar record supported by adequate documentary evidence. A cancelled check payable to a named payee *will not*, by itself, support a business expenditure without other evidence that the check was used for a certain business purpose. A cancelled check together with a bill from the payee will ordinarily establish the element of cost.

If you entertain many people, you do not have to record each name if a readily identifiable class of individuals is involved. For example, if you entertain all the stockholders of a small corporation a designation such as "all the stockholders of Acme Mousetraps" is sufficient.

The IRS may require additional information to establish reliability or accuracy of records, statements, testimony, or documentary evidence before a deduction for entertainment, travel, or similar expenses is allowed. An entertainment facility is any property used in connection with entertainment such as a yacht, hunting lodge, fishing camp, swimming pool, tennis court, bowling alley, automobile, airplane, apartment, hotel suite, or a home in a vacation resort. The expenditures attributable to the maintenance, preservation, or protection of the entertainment facility (including depreciation) are not deductible unless you can show that the facility is used *more than 50 percent* for business purposes. Generally, a dwelling unit will not qualify as an entertainment facility if it is used as a personal dwelling unit for the greater of either 14 days or 10 percent of the number of days the home is rented during the year.

Expenditures of the entertainment facility that can be deducted as entertainment expenses include: depreciation, rent, utilities, repairs, insurance, compensation paid to caretakers or security personnel, and other generally accepted operating expenses. Interest, taxes, and casualty losses on the facility are not deducted as entertainment expenses but rather as taxes, interest, and casualty losses.

Club dues or fees paid to any social (for example, country club), athletic, or sporting club or organization are treated as expenditures for an entertainment facility if the club is used more than 50 percent for business purposes. You may deduct the portion of your dues directly related to business (if this represents over 50 percent of total usage). For example, your dues in a club are $100 a year, and you use it 60 percent for the furtherance of business — 20 percent for business meals, 25 percent for directly related entertainment, and 15 percent for associated entertainment. Since more than 50 percent of your use of the club is to further your trade or business, you are entitled to a deduction. But you can only deduct 45 percent of your club dues during the year (20 percent for business meals and 25 percent for directly related entertainment). Although you may consider the associated entertainment expenses in determining whether you use the club primarily for business, the portion of dues attributable to that use is not deductible.

There are no rigid criteria for determining whether more than 50 percent of the use of the facility was for business purposes. There are, however, some specific tests that can be used as guidelines.

One guideline is the *number of days used for business* in relation to the total number of days. If you use the facility 100 days out of the year and 51 or more of these days are used for business, then the facility is considered deductible. If the primary use of a facility during the day is of a business nature, it is counted as a day of business use. If the facility is used for substantial business discussion on a particular day, that day will be considered a day of business use even though the facility was used on the same day for personal or family purposes not involving entertainment of others. The primary use test is satisfied in the case of automobiles and airplanes if more than 50 percent of the mileage driven or hours flown during the tax year is for business purposes.

Director, stockholder, or employee meetings; trade association meetings; and the cost of providing entertainment to the public as a means of advertising or promoting goodwill in the community are all deductible expenses generally.

Expenses for *business gifts* made directly or indirectly to any individual are allowed, but only up to $25 total value per person per year. The following are *not* considered gifts:

1. An item costing $4 or less, if the name of your company is clearly and permanently imprinted on it, and if it is one of a number of identical items you distribute to other people. Such items include pens, desk sets, plastic bags, and additional promotion items. These are considered generally as advertising expenses.

2. A sign, display rack, or other promotional item to be used on the business premises of the recipient
3. An item of tangible personal property costing not more than $100, if awarded to the employee because of length of service or for safety achievement. This is considered part of the employee's gross income.

Any item that may be considered entertainment or a gift will be considered customarily as a gift.

QUESTION: Are you allowed to deduct entertainment expenses for spouses of customers or for your own spouse?

ANSWER:
Yes. Ordinarily the portion of an otherwise deductible entertainment expense that is allocated to the spouse of a person engaged in substantial business discussion will be considered associated with the active conduct of your business. Therefore, you can deduct the cost of entertainment allocated to your spouse or the spouse of a business customer.

QUESTION: Are entertainment expenses that occur after a business discussion, or prior to it, deductible?

ANSWER:
If it occurs on the same day, yes. If it occurs on a previous or subsequent day, maybe. Entertainment occurring on the same day as the business discussions will be considered as directly preceding or following the business discussion, and are deductible. However, if the entertainment does not occur on the same day, the facts and circumstances of each case will have to be considered. Among the facts to be considered are the place, date, duration of the business discussion, whether you or your business associates are from out of town, and, if so, the dates of arrival and departure, and the reasons the entertainment and discussion did not take place on the same day.

For example, if a group of business associates comes from out of town to your place of business to hold a substantial business discussion, the entertainment of those business guests and their spouses on the evening before, or on the evening of the day following, the business discussion would be regarded as directly preceding or following it.

QUESTION: When are business meals not deductible as entertainment expense?

ANSWER:

Business meals are not generally deductible when they are reciprocal meals or meals in places where entertainment is a major attraction and there is no possibility of engaging in the active conduct of business. Reciprocal meals are considered so when a group of businesspersons takes turns buying lunch for each other in a regular manner. Meetings at nightclubs, theaters, sporting events, or essentially social gatherings, such as cocktail parties and situations in which you meet with a group (including persons other than business associates) may be considered circumstances where there is little or no possibility of engaging in active conduct of business. You may overcome these presumptions by establishing that you did engage in a substantial business discussion by the methods described previously.

Interest Expense

Interest is defined as the compensation allowed by law or fixed by the parties for the use (or forbearance) of money. A business can deduct all interest paid or accrued in the tax year on business debt. The interest paid must be on a debt under which you have a valid obligation to pay a fixed and determinable sum of money. This debt is generally referred to as a *liability.*

The liability must be your liability or you cannot deduct the interest paid. An individual, for instance, cannot deduct interest paid on the debt of a corporation. In the special case when you purchase property and pay interest owed by the seller, you cannot deduct the interest but must capitalize it (make it part of the cost of the property).

Sometimes, interest in the form of a discount is subtracted from the proceeds of a loan at the time it is made. This type of interest deduction can be made only at the time that it is due to be paid. Even though the interest is paid at the beginning of the loan, it is thought to accrue ratably over the period of indebtedness. You must deduct the interest only in the year the liability to pay it accrues. For example, Acme Mousetraps borrowed $1,000 from the bank on October 1 1978 and signed a six-month note bearing an annual interest rate of 7 percent. Acme is on the cash basis for accounting. The bank discounted the note and deposited $965 ($1,000 less $35 interest) in Acme's account. On March 1 1979 Acme issued a check to the bank for $1,000 in payment of this note. Although Acme did not have an interest deduction on its calendar-year income tax return in 1978, when the bank discounted the note, the company could deduct $35 interest on the 1979 return.

If, in this example, Acme had been on the accrual method of accounting, it would have been allowed to deduct $17.50 (October, November, and December interest) in 1978 and the balance (for the last three months of the loan), $17.50, in 1979.

Interest paid on *mortgages* is deductible. In general, monthly payments on mortgages include both principal and interest. Only the interest is deductible. If you prepay your mortgage and pay the lender a penalty for this privilege, this payment is deductible as interest. Points on a mortgage, that is, charges paid by a mortgagor-borrower to a lender as loan obligation fees, maximum loan charges, or premium charges, are deductible as interest. However, expenses incident to acquiring a mortgage loan (mortgage commissions, abstract fees, recording fees, and the like) are not deductible, either as interest or business expenses. These expenses are capital expenditures, but they are *not* added to the basis of the property (cost of the property purchased), but rather are deductible on a pro-rata basis over the life of the mortgage (not the life of the asset).

Prepaid interest (interest you pay in cash in advance) is *not* deductible when paid, but as in the discounted note just mentioned, it accrues ratably over the period of the indebtedness.

Items *not* deductible as interest are: capitalized interest, cost keeping, commitment fees, tax penalties, and interest on tax-exempt income. Capitalized interest is interest paid as a cost of property purchased (as when you pay the interest of the seller), or when you, as a taxpayer, elect to capitalize your mortgage payments as part of the cost of the property. Commitment fees paid as current charges for making business funds available on a standby basis, and not for the use of funds, are not considered interest payments. They are considered as a business expense, however. Penalties on deficiencies or underestimating tax are not interest and therefore are not deductible. Fines and penalties, regardless of their nature are not deductible. Interest relating to tax-exempt income is not deductible. No deduction is allowed for interest on a debt incurred or continued for the purpose of purchasing or carrying tax-exempt securities.

Insurance Expense

If you carry business insurance to protect your company against losses by fire or other hazards, the premiums paid are deductible as business expenses. The following are sample deductible expenses:

Premiums on fire, theft, flood, or other casualty insurance
Merchandise and inventory insurance
Credit insurance

Employee's group hospitalization and medical insurance
Premiums on employer's liability insurance
Malpractice insurance
Public liability insurance
Workmen's compensation insurance
Overhead insurance
Use and occupancy insurance and business interruption
Employee performance bonds
Expenses for bonds the business is required to furnish either by law
or by contract
Automobile and other vehicle insurance (unless you use the Standard Mileage Rate to compute auto expense).[1]

Most life insurance premiums are *not* deductible as business expense. Premiums you pay or incur on your own life insurance policies are personal expenses, and are not deductible. Contrary to popular belief, if you take out a policy on your life or on the life of any other person financially interested in your business in order to procure or protect a loan (required by the bank), the premiums paid *are not deductible*.

Key man insurance premiums you pay or incur on a life insurance policy covering any officer or employee *are* deductible, but only if:

1. The premium payments are an ordinary and necessary business expense in the nature of additional compensation
2. The total amount of all compensation, including insurance premiums, paid to the person is not unreasonable
3. The policy does not directly or indirectly state that you are a beneficiary.

Life insurance on one partner is not deductible. If a partner, whose continued services are essential to the success of the business, takes out insurance on his or her own life naming copartners as beneficiaries to induce them to retain their investments in the firm, then the essential partner would be a direct or an indirect beneficiary. A business cannot deduct its share of premiums paid on a life insurance policy purchased on the life of an employee under the so-called split-dollar plan. Under the split-dollar plan, the business and the employee join in buying an insurance policy in which there is a substantial investment element on the employee's life.

---

[1] Premiums paid for workmen's compensation on behalf of partners are *not* deductible by a partnership as amounts paid on behalf of employees, since partners are not considered employees of the partnership.

QUESTION: Are funds used for a self-insurance reserve deductible?

ANSWER:

You cannot deduct as an insurance expense periodic amounts credited to a reserve for self-insurance equal to the estimated premiums you otherwise would have paid an insurance company for business insurance. This applies even though you are unable to get business insurance coverage for certain business risks. However, actual losses are deductible.

Tax Expense

Various taxes, imposed by federal, state, local, and foreign governments incurred in the ordinary course of business or trade are deductible. Those taxes that are not deductible include: federal income, estate and gift taxes; state inheritance, legacy, and succession taxes; and assessments for local benefits. Assessments for local benefits are those that tend to increase the value of your property (such as assessments for construction of streets, sidewalks, public parking facilities, and water and sewage systems).

Taxes that are deductible as business expenses are broken down into broad categories:

Real property taxes
Income tax
Other taxes
Employment taxes (payroll, Social Security, and the like).

Next to income tax, the greatest tax paid by business people is *real property taxes*. Ordinarily, a business can deduct all taxes imposed on real property that the business owns. Sometimes the business can elect to capitalize expenditures for taxes as a cost of the property. Local assessments for maintenance, repairs, or interest charges for benefits such as streets, sidewalks, and water and sewage systems are deductible as a business expense (even though assessments for construction of these projects are not deductible).

Taxes levied by a special taxing district that was in existence on December 31 1963 are deductible to the extent levied for the purpose of retiring debt that existed at that date. A special taxing district covers at least one county, includes at least 1,000 persons subject to its taxes, and levies annual assessments, at a uniform rate, on the same assessed value of real property that is used for the real property tax. If real estate is sold, then the deduction for real estate taxes must be apportioned between the buyer and the seller according to the number of days in the real property tax year that each held the property. The dividing date is the date of sale.

State or local income taxes imposed on a corporation are deductible as business expense. However, state or local income tax is not deductible by an individual as a business expense, but can be deducted in computing the individual's income tax liability if deductions are itemized. A state tax on gross income (as distinguished from net income) directly attributable to business carried on by a partnership or an individual is deductible as a business expense.

In addition to real property taxes and income taxes, there are other taxes that can be deducted as business expenses. These taxes include: personal property tax, registration fees, sales taxes, state unemployment compensation or disability contributions, gasoline taxes, compensating use taxes, and corporate franchise taxes.

If state law imposes a sales tax on the seller or retailer and allows the seller or retailer to state it separately or pass it on to the consumer, then the consumer (if a business) may deduct, as a business expense, sales tax paid in purchasing property used in business.

A compensating use tax may be deductible as a general sales tax. This tax generally is imposed on the use, storage, or consumption of an item brought in from another taxing jurisdiction.

Any taxes paid on gasoline, diesel fuel, other motor fuels, and on lubricating oils that are used in the business are deductible. These taxes usually are included as part of the cost of the fuel itself and are not deducted as a separate item. You may also be entitled to a credit for tax paid on fuels and lubricants used for nonregistered vehicles. A tax of 4 cents on a gallon on certain fuel is charged. If the fuel is used in a vehicle not required to be registered for use on highways, a 2-cents-per-gallon rate applies. Therefore, you may obtain a credit or refund of 2 cents a gallon if you paid the full 4 cents tax.

A special rule applies to motor vehicle sales taxes. If the rate of a state or local sales tax on motor vehicles is higher than the general sales tax rate, then the only amount deductible is the amount of tax paid had the general rate been used. The excess should be treated as part of the cost of the asset.

If you have one or more employees, you are required to withhold federal income tax from their wages and you may also be subject to the Federal Insurance Contributions Act, FICA, (Social Security) and the Federal Unemployment Tax Act, FUTA (unemployment insurance).

These taxes are all considered *employment taxes*. Every employer subject to employment taxes is required to have an *"employer identification number."*

Under common law rules, every individual who performs services subject to the "will and control of an employer, both as to what shall be done and how it shall be done" is an employee. It does not matter that the employer permits the employee considerable discretion and freedom of action, so long as the employer has the *legal right* to control both the method and the result of the services.

Generally, if under the common law rules individuals are not employees, there is no liability for federal income tax withholding. For the Social Security taxes under FICA, the term *employee* also means any individual who performs services for remuneration under the following conditions:

1. As agent-drivers or commission-drivers engaged in distributing meat products, vegetable products, fruit products, bakery products, beverages other than milk, or laundry or dry-cleaning services for their principals.
2. As full-time life insurance salespersons.
3. As homeworkers performing work according to specifications furnished by the persons for whom the services are performed, on materials or goods furnished by such persons and required to be returned to them or persons designated by them.
4. As traveling or city salespersons engaged on a full-time basis in soliciting and transmitting orders on behalf of their principals from wholesalers, retailers, contractors, or operators of hotels, restaurants, or similar establishments for merchandise for resale or supplies for use in their business operations. Such activities do not include sideline activities on behalf of some other person.

Individuals within any of these categories are employees for Social Security purposes if:

1. The service contract states or implies that substantially all of the services are to be performed by the individual, personally.
2. The investment in facilities (other than in transportation facilities) used in the performance of services is not substantially theirs.
3. The services are such that they represent a continuing relationship with the persons for whom they are performed.

For FUTA purposes, the term employee means the same as for Social Security (FICA) tax except that it does not include insurance salespersons or homeworkers.

If your company is required by law to deduct and withhold income tax from wages or is liable for Social Security taxes, you must file a quarterly return, IRS Form 941. Under no circumstances may a return cover a period of more than one calendar quarter. Form 941 combines the Social Security taxes (including hospital insurance) and income tax withholding. Form 941E is used for reporting income tax withheld from wages, tips, annuities, and supplemental unemployment compensation benefits when no FICA (Social Security) coverage is required.

You are required by law to deduct and withhold income tax from the salaries and wages of your employees, and you are liable for the payment of that tax, whether or not you collect it from your employees. If, for example, you deduct less than the correct tax from your employees' wages, you are liable for the full amount of the correct tax.

Remember, amounts of deductions allowed, business responsibility in these matters, and special rules for withholding and other taxes change frequently, and it is best to consult the IRS *Publication 15* "Employer's Tax Guide," available free from any office of the IRS, before accounts are set up or any special steps are undertaken.

In general, an employee's *income tax withholding allowances* correspond with the exemptions to which the employee will be entitled in computing income tax on his annual return. Each employee must furnish to the employer a Form W 4. The Form W-4 is used to indicate the number of allowances that an employee wishes to claim for withholding tax. Do not confuse the Form W-4 with the Form W-4E discussed earlier. The Form W-4E is used to certify that an employee is *exempt* from withholding tax. Any time an employee desires to change his number of deductions, a new Form W-4 should be filed.

An employee may claim a special withholding allowance if the employee is single with only one employer, or married with only one employer and the employee's spouse is not employed. Also, if an employee is subject to excessive income tax withholding because large personal itemized deductions are claimed, the employee may claim additional withholding allowances.

The amount to be withheld is computed on gross wages before any deductions for Social Security tax, pension, union dues, insurance, and other authorized deductions are made. It may be determined by several methods, the most common of which is the percentage method or the wage-bracket-tables method. To compute the income tax to be withheld using the percentage method, you multiply the dollar amount of one withholding allowance by the number of allowances claimed on Form W-4, then subtract that amount from the employee's wages. Under the wage-bracket method, the tables used (in *Publication 15*) are based on wage ranges to compute the income tax to be withheld. These tables are provided for daily, weekly, biweekly, semimonthly, and monthly payroll periods. Three other methods, less frequently used, are the quarterly average wages, annualized wages, and cumulative wages methods. These usually produce the same result as the percentage and wage-bracket methods.

Employee tips, either cash or charge, received in the course of employment must be reported to the employer before the 10th day of the month following the month the tips were received. You, as the employer, must collect both employee Social Security (FICA) and income tax on tips reported by the employee from wages due the employee or from other funds the employee makes available. However, employers are *not liable* for employer taxes with respect to tip income received by their employees except to the extent of FICA tax on wages equal to the minimum wage.

Other Business Expenses

Ordinary and necessary business expenses that you pay or incur in your business during the year are deductible for the year paid or incurred. There are certain expenses for which no deduction is allowed at any time and there are other expenses that are not deductible in the current tax year, but are deductible in other tax years.

The following expenses are generally deductible:

1. Heat, light, and power.
2. Incidental supplies and materials such as office supplies, and wrapping paper.
3. Advertising that bears a reasonable relationship to your business activities, including goodwill advertising to keep your name before the public, are deductible.
4. Licenses and regulatory fees.
5. Charitable contributions made in cash or other property are deductible, subject to certain limitations.

Contributions to most recognized, nonprofit organizations — including religious, public assistance, and educational — in U.S. states or possessions, are deductible if the amount is not in excess of 5 percent of the company's taxable income. A special rule is that a corporation (other than

Subchapter S) is allowed a deduction for up to half of the appreciation on certain types of income property contributed to a public charity or a private operating foundation.

IRS *Publication 78* has a cumulative list of all organizations to which a contribution is deductible:

1. Donations to business organizations and chamber of commerce dues.
2. Management survey expenses.
3. Lobbying expenses.
4. Franchise, trademark, or trade name expenses related to a transfer, sale, or other disposition are deductible as business expenses if payments are contingent on the productivity, use, or disposition of transferred items. If the costs for these items are part of a purchase price of a capital asset, however, they must be capitalized and depreciated over their expected life.
5. Educational expenses for your employees or yourself (along with meals, lodging, and transportation expenses connected with education) can be deducted if you can show that the education maintains or improves skills required in your trade, business, or profession.
6. Commitment fees or standby charges you incur in a mortgaging agreement, under which funds for construction are made available to you in stated amounts over a specified period, are deductible.
7. Net operating losses and other losses attributable to your business or trade can be deducted. This includes losses from sales or exchanges.

The following expenses are generally *not deductible*:

1. Costs of mailings to stockholders urging action on their part to influence legislation are not deductible.
2. Educational expenses incurred to meet the *minimum* requirements of your present trade, business, or profession and expenses incurred to qualify for a new trade, business or profession are not deductible.
3. Federal income, estate, and gift taxes and state inheritance, legacy, and succession taxes.
4. Fines and penalties paid to any government, or to any agency or instrumentality thereof, for violation of the law are not deductible. This includes fines paid because of a conviction for a crime;

paid as a penalty in a government civil action; paid in settlement of actual or potential liability; or forfeited as collateral posted in connection with a proceeding which could result in the imposition of a fine or penalty.

5. Bribes, kickbacks, and related payments.
6. Gifts or contributions to political parties and candidates.
7. Commissions or finders' fees paid to locate money that you can borrow.
8. Reserves for anticipated liabilities.

QUESTION: *If I were awarded money in a legal suit and the court's judgment were reversed, could I declare the repayment of this money as an expense?*

ANSWER:
Yes.

In the past few years many companies with government contracts were required to make certain structural allowances in their buildings for the handicapped (ramps and support bars are examples). Before 1980, you can deduct the expenses for making a facility or public transportation vehicle, owned or leased by the business, more accessible to and usable by handicapped and elderly individuals. The deduction is limited to $25,000 for the tax year in which the expense is paid or incurred. These expenses may be capitalized instead of written off in the year paid.

NET INCOME OR LOSS

The final step in determining how your business did for the year is to calculate your net income (profit) or loss. Total income minus all the expenses of the business and the cost of sales gives you *net profit* or *loss*. If your company is a sole proprietorship, the net profit or net loss for the year from your business becomes part of your personal income on your individual income tax return. If you are a member of a partnership, your portion of the partnership net profit or loss becomes part of your income for tax purposes. A sole proprietorship fills out IRS Form 1040 when he or she determines profit or loss; a partnership uses Form 1065, which is then brought over to a Form 1040. In other words, in a sole proprietorship or a partnership, the individual owners pay income tax on the business. In a corporation, the corporation itself pays the income tax on its earnings. Any income after taxes may be distributed to the stockholders.

A *net operating loss* is the excess of allowable deductions over and above gross income. If you have a net operating loss, you can carry the loss as a deduction to certain tax years to reduce your tax liability or obtain a refund of all, or part of, any income tax already paid in the present year.

For individuals, net operating loss is computed in the same way as your taxable income, except that:

1. You may not deduct a net operating loss carryover or carryback from any other year.
2. You may not use capital losses in excess of your capital gains.
3. You cannot deduct 50 percent of the excess of a net long-term capital gain over a net short-term capital loss.
4. You may not claim any personal exemptions or exemptions for dependents.
5. You cannot use nonbusiness deductions in excess of your non-business income.

Shareholders of a Subchapter S corporation may be entitled to deduct their pro-rata shares of the corporation's net operating loss, subject to some limitations. But this income is treated as nonbusiness income for the shareholders when computing a loss.

Exhibit 2.6 is an example of how net operating loss might be calculated (from IRS *Publication 334*).

Loss Carrybacks and Carryforwards

If your business has a loss in any given year, the IRS allows you to carry back that loss to the three previous years or carry forward that loss to the next seven years. You can elect to carry back three years and carry forward seven years, or only to carry forward for seven years, or not to carry the loss forward or backward.

If you choose to carry back, then net operating losses must be carried back to the third tax year preceding the year in which it was sustained (if the loss occurred in 1977, you carry back the loss to 1974). Any amount of the loss not used to offset taxable income for the third preceding year is carried to the second preceding year. Any amount of the loss not used to offset taxable income for the third and second preceding years must be carried to the first preceding year. If you have a loss in 1977, you carry it back to 1974. If the loss is not used up, you apply it against 1975. If there is still some amount of loss left, you apply it to taxable income in 1976. If the loss is not entirely used to offset taxable income in the three preceding

EXHIBIT 2.6
Calculating Net Operating Loss

Example of net operating loss: You began operation of your retail shoe business in 1975 and had a net operating loss of $185 for that year. You had no taxable income in 1972, 1973, or 1974. During the tax year 1976 you had the following income and deductions:

INCOME

Salary earned as part-time helper in gas station (salary is business income)	$ 865
Interest on savings	425
Net long-term captial gain on sale of real estate used in business	2,000
Your total income	$ 3,300

DEDUCTIONS

Net operating loss carryover from 1975	$ 185
Net loss from business (gross receipts $67,000 minus expenses $72,000)	(5,000)
Net short-term capital loss on sale of stock	500
Net loss from rental property	150
Deductions for excess of net long-term capital gain over net short-term capital loss (50% of $1,500)	750
Personal exemption	750
Itemized deductions	560
Small business investment company stock loss	300
Loss on small business stock	700
Your total deductions	$ 8,895
Your deductions exceed your income by	($ 5,595)

To determine your net operating loss, the following adjustments must be made:

Deductions in excess of income		($ 5,595)
Estimate your net operating loss carryover from 1975	$185	
Eliminate your nonbusiness net short-term capital loss	500	
Eliminate your 50% deduction for net long-term capital gain	750	
Eliminate your personal exemption	750	
Eliminate the excess of your nonbusiness deductions (itemized deductions, $560) over your nonbusiness income (interest, $425)	135	
Total adjustments to net loss		$ 2,320
Your net operating loss for 1976		($ 3,275)

years, the balance may be carried forward to the seven succeeding years in order of their occurrence. Two examples from IRS *Publication 334* are shown in Exhibits 2.7 and 2.8.

EXHIBIT 2.7

Example 1: You started in business in the calendar year 1976 and had a $42,000 net operating loss for the year. Before 1976 your income consisted of wages. Your taxable income (after necessary adjustments) in the other years to which the loss may be carried back or forward is as follows:

Year	Carryback or carry-over	Adjusted taxable income	Unused carryback or carry-over
1973 3d preceding year	$42,000	$ 2,000	$40,000
1974 2nd preceding year	40,000	3,000	37,000
1975 1st preceding year	37,000	5,500	31,500
1976	Net operating loss year		
1977 1st succeeding year	31,500	7,000	24,500
1978 2nd succeeding year	24,500	3,800	20,700
1979 3d succeeding year	20,700	5,700	15,000
1980 4th succeeding year	15,000	6,000	9,000
1981 5th succeeding year	9,000	2,500	6,500
1982 6th succeeding year	6,500	3,000	3,500
1983 7th succeeding year	3,500	3,300	200

The $200 carryover remaining at the end of 1983 may not be used in 1984 or any other year.

If you have more than one net operating loss to be carried to the same tax year, apply the loss from the earliest year first. For example: You had net operating losses in the calendar years 1977 of $3,000 and 1978 of $5,000. Your adjusted taxable income in 1974 was $2,500. You carried the $3,000 loss from 1977 to 1974, leaving an unused portion of $500. You have two losses to be applied to 1975. You first apply the $500 unused loss from 1977 and then the $5,000 loss from 1978.

If you make a claim of a net operating loss deduction, you must file with your return, for the year of the deduction, a concise statement setting forth all related facts, including a detailed schedule showing how the deduction was computed.

EXHIBIT 2.8

Example 2: The facts are the same as in *Example 1* except that your adjusted taxable incomes for 1981, 1982, and 1983 are $8,000, $5,000, and $6,000 respectively. You elect to forgo the carryback period for the loss and carry the loss forward 7 years.

Year 1976 Net operating loss Year	Carryover	Adjusted taxable income	Unused carryover
1977 1st succeeding year	$42,000	$ 7,000	$35,000
1978 2nd succeeding year	35,000	3,800	31,200
1979 3d succeeding year	31,200	5,700	25,500
1980 4th succeeding year	25,500	6,000	19,500
1981 5th succeeding year	19,500	8,000	11,500
1982 6th succeeding year	11,500	5,000	6,500
1983 7th succeeding year	6,500	6,000	500

The $500 carryover remaining at the end of 1983 may not be used in 1984 or any other year.

3

Financial Statements:
The Balance Sheet

The balance sheet — a summary of assets of the business and claims against those assets — includes claims of other businesses and individuals (liabilities), as well as claims of the owners (equity). *Accounting Terminology Bulletin No. 1* of the American Institute of Certified Public Accountants (AICPA) defines the balance sheet as: "A tabular statement or summary of balances (debit and credit) carried forward after an actual or constructive closing of books of account kept according to principles of Accounting."

The balance sheet fleshes out the accounting equation:

$$\text{Assets} = \text{Liabilities} + \text{Equity}$$

The balance sheet is based on historical cost. Assets are stated at their original cost, less depreciation (if any); common and preferred stock are recorded at the original amount received for the stock; and liabilities are recorded at the amount owed. Historical cost is the norm of choice, for it minimizes the extent to which the accounts are affected by the owner's personal opinions. For instance, if the value were set at present market value, then the people responsible for the accounts would have to appraise the current market value. People often have different ideas as to what comprises market value. However, although the cost of a piece of equipment is the cost of a piece of equipment (a rose is a rose), its expected life and rate of depreciation leave room for differences of opinion and value judgments.

An example of a balance sheet is shown in Exhibit 3.1. This information for Fixit Fuzz Company shows the typical categories and items of a balance sheet. Assets are on the left (or presented first); liabilities and equity (capital) are on the right (or presented last). The first items of

---

EXHIBIT 3.1
Balance Sheet of Fixit Fuzz Company, Inc.
December 31, 198X

Assets:

Current Assets

Cash	$ 12,000	
Accounts Receivable	119,000	
Notes Receivable	7,800	
Inventories at Cost (LIFO)	235,200	
Prepaid Assets	26,000	
Total Current Assets		$ 400,000

Fixed Assets

Land	45,000	
Buildings and Improvements	230,000	
Equipment and Vehicles	497,000	
Furniture and Fixtures	31,456	
Less: Accumulated Deprec.	(212,456)	
Total Fixed Assets		$ 591,000

Other Assets

Investment in Subsidiaries	49,000	
Goodwill	76,000	
Research and Development	82,000	
Less: R&D Amortization	(51,000)	
Total Other Assets		$ 156,000
Total Assets		$1,147,000

EXHIBIT 3.1
continued

Liabilities:
Current Liabilities

Accounts Payable	$ 98,500	
Notes Payable	7,340	
Accrued Taxes	103,182	
Accrued Salaries	10,340	
Provision for Pensions	56,300	
Total Current Liabilities		$ 275,662

Long-Term Liabilities:

Notes Payable	28,503	
Bonds (8½% due 1985)	310,635	
Total Long-term Liabilities		$ 339,138
Total Liabilities		$ 611,800

Equity

Capital Stock	100,000	
Paid-in Surplus	120,000	
Retained Earnings	315,200	
Total Equity		$ 535,200
Total Liabilities and Equity		$1,147,000

assets are the current assets; the first items of liabilities are the current liabilities. These current assets are followed by fixed assets and other assets.

Current liabilities are followed by long-term liabilities. *Current assets* are assets that can be converted to cash within one year. *Current liabilities* reflect a one-year period, but they are debts that will be repaid within the next year. *Fixed assets* — assets that will remain for more than one year — are generally (with the exception of land) depreciable or amortizable. Other assets are assets that cannot be converted into cash within one year and are usually not depreciable or amortizable. However, other assets may include patents or intangibles that are amortized. Long-term liabilities are debts that will take more than one year to pay off. In accounting, more than one year is considered *long-term*.

The equity (or capital) portion of the balance sheet shows the basic components of the owner's investment and retention of capital in the business: stock, paid-in surplus, and retained earnings. In proprietorships and partnerships, this section may contain owners' cumulative equity only in the business (owners' equity) and the retained earnings for that period (sometimes stated simply as net profit).

ASSETS

An asset is defined as property that is used in the trade or business. Either directly or indirectly, this property contributes toward earning the income of the business. In general, assets are productive items that contribute to income and are tangible property, or promises of future receipt of cash (accounts receivable), or investments made in the business that are not considered expense.

The *Accounting Terminology Bulletin No. 1* of AICPA, mentioned earlier, defines assets in this way:

> The word asset is not synonymous with or limited to property but includes also that part of any cost or expense incurred which is properly carried forward upon a closing of books at a given date. Consistently with the definition of balance sheet, . . . the term asset, as used in balance sheets may be defined as follows: Something represented by a debit balance that is or would be properly carried forward upon a closing of books of account according to the rules or principles of accounting (provided such debit balance is not in effect a negative balance applicable to a liability), on the basis that it represents either a property right or value acquired, or an expenditure made which has created a property right or value acquired, or an expenditure made which has created a property right or is properly applicable to the future. Thus, the plant, accounts receivable, inventory, and a deferred charge are all assets in balance-sheet classification.

The following are types of assets.

Current Assets: Cash, accounts receivable, inventory, notes receivable (within one year), short-term investments, prepaid expenses and deposits that will be applied to expense within one year, and other cash equivalents.

Fixed Assets: Equipment, improvements, land, buildings, automobiles and trucks, furniture, fixtures, and other tangible property or costs of tangible property.

Other Assets: Goodwill, patents and copyrights, organizational expense, investments in subsidiaries, some research and development expenditures, and other costs that are capitalized, but are not attributable to fixed or current assets.

CURRENT ASSETS

Current assets consist of assets in which the flow of funds is one of continuous circulation or turnover in the short run. They include cash on hand, or in banks, that is subject to withdrawal for current use and other assets that are expected to be converted to cash or will be sold, consumed, or converted within the normal operating cycle (usually one year). In some companies, inventory is not consumed or converted within one year, but, nevertheless, is considered a current asset.

In some instances, units of certain types of items will be shown as current; in other instances they will not. In natural resource industries, the start-up costs of a process is so expensive that the company may continue to produce inventory (the raw material) even though an excess already exists. In this case, only the inventory that can reasonably be expected to be sold in the next year will be listed as a current asset, and the balance will be either a fixed or other asset.

In addition, if your company has a long-term note receivable from a customer that will be only partially paid in the next year, then the portion that will be paid after the next year will *not* be a current asset. Current assets include cash or cash equivalents, accounts or notes receivable, inventories, and prepaid items (variously called prepaid expense or pre-paid assets).

Cash represents money on hand or on bank deposit subject to demand, such as a checking account. Bank deposits subject to restrictions (cannot be withdrawn without penalty for three months, for example) are accounted for as investments, not as cash.

Temporary investments, such as government bonds and certificates of deposit and other restricted accounts, are listed as current or other assets, depending on your intent in using the money. To be listed as a current asset, investments should be readily convertible to cash to be used in financing other current assets or in reducing current liabilities. If the temporary investments are to be converted to cash to use for long-term purposes (such as to purchase equipment), they are not current assets and should be listed as other assets. Investments in the capital stock of subsidiaries, representing long-term investments, should not be listed as current assets. The common practice is to show investments on the balance sheet at the lower of their cost, or market valuation, at the date of the balance sheet.

Notes and accounts receivable (sometimes known as trade receivables) represent amounts, attributable to company sales that are owed to the company. Other types of receivables in significant amounts are shown separately as *Accounts Receivable, Other,* or by separate specific classifications. This listing is in keeping with the accounting convention of making full disclosure of material facts. The AICPA rule states: "Notes or accounts receivable from officers, employees, or affiliated companies must be shown separately and not included under a general heading such as notes receivable or accounts receivable."

Notes receivable are the debts of customers or borrowers, acknowledged by them in signed written agreements (promissory notes), committing them to certain scheduled payments. Notes receivable must be listed separately from accounts receivable, when they constitute a significant portion of total receivables.

Accounts receivable (customer debt on open account) are customer debts in which no promissory notes are involved. They are usually documented by purchase orders or sales slips signed by customers.

Neither notes nor accounts receivable that will not be collected within a year should be listed as current assets. Generally speaking, if both accounts and notes receivable are shown separately, then accounts receivable is listed first on the balance sheet. However, such listing is not required.

If receivables are pledged as security (collateral) for loans, this fact should be explained in a footnote accompanying the balance sheet.

An *allowance for bad debts* is usually included as an offset to receivables, since companies depend on the convertibility of receivables for income. To account for such losses, both conservatism and proper matching of costs and revenues require that an estimate of probable loss from bad debts be charged against the sales of each period, rather than waiting until individual accounts prove to be uncollectible.

The term *inventory* applies to:

1. Goods on hand, available for sale, which were produced or acquired for that purpose
2. Goods being produced for the purpose of sale
3. Raw materials, manufactured parts, and supplies intended to be used in the regular course of operations for the production of goods or furnishing of services for sale.

A physical count of inventory is required by the IRS and is common practice. Some companies have a continuous (perpetual) inventory system aided by manual or electronic records that show the expected inventory at any given time or at the reorder point. When a given company has inventory divided into several different categories (types of raw material, types of finished products, for example), then for reporting purposes, the company divides inventory into three groups: raw material, goods in process, and finished goods.

Prepaid expense are payments made in advance for some expenses that are assets in later accounting periods. Such items include prepayments of rent, insurance premiums, and interest. Accounted for as prepaid expense at the time of payment, these payments are an anticipated asset that saves the company from future expense.

FIXED ASSETS

Since items of property, plant, and equipment are commonly referred to as fixed assets, because of their permanent nature, it follows that they are not subject to the rapid turnover associated with current assets. Fixed assets are used in connection with producing or earning revenue and are not for sale in the ordinary course of business.

Since fixed assets have an expected useful life in excess of one year, the cost (or other basis) of an asset is recovered through annual depreciation deductions. Amounts paid for these business assets are considered to be capital expenditures.

Fixed, and other business assets may be acquired in several ways. These include, but are not limited to:

1. Outright purchase for cash, or for a cash down payment plus a note for the remainder of the purchase price
2. Outright purchase as above, except that a used asset also has trade-in value
3. Inheritance
4. Gift
5. Conversion to a business asset of property held for personal use
6. Exchange of another asset
7. Transfer to a corporation in exchange for stock.

For fixed assets, all costs, including freight, installation, and testing are capital expenditures. The costs incurred in the construction of your own business assets are also considered capital expenditures. Interest, certain taxes, and carrying charges may, at your election, be treated as capital expenditures.

Fixed assets are recorded on the balance sheet and in the books at their historical cost or fair market value at the time of purchase. In addition, the balance sheet shows the depreciation charged against the asset, and therefore shows the worth of the assets at cost minus accumulated depreciation.

Customarily, the basis of value for a fixed asset is its cost. The cost of property is the amount you pay for it either in cash, debt obligations, or other property. If property is acquired on time-payment arrangements, under which either no interest or only a low interest is charged, then the basis of your property may be the purchase price, less an amount considered to represent interest.

Other items of cost that are added to the cost of the property to serve as a basis for depreciation, including the total cost of the property kept in your books, are:

1. Taxes you agree to pay on a purchase of real property if those taxes were obligations of the seller
2. Purchase commissions, legal and recording fees required to take possession of the property
3. Assumption of a mortgage (when you acquire property, subject to an existing debt, the basis is the amount you pay for the property, plus the unpaid debt you assume)
4. Compensation paid to your employees for personal services rendered in the construction of property.

Some cases require that a basis other than cost be used. In these cases *fair market value* is called for. According to the IRS, *fair market value* is the price at which the property would change hands, between a willing buyer and a willing seller, with neither one being under any compulsion to buy or sell, and both having reasonable knowledge of all relevant facts.

One principal debate in financial and accounting theory concerns the validity of taking assets at their historical value. Due to the rapid inflation in recent years, assets are being carried on company balance sheets at amounts that show little relation to current economic values. (The replacement cost of equipment in the steel industry, for industry, for instance, is three times the historical cost.) This practice tends to understate actual value of assets while, at the same time, overstating income.

The Securities and Exchange Commission (SEC) required (in 1977) not only that 1,000 of the nation's leading industrial companies calculate and disclose the historic cost of fixed assets and inventories, but also that they determine today's cost of replacement. This action, no doubt, represents a trend that has far-reaching implications. Lee J. Seidler, professor of accounting at New York University's Graduate School of Business Administration, remarked that "It's the biggest single change in accounting in the United States since the introduction of the income tax" (Business Week, Oct. 17, 1977).

Many accounting problems arise because economists and accountants view profits in two different ways. Most economists insist that profits are funds that could be taken out of the business without impairing its capital. Accountants, on the other hand, have been content to match the current revenues that come in from the sale of finished goods or services with the company's costs for such things as labor and raw materials to produce those products. The two profit concepts produce moderately consistent results, as long as price levels are reasonably stable. When there is rapid general inflation or even a sudden change in a key commodity price, however, the results can be diverse.

Once the basis cost of the fixed asset is determined, the next problems are to determine the useful life of the asset, as well as the most satisfactory type of depreciation procedure for this particular property. All fixed assets except land are depreciable. The reason behind this nonappreciability of land lies in the fact that theoretically, at least, land never gets used up or wears out, and furthermore, land almost never loses its value.

Depreciation accounting is described in Accounting Terminology Bulletin No. 1 (AICPA) as: "a system of accounting which aims to distribute the cost or other basis value of tangible capital assets, less salvage (if any), over the estimated useful life of the unit (which may be a group of assets) in a systematic and rational manner. It is a process of allocation, not valuation."

The three main components of determining depreciation are: the estimated useful life of the fixed asset, the probable salvage value of the asset, and the most appropriate system of allocating its cost over its estimated life.

The economic life of a capital asset largely depends on the factors of physical wear and tear, obsolescence, and inadequacy. Estimating useful life generally involves experience, judgment, and some subjective reasoning. The IRS pamphlet, Depreciation Guidelines and Rules, lists service lives for broad classes of depreciable assets that they consider to be appropriate in arriving at taxable income. Although these guidelines are widely used, they are meant only as guidelines and sometimes may not exactly fit your case. A factor critical to forecast in the life of a tangible capital asset is obsolescence, since obsolescence is difficult to predict. The factor of inadequacy is somewhat akin to obsolescence; it may mean that a machine, for instance, cannot produce to the capacity needed to maintain competitive ability.

Accounting for Fixed Assets

Some of the most crucial accounting problems faced by companies today involve fixed assets (property, plant, and equipment). Three problems of this type are:

1. Determining the cost of depreciable assets acquired
2. Estimating the useful life of these assets
3. Selecting the most appropriate manner in which to amortize the cost of the asset over its useful life.

When determining the cost of the asset acquired, this accounting rule that can generally be followed: All costs incurred that would not have been incurred had an asset not been acquired, should be accounted for as costs of that asset. Thus, when a machine is purchased, the price paid (invoice price) as well as freight and delivery costs represent the cost. Other costs related to purchase also would be charged to expenses. This procedure is referred to as *expensing* costs, as opposed to *capitalizing* costs, by adding them to the book cost of the asset.

The following items involved with the purchase are expensed, in most cases, and therefore expensed rather than capitalized: time and expenses of an engineer in investigating and selecting the machine purchased; time and expenses of the purchasing agent; or the time and expense of anyone at your company who is involved in the setting up or purchase of a machine. All these expenses are overhead expenses and cannot be added to the cost of the machine.

Installation costs, however, and the cost of trial runs, if it represents a large amount of material, are accounted for as the cost of the machine acquired. Such costs include fees, travel, and living expenses of people involved in the supervision or installation.

In many borderline situations, however, the judgment of an expert may be called for. Clarence B. Nickerson, in his book *Accounting Handbook for Nonaccountants*,* uses the example of a situation wherein the floor under

---

*Clarence B. Nickerson, *Accounting Handbook for Nonaccountants*, 2nd ed. (Boston: CBI Publishing Company, Inc., 1979).

a newly installed machine, had to be replaced due to the machine's excessive weight. In such a case, since it could be argued that the floor had to be strengthened as a result of acquiring the new machine, it follows that the cost of the strengthening should be part of the cost of the machine. On the other hand, it could be argued that the floor had not been constructed properly to house machinery and that strengthening the floor makes the building more valuable. Therefore, the cost should be capitalized as part of the building asset. It also could be said that the floor had weakened and the repair should be charged to maintenance expense for the period. None of these approaches is strictly the right one, and any one approach could be legitimately taken.

The invoice price of a machine should not, in every case, be considered as the true purchase price. When trade-ins are involved, as is frequently the case, the appropriate figure to be recorded for the cost of the unit purchased is the amount that would be paid if the machine were purchased for cash with no trade-in.

When a company produces a machine for its own use, it is obvious that the direct cost of labor and materials is a cost of the machine. But there are problems in determining the indirect overhead expenses to be allocated.

If a division of a large company sells a machine that it ordinarily produces to another division, then the price of the machine should be the same charged to other customers. This is easily rationalized. If, however, a company or division produces a machine for its own use, a more selective judgment is called for in determining actual cost. The first (or only) model of a new machine that the company builds for its own use customarily involves research, development, and experimental costs that are far higher than costs of building future models. If this is the first of several machines to be built, then many accountants favor expensing these costs, rather than capitalizing them. This conservative procedure avoids charging the first model for costs that will also benefit subsequent models. However, if the first model is the only machine of its kind that will be built, then all of the research, development, and experimental costs connected with it are part of its cost, or, according to FASB *Statement No. 2*, may be required to be expensed.

Ultimately, then, the costs are added to a machine, over and above direct costs of labor and materials, is a matter of company judgment and the cost accounting practiced by the company, rather than a matter of dogma.

Generally, costs of moving machinery from one part of the plant to another to increase productivity should be expensed. Because of the uncertainty of benefits to be gained from such a move, conservatism is called for. Since installation costs of the original placement are already part of the cost of the machinery, it follows that moving it negates this portion of the cost (the original installation is now worthless). However, taking the original installation as a loss and adding the new installation costs involves complex bookkeeping. Expensing the cost of moving is a more economical solution.

If a company purchases a site with the intention of demolishing the existing buildings and building new buildings, then the cost of the demoliton is considered a cost of the land. In general, all of the costs involved in connection with the construction of a new building, up to the point of occupancy, are accounted for as its costs. The costs include such items as architect's fees, permits, and the wages of guards, as well as items involved in the physical construction of the building. If the construction is not on a fixed-priced basis, then the total cost includes the costs of errors and delays.

Expenditures for minor repairs and ordinary maintenance that do not prolong the useful life of property beyond that anticipated when it was purchased (or constructed) can be charged as expenses at the time they occur. Major repairs, which prolong the life of the property, are capitalized also. Similarly, attachments or alterations that increase the usefulness of the property, or change it in some way, are capitalized.

Income taxes influence whether a repair or maintenance expenditure is capitalized or expensed. From a tax standpoint, the general policy is to expense an item if there is any possible justification for doing so. The problem of estimating the useful life of an asset revolves mostly around the judgment of obsolescence of an asset. The exception to the guidelines occurs when estimating useful lives of individual items — especially new types of machinery and equipment, for which you have no precedent. Over and above the IRS guidelines, management of any company must consider how quickly these assets will become outmoded or inadequate.

Tax Treatment for Sales, Exchanges, and Trade-ins of Fixed Assets

Exchanges, sales, and trade-ins of property; plant equipment for new property; plant and equipment; or these trades plus cash — all these fall into two categories: taxable exchange and sale and nontaxable exchange. Nontaxable exchanges include exchange of property for like-kind of property and involuntary conversion or exchange.

Taxable Exchange

To be a taxable exchange or sale, some loss (deductible) or gain (taxable) must be a result of the exchange of property for either property or cash. Gain is the excess of the amount realized from a sale or exchange of property over the *adjusted basis* of the property transferred. Loss is the excess of the adjusted basis of the property over the amount realized.

The amount realized from the sale or exchange of property is the sum of any money received, plus the fair market value of any property or services received. Also included in the amount realized are liabilities assumed by the purchaser. Liabilities attached to the property acquired, such as real estate taxes and a mortgage, are also included. Costs of transferring the property, such as selling expenses, are deducted from the amount realized.

For example: Kasko Kots, Inc., purchased their business building four years ago for $70,000 and later added $20,000 in improvements (a total of $90,000 value before depreciation). Straight-line depreciation of $10,000 has been claimed (asset book value is $80,000). Kasko sells the building for $100,000 cash, plus other property that has a fair market value of $20,000. The buyer assumes the seller's accrued real estate taxes of $3,000 and a mortgage of $17,000. Selling expenses were $4,000. Kasko's gain on the sale is computed as shown in Exhibit 3.2. Taxable gain on a sale or exchange is calculated in different ways for *personal property* and for *real property*. As defined by the IRS *Publication 334, personal property* includes what is generally referred to as personal property for state tax purposes (equipment, furniture, and other items) plus an elevator or escalator, and real property to the extent that it uses amortization deductions for pollution control facilities and on-the-job training and child-care facilities, and a special purpose structure or storage facility. *Real property* is land and buildings, except those parts of buildings included in personal property.

Gain from the sale, exchange, involuntary conversion, or other disposition of depreciable personal property, including a sale and lease-back transaction, must be reported as ordinary (not capital-gains) income.

For example, on January 1, 1969 you bought a machine for $6,000. You claimed $600 depreciation on it for each year and sold it for $2,000 on July 1, 1978. The adjusted basis on the date of sale was $300 ($6,000 less $5,700, which represents $600 per year depreciation between 1969 and 1978 (9 years) plus $300 for the half year in 1978). Therefore, your gain was $1,700 on the sale. Since the gain ($1,700) was less than the total depreciation after 1961 ($5,700), the entire gain must be included as ordinary income.

EXHIBIT 3.2
Gain on Sale

Amount realized:		
Cash	$100,000	
Other property (fair market value)	20,000	
Real estate taxes (assumed by buyer)	3,000	
Mortgages	17,000	
Total	$140,000	
Less: Selling Expenses	4,000	
		$136,000
Adjusted basis:		
Cost of building	$ 70,000	
Improvements	20,000	
Total	$ 90,000	
Less: Depreciation	10,000	
		80,000
Gain		$ 56,000

On real property, gain is calculated as personal property if the following apply:

1. Depreciation is computed on the property using the straight-line method (or any other method resulting in depreciation not in excess of that computed by the straight-line method), and you have held the property more than a year.
2. A loss is realized on the sale, exchange, or involuntary conversion of property.
3. You dispose of low-income rental property that was held for 16 2/3 years or more. (In the case of low-income rental housing for which the special 60-month depreciation for rehabilitation expenditures was allowed, the 16 2/3 years begin when the rehabilitated property was placed in service.)

Otherwise, real property disposal by sale or exchange must be calculated by a special formula to determine what portion of the gain is to be treated as ordinary income. Because of the rather complex nature of the procedure, a diagram (Exhibit 7.5) with an explanation of the procedure step by step appears in Chapter 7.

OTHER ASSETS

Other assets are all assets that are not current and cannot fit into the fixed-asset category, such as goodwill, research and development. Prepaid deposits that probably will not be applicable in the next year can also be considered another asset. This asset is rather straightforward — it is the deposit you made on last month's rent, telephones, and utilities. It has to be carried as an asset, not charged as an expense.

Long-term Investment

Many of the larger businesses make long-term investments in other companies for the purpose of earning revenue, directly or indirectly. Customarily, these investments are in common stock, but they also can be in the form of preferred stock or bonds, loans, or even investments in property, plant, or equipment that are not related to the principal business of the company. Long-term investments are commonly listed in the investor's balance sheet as a single item between current assets and fixed assets.

Common stocks, like fixed assets, are recorded at historical cost, including brokerage fees. Accounting is simple, if stocks are paid for in cash. If some basis other than cash is used to pay for the stocks, then the value of the stock acquired is based on the fair market value of the stock acquired, on the fair market value of the net assets underlying the stock acquired, or on the fair market value of the stock or other property given in exchange for the stock acquired.

If the investing company has *significant direct or indirect* influence over the affairs of the company whose stock they buy, it is not adequate accounting simply to carry the investment at historical cost or to record income on the investment only as dividends received.

The Accounting Principles Board in *Opinion No. 18, The Equity Method for Investments in Common Stock* concluded that investments in common stock of unconsolidated foreign or domestic subsidiaries should be accounted for by the equity method in consolidated financial statements. They also concluded:

. . . the parent companies should account for investments in the common stock of subsidiaries by the equity method in parent-company financial statements prepared for issuance to stockholders as the financial statements of the primary reporting entity.

. . . that the equity method best enables investors in corporate joint ventures to reflect the underlying nature of their investment in those ventures.

. . . that the equity method of accounting for an investment in voting stock gives it the ability to exercise significant influence over operating and financial policies of an investee even though the investor holds 50 percent or less of the voting stock.

In order to achieve a reasonable degree of uniformity in application, the (Accounting Principals) Board concludes that an investment of 20 percent or more of the voting stock of an investee should lead to a presumption that in the absence of evidence to the contrary an investor has the ability to exercise significant influence over investee. Conversely, an investment of less than 20 percent of the voting stock of the investee should lead to the presumption that an investor does not have the ability to exercise significant influence unless such ability can be demonstrated.

In accounting by the equity method, the investment is entered first in the investor's accounts at its cost plus brokerage. Thereafter, the investment account, or subdivision of it, is either increased each period for the investor's share of the investee's realized net income, or decreased for its share of a loss. At the same time, the amount of this income or loss is recorded in the investor's income accounts and later is shown as a separate item on its income segment. In arriving at the amount of net income, or loss, intercompany gains or losses are eliminated, as in preparing consolidated statements.

Thus, under the equity method, the balance in the investment account at the close of an accounting period represents the ownership claim (equity) on that date of the investor in the investee. In other words, the balance in the investment account represents the unamortized cost of the investment plus the investor's claim for its share of the earnings realized, and retained by the investee, since the date of the investment. In addition, it includes any unpaid balance of advances or loans made by the investor in the investee.

When the power to control a subsidiary company (investee) lies in the ownership of a majority (more than 50 percent) of the outstanding stock, it is a common practice for the parent company to report the combined financial affairs of parent and subsidiaries in what are known as *consolidated financial statements*. The parent company presents financial statements of itself and its subsidiaries consolidated. The assets and liabilities of the parent and subsidiaries are combined in a consolidated balance sheet, while parent and subsidiary revenues and expenses are brought together in a consolidated income statement.

In summary, if the long-term investment in stock is less than 50 percent of the purchased company's outstanding stock, then one figure, a *long-term investment* figure, will appear on the investor's balance sheet. If the investor owns *more than* 50 percent of the stock, then the investor and the investee's balance sheets and income statements are combined or consolidated. If the investor owns 20 percent or less of the stock, then generally speaking, the investment is carried at cost. If the ownership is more than 20 percent of the stock, but less than 50 percent, the investment account will be kept on the equity basis.

Goodwill

All companies consider that they have some goodwill in their business if they have operated successfully for a number of years. However, goodwill appearing on a balance sheet arises only in connection with the purchase of another company. This occurs when the total price paid is in excess of the values that can be assigned to the net tangible assets and net identifiable intangible assets (such as patents) acquired.

For example, let us assume that $1 million is paid for a company, and by means of appraisals or other determinations, $800,000 of this was paid for tangible assets and identifiable intangible assets, net of the liabilities that also had to be taken over. In this case, the assumption would be that $200,000 was paid for goodwill.

As long as the company that was acquired is not resold or abandoned, goodwill cannot be amortized as an expense or loss for income tax purposes. If the acquired company is later sold or abandoned, goodwill can be taken into account for tax purposes in arriving at the gain or loss on disposal.

Research and Development

FASB *Statement No. 2* concludes that, with some specific exceptions, all research and development costs — materials, equipment, facilities, wages, contract services, allocated indirect costs and intangibles without an alternative use purchased from others — must be charged to expense when incurred. The exceptions are:

1. Research and development costs incurred for others under con-
    tract.
2. Activities unique to companies in the extractive industries, such
    as prospecting, exploration, and drilling.
3. Regulated enterprises that continue to defer research and de-
    velopment costs for financial statement purposes in accordance
    with Addendum to APB *Opinion No. 2* ("Accounting for the
    Investment Credit").
4. Materials, equipment, facilities, or purchased intangibles used in
    research and development activities that have alternative future
    uses.

The statement requires disclosure of the total research and development costs charged to expense in each income statement period. For
regulated companies subject to the APB *Opinion No. 2,* the following must
be disclosed:

1. Accounting policy followed, including amortization method.
2. Total research and development costs incurred and deferred in
    each income statement period presented.

LIABILITIES AND CAPITAL

Liabilities include all debts of the company — amounts of money owed
but not yet paid. *Capital* or *equity* is the amount of money that the owners
of the business have invested in the business and includes the amount
with which they started the company, plus any money that has accumulated in the company since its inception.

Current Liabilities

On the right-hand side of the balance sheet, short-term debts are grouped
under the title Current Liabilities. *Current liabilities* are those debts existing as of the balance sheet date that will fall due for payment within one
year or within the normal operating cycle of the business. It is a statement
of short-term indebtedness, as of the balance sheet date, arising from
financial transactions that have already taken place.
   Some current liabilities include:

1. Accounts payable (money owed for inventory, outside labor, and related accounts)
2. Notes payable (the notes or portions of notes that are due to be paid within a one-year period)
3. Accrued expenses (like income tax payable, tax payable, salaries payable, rent payable)
4. Trade payables
5. Provision for pensions

Long-term Liabilities

Long-term, or *fixed, liabilities* are those debts that will be paid in a period longer than one year.

A major source of funds for most companies consists of some form of long-term debt. For the larger corporations, this indebtedness is commonly in the form of bonds paying interest at a specified rate. The two major classifications of bonds are mortgage bonds and debentures.

Mortgage bonds are backed by specific stated properties that may be claimed by the bondholders if the terms of the indenture are not met, and particularly, if the issuing company ceases to exist. *Debentures,* on the other hand, have only a general claim on the assets of a company.

Bonds are described in a balance sheet as to type, rate of interest, and due date. The issuing company records the bonds at their face value and maintains a separate record of the premium or discount and expense involved in the issue. These separate accounts are amortized over the life of the bonds, generally on a straight-line basis. Other long-term liabilities include: 1. mortgages on buildings and land; 2. loans for equipment, furniture, and fixtures; and 3. most government-guaranteed loans (such as Small Business Administration loans).

Owners' Equity (Capital)

To an accountant, capital means the owner's equity in the business, which consists of the owner's claim to funds that he has invested in his business and the earnings he has kept in the business over the years.

In a single proprietorship, the owner's equity is usually shown as a single balance sheet figure covering both the capital he has put in the business and the net earnings he has left there. Although only one figure is used, the owner of a sole proprietorship may choose to keep the money that he put from his personal resources into the business separate from the earnings that he has put back into the business. The owner could have a separate account for paid-in capital (what he personally puts in) and for retained earnings (money put back into the business from profits after taxes).

In a partnership, the owners' equity is usually shown on a balance sheet broken down by individual partners, unless it is a very large partnership. But the owners' equity usually is not separated by paid-in capital and retained earnings. However, for internal management use, separate partners' accounts are usually maintained for such items as paid-in capital, share of net earnings retained, owners' drawings (salary), and for loans to or from the partnership.

In a corporation, the owners' equity is shown in a balance sheet in at least two parts: *Capital Stock* (or paid-in capital) and *Retained Earnings* (formerly called surplus, a term no longer preferred).

In most cases the capital stock is shown at a *par* or *stated value* (the management determined stated value of the stock, not the market value). The difference between the par value and the amount paid initially for the stock by the stockholders, less costs connected with the issue, is shown as capital in excess of par or stated value, as paid-in surplus, or as capital surplus.

Paid-in capital, no matter how it is shown, is kept separate from retained earnings. This is done both because paid-in capital is usually the limit of the liability of stockholders to creditors and others who may have or make claims on the company and because retained earnings are legally available for dividends, even though it is likely that, for the most part, they will be retained by the company as permanent capital.

Some corporations have preferred stock in addition to common stock, paid-in surplus, and retained earnings. In some cases, particularly in foreign countries, corporations maintain also reserves of one kind or another that, as of the balance sheet date, and until required for some other purpose, represent ownership claims.

Preferred stock is a class of stock that has a preferred claim over common stock as to dividends, if a company is successful, and as to recovery of investment, if the company is not successful. The obligation to pay dividends on preferred stock is conditional on the company's earning a profit and on a formal declaration of a dividend by the company's board of directors. The amount of dividend that is paid on a preferred stock is stated on the stock certificates and in the balance sheet description of stock. The amount is stated either as a given number of dollars per share of stock or as a percentage of the par value of the stock.

Another type of preferred stock is *convertible preferred stock*. This is a type of preferred stock that later can be converted to common stock at a given ratio at the option of the holder.

Preferred stock does not usually have as complete voting rights as common stock. Generally, it does have the right to vote on proposals for increasing the number of shares of preferred stock or the sale of senior securities and full voting rights, if the company gets into specified difficulties.

Stock, including preferred, is either *par* (has a value assigned to it) or *no par* (has no value assigned to it). Par value is an arbitrary amount assigned to a share of stock that has no necessary relationship to market value. For accounting purposes, no par stock is assigned stated value per share by the issuing company, and this is the basis on which the stock is presented in the balance sheet.

The excess price, above either the par or the stated value received at the time the stock is sold initially, is entered in an account entitled Paid-in Surplus. This figure appears as a separate item in the capital section of the balance sheet. The most logical and forthright manner in which to display any type of stock in a balance sheet is at the amount received from its initial sale net of expenses connected with its issue. Some companies avoid the artificial separation of paid-in capital into stated value and paid-in surplus by reporting stock at its initial selling price.

If a corporation has only one type of stock outstanding, this stock is often shown in the balance sheet as Capital Stock. If the company has more than one type of stock, this same capital stock would be called Common Stock. Sometimes a company has Class A and Class B common stock, only one class of which has voting rights; but this practice has passed into disfavor in the United States, primarily because the New York Stock Exchange refuses to list stocks of companies that do not give voting power to their common stockholders.

Shares of a company's own stock, which it has purchased and is holding for some purpose, are accounted for as Treasury Stock. At the time of purchase, the shares are recorded at their cost and carried at this valuation until sold or retired. Treasury stock is usually shown in the balance sheet as a deduction from stockholders' equity, with the type of stock and the number of shares also being stated.

STATEMENT OF RETAINED EARNINGS

Most corporations are required to show their retained earnings in the *Statement of Retained Earnings*, which shows the retained earnings at the beginning of the period and adjustments to retained earnings for the profit or loss for the period, dividends declared, and items, if any, of the following type:

1. Adjustments or changes or credits resulting from transactions in the company's own capital stock
2. Transfers to and from accounts properly designated as appropriated retained earnings (such as general purpose contingency reserves or provisions for replacement costs of fixed assets)
3. Adjustments made pursuant to a quasi-reorganization.

Exhibit 3.3 is an example of a statement of retained earnings.

EXHIBIT 3.3
Statement of Retained Earnings

	For the Years Ending	
	Dec. 31, 1979	Dec. 31, 1980
Retained earnings at beginning of the period	$ 100,320	$ 212,431
Net Income for Period	112,111	157,900
	$ 212,431	$ 370,331
Common stock dividend — 5% (4,320 shares and $435 cash for partial shares)	—0—	$ 43,645
Retained earnings at end of period	$ 212,431	$ 326,696

The Funds Statement

All companies are now required to have a Funds Statement along with their Income Statement and Balance Sheet. The purpose of the funds statement is to trace the flow of working capital during the accounting period. *Working capital* is the excess of current assets over current liabilities.

The funds statement helps to answer such questions as:

1. Where did profits go?
2. Why were dividends not larger in view of the profits made?
3. How was it possible to distribute dividends in the face of a net operating loss?
4. How was the expansion in plant and equipment financed?
5. What happened to the sale of additional stock and the proceeds from the sale of fixed assets?
6. How was the retirement of debt accomplished?
7. What brought about the increase or decrease in working capital?

The statement can be divided into sources of funds (working capital) and application of funds (working capital), as shown in Exhibit 3.4. A sample funds statement is shown in Exhibit 3.5.

EXHIBIT 3.4
Sources and Application of Funds

Sources of Funds	*Application of Funds*
Increases in long-term debt (+)	(−) Decreases in long-term debt
Increases in owners' equity (+) ●through an increase in contributed capital ●through increase in retained earnings	(−) Decreases in owners' equity ●through decrease in contributed capital ●through decrease in retained earnings ●through operations ●through dividends
Decreases in fixed assets (−) ●through sale ●through depreciation	(+) Increases in fixed assets

---

EXHIBIT 3.5
ACME MOUSETRAPS, INC.,
Funds Statement For the Period Ending
Dec. 31, 197X

Source of Funds:

Operations: net income	$25,316	
add depreciation	5,720	$ 31,036
Sale of Stock		10,000
Total Sources		$ 41,036

Use of Funds:

Purchase of fixed assets	$ 4,750	
Cash dividends paid	10,000	
Retirement of long-term debt	17,812	$ 32,562
Net Increase in Working Capital		$ 8,474

4

Cash Management

Net profits are not net cash income, nor are sales necessarily cash income. In other words, net profit is not the total cash a business earns during the year, and sales, in most cases, are not equivalent to the total cash income.

Net income on the income statement — even net income after tax — does not include the payments for principal loan repayments, purchase of capital assets, payment of dividends, or (in the case of a proprietorship or partnership) owners' draw. All these are cash expenditures not considered expense, in the income statement sense, and therefore do not appear on the income statement as a reduction in net income. If sales are based on shipments, as they are in an accrual accounting system, then cash does not come from the sales until the accounts receivable are collected.

The failure to understand the difference between sales and cash inflow, as well as between net profit and net cash inflow, has forced many businesspersons into binds. This misunderstanding is so deep in our society that even business books, from time to time, misrepresent the situation.

LIQUIDITY

The amount of cash that is immediately available to a company is termed its *liquidity*. A measure of financial soundness, liquidity refers to a firm's ability to pay its obligations when they become due. Liquidity denotes cash or other resources that can be readily converted into cash. It is usually measured in terms of one-year periods.

If it were not necessary to be liquid to a certain extent then there would be no incentive to keep resources in the form of cash or cash equivalents. The reason that there is no incentive to keep cash is that cash or cash equivalents have little or no earning power in most business enterprises (except for financial lenders). The earning power of a firm's varied assets are shown graphically in Exhibit 4.1.

EXHIBIT 4.1
Illustrative Earning Power of Assets

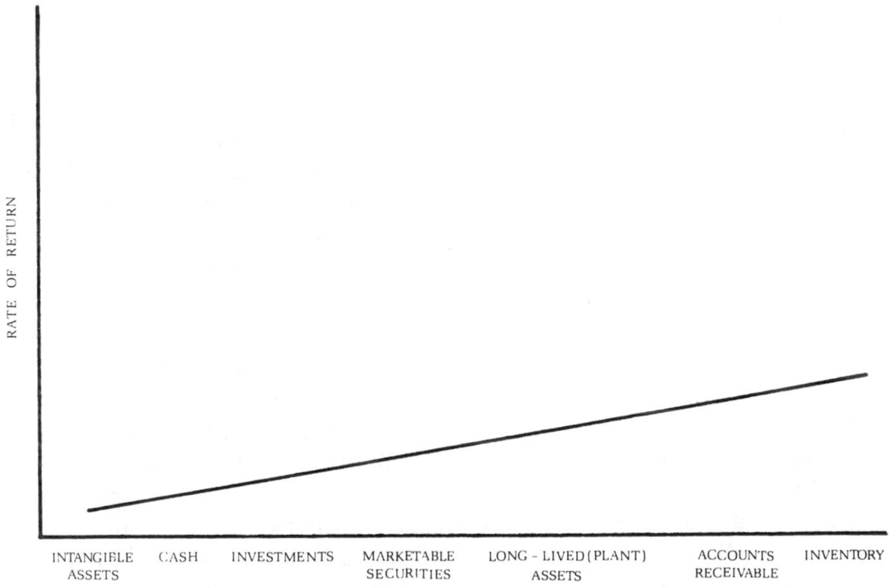

RATE OF RETURN

| INTANGIBLE ASSETS | CASH | INVESTMENTS | MARKETABLE SECURITIES | LONG - LIVED (PLANT) ASSETS | ACCOUNTS RECEIVABLE | INVENTORY |

THE FINANCIAL RESOURCE CYCLE
AND THE CASH RESERVOIR

The term *cycle* refers to the inception, transformation, and completion of a process. When applied to cash, the *cash cycle* refers to the amount of time required for cash in one state to go through sequential steps and return to the original state.

Exhibit 4.2 illustrates the cash cycle for businesses that are on a cash

---

EXHIBIT 4.2
Cash Cycle

CASH BASIS

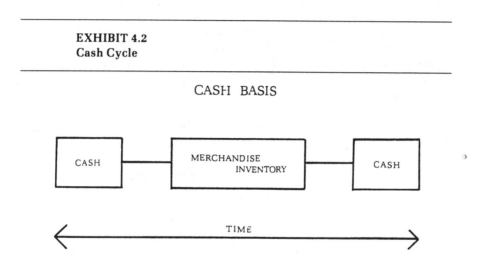

ACCRUAL BASIS

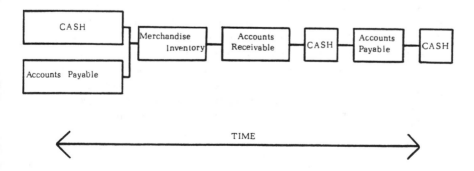

accounting basis and also shows the cash cycle, which includes additional steps for firms on the accrual accounting basis.

If accounting is on a cash basis, then the cash cycle consists of taking cash and purchasing merchandise, which is then sold for cash.

If a firm's accounting is on an accrual basis, then the cash cycle consists of taking cash and credit (accounts payable) and purchasing inventory. The inventory is then sold and converted to accounts receivable, which, in turn, is converted to cash. The cash from accounts receivable is used to pay accounts payable and the balance of the cash returns to its original state in the accrual cash cycle.

Understandably, the buying of merchandise and the paying of accounts payable are not the only uses of cash and cash sales, nor is the conversion of accounts receivable the only means of getting cash into the business. Debt, capital invested in the business, conversion of fixed assets to cash, and other income outside of sales are all stimulated by cash inflow. Cash expenditures are used for operating expenses, taxes, principal loan repayment, dividends or draw, purchase of assets, and investments, in addition to repayment of payables and purchase of inventory. Exhibit 4.3 shows the cash inflows and outflows of a business, using an analogy of a cash reservoir and a reservoir of water, wherein cash is substituted for water.

The exhibit indicates that all cash inflow except retained earnings comes from outside the company. By extending the analogy, we can see how cash comes from the outside — like rain, collecting in the debt, equity, cash sales, collection of accounts receivable, and sale of assets holding tanks, which all drain into a cash reservoir. The circle control valves are the controls that management uses to release a specific quantity from each holding tank.

Cash drains out of the cash reservoir into the holding tanks for increase in assets, payment of expense, reduction of liabilities, other payments, and retained earnings. *Retained earnings* are the amounts of cash retained by the business after everything is paid. These retained earnings are pumped back up the equity cash inflow holding tank and funneled back into the cash reservoir. All other cash outflows are funneled into rows of drainage ditches such as taxes, dividends, owners' draw, and legal settlements running from the *other payments* holding tank; fixed assets, investments, inventory, and prepayments for the increase assets tank; operating expense and cost of sales from their tank; and accounts payable and notes payable from the reduce liabilities holding tank. Note that each drainage row has a shut-off valve connected to it for management to regulate the flow.

EXHIBIT 4.3
Cash Inflow and Outflow as a Cash Reservior

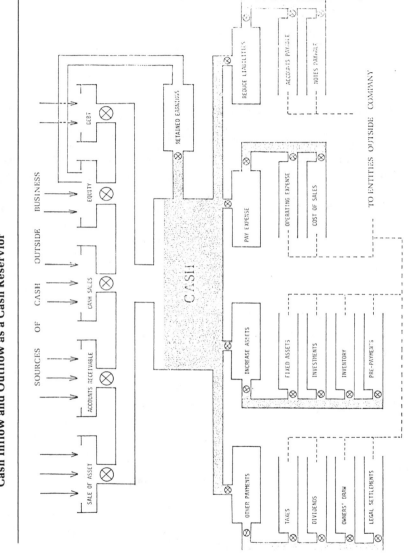

Source and Uses of Cash

The term *cash* that we have used in this chapter includes negotiable money orders and checks, and balances in the business and also in the business's bank accounts.

It is clear from the previous example where cash comes from and for what it is used. The following list summarizes these sources and uses of funds:

Sources

1. Conversion of assets to cash (including collecting accounts receivable, selling fixed assets, cashing in on investments, or any other conversion of an asset directly to cash).
2. Increase in liabilities, such as cash loans, or other credits which have the effect of postponing cash payments. Obtaining a working capital loan from a bank is an obvious example of increasing a liability for cash.
3. Increase in owners' equity either through additional, contributed cash (through the sale of stock or owners' contributions) or through the retention of cash from operations (retained earnings). Cash inflow comes from cash sales and conversion of accounts receivable, but, theoretically, these sales come through owners' equity after expenses and other payments.

Uses

1. Investment in other assets. (Purchase of inventory, fixed assets, investments, and other assets.)
2. Decrease in liabilities such as payment of loan payments (principal paid after tax and interest paid out of expenses) or reduction in accounts payable.
3. Decrease in owners' equity caused by net loss or other nonexpense and non-asset-increasing expenditures.

Exhibit 4.4 uses a balance sheet to show sources or uses of cash.

EXHIBIT 4.4
Sources and Uses of Cash in a Balance Sheet

Balance Sheet Item	Cash	
	Sources	Uses
Cash	+	−
Current Assets Other than Cash	−	+
Fixed Assets	−	+

Balance Sheet Item	Cash	
	Sources	Uses
Liabilities	+	−
Owners' Equity:		
Contributed Capital	+	−
Retained Earnings:		
Income	+	−
Expenditures	−	+

+ Indicates increase
− Indicates decrease

Examining the chart, it is apparent that an *increase* in cash equates with a *decrease* in current assets other than cash, expenditures, or fixed assets, or an increase in cash, liabilities or owners' equity (through direct contribution or increased retained earnings caused by an excess of income over expense).

A decrease in cash equates with an increase in current assets other than cash, expenditures, or fixed assets; or a decrease in the cash asset, liabilities, or owners' equity.

Consider two accounts — cash and inventory (another current asset). If inventory increases, then cash decreases. Conversely, inventory is increased by paying cash for it. If we sell inventory for cash, then cash increases. Admittedly, inventory might be bought on credit. This procedure will increase accounts payable and increase inventory. Inventory also could be sold for credit, which would increase accounts receivable and decrease inventory. But ultimately, these transactions result in either decreases or increases in cash. Purchasing or selling on credit avoids the immediate payment or receipt of cash. If accounts payable are paid (a payment is made to a vendor) then cash decreases. If accounts receivable are collected, we increase cash.

PROFIT VERSUS CASH FLOW

One frequent cause for mismanagement of cash is the belief that profits and cash are the same. Mistakenly, it is assumed that if a firm makes a profit, then this profit will automatically be reflected in an identical increase in the amount of cash in the till. As discussed in the first part of this chapter, cash and profit are not synonymous. This section discusses the difference, which can be summed up in the often-heard statement that, "Profit is an opinion, but cash is a fact."

Profit, as measured by the accountant, is a technical expression that represents the excess of revenues over expenses. These revenues and expenses are not necessarily cash inflows and cash outflows. Rather they are the result of the consistent application, from accounting period to accounting period, of traditional accounting principles of matching and conservatism.

Profit, in short, is a complex concept; its ramifications, and the rules covering it, cannot be explained fully in this book. Cash, on the other hand, is a simpler concept. Simply stated, *cash flow* is the difference between the inflow and outflow of cash in a business bank account.

Capital Expenditure and Depreciation

Capital expenditure is the acquisition of a physical item of a long lasting nature, such as a plant, equipment, and motor vehicles. Since these capital items last for several years, the accounting concept of matching does not charge the cost of the item against profits in the year of acquisition, but rather seeks to spread its cost over its estimated working life. This procedure of spreading is called *depreciation*. Profit is thus arrived at after charging depreciation. For cash, on the other hand, there is an immediate outflow when the capital asset is acquired and payment made. From this, three facts emerge:

1. Cash flow from operations is basically profit before charging depreciation.
2. In any year in which capital expenditures are incurred, the total cash flow of the firm could be negative, despite having made a profit.
3. In any year in which no capital expenditure or other payments are made, the total cash flow will be higher than profit, by the amount of the depreciation charge.

Exhibit 4.5 gives figures supporting a case in point. Mr. Harry Zigelswitzer has a street vendor's cart in New Orleans and sells "Harry's Original Peanut Bags" to the tourist trade. He buys his inventory, four-color peanut bags, for cash and sells all his bags for cash ($2 each). In the first year of operation, Harry bought a street vendor's cart for $3,000; the cart is estimated to have a useful life of five years. The result of his first five years of operation, expressed in both profit (or loss) terms and cash flow terms, is shown in Exhibit 4.5. (Note the differences between profit, cash flow from operations, and total cash flow.)

Inventories and Cash Flow

When computing profit, the matching concept of accounting will normally deduct the cost of inventory only at the time the inventory is sold. For the cash till, however, there is an immediate outflow as soon as the inventory is acquired. It follows that in any accounting period during which the amount of the unsold inventories increases, there will be a cash outflow not reflected in a reduction of profits. It also follows that in any

EXHIBIT 4.5
Harry's Original Peanut Bags Profit and Loss, Cash
Flow — 5 Years

	Year 1 $	Year 2 $	Year 3 $	Year 4 $	Year 5 $
Cash Sales	24,000	24,000	21,000	21,000	24,000
Less: Purchases	12,000	12,000	10,000	12,000	12,000
Other Exp.	10,000	10,000	10,000	10,000	10,000
Total Expense	22,000	22,000	20,000	22,000	22,000
Cash Flow from Operations	2,000	2,000	1,000	(1,000)	2,000
Less: Depreciation*	600	600	600	600	600
Profit (Loss)	1,400	1,400	400	(1,600)	1,400
Cash Flow from Operations	2,000	2,000	1,000	(1,000)	2,000
Capital Expenditure	(3,000)	0	0	0	0
TOTAL CASH FLOW	(1,000)	2,000	1,000	(1,000)	2,000

*Depreciation is calculated straight line, no salvage, or 3,000/5 = $600

period during which the amount of the unsold inventories decreases, there will be a cash inflow that is not reflected by an increase in profits.

Note that in Exhibit 4.6 gross profit is higher than cash flow in the first period because in this period, more inventory was purchased than sold. In the second period, the total amount of inventory purchased and sold was the same; thus, gross profit and cash flow are the same. In the last period, less inventory was bought than sold, which produces a cash flow higher than gross profit for that period.

Credit and Cash Flow

The theory and practice of accounting require that income be declared when the goods are shipped to a customer, even if payment is not forthcoming for 30 days or more. Similarly, purchases of supplies are

EXHIBIT 4.6
Harry's Original Peanut Bags Quarterly Cash Flow,
First Year

	Period 1	Period 2	Period 3
#Bags bought for cash	4500	3000	3500
#Bags sold for cash	3000	3000	3000
#Closing Inventory	1500	1500	1000
Computation of Profit			
Sales	$6,000	$6,000	$6,000
Opening Inventory	-0-	1,500	1,500
Purchases	4,500	3,000	2,500
Closing Inventory	1,500	1,500	1,500
Cost of Goods Sold	3,000	3,000	3,000
GROSS PROFIT	$3,000	$3,000	$3,000
Computation of Cash Flow			
Sales	$6,000	$6,000	$6,000
Purchases	(4,500)	(3,000)	(2,500)
Net Cash Flow	$1,500	$3,000	$3,500

considered expenditures although these purchases are made on a line-of-credit basis and will not be paid for a period of time. If a sale is made on credit, then there is no cash income until the account receivable is paid, and there is no cash outflow for supplies purchased until the account payable is paid by check. In effect, an extension of credit to a customer is equivalent to an outflow of cash because the item sold had cost you, the seller, money, yet you are not receiving cash for its sale. The following factors become evident:

1. In any accounting period during which there is an increase in the amount of credit extended to customers (known in accounting terms as *accounts receivable* or just *receivables*), cash flow from operations will be reduced by this amount.
2. In any accounting period during which there is an increase in the amount of credit taken from suppliers (accounts payable or

payables), cash flow from operations will be increased by this amount.

Exhibit 4.7 shows the cash flow and gross profit (sales minus cost of goods sold) implications of Harry's Original Peanut Bags for the second year of operations (periods 5 through 8, each period representing a quarter of a year). Each unit purchased or sold represents $1 of cost. Gross profit is the number of units sold, times $1 gross profit, per item. Net cash flow is the cash income minus the cash outgo. Amounts still owing on sales (accounts receivable) and on purchases (accounts payable) do not consider payment of payables or receipt of cash for receivables.

Note that in period 5 there was no effective difference between net cash flow and gross profit because as much inventory was sold for cash as was purchased for cash. In period 6, goods were sold on credit, but purchased with cash, resulting in a negative cash flow. In period 7, goods were sold for cash and bought on credit, which had an increasing effect on

---

EXHIBIT 4.7
Harry's Original Peanut Bags Quarterly Cash Flow,
Second Year

Period	Action	Gross Profit $	Net Cash Flow $	Amounts Still Owing On Sales	Purchases
5	Buy 6,000 units for cash, sell 6,000 units for cash	6,000	6,000	None	None
6	Buy 6,000 units for cash, sell 6,000 units on credit	6,000	(6,000)	12,000	None
7	Buy 6,000 units on credit, sell 6,000 units for cash	6,000	12,000	None	6,000
8	Buy 6,000 units on credit, sell 6,000 units on credit	6,000	-0-	12,000	6,000

cash flow. In period 8, all goods were bought and sold on credit, therefore there was no cash flow.

From these discussions it is apparent that profit and cash flow are not the same. Furthermore, it is apparent that it will be a coincidence if these two quantities are identical in amount. Moreover, these causes of disparity constantly are evident during normal operations: multi-direction disparities are prevalent.

Growth, Inflation, Timing, Management, and Cash Flow

Consider the impact of the following points, previously discussed, in terms of the consequences of growth:

1. If it is necessary in a growth situation for capital expenditures to continue at a high level, then total cash flow will be negative, despite profitable sales. This situation results when capital expenditures represent cash outlays that usually do not produce immediate cash inflows.
2. Inventories must increase to meet growing demand, which means that cash flow will be reduced, despite the profit made.
3. Both the amount of credit given to customers and taken from suppliers must increase, but the amount of the increase in accounts receivables is likely to exceed the amount of the increase in payables. This means that cash flow will be reduced.
4. Finally, cash flow from operations may be low because profit will be low until volume is built up and margins are established.

A firm undergoing a period of rapid growth is in a vulnerable position because everything is working against cash flow of the firm. During this time, a firm is in a critical need of financing, but banks and other financial lenders are cautious about lending to a firm with growing pains. The momentum is usually hard to stop both physically and mentally. Cash management is essential at times of rapid growth.

Many firms try to finance their growth through accounts receivable financing, which causes problems. Not only is it expensive, but only 80 percent of the receivables (previous months sales) are typically financed. Imagine the problems of a firm that is growing at 20 percent per month in sales and has an 80 percent cost of goods sold. In January, the firm has sales of $100,000 and cost of goods and labor of $80,000. In February, the bank finances its $100,000 in receivables by advancing it $80,000; but in February the firm has sales of $120,000 and a cost of sales of $96,000 (80 percent of sales). There is a $16,000 short-fall in cash flow on cost of goods sold, alone (in addition to operating expenses). This short-fall in cash flow can be financed from extending payables for a longer period, but after several months of 20 percent growth, this alternative is no longer viable. If the firm cannot get additional financing or additional capital, it is headed for insolvency.

Inflation also has a negative effect on cash flow. The impact of growth is one of volume changes that are reflected in cash values. But it is the *value* of the products, not the *volume*, that really counts in the cash till. Consider the following impact of inflation during any accounting period:

1. The values of capital expenditure continue to increase beyond the depreciation charge (which was based on the original cost of the existing assets, not their inflated value).
2. The values of inventories increase irrespective of volume.
3. The value of the credit given to customers exceeds that taken from suppliers.

Then where is the difference between growth and inflation? *Inflation* is growth in dollar terms. Therefore, in periods of rapid inflation a firm must expect to find itself in an unfavorable cash flow position since the firm is growing too fast. A firm that tries to grow in times of rapid inflation faces many difficulties.

We have seen how the application of accounting concepts to the determination of profit can create problems when analyzing the amounts of cash flow. The timing at which the amounts flow also creates a problem. Cash inflows and outflows do not always flow smoothly over a period of time. Some cash outflows do flow smoothly; monthly salaries, for example, are fairly constant from month to month. However, many cash outflows must be paid in one lump sum rather than periodically throughout the year. For example, property tax is usually paid twice yearly, state and federal taxes are customarily paid quarterly, and local taxes are generally paid annually. A company that extends bonuses to employees usually does so on an annual basis. In a seasonal business, cash inflows from customers may be higher at one time of the year than in another. In scrutinizing the foregoing financial situation, it would be easy to visualize three firms with an identical cash balance at the beginning and at the end of the year, but with vastly different patterns of cash flow during the year. Cumulative cash inflow graphs appear in Exhibits 4.8 and 4.9. Interestingly, in each case both the opening and the closing cash

EXHIBIT 4.8
Cash Flow Over Time

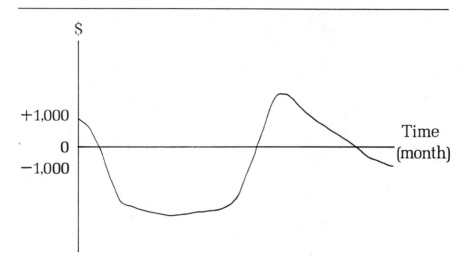

EXHIBIT 4.9
Cash Flow Over Time

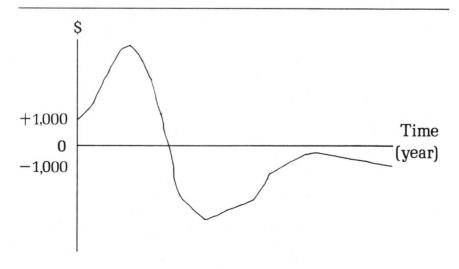

positions are identical, but each situation has a vastly different requirement for finance and availability of surplus.

Most retail businesses have their greatest sales in November and December, when there is considerable Christmas shopping. Toy manufacturers, however, have their biggest sales months in September and October, when retail stores are ordering toys for the forthcoming Christmas season. Toy manufacturers may have as much as 50 percent of their total annual sales in just two months. Ski resorts have business amounting to only about 5 percent of their total annual sales in summer months, but will receive perhaps 90 percent of their total sales in only three winter months. Travel agencies, on the other hand, do most of their business in the summer months. Different businesses, even those located in close proximity, may have entirely opposite cash flows.

A firm can still be in serious financial difficulties despite having correct forecasts of cash flow amounts, if the forecast of their timing is incorrect. Most amounts are two dimensional — a quantity multiplied by a price. Cash flow amounts add a third dimension — time. The time dimension is the root of various problems created by the accounting concepts discussed:

QUESTION: What specific areas of management decisions are involved
            with cash flow?

ANSWER:
Cash movement does not flow of its own accord — it can do so only as a direct consequence of management decisions. Ten decision areas determine cash flows for a firm and set up the difference between profit and cash flow:

1. Operating decisions: the same range of decisions which contribute to profit before charging depreciation.
2. Capital expenditure decisions: the acquisition or disposal of plant, equipment or such other assets of a long lasting nature which result in a depreciation charge against profits.
3. Inventory decisions: changes in the amounts tied up in stocks of raw materials, finished goods, work-in-process, sub-assemblies, and service spares. Increases in inventory create a negative cash flow. Decreases in inventory effectively create a positive cash flow because cash outflow for replacement is avoided.
4. Customer credit decisions: the length of time the customer is permitted before he or she pays for invoiced sales (note that profit on sales is normally computed as soon as the invoice is

sent). An increase in customer credit delays cash inflow — reduction of credit accelerates it.

5. *Supplier credit policies:* the length of time taken before materials, services, and other items are paid for. An increase in supplier credit effectively creates a positive cash flow, in that it delays cash outflow—reduction of credit accelerates cash outflow.

6. *Other accepted credit terms* (an extension of point 5): for example, rent, telephone, electricity, and certain taxes where it is normal to pay or receive, at periodic intervals, in advance or in arrears. The accounting process will tend to smooth out the charge against profits.

7. *Tax on profits* (an extension of point 6): Tax on company profits is due and payable at certain dates predetermined by law and consequently has a significant impact on the patterns of cash outflows.

8. *Financial obligations:* interest and dividend payments plus any contractual repayments of capital arising from past financial decisions.

The impact of these groups will determine the net cash surplus or deficit at time, which leads to a final pair of groups:

9. *Investing decisions:* the use of surplus funds by the purchase of investment or, conversely, the liberation of funds by the sale of such investment.

10. *Financing decisions:* the acquisition of new money either from shareholders or by borrowing from an outside firm (bank), including the use of installment purchasing or leasing to finance capital expenditure decisions.

Cash Flow and the Cash Account

The cash account is the most active of all business accounts. Receipts from sales (either in cash or payment of accounts receivable), receipts from the sale of assets, receipts from capital investment of the owners, and receipts of loan proceeds — all these go through the cash account. Disbursements for payment of expenses, cost of goods sold, repayment of a liability, payment of dividends or owner's draw, and the purchase of assets — all these also go through the cash account. The cash account is the only account that is used in transactions with all the other groups of accounts: assets, liabilities, capital, cost of goods sold, income, and expenses.

Cash transactions in the cash account can be divided roughly into cash receipts and payments and cash documentation in original vouchers, journals, and ledgers. Cash receipts are cash to the company, either as a result of product sales or assets, or as capital investment or liability proceeds. Cash documentation involves the bookkeeping system of the company from the original voucher (such as a sales receipt) to the journals (cash receipts journal) to the ledgers.

Cash Receipts and Payments

The principal cash events and their related vouchers are shown in Exhibit 4.10. These vouchers initiate the processing of cash data. A cash receipt indicates that the firm has received cash; a check indicates that a payment has been made; an adjustment voucher informs the system to record bank charges in an effort to reconcile a cash account with its related bank statement.

The concept of cash receipt, relocation, and disbursement can be seen in terms of how it affects journal entries. (See Exhibit 4.11.)

Cash Documentation

Specialized records called *journals* record the many repetitive transac-

---

EXHIBIT 4.10
Cash Events and Vouchers Required

Event	Voucher
Cash is received	1. Receipt (sales receipt, check cash)
	2. Draft (bank deposit slip)
Cash is relocated	3. Record of deposit (relocation of cash to a bank account)
	4. Transfer (relocation of cash from one business or division to another or from one bank account to another)
Cash is disbursed	5. Bank adjustment (reduction from bank account for bank service charges and adjustments)
	6. Petty cash fund
	7. Check or money order

EXHIBIT 4.11
Cash Actions and Journal Entries

Event/Voucher		Notation	Accounts	Debit $	Credit $
Cash is received					
1. Receipt voucher					
	a)	Cash provided as equity from owners	Cash	5000	
			Equity		5000
	b)	Cash provided by long-term creditors	Cash	2500	
			Long-term Liability		2500
	c)	Customer pays cash on account	Cash	150	
			Accts. Rec.		150
	d)	Fixed assets sold for cash	Cash	1000	
			Fixed Asset		1000
	e)	A sale is made for cash	Cash	1500	
			Income		1500
Cash is relocated:					
3. Deposit					
	f)	Cash is deposited Bank	X Bank	9750	
			Cash		9750
	g)	Cash is transferred from X Bank to Y Bank	Y Bank	5000	
			X Bank		5000
Cash is disbursed:					
5. Adjustment					
	h)	X Bank service charges are recorded	Bank Chgs.	5	
			X Bank		5

EXHIBIT 4.11
continued

Event/Voucher	Notation	Accounts	Debit $	Credit $
6. Petty Cash	i) Postage stamps are purchased	Misc. expense Cash	50	50
7. Checks	j) Merchandise is purchased with a check from X Bank	Inventory X Bank	900	900
	k) A payment is made to long-term creditors from X Bank	Long-term liab. X Bank	500	500
	l) Owner takes draw from Y Bank	Owners Draw (Equity) Y Bank	1000	1000
	m) Payment is made to Vendor from Y Bank	Accounts Pay. Y Bank	250	250
	n) A fixed asset is purchased with a check/Y Bank	Fixed asset Y Bank	2500	2500
	0) Wages, rent, & exp./Y Bank	Expenses Y Bank	400	400
		TOTAL	30505	30505

tions involving cash receipts (payments of accounts receivable and cash sales) and payments (such as rent expense and reduction of accounts payable).

The *cash receipts journal* is a specialized record of all cash receipts (Chapter 1).

A *petty cash* (or *imprest*) *fund* record is used to keep track of the many small cash or check payments that most organizations find necessary to use for such items as postage stamps, taxi cab fares, collect-postage items, freight charges, and various incidental expenses. A petty cash fund permits immediate cash or check payments within a per-event limit (of, say, $10 or $20) without meeting the approval requirement for the major check or cash disbursements. Where checks are used, a special petty cash checking account is maintained for that purpose (Chapter 1).

In a petty cash fund, reimbursement is a fixed amount each period or whenever the fund balance is low. There is a periodic, usually month-end, transfer of the petty cash expenses to specific expense ledger accounts. In an imprest fund, reimbursement is an amount necessary to restore the fund to an approved maximum level (of, say, $200), based on actual disbursements. Expense items are transferred when reimbursement is requested.

The process of *posting* consists of recording the original events from the journals (cash disbursements journal, cash receipts journal, for example) into the ledger accounts. Using the T-account ledger format, the events as discussed in the previous table on journals would be recorded as shown in Exhibit 4.12.

Notes on T-Account Illustration:

1. A T-account is a simplified representation of a ledger account that is used to illustrate dollar flow under the debit-credit convention. The following is the typical format and content of a real ledger account:

Date	Description	Debit	Credit $
1/6/79	Capital	5,000	
1/7/79	Long-term liability	2,500	
1/9/79	X Bank		9,800

EXHIBIT 4.12
Balance Sheet T-Accounts (1)

Cash			
a)	$ 5,000	f)	$ 9,750
b)	2,500	g)	50
c)	150		$ 9,800
d)	1,000		
e)	1,500		
	$10,150		
Bal. $	350		

X Bank			
f)	$ 9,750	g)	$ 5,000
		h)	5
		j)	900
		k)	500
	$ 9,750		6,405
Bal. $ 3,345			

Y Bank			
g)	$ 5,000	l)	$ 1,000
		m)	250
		n)	2,500
		o)	400
	$ 5,000		$ 4,150
Bal. $	850		

Accounts Receivable			
$ 1,200	(3)	c)	$ 150
Bal. $ 1,050			

Merchandise Inventory			
$ 3,000	(3)	$ 2,800	(5)
900			
j)	3,900	$ 2,800	
$ 1,100			

Accounts Payable			
m)	$ 250		$ 3,000 (4)
		Bal.	$ 2,750

Long-term Liabilities			
k)	$ 500	b)	$ 2,500
		Bal.	$ 2,000

Capital (Owner's Draw)			
l)	$1,000	a)	$ 5,000
		Bal.	$ 4,000

Income		
	$ 1,200	(3)
e)	1,500	
Bal.	$ 2,700	

Cost of Sales	
$ 2,800 (5)	

Expenses	
h)	$ 5
i)	50
o)	400
	$ 455

Fixed Assets		
n)	$ 2,500	d) $ 1,000
Bal.	$ 1,500	

2. In this example, there is a distinction between *cash* and *bank* transactions. In other texts, cash is often used generically to refer to all forms of cash and checking transactions.

3. This entry does not involve cash at this point. A sale has been made *on account*. The notation for this event in the general journal would be:

    Increase (debit) accounts receivable $1,200

    Increase (credit) income $1,200

4. This is similar to the foregoing event; here, merchandise inventory has been purchased on account with the following notation:

    Increase (debit) merchandise inventory $3,000

    Increase (credit) accounts payable $3,000

    Suppliers of inventory are called *vendors*.

5. There are two transactions for each sales event — recording the event at the *selling* price, and recording the event at the *cost* price. This entry records the cost of sales for the period:

    Increase (debit) cost of sales $2,800

    Decrease (credit) merchandise inventory $2,800

QUESTION: *How does the cash movement in the books break down into receipts and payments (cash income and outgo)?*

ANSWER:

Receipts

1. From customers; that is, collections of accounts receivable or notes payable.
2. From cash sales not involving credit.
3. From miscellaneous repetitive sources; that is, rent income, interest income, dividends, and royalties.
4. From miscellaneous, nonrepetitive sources, as sale of surplus assets or investments and new sources of finance (bank borrowings, loans, equity investment from outside).

Payments

1. To suppliers of raw materials or other supplies, as reduction of accounts payable or notes payable.

2. To employees for salaries and labor-related expenses, as taxes, insurance, pension, and other expenses.
3. Utilities and other services where payment is made on a regular basis (telephone, accounting, and maintenance).
4. Other operating expenses (supplies, small tools, fees).
5. Settlement of tax liabilities (federal, state, and local).
6. For capital expenditures, for example, the acquisition of land, buildings, plant and equipment: representing significant but irregular payments.
7. To meet financial obligations:
    a. Of a regular nature, as interest and dividend payments.
    b. Of an irregular nature, as repayment of loans.
8. For any other purpose of a significant, irregular, or extraordinary nature, as settlement of litigation.

THE CASH TANK METHOD OF CASH MANAGEMENT

W.C.F. Hartley in his book *Cash: Planning, Forecasting, and Control* describes an easily visualized method of cash management called the *cash tank*. It is similar to the illustration used at the start of this chapter, equating cash to a liquid in a reservoir whose inflow and outflow are controlled by management by means of control valves.

The level of liquid (cash) in the tank can be controlled only by one of two courses of action:

1. Reducing or eliminating outflows by adjusting the valves on one or more of the outlet pipes.
2. Increasing inflows by adjusting the valves on one or more of the inlet pipes.

A schematic diagram (Exhibit 4.13) of such a liquid flow system shows the main tank, feeder tanks, and inlet and outlet pipes with the control valves pictured as a spoked wheel. The control valve regulates both the rate and timing of the flow.

Against the background of this physical model of liquid flow a cash flow system that adopts the same concepts is easily envisioned. Only three feeder tanks have been used, representing the three major sources: income from operations; new financing (from debt or capital injection); and liquidation of assets.

EXHIBIT 4.13
Cash Tank Analysis

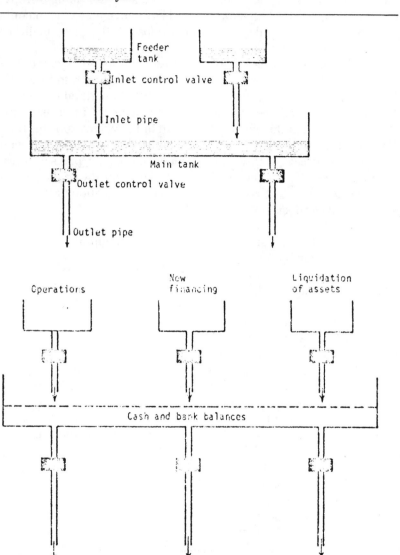

Similarly, each group of inflows has its counterpart group of outflows: appropriations of profit (payment of all expenses out of income plus payment of taxes, owners' draw, and dividends); servicing or repayment of borrowings; and acquisition of assets. If management is to control the level of cash in the tank, then these groups are the three main designations of inflow and outflow to be tackled.

A cash tank analysis highlights those areas of management responsibility in which decisions were made that caused cash to flow. Pursuing the tank analogy to its conclusion, the cash-tank method concentrates on the valves that must be controlled by management in order to preserve the level of cash in the bank. Adjustment of the valves controls the rate of timing of cash flow in from the feeder tanks via the inlet pipes (representing sources of cash inflows), or through the outlet pipes (representing cash outflows). The valves will, in fact, represent the management decisions discussed in the first question-and-answer portion of this chapter. In summary, these decision areas are:

1. Operating decisions — culminating in potential cash flow from operations before tax.
2. Capital expenditures decisions:
    a. acquisition (purchase)
    b. disposal (sale)
3. Inventory decisions:
    a. increases in inventory
    b. decreases in inventory
4. Customer credit decisions:
    a. increase or extension of credit
    b. reduction of credit
5. Supplier credit policies:
    a. increase in the time or amount of credit you receive
    b. decreases in credit
6. Other accepted credit terms
7. Taxes on profit
8. Financial obligations:
    a. interest payment
    b. dividend payment
    c. repayment of borrowed capital
9. Investing decisions — use of temporary surplus funds:
    a. purchase
    b. sale
10. Financing decisions — acquisition of new money:
    a. from stockholders, partners, and other sources
    b. by borrowing

Forecasting Cash Movements

Because cash flow is crucial to a firm, it is essential that management attempt to forecast the likely pattern of future cash flows, if only as a minimum precaution against business failure. Such a forecast will not always prove to be precisely accurate, but nevertheless it will create reliable signals to indicate the type of action needed. A good forecast is not necessarily the one that turns out to be right but the one that, as the future unfolds, provides the basis for guiding appropriate and timely management action. (See Exhibit 4.14.)

Advantages to a firm that maintains a systematic approach to cash forecasting include:

1. Avoiding costly mistakes. Short of bankruptcy, many firms suffer the financial consequences of ill-considered or hastily undertaken ventures. A cash forecast will reveal in advance the potential impact on cash flow of any venture. Revealing the possible consequences in advance should allow sufficient time to reconsider the venture or its timing. Foresight can prove better than hindsight.
2. Assisting management control. The cash forecast will warn of an impending cash problem and indicate steps that management might take to reduce or eliminate its impact.
3. Increases confidence by the lender. It becomes less difficult to raise funds when required if management can demonstrate that it is attempting to be in command of the situation by predicting the amount of additional funds that will be required. It could be too late to attempt to raise funds after the onset of financial difficulties.
4. Improved utilization of capital. Not only is it the function of a cash forecast to indicate cash deficiencies or requirements for finance, but also it will indicate if cash surpluses are likely to arise. In these circumstances, management can take appropriate measures to use the cash surplus to maximum advantage.

Earlier in this chapter the importance of timing in cash flow was stressed. The time dimension must be restressed at this stage because a cash forecast attempts to forecast not only quantities, but also the timing of cash flow. Although all the quantities of future cash flows have been forecast correctly, the firm could still find itself in considerable financial difficulty, if the forecast of the timing were seriously wrong; or if, for example, all the cash inflows, though forecast correctly in amount, came one month later than expected. Exhibit 4.15 demonstrates the importance

EXHIBIT 4.14
Cash Flow Example

CASH FORECAST (SIMPLIFIED)

	JAN	FEB	MAR	APL	MAY	JUN	TOTAL
Forecast inflows	100	200	300	200	200	-	1000
Forecast outflows	-	80	160	240	160	160	800
Monthly cash surplus (deficit)	100	120	140	(40)	40	(160)	200
Cumulative cash surplus (deficit)	100	220	360	320	360	200	200

ACTUAL CASH FLOWS FOR THE SITUATION FORECAST ABOVE

	JAN	FEB	MAR	APL	MAY	JUN	TOTAL
Actual inflows	-	100	200	300	200	200	1000-
Actual outflows	80	160	240	160	160	-	800
Monthly cash surplus (deficit)	(80)	(60)	(40)	140	40	200	200
Cumulative cash surplus (deficit)	(80)	(140)	(180)	(40)	nil	200	200

EXHIBIT 4.15
Budget Format

CASH BUDGET
For the Fiscal Year, 19 —

Details	First Quarter	Second Quarter	Third Quarter	Fourth Quarter	Total
OPERATING SOURCES					
Cash sales	$ 50,000	$ 50,000	$ 100,000	$ 250,000	$ 350,000
Collections on accounts receivable	450,000	400,000	600,000	850,000	2,300,000
TOTAL OPERATING SOURCES	500,000	450,000	700,000	1,100,000	2,650,000
USES					
Cash purchases	40,000	40,000	75,000	100,000	255,000
Payments on accounts payable	460,000	260,000	325,000	400,000	1,445,000
Cash operating expenses	200,000	200,000	250,000	300,000	950,000
TOTAL OPERATING USES	700,000	500,000	650,000	800,000	2,650,000
NET OPERATING CASH	$ (200,000)	$ (50,000)	$ 50,000	$ 300,000	$ 100,000
NONOPERATING SOURCES					
Interest income	5,000	5,000	5,000	4,000	19,000
Sale of investment	-	-	50,000	-	50,000
Sale of fixed assets	25,000	-	-	-	25,000
Contributed capital	-	50,000	-	-	50,000

EXHIBIT 4.15
continued

Loans, bonds or other forms of long-term creditors' equity	170,000	-	-	-	170,000
TOTAL NONOPERATING SOURCES	200,000	55,000	55,000	4,000	314,000
USES: Interest expense	-	2,500	2,500	2,500	7,500
Investments	-	-	-	50,000	50,000
Purchase of fixed assets	-	-	-	150,000	150,000
Repayment of creditors' equity	-	-	-	170,000	170,000
Dividends	-	-	-	25,000	25,000
Repurchase of owners' equity	-	-	-	-	-
TOTAL NONOPR. USES	-	2,500	2,500	397,500	402,500
NONOPERATING CASH	$ 200,000	52,500	52,500	(393,500)	(88,500)

of timing. Notice that the forecast and actual quantities of both inflow and outflow are identical, and therefore the actual total cash position remains exactly the same as planned. However, the actual outflow is required one month earlier than expected, whereas the cash inflows occurred one month later than planned. The forecast showed a favorable, cumulative cash position throughout the six months, but the actual cash was considerable and continuously negative until the end.

There are two types of cash forecasts:

1. The short-term forecast
2. The long-term forecast

The two types of cash forecasts, having slightly different objectives and orientation, will be dealt with separately.

The Short-term Cash Forecast

The short-term (or short-range) cash budget covers the length of a cycle from investment of cash to its recovery in such terms as inventory, receivables, and deferred charges. The period covered is generally the cash cycle discussed earlier in this chapter.

The prime objective of a short-term cash forecast is to ensure that a firm can pay its debts in the immediate future. It is oriented towards the guidance of appropriate management control action in the short term. Consequently, such a forecast needs to be up to date and reasonably detailed. It should be prepared at frequent intervals and cover the next six to twelve months.

Long-term Cash Forecast

A long-term (or long-range) cash forecast covers the length of a cycle from investment of cash to its recovery from such items as plant and equipment, market development, and research. Since this period is viewed as being the maximum length of time from which sales trends, technology, and the products of market development and research can be projected with sufficient certainty to yield a reliable cash forecast, it follows that the period most commonly used for this purpose is from three to five years. In cases where long-term cash flow is certain, as with ground rents, mortgage loans or long-term leases, it could be projected accurately for periods up to ninety-nine years or more.

The object of preparing a cash forecast over the longer term is to indicate the financial consequences of future strategic courses of action and to assist in long-term financial planning. This objective is quite different from that of short-term forecasts. The long-term forecast is prepared annually. Its orientation will be toward the financial consequences of and interrelationship between strategic management decisions.

BUDGET FORMAT

A format for a short-term cash budget is shown in Exhibit 4.15. Its purpose is to project the operating cash position for a specified period and to enable management to plan for nonoperating sources and uses given a knowledge of the operating cash deficiency or surplus. For example, an operating cash deficit of $200,000 is budgeted for the first quarter. A further deficit of $100,000 is indicated for the second quarter. In quarters three and four, respectively, surpluses of $150,000 and $200,000 are projected. Having this information in advance aids management in cash planning.

In the first quarter management elects to raise the needed cash by using its interest income, by selling fixed assets, and by securing a $170,000 loan. The second quarter sees the deficit decrease by $55,000 in contributed equity and interest income.

Cash Control

In general, there are considered to be two types of control in the cash system: stewardship controls and management control. Each shall be discussed.

Stewardship Controls

Stewardship controls are designed to accomplish two things:

1. The proper receipt of all cash to the organization
2. The proper disbursement of all cash by the organization.

Cash is more subject to theft than any other asset, and a large percentage of business transactions involve the receipt and disbursement of cash. For these reasons, strict stewardship controls are needed to prevent misappropriation of cash. Two forms of embezzlement should be noted:

1. *Lapping:* The theft of cash received from one customer but

credited to that customer's account at a later date by using cash received from another customer.

2. *Kiting:* a. Cashing an unrecorded check in one bank, and covering it with a check drawn on another bank

   b. Opening a bank account with a fraudulent check (usually originating in a different city or state to lengthen clearing time), and then drawing most of the amount out before the bank discovers the error.

Embezzlement by these and other methods can be guarded against by maintaining a system of internal controls over the handling of cash. The following are general principles for controlling cash receipts and cash disbursements.

Among effective general principles for controlling *cash receipts* are:

1. The immediate separation of cash from its documentation. For instance, people who record cash transactions should not write checks or make deposits. Documentation is channeled to the accounting department and cash to the cashier. The records can then be compared.
2. The function of cash handling must be distinct from maintaining the accounting records. Neither party should have access to or supervise the recordkeeping of the other.
3. If possible, there should be a daily deposit of all cash receipts into the bank.
4. The party responsible for cash receipts should not also be responsible for cash disbursements.

The following are general principles for controlling *cash disbursements:*

1. All disbursements should be made by check. Issuing a check should require approval of more than one person. A cancelled check is proof that payment was made and payment by check provides a permanent record of disbursements.
2. Checks should be prenumbered. Spoiled checks should be marked *void.*
3. If possible, checks should be signed by one person and countersigned by another.
4. Supporting invoices and other documentation should be perforated or marked *paid* in order to prevent double payment for the same item.

5. A system for approving payments should underlie the issuance of checks. The person who approved the payment should not be the person who issues the check.

Note that stewardship controls place a repeated emphasis on the principle of *separation of duties*. Underlying this principle is the observed fact that the odds of embezzlement are decreased significantly if an act of dishonesty requires the collusion of two or more persons.

Management Controls

Management control has as its principal purpose *optimizing* the company's cash position. This is true if the company has a cash surplus or a cash deficit.

Excess cash denotes poor management, since these cash resources can usually produce a higher return if they are converted to some other form of asset (such as investments). Contrary to popular thinking, a large cash balance is not a reliable indicator of an organization's good health; it may be just the opposite. Too little cash is also hazardous and may require unscheduled borrowing of funds on adverse terms, or the untimely disposition of the firm's assets.

QUESTION: How does one optimize cash position?

ANSWER:
The application of management controls in administering cash has had some impressive results.

Cash forecasts and budgets (Chapter 11) are the principal techniques for the management control of cash. Cash budgets may be prepared for any period of time. They serve as management controls for the following reasons:

1. They emphasize the timing of future cash events.
2. They indicate periods when cash surpluses or shortages are likely to occur, thus enabling management to:
    a. Convert temporary surplus cash into investments.
    b. Arrange in advance for financing for periods where shortages are indicated.
3. They facilitate the scheduling of loan repayments.
4. By distinguishing postponable from nonpostponable disbursements, they provide management with a basis for deciding priorities and for relating postponable needs to periods where optimum financing is possible.

5. They provide guidelines for controlling disbursements, in that expenditures for a particular account cannot exceed budget without special approval.

Financial cash flow ratios are another technique for optimizing management controls of cash.

One ratio for doing this is the *average daily disbursements ratio*. This is a simple ratio that tells you the amount of money your company spends on the average each day. The formula can be represented as follows:

$$D_a = \frac{D_t}{N_p}$$

Where: D_a = average daily disbursements

D_t = total disbursements for a period

N_p = number of days in the period

Once you know the average amount of money the firm spends daily (the average daily disbursements above), then it is easy to find out how long your cash reserve will last if there is no income. You multiply the average daily disbursements by the number of days to be covered by the cash reserve, as follows:

$$C_b = N_r \times D_a$$

Where: C_b = cash balance

N_r – number of days covered by the cash reserve

D_a = average daily disbursements (from the previous formula)

If a person wants to find out how many days the cash reserve will last, just turn the formula around like this:

$$N_r = \frac{C_b}{D_a}$$

Other ratios also assist management in controlling cash flow, such as break-even and cash break-even formulas and accounts receivable and inventory ratios. These ratios will be discussed in the chapter on budgeting, Chapter 11.

Cash discounts are another technique for management control. *Cash discounts* are inducements to pay accounts within a specified period of time. Cash discount terms are usually quoted on vendors' invoices. For example, the cash discount expression 2/10, n/30 means that a 2 percent discount can be subtracted from the face amount of the invoice if payment is made within 10 days of the invoice date. The full amount is due within 30 days of the invoice date, and no discount is allowed if payment is made after the 10th day.

Cash discounts are received where the firm purchases items, or given where the firm sells items. The accounting records are kept on the assumption that (a) all discounts are taken (net price method) or (b) all discounts are not taken (gross price method). Exhibit 4.16 is an example of these methods.

The choice of method — net price or gross price — should agree with management's policy regarding cash discounts. If the policy of the company is to take discounts, then the net price method should be used. This method will highlight exception to policy when discounts are *not* taken.

There is an implied interest rate in the discount formula. The two-percent discount in the expression 2/10, n/30 is equivalent to a 36 percent annual interest rate. The formula for computing this is:

$$I_r = D_r \left(\frac{F_y}{O_p} \right)$$

Where: I_r = effective annual interest rate

D_r = discount rate (the 2 percent in 2/10, n/30)

F_y = financial year consisting of 360 days

O_p = option period (20 days in 2/10, n/30)

The firm will pay either on the 10th or the 30th. Paying before the 10th will not increase the discount, but will decrease cash flow; whereas paying between the 11th and the 30th will not give the company a discount and will decrease its cash flow. Therefore, the option period is 20 days (difference between 10 and 30).The cost of *not* taking the discount is 2 percent for 20 days. There are 18 twenty-day periods in a year, hence 18 × 2 percent = 36 percent effective annual interest rate.

For example: Your Company, Inc., purchases materials subject to cash discounts on terms 3/10, n/30. During the twelve months of 1978 these purchases amounted to $600,000. No cash discounts were taken.

QUESTION: *If Your Company, Inc., could borrow the necessary cash from a bank (at 15 percent interest) on the tenth day of each month and repay the loan on the thirtieth of the same month, what effect would this have on net income for the period?*

EXHIBIT 4.16
Examples of Cash Discount Technique

On March 15, 1979, Your Company, Inc., sells My Company, Inc., merchandise priced at $1,000 on terms 2/10, n/30. The invoice has the same date. Entries in Your Company's records under the net price method would be:

Data/Transaction	CASH		ACCOUNTS RECEIVABLE		SALES		CASH DISCOUNTS NOT TAKEN	
	Debit	Credit	Debit	Credit	Debit	Credit	Debit	Credit
a) March 15. . . .			$ 980			$ 980		
b) March 25—if discount is taken.	$ 980			$ 980				
c) March 15—if discount is not taken. . . .	$1000			$ 980				$ 20

The entries in X Company's income statement if (b) or (c) occurs would be:

(b) Sales .... $ 980
(c) Sales .... $ 980
    Add: Cash discounts not
        taken by client(s) $ 20
                   $1,000

EXHIBIT 4.16
continued

Entries in Your Company's records under the Gross Price Method would be:

Date/Transaction	CASH Debit	CASH Credit	ACCOUNTS RECEIVABLE Debit	ACCOUNTS RECEIVABLE Credit	SALES Debit	SALES Credit	CASH DISCOUNTS NOT TAKEN Debit	CASH DISCOUNTS NOT TAKEN Credit
a) March 15			$1,000			$1,000		
b) March 25—if discount is taken.	$ 980			$1,000			$ 20	
c) March 15—if discount is not taken.	$2,000			$2,000				

The entries in Your Company's income statement if (b) or (c) occurs would be:

(b) Sales. $2,000
Less: Cash discounts taken by client (s). . . . . $ 40
$1,960
$2,000

(c) Sales. . . . .

EXHIBIT 4.16
continued

Entries in My Company's records under the net price method would be:

Date/Transaction	CASH		ACCOUNTS RECEIVABLE		SALES		CASH DISCOUNTS NOT TAKEN	
	Debit	Credit	Debit	Credit	Debit	Credit	Debit	Credit
a) March 15.			$ 980			$ 980		
b) March 25— if the discount is taken		$ 980		$ 980				
c) March 15— if the discount is not taken.	$1,000			$ 980				$ 20

The entries in Y Company's income statement if (b) or (c) occurs would be:

(b)	Purchases (Cost of Sales).	$ 980
(c)	Purchases (Cost of Sales).	$ 980
	Add: Cash discounts not taken.	$ 20
		$1,000

EXHIBIT 4.16
continued

Entries in My Company's records under the gross price method would be:

Date/Transaction	CASH Debit	CASH Credit	ACCOUNTS RECEIVABLE Debit	ACCOUNTS RECEIVABLE Credit	SALES Debit	SALES Credit	CASH DISCOUNTS NOT TAKEN Debit	CASH DISCOUNTS NOT TAKEN Credit
a) March 15.			$1,000			$1,000		
b) March 25 — if the discount is taken		$ 980		$1,000				$ 20
c) March 15 — if the discount is not taken		$1,000		$1,000				

The entries in *Y Company's* income statement if (b) or (c) occurs would be:

(b) Purchases (Cost of Sales) $1,000
    Less: Cash discounts taken. . .   20
    Purchases (Cost of Sales) $ 980

(c) Purchases (Cost of Sales) $1,000

ANSWER:

Interest and bank charges for Your Company can be computed by the following formula:

$$I_a = \frac{P_d}{F_y} \times I_r \times A$$

Where: I_a = interest in dollars that the bank charges

P_d = period for which the funds are borrowed in days

I_r = annual interest rate

A = amount borrowed

Using the figures in the example, the calculation works as follows:

$$I_a = \frac{20}{360} \times .15 \times 582{,}000$$

$$I_a = \$4{,}850$$

The amount borrowed would be $582,000 ($600,000 times 0.97 [100 percent minus a 3 percent discount]) for a period of twenty days. In our example, the bank would charge $4,850 in interest. The cost of losing the cash discount can be computed.

$$.03 \times \$600{,}000 = \$18{,}000$$

Income would be improved by $13,150 ($18,000 − $4,850) if cash could be borrowed from the bank in order to take advantage of the cash discount.

The point is that discounts allowed on purchases can have an effective interest rate higher than a banker would charge to borrow the money. Since the effective interest rate on a 2 percent discount in ten days is 36 percent per annum, it might be wise to take discounts any time they amount to 2 percent or more.

Money float is also a very effective management cash control technique. *Float* is cash in transit or suspense. For example, for the period between the time a check is written and the time it *clears* the payor's bank account, that amount of cash is in float. Many large companies pay their employees on the West Coast with checks drawn on East Coast banks so that the time between when the check is written, cashed at a West Coast bank, shipped to an eastern bank, and subtracted from the company's account is lengthy. The company can use the cash during this time interval. Here are some more examples of float:

1.   *Disneyland coupons:* Visitors to Disneyland exchange money for coupons at the gate. They may not use all of the coupons in one day, and

keep the rest for a return visit days, weeks, months (or never) in the future. Disneyland, of course, has been paid for the unused coupons so that it gets float on the money.

2. *Traveler's checks:* Bank of America, CitiBank, Cooks, and American Express Company trade their traveler's checks for cash. (The money you pay for the checks, if any, goes to the bank as a handling fee.) People who exchange cash for traveler's checks takes a vacation, during which they periodically cash the traveler's checks. Meanwhile, the issuing company (American Express) has invested the cash it received. With a continuing stream of clients, the issuing company always has a substantial amount of float invested, earnings from which constitutes the company's source of income.

3. *Trade dollars:* A group of merchants wishes to encourage business among themselves as a group. The promoters issue trade association dollars in exchange for real money. For as long as the trade dollars remain in circulation within the group, the promoters can benefit from the investment of the float.

4. *Gift certificates:* Rather than purchase an item from a retail store, many people buy gift certificates for relatives and friends. Until the relatives and friends spend these certificates, however, the company that issues them (the retailer) can use the money as float.

These examples are how float can be created. Even though most businesses do not create float, they can utilize it. For example, analysis of check-clearing processes can permit a judicious pairing of cash reserves.

Bank reconciliations can be useful in developing statistical float data in addition to their usefulness in achieving agreement between the cash and the bank accounts. Float works two ways in a checking account. When deposits are made a float of from two to three days is usually required before the checks clear the payor's accounts. This is *negative float*, for until the deposits are cleared, the firm may not issue checks or make withdrawals. On the other hand, checks issued by the firm are float until they have cleared the firm's bank account. This is *positive float*. The difference between negative and positive float is *net negative* or *net positive* float. If the minimum float period is two days (based on mailing and clearing time), we can readily compute minimum float.

In addition, some clients may be in distant locations or they may simply be slow depositors. To refine our measurement of float, we can analyze checks outstanding at the end of each month and *age* them according to various time periods. (See Exhibit 4.17.)

With sufficient aging data and experience, we have a basis for calculating probable float. You can calculate the percentage of total checks cashed

EXHIBIT 4.17
Aging of Checks Paid

Checks Outstanding	0-30 Days	31-60 Days	61-90 Days	Over 90 Days
No. 1012				$ 500
1015			$1,000	
1023			500	
1032		$1,500		
1035		500		
1041	$ 500			
1046	2,000			
1048	2,500			
	$5,000	$2,000	$1,500	$ 500

in less than thirty days, less, than sixty days and other designated timings. You could then figure that a certain number of your checks are going to be outstanding, so that you could actually write checks for that percentage more than your cash balance in the bank. You could also get an idea of how long a certain company takes to cash checks. Float analysis can, in this way, be a useful management cash control tool.

MANAGEMENT DECISIONS IN A CASH DEFICIT SITUATION

The existence of, or the anticipation of, a cash deficit does not automatically imply that the firm must search for additional financing outside of the company. Management's initial response should always be to attempt to eliminate or to reduce the deficit by finer internal control of the cash flow. Management should consider the cost of alternative ways of dealing with a deficit. Internal management action can cost less than a new external source of financing. Even if an external source has to be found, this source might prove merely a bridging operation pending the ability to bring on-stream an alternative internal source.

The size, duration, and degree of warning are critical factors in the selection of appropriate management action, be it time-related, volume-related, or one-time occurrences. Let us consider some specific actions that might be taken that do not require major volume or scale cuts in levels of activity or expense, or large-scale divestments. These are pertinent areas of management decisions:

1. Collections from customers
2. Rents and interest received
3. Sale of assets
4. Payments to suppliers
5. Wages, salaries, and labor-related expenses
6. Other payments
7. Taxes
8. Purchase of buildings, plants, and equipment
9. Interest, dividend payments, and capital repayments.

1. *Collections from customers:*

QUESTION: *Is it possible, either over the whole range of customers or in specific cases, to accelerate the rate of cash collections?*

ANSWER:

The amount to be collected is a function of sales invoiced and the collection period. Leaving aside the question of sales volume, can anything be done to speed up the time between shipment of the goods and collection of cash? Administrative activities concerned with invoicing, presentation of statements or other demands to the customer, control over the collection period, and the mechanics of cash collection and banking should be carefully examined to confirm that no unnecessary delay has crept in. One day's delay in presenting an invoice could delay cash inflow by one month if the invoice by chance fails to get into the customer's current accounting period. Checks collected by traveling salespersons do not ease the liquidity position until they are deposited at the bank.

Generally speaking, the use of cash discounts to accelerate cash collections should be avoided because the cost of such an action could be considerable. Besides, there is always the customer who will take the discount but will still pay the money late, a practice that causes all sorts of problems.

2. *Rents and interest received:* It may be possible to renegotiate terms of rentals or notes receivable in such a way as to have an accelerating effect on cash inflows whether by earlier or more frequent (biweekly) payments.

3. *Sales of assets:* Without considering large-scale divestment of

assets, management may review its current investments in fixed assets, inventories, or other short-term deposits. Are there any individual items that represent redundant assets, the ongoing rate of return of which no longer justifies retention? Many businesspeople prefer to hoard rather than divest. By doing so, however, they could be denying themselves the opportunity of cash inflows with a very low price tag, relying instead on an alternative source which may be more costly.

4. *Payments to suppliers:* Indiscriminate curtailment of payments to suppliers is not recommended. However it may be possible to negotiate extended credit terms, either generally, or specifically with certain suppliers. Alternatively, new sources of supply may be sought that offer better terms. The value of interest saved arising from better credit terms may even justify payment of a slightly higher price to the new supplier.

The equivalent percentage per-annum cost of losing cash discounts by delaying payment to suppliers who offer a discount must be carefully weighed. Sometimes loss of cash discounts from suppliers by delaying payment to them could represent a high price to pay for what is effectively a source of cash inflow.

There is a natural delay (float) between the time a check is written and the time it is charged against the firm's bank account. This float can be of considerable value to a firm's cash flow. Simple procedures such as using third-class mail instead of first-class mail for the checks sent to suppliers can help this process. It might be a good idea to make a study of how businesses cash their checks, as suggested in the previous section on float.

The amount payable to suppliers is determined not only by credit terms but also by the level of purchases. The amount paid for inventories depends on management decisions about the volume of production, the level of inventories, and the frequency of ordering or delivery of purchased items.

5. *Wages, salaries, and labor-related expenses:* The selection of a production policy for meeting seasonal peaks in demand will have its impact on the pattern of wage payments. A policy that maintains a constant level of production (allowing inventory to act as a buffer) will create a different pattern of wage cash flow than a policy that allows production levels to vary in harmony with peaks and troughs in demand. Ordinarily little can be done about wages in the short run when the level of production or the staff level is constant.

6. *Other payments:* Little can be done about other expenses (rent, and utilities) in the short run. The only advice that can be offered is that the firm take the maximum allowable time and amount of credit.

7. *Taxes:* With taxes there is also little that can be done. It is usually

possible, however, to get short extensions in time, and sometimes a firm can make partial payments (although penalties are charged on the amounts remaining unpaid).

8. *Purchase of buildings, plant, and equipment:* This item leaves considerable room for management control. The capital investment decision itself clearly has its impact on cash flow. Management must carefully choose the date on which each project is to start. Similarly, the nature of the project itself will affect cash flow — for example, whether the project is labor or capital intensive. Cash flow beyond the time of the capital decision should be considered. Alternative methods of payment are normally available and should be considered. Deferred payment terms might be negotiated instead of outright purchases; installment terms may be available and leasing might be considered (see leasing chapter, Chapter 9).

9. *Interest, dividend payments, and capital repayments:* Payment of interest on and repayment of borrowed money are contractual liabilities and default can have consequences. Payment of dividends is more a moral than a contractual obligation; but if stockholders' expectations of a dividend are not fulfilled, then this situation could cause an adverse effect on market price of shares. There are, however, some things that management can do. The amount of the dividend can be determined, and management can exercise control through determination of the dates of payment, of interest, and other applicable expenses. For example, it would seem senseless to select a date for payment of interest or dividend that coincides with a period of peak seasonal inventory (which normally implies high negative cash flow) or with the date of payment of tax on corporate profits.

QUESTION: *What is the best way for management to deal with a cash surplus?*

ANSWER:

Contrary to popular thought, a cash surplus is not necessarily a good thing because the amount of the surplus in effect indicates underutilization of resources by the firm. A cash surplus, unless beneficially employed can only detract from the overall rate of return currently being earned by the firm on its total capital employed.

If the cash surplus is actually retained in cash, it will earn precisely nothing (and it is likely to fall in value due to the eroding effect of inflation). On the other hand, the surplus may be placed on deposit with the bank earning a normal rate of interest. But there are usually better ways to invest the money. Potential management actions that might be taken depend on the size of the cash surplus, the period of time for which it is available, and the degree of notice that management received that the cash surplus was becoming available. However, the following actions might be worth considering:

1.   If the cash surplus is likely to be available permanently or for an extended period of time, then steps should be taken to deploy it profitably within the business, if possible. A planned phase of re-equipment, expansion, or addition to the product range might be a good idea. Remember, money invested in one's own firm gives the most control and profit. These expenditures, however, should be well planned.

2.   If the surplus is available for a shorter period of time, several formal short-term investment opportunities present themselves, such as investment in government bonds or treasury notes, term deposits with banks, and even overnight lending to the money market, which earns a return. Any rate of return is better than none, but it is important that this type of investment be both secure and easily liquidated. Short-term cash surpluses should never be used for speculative investments or for investments that cannot be liquidating in the short term. Most banks offer interest on checking accounts if a minimum balance is maintained. Advantage should be taken of these accounts.

3.   Several other time-related actions are alternative means of deal-ing with short-term cash surpluses, such as the earlier payment of amounts owing to suppliers and the earlier purchase of materials. Any action of this type should be undertaken only after careful evaluation of rate of return on this investment. Paying earlier may take advantage of discounts offered by suppliers. Similarly, by taking delivery of materials earlier, it may be possible to negotiate a conces-sionary price with the supplier. Most suppliers also offer lower prices on materials that are ordered in large amounts. If the inventory is the kind that turns over rapidly, purchasing large amounts at a cheaper price may be to the firm's advantage. After taking into account storage and other costs involved in taking early or large deliveries, it is possible to work out the equivalent per-annum rate of return represented by the net savings earned by this transaction.

4.   If the cash surplus is permanent and no alternative use presents itself, early repayment of loans or other capital should be considered as a last resort. The rate of return earned on this use of the surplus cash is, of course, the amount saved in future interest on the capital repaid.

QUESTION: *What are the management decisions involved with good cash control of inventories?*

ANSWER:

The goal of inventory management is to have zero inventories that are not immediately sold; but clearly this is impossible. In theory, a firm must carry inventory to smooth out any imbalance in production-marketing efforts, to ensure that all reasonable demands can be met as expeditiously as possible and to provide a hedge against failure in delivery or escalation of delivery price. Are the firm's inventory levels down to the minimum necessary to achieve these theoretical goals? Over and above the minimum, how much inventory results from bad ordering, an over-cautious attitude to the risk of stock-out, the residue left in the wake of design modifications and other changes of plan, or simply just from what is left over from production? The amount of finished goods that must be carried to ensure 100 percent customer satisfaction could be crippling — a considerable liberation of cash might be achieved by acceptance of something less than 100 percent service cover. It is estimated that in many industries, 50 percent of the items amount for more than 70 percent of the sales. The chapter on inventories (Chapter 6) discusses the various techniques of inventory adjustment covering different degrees of mathematical sophistication: here our emphasis is on four points of decision:

1. Minimum safety levels must be fixed by a senior level manager because once fixed, cash will be committed to inventory more or less permanently.
2. The total amount of inventory held at any one time is a function of the minimum safety stock plus a fluctuation amount determined by the relationship between the delivered quantity and the demand. The higher the delivered quantity, the higher the average overall inventory level and the greater the amount of cash tied up. Thus, the essential levels that should be determined in addition to the minimum safety levles are the delivered quantities.
3. A further determinant of the total inventory volume is the number of locations at which minimum levels are held. The lowest overall inventory level is usually achieved if only one central pool of inventory is maintained. On the other hand, many practical reasons demand a degree of duplication. However, such duplication should be kept to the minimum consistent with efficient and economical production and sales activity and again should be the decision of senior level management.

4. Another aspect of duplication that causes an unnecessary amount of cash to be tied up in inventory is the uncontrolled expansion of the range of items carried. The number of items held in stock should be reviewed at intervals to establish whether it is possible to reduce the range by standardization of materials, components, or stores. Any redundant items thus weeded out should be converted into cash.

Of course, one must not overlook the possibility that cash committed to inventory may be a good investment in the light of potential windfall profits that can be earned by avoiding future price escalations, especially in times of rapid inflation. But remember, gambling your cash on continued inflation is just that — a gamble. It must be carefully weighed against the possibility of a price decrease. Some industries, such as solid-state electronics, are continually faced with price decreases even in time of rapid inflation.

5

Receivables

Chapter 5 discusses *receivables*, a term that generally speaking, suggests claims for money and goods due from other businesses. The various types or categories of receivables include:

1. Accounts receivable (due from customers)
2. Notes receivable (due from those who owe money and who have signed a negotiable instrument or note)
3. Deposits receivable or returnable
4. Claims against various parties (governments, lawsuits)
5. Advances to employees, officers, stockholders

CURRENT VERSUS NONCURRENT

Receivables can be listed as current or as long-term assets. To be classified as a current asset, a receivable should be convertible into cash within one year's time; otherwise it should be classified as a noncurrent asset.

QUESTION: How should receivables be valued if they are due in more
                      than one year?

ANSWER:

Receivables should be stated at their net realizable cash value. Initially, they may be stated at the invoice price of the sale, if, for example, a credit sale for $100 is recorded. However, not all receivables are collectible. Therefore, if receivables are to stated at their net realizable cash value, then an estimate of the amounts of receivables that will not be collected is required. In other words, an allowance for bad debts or uncollectible accounts should be deducted from receivables. Estimating allowances for bad debt will be covered in a following section.

DISCOUNTING

Since it is commonly understood that a dollar today is worth more than a dollar tomorrow it follows that today's dollar can be invested or loaned and thus produce interest.

For example, if $100 is loaned at 6 percent, then by the end of a year, it will be worth $106, assuming that principal plus interest is collected from the person to whom the money is loaned. On the other hand, if a customer buys goods worth $100, but says that it is to be repaid in one year's time, goods have not been sold for $100 — but sold for $94 only,(100 × .94), assuming that the money could earn 6 percent interest.

A ruling by the Accounting Principles Board (APB),[1] *Opinion No. 21*,[2] requires that interest be imputed on receivables. This means that if a customer is allowed liberal or lengthy terms for payment, without interest on the amounts owed, or interest at an unrealistically low amount, then the amount of the sale and the amount of the receivable should both be reduced by a realistic level of interest on the amounts receivable. This interest is taken into income over the term of the receivable.

Example: A machine is sold to a customer for $1000 with the following terms: $100 down, balance payable in three annual installments of $300 each plus accrued interest. The unpaid balance will accrue interest at 4

----

[1]The APB was the official rule-making body of accounting between 1959 and 1973. It has been replaced by the Financial Accounting Standards Board.

[2]Issued in 1971.

percent. However, similar loans to this class of customer would normally
require interest at 6 percent

$$Amount\ of\ Sale = \$968 \quad composed\ of:$$

$100	down payment
900	receivable
72	interest at 4%[1]
$1,072	
(104)	less interest at 6%[2]
$ 968	

$$Amount\ of\ Receivable = \$868 \quad composed\ of:$$

$968	Amount of Sale
100	Less: Cash Down
$868	

1. $(900 \times .04) + (600 \times .04) + (300 \times .04)$
2. $(900 \times .06) + (600 \times .06) + (300 \times .06)$

At the end of the first year, cash received of $336 is recorded.[3] Also
recorded is interest income of $52.[4] The difference between the amount of
interest income recorded ($52) and the cash interest received ($36)
increases the carrying amount of the receivable from $568 ($868 − $300)
to $584.

Note that reducing sales and receivables for imputed interest is
required for companies that issue financial statements that conform to
generally accepted accounting principles. This procedure is not acceptable
for tax purposes, except in certain limited circumstances.

Example: Your Company, Inc., wishes to maintain a cash balance equal
to 20 days of average daily disbursements. Total disbursements for the
year is scheduled to be $360,000. The calculations will be based on a
standard financial year of 360 days.

1. $D_a = \dfrac{\$360,000}{360}$

   $D_a = \$1,000$
2. $C_b = 20 \times \$1,000$

   $C_b = \$20,000$

[3] $300 + (900 \times .04)$
[4] $868 \times .06$

QUESTION: What is the best way to calculate estimated bad-debt
            expense? How does the IRS view bad-debt expense and
            allowances?

ANSWER:

The points made in the following discussions will be helpful.

Bad-Debt Expense

When sales are made on credit, it must be expected that some customers
will not pay, unless you have an extraordinarily effective collection
procedure.

There are four principal methods of calculating estimates of bad-debt
expense:

1. Percentage of sales
2. Percentage of credit sales
3. Percentage of outstanding receivables
4. Aging receivables

All four methods are currently in use. The percentage of credit sales
and the percentage of outstanding receivables are most commonly used.
The aging method, however, probably gives the most accurate figure for
bad-debt expense and with increased use of computers should become
widely used.

Percentage of Credit Sales

When a percentage-of-sales approach is employed, a company's past
experience with uncollectible accounts is analyzed. If there is a stable
relationship between the previous year's charge sales and bad debt, then
that relationship can be turned into a percentage and used to determine
the current year's bad-debt expense. (See the first part of Exhibit 5.1.)

Percentage of Outstanding Receivables

Using past experience, a company can estimate the percentage of its
outstanding accounts receivables that will become uncollectible, without
identifying specific accounts. This procedure provides a reasonably accurate picture of realizable value of the receivables at any time but does not
fit the concept of matching costs and revenues as well as the percentage-
of-sales approach. It has the same weakness as the percentage-of-sales

---

EXHIBIT 5.1
Bad-Debt Expense

Percentage of Credit Sales Method
of Estimating Bad-Debt Expense

Year		Credit Sales	Actual Bad Debts
19×3		$1,000,000	$ 15,000
19×2		900,000	12,000
19×1		800,000	12,000
	TOTAL	$2,700,000	$ 39,000

$$\text{Percentage} = \frac{\$39,000}{2,700,000} = 1.44\%$$

19×4	Credit Sales: $1,200,000	
19×4	Estimated Bad Debt Expense:	$1.44\% \times \$1,200,000 = \$17,280$

---

approach in that past experience must predict the future. (See the second part of Exhibit 5.1.)

Aging of Accounts Receivable

A more sophisticated approach than the percentage of outstanding receivables method is to set up an aging schedule. Such a schedule indicates which accounts require special attention by providing the age of the receivable. (See Exhibit 5.2.).

The amount $189 indicates the bad-debt expense to be reported for the year, but only if this is the first year the company has been in operation. In subsequent years, the allowance for doubtful accounts balance is adjusted to the amount determined by the aging schedule. An aging schedule is not only prepared to determine bad-debt expense, but also serves as a control device, to determine the composition of receivables and to identify delinquent accounts. The estimated loss percentage developed for each age category is based on previous loss experience and the advice of persons in your business who are in charge of granting credit. The aging approach is sensitive to the actual status of receivables, but as with all estimates it may overstate or understate the actual loss from uncollectible accounts.

EXHIBIT 5.1
continued

Percentage of Accounts Receivable
Method of Estimating Bad-Debt Expense

Year	Accounts Receivable (End of Year)	Accounts Receivable That Become Bad Debts
19×3	$150,000	$ 15,000
19×2	140,000	12,000
19×1	135,000	12,000
TOTAL	$425,000	$ 39,000

Percentage: $\dfrac{\$39,000}{\$425,000} = 9.2\%$

19×4   *Ending Accounts Receivable: $160,000*
19×4   *Estimated Bad-Debt Expense: 9.2% × $160,000 = $14,720*

EXHIBIT 5.2
Aging Schedule

Name of Customer	Balance 12/31	Under 60/da	61–90 Days	91–120 Days	Over 120/days
Customer A	$ 1,000	$ 800	$ 200	$	$
Customer B	3,000	3000			
Customer C	600				600
Customer D	750	600		150	
	$ 5,350	$ 4400	$ 200	$ 150	$ 600

	Summary		
Age	Amount	Percentage*	
Under 60 days	$4,400	1%	$ 44.00
61-90 days	200	5%	10.00
91-120 days	150	10%	15.00
Over 120 days	600	20%	120.00
Bad-Debt Expense or Allowance for Doubtful Accounts			$ 189.00

*Percentages based on experience.

Designing a Credit Policy

Receivables result from selling on credit, and the essence of credit sales lies in the trade-off between increased sales and increased collection costs. Credit sales can be increased indefinitely in most businesses simply by liberalizing credit agreements. However, the increased sales become unprofitable when the costs of collection exceed the profit margin. Therefore, a balance between increased sales and collection costs must be sought.

Credit rating services, such as Dun and Bradstreet and TRW Credit Data, are useful sources of data for making credit decisions, but rating services cannot make credit granting decisions; they only provide the historical background on a prospective customer.

In making a credit decision, an assessment of a customer's financial position and short-term liquidity is necessary. The most commonly used financial ratio for assessing short-term credit risk is the ratio of current assets to current liabilities. Based on recent research in the area of prediction of bankruptcy, a better ratio is cash flow to total debt.

Cash Flow to Debt Ratio

(Cash flow is approximated by adding depreciation expense to net income and subtracting purchases of fixed assets and dividends.) The ratio of cash flow to total debt will vary by industry, but a ratio of 1:4 may be an expected average. For public companies, the data is easily obtainable. For privately owned firms, the data will be sought by other means, principally request of the potential customer.

Z Score

Another method of credit analysis is the so-called Z score, which was developed by Edward Altman as a predictor of bankruptcy.[5] Five ratios are incorporated in the Z score:

1. Working capital/Total assets
2. Retained earnings/Total assets
3. Earnings before interest and taxes/Total assets
4. Market value of stock/Liabilities
5. Sales/Total assets

The Z score is calculated as follows:

[5]E. Altman, "Financial Ratios, Discriminant Analysis and the Prediction of Corporate Bankruptcy," *Journal of Finance* (September 1968).

$$Z = 1.2 \text{ (Ratio 1)} + 1.4 \text{ (Ratio 2)} + 3.3 \text{ (Ratio 3)} +$$
$$.6 \text{ (Ratio 4)} + \text{(Ratio 5)}$$

In assessing the Z score, a value greater than three indicates that the customer is probably a sound credit risk in the near term future (two to three years) and a score less than 1.8 indicates that the customer is a poor credit risk. (See Exhibit 5.3.)

RECEIVABLES INFORMATION SYSTEM

In general, a credit policy should be based on the typical credit terms in your industry, and businesses should expect to meet the terms provided by others in the industry. Customers who are poor credit risks require stricter terms. A way to formulate a sound credit policy is to develop a credit information system, sometimes called a *credit scoring system*. This system is based on the five Cs of credit: character, capacity, capital, collateral, and conditions, as defined on the next page.

EXHIBIT 5.3
Calculation of Z Score

Data were gathered on two companies for the year 1970. The companies are General Electric and Dolly Madison. Dolly Madison subsequently declared bankruptcy in 1971.

	1970 Data	
	General Electric	Dolly Madison
Total Assets	$6,198,506,000	$ 92,433,129
Total Liabilities	3,533,498,000	68,103,083
Stockholders Equity	2,665,008,000	24,330,046
Working Capital	684,505,000	1,721,490
Retained Earnings	1,874,136,000	9,894,433
Market Value of Stock	3,723,335,787	8,799,983
Sales	8,726,738,000	13,740,807
Earnings before Interest and Taxes	660,466,000	Deficit

EXHIBIT 5.3
continued

		Ratios	
		General Electric	Dolly Madison
1.	Working Capital:		
	Total Assets	.1104	.0186
2.	Retained Earnings:		
	Total Assets	.3024	.1070
3.	Earnings before Interest and Taxes		
	Total Assets	.1869	(Deficit)
4.	Sales Market value of Stock		
	Liabilities	1.0537	.1292
5.	Sales Total Assets	1.4079	.1487
Z Score		**3.0613**	0.3983

1. *Character:* The probability that a customer will try to honor his obligations; measured by past payment history. Interviews and references can supply relevant information.
2. *Capital:* Measured by the financial position of the firm as indicated by total assets, net worth, or debt-to-equity ratio.
3. *Collateral:* Represented by assets the customer may offer as security.
4. *Capacity:* Measured by the consistency of profitable operations.
5. *Conditions:* The state of the economy and the state of the industry in which the customer operates.

An illustration of a credit scoring chart appears in Exhibit 5.4.

How to Develop Credit Scores

Based on data supplied in the customer's credit application, assign points in each rating category, then decide a cut-off point. The sum of the points in each category provides the customer's credit score. As shown in Exhibit

EXHIBIT 5.4
Credit Scoring Chart

Character					Points
Subjective Measure	Excellent	Good	Fair	Marginal	
Points	5	3	1	0	☐
Capacity					
Years of Profit	15+	10–15	5–10	2–5	
	5	4	3	2	☐
Capital					
Debt/Equity Ratio	0–.10	.10–.25	.25–.80	.50–1.00	
	5	3	3	1	☐
Collateral					
Type	Mortgage	Securities	Pledge	None	
	5	4	2	1	☐
Conditions					
Sales Growth in Customer's Industry	Growth in past 4 quarters	Growth in past 2 quarters	Stable	Decline	
	5	4	2	0	☐
			TOTAL SCORE		

5.4 points range from one to five, but you can set your own range to suit the facts of your industry.

As indicated previously, aging accounts is a useful technique in that it directs attention to the most troublesome areas and may indicate necessary changes in credit granting policy. If the data are available, another useful technique is analysis of payment history by customer class or category. Results of this technique will disclose that certain categories of customers are more trouble than they are worth and that credit should either not be granted or granted only on restricted terms.

Payment Stimulation Techniques

The essence of control over receivables is to minimize the amounts of money tied up in receivables while maximizing sales in your particular market. Minimizing the investment in receivables may be facilitated by payment stimulation techniques. Ways to speed up the payment of receivables include:

1. Discounts for early payment
2. Add on interest for payment after a certain date
3. Dunning letters that become increasingly threatening as time passes
4. Personal telephone calls
5. Outside collection services
6. Legal action

Clearly you would like to stimulate payment with the method that costs least in terms of expense and customer alienation. There is a trade-off between the severity of the stimulation technique and maintenance of customer satisfaction. You should relate the severity of the technique to the age of the receivable.

QUESTION: *How can I turn receivables into cash?*
ANSWER:

Beware of Discounts

Unless a discount policy has the effect of stimulating increased sales, it is often more costly than it seems. For example, a discount of 2 percent for payment within 10 days (2/10 net 30) actually amounts to a loan to your customer for 20 days (30 days less 10 day discount period) at 2 percent or, in other words, approximately 36 percent per annum. This may seem attractive, but the other side of the coin is that when the discount is taken this interest is a cost to you. Nevertheless, it may be necessary to grant discounts in order to meet the competition in your industry.

BAD DEBT AND THE IRS

The tax law divides loans, the receivables therefrom, and the potential bad debt thereon, into three general categories:

1. Business bad debt
2. Nonbusiness bad debt
3. Personal bad debt

Personal bad debt is generally not deductible at all unless it is fully supported by signed legal agreements for repayment and evidences a business purpose, which converts the bad debt from a personal one into a nonbusiness bad debt, with an investment purpose. For example, a father makes a loan to his son, so that the son can start a business. If there are no signed agreements with specific repayment terms, the debt would not be deductible in the event the son could not repay. However, if the agreement is specific as to times and terms of repayment and if the father did expect repayment and the son could not repay, then the debt would be deductible as a capital loss, which could offset capital gains, or be subtracted in arriving at adjusted gross income up to a limit of $1000 per year.

Business Bad Debt

Business bad debt is deductible in full against ordinary income. Two methods are used to determine the amount of the bad-debt deduction. Using the *specific-debt* or *specific charge-off* method, the taxpayer deducts in each year the specific debts that become worthless in that year. This method is used primarily by taxpayers who do not want to estimate a reserve for bad debts. It is not a generally accepted accounting principle for audited statements and therefore should be used only by businesses not issuing audited statements.

The other accepted method of deducting bad debt for tax purposes is the reserve method, under which the taxpayer carries a reserve in the amount that he (and the IRS) considers sufficient to cover his bad debt losses. Under this method, the taxpayer makes an addition to the reserve each year so that the reserve remains at a figure sufficient to cover expected bad debt. The taxpayer deducts the amount added to the reserve each year and charges against the reserves the debts that become worthless. (See Exhibit 5.5.)

Reasonableness of Addition to Reserve

The reasonableness of the addition to the reserve for bad debt is determined by the past experience of the business and is generally checked carefully by IRS field auditors.

The Internal Revenue Regulations provide as follows concerning reserves for bad debt:

Section 1.166-4. Reserve for Bad Debt

a. *Allowance of deduction.* A taxpayer who has established the reserve method of treating bad debt and has maintained proper reserve accounts for bad debt or who, in accordance with paragraph (b) of Section 1.166-1, adopts the reserve method of treating bad debt may deduct from gross income a reasonable addition to a reserve for bad debts in lieu of deducting specific bad debt items.

EXHIBIT 5.5
Calculation of Reserve for Bad Debt

Assume:

Volume of charge sales..$1,000,000

Notes and Accounts Receivable:

Beginning of Year..$ 80,000

End of Year..$ 90,000

Amount of debts which have become wholly or
partially worthless and have been charged against
reserve account...$ 2,500

Reserve for Bad Debts:

Beginning...$ 2,700

Estimated percentage of bad debts..3%

Calculation of Reserve:

Beginning	$2,700
Less: Charge-offs	(2,500)
	$ 200
Add: Addition to Reserve	
(3% × $1,000,000)	3,000
ENDING BALANCE	$3,200

---

   b.   *Reasonableness of addition to reserve* — (1) *Relevant factors.*
What constitutes a reasonable addition to a reserve for bad debt
shall be determined in the light of the facts existing at the close of
the taxable year of the proposed addition. The reasonableness of
the addition will vary as between classes of business and with
conditions of business prosperity. It will depend primarily upon
the total amount of debt outstanding as of the close of the taxable
year, including those arising currently as well as those arising in
prior taxable years, and the total amount of the existing reserve.
(2) *Correction of errors in prior estimates.* In the event that
subsequent realizations upon outstanding debt prove to be more
of less than estimated at the time of the creation of the existing
reserve, the amount of the excess or inadequacy in the existing
reserve shall be reflected in the determination of the reasonable
addition necessary in the current taxable year.

   c.   *Statement required.* A taxpayer using the reserve method shall
file with his return a statement showing:

1. The volume of his charge sales or other business transactions for the taxable year and the percentage of the reserve to such amount;
2. The total amount of notes and accounts receivable at the beginning and close of the taxable year;
3. The amount of the debts which have become wholly or partially worthless and have been charged against the reserve account; and
4. The computation of the addition to the reserve for bad debt.

Frequently, dealers in property, such as automobile and appliance dealers, discount their installment contracts with a bank or finance company. For example, a General Motors Pontiac dealer may help customers finance their purchases through General Motors Acceptance Corporation. The finance company, or bank, accepts these installment contracts receivable often with full recourse against the dealer, in effect, requiring him to guarantee payment of the customer's installment contract. Usually a reserve account, or holdback, on the proceeds of its loan to the dealer secures this guarantee. This reserve account poses a problem for the dealer because he has sold his receivables, or pledged them for a loan. Thus, it is not clear that he should be allowed a deduction for an addition to a reserve for bad debt; yet, as a guarantor, he has a residual liability to pay if the customer does not. The *Internal Revenue Code* allows the dealer, in these circumstances, to set up a reserve for bad debt, additions to which are deductible.

Bad-Debt Reserves of Small Business Investment Companies

The *Internal Revenue Code* provides that a company operating under the *Small Business Development Act of 1958*, or a so-called business development corporation chartered by a state, can use its own loan loss experience in determining its reserve or it can use the average loan loss experienced of all small business development companies if that is greater.

Bad-Debt Reserves of Mutual Savings Banks and Savings and Loans

Mutual savings banks and savings and loan associations that are not corporations may use one of three methods of computing the addition to a reserve for bad debt:

1. Experienced method
2. Percentage method (same as banks)
3. Percentage-of-net-income method

The percentage-of-net-income method allows the savings and loan association to calculate deductible addition to a reserve for bad debt that is equal to approximately 40 percent of net income.

Deduction of Bad-Debt Losses on Loans Made to a Corporation by a Stockholder

A common problem arises when the small businessperson makes advances to a corporation in which he or she is both an employee and a controlling stockholder; or perhaps he or she may be called on to guarantee bank loans or to make other guarantees to the corporation. The Supreme Court has ruled that a bad debt resulting from a stockholder's advances to a corporation or payments on a guarantee is a nonbusiness bad debt in which the stockholder, although active in management, primarily looks for a return in the form of dividends, or an enhancement in the value of his or her stock. This means that losses from unrepaid loans made to your business would only be deductible as capital losses, which means a limit of $3000 per year, with an unlimited carryover to offset future years' incomes.

Characterization of Loans Made to Employees, Officers, and Stockholders

Both auditors and the IRS are often concerned about loans and advances made to and receivables from employees, officers, and stockholders of the business. Ordinary loans made to nonofficer, nonstockholder employees should cause little concern if properly documented and disclosed in the financial statements.

Receivables from officers are immediately suspected by auditors and the IRS and are doubly suspect if the officer is also a stockholder. Most major accounting firms pay special attention to so-called "related party transactions," which includes all transactions between the corporation and principal officers and stockholders. Auditors will insist that all such transactions be fully disclosed in audited financial statements. The IRS may attempt to construe such loans as compensation to the officer or as dividends to the stockholder. Legal documentation with specified repayment terms and no prior intention to cancel the obligation should prevent characterization of the loan receivable as something else.

Deferring Tax on Installment Sales Receivable

Even though it is not a generally accepted accounting principle to which auditors will attach a clean opinion, the *Internal Revenue Code* provides that the installment method of accounting can be used for tax purposes. This means that taxes on the uncollected portion of installment contracts receivable do not have to be paid until the cash is collected. This provision is available to all dealers in personal property who regularly sell on the installment basis and to others who occasionally sell real property or personal property, if the amount received in the year of sale is 30 percent or less of the selling price.

Example 1: A business sells $100,000 worth of merchandise on the installment plan. The company's normal gross profit margin is 40 percent. In the current tax year, it collects $50,000 from customers. How much taxable income before operating expenses would it report?

Answer:

$20,000 ($50,000 × 40 percent)

What would they report as gross profit on financial statements?

Answer:

$40,000 ($100,000 × 40 percent)

Assuming the company's operating expenses were $10,000 and the income was $10,000 and the income tax rate is 50 percent, how much will it pay in taxes?

Answer:

$5,000	($20,000	Gross Profit
Less:	10,000	Operating Expense
	$10,000	Taxable Income
	$ 5,000	Taxes Payable)

What will the tax expense reflected in the financial statement be?

Answer:

$15,000	($40,000	Gross Profit
Less:	10,000	Operating Expense
	$30,000	Income before Tax
	15,000	Income Tax Expense
	$15,000	Net Income)

The difference between the income tax expense reflected in the financial statements ($15,000) and the tax payable ($5,000) to the government will be reflected in the balance sheet as a deferred tax payable, which is classified among the liabilities.

Example 2: An individual sells a house for $100,000. The buyer assumes a $20,000 mortgage, makes a down payment of $30,000, and agrees to pay the balance of $50,000 over 10 years. The house cost the seller $60,000. How much profit would the individual report in the year of sale?

Answer:

$15,000

Explanation: The gross profit is $40,000 ($100,000 − $60,000). The installment method of reporting may be used because the cash received ($30,000) is not greater than 30 percent of the selling price ($100,000). The profit to be reported is the ratio of the gross profit ($40,000) to the contract price ($80,000; $100,000 − $20,000 mortgage assumed) times the cash received.

ACCOUNTS RECEIVABLE FINANCING AND FACTORING

If you are in a business that is growing rapidly, you may need additional working capital; but your balance sheet does not support unsecured borrowing from a bank. In such circumstances, it often is possible to borrow on a secured basis by pledging or assigning valid accounts receivable as collateral for the loan. Often, this type of loan is available from your bank or from a subsidiary of a bank that specializes in commercial financing. For businesses with higher degrees of risk, commercial finance companies or factors may be the appropriate source of funds.

The type of financing and the terms of the loan will vary by the character of the industry you are in and by the institution providing the financing. However, the two basic categories of this type of financing are receivables financing and factoring.

Receivables Financing

In *receivables financing*, receivables act as collateral for a loan. Since many types of industries employ loans of this type, it follows that the typical company applying for such a loan is fast growing, highly seasonal, and needs cash in order to operate. Financial institutions will take considerable care in validating the value of receivables as collateral in this type of financing. The cost of receivables financing is high compared to the cost of term loans. Whereas the rate on term loans usually equals prime rate plus 1 percent, the rate on receivables loans may be prime plus 4 or 5 percent.

However, there are considerations that make receivables loans attractive. Interest is computed on an average daily balance basis with receivables loans, whereas with term loans, interest is computed based on the term. No compensating balances are required with receivables loans. Interest on the nonusable, compensating balance at a rate of prime rate plus 1 percent may exceed the additional interest required on a receivables loan.[6]

Factoring

Factoring is distinguished from receivables financing because in factoring the outstanding receivables are usually sold outright and without recourse to the factor. The two types of factoring are maturity factoring and discount factoring.

In maturity factoring, no funds are remitted by the factor until the receivables are collected. The factor, in essence, serves as the credit department of his customer. Typically, the factor knows the customers of the client better than the client knows them and is able to determine the credit worthiness of a customer and the collectibility of the receivable. The factor maintains credit files on customers in industries in which factoring is common and has staffs of auditors and loan officers to assist collection procedures. For this service, the client pays approximately 1 percent of outstanding receivables as a factoring fee but is relieved of collection and credit burdens. In discount factoring, the factor buys the receivables outright and without recourse to the seller. It is not as commonly available as maturity factoring. Factoring is not widespread outside of the textile and garment industries.

QUESTION: What is the basic difference between assigning, pledging, and factoring receivables?

[6]The break-even point is defined by the formula:
$$P = \frac{.03 - .04R}{R}$$
where P = Prime rate in decimal, R = compensating balance of in decimal.

EXHIBIT 5.6
Comparative Balance Sheets With and Without Factoring

Without Factoring

Assets		Liabilities	
Cash	$ 10,000	Accounts Payable	$200,000
Accounts Receivable	300,000	Note Payable	100,000
Inventory	150,000	Net Worth	160,000
Total	$460,000	Total	$460,000

Current Ratio:

$$\frac{460,000}{300,000} = 1.53$$

With Factoring

Assets		Liabilities	
Cash	$ 10,000	Accounts Payable	$100,000
Due from Factor	100,000	Net Worth	160,000
Inventory	150,000		
Total	$260,000	Total	$260,000

Current Ratio:

$$\frac{260,000}{100,000} = 2.6$$

ANSWER:

Improvement of financial ratios by factoring

Balance sheet financial ratios may be made to appear more favorable through factoring. See Exhibit 5.6, which presents an example of comparative balance sheets, with and without factoring. Without factoring, the company requires a $100,000 bank loan and incurs $200,000 of payables, while having $300,000 receivables outstanding. The current ratio is 1.53:1 without factoring. With factoring, the receivables are sold and $200,000 is realized, leaving $100,000 due from the factor. The $200,000 is applied to reduce the accounts payable to $100,000 and to pay off the note. The current ratio is increased to 2.6:1.

6

Inventories

QUESTION: Why should you be concerned with inventories?

ANSWER:

Since inventories are one of the most important assets an enterprise possesses, it follows that the description and measurement of inventory require careful attention. The sale of inventory at a price greater than cost is the primary source of income to many businesses. Matching inventory cost to revenue is necessary for the determination of net income. Inventories are particularly significant for they affect both the balance sheet and the income statement.

DEFINITION OF INVENTORIES

Inventories are defined as assets that are held for sale in the ordinary course of business, or goods that will be used or consumed in the production of goods to be sold. Assets awaiting resale may be excluded from inventory because they are not normally sold in the ordinary course of business. Such assets include plant and equipment items that are being retired or securities held for investment.

QUESTION: What are the usual classifications of inventories?

ANSWER:

Inventories are typically considered within the setting of a trading concern. A trading concern purchases its merchandise in a form ready for sale to customers. This merchandise reflects the cost assigned to unsold units on hand at the end of the period, such as merchandise inventory. Customarily, only one inventory account appears in the financial statements of a trading concern.

Most larger businesses are not merchandising operations, but rather are manufacturing concerns whose purpose is to produce goods to be sold to merchandising firms (either wholesale or retail). A manufacturing firm normally has three inventory accounts: raw materials, work in process, and finished goods.

The cost of goods and materials on hand but not yet placed into production is considered raw materials inventory. For example, raw materials are items such as plastic to make toys or steel to make a car. These materials can be traced directly to the end product. At any given time in a continuous production process, some units have not completed the process cycle. The cost of the raw material for a partially completed product plus the cost of labor applied specifically to the material as well as a share of the overhead costs comprise the work-in-process inventory. The costs of completed but unsold units on hand at the end of the period are reported as finished goods inventory.

An example of the three categories of inventories is:

CURRENT ASSETS
Inventories

Finished goods	$200,000
Work in process	15,000
Raw materials	20,000
Other materials and supplies	30,000

QUESTION: What is the difference between inventories and supplies?

ANSWER:

The distinction between inventories and supplies is that inventories become products to be sold, or at least part of a product to be sold, whereas supplies are consumed. If supplies include lubrication oil for a machine, then inventory include products manufactured by the machine.

From a managerial perspective, inventories are an important asset. The investment in inventories, usually the largest current asset in manufacturing and retail firms, is often a significant portion of the firm's total assets. Significantly, it is from inventories that sales are made and customers are satisfied. This fact is the crux of managerial decisions pertaining to inventories. If unsalable items accumulate in inventory, then a potential loss exists. If products ordered or desired by customers are not readily available in the style, quality, and quantity required, then sales and customers may be lost. Inefficient purchasing, faulty manufacturing, or inadequate sales efforts result in excessive or unsalable inventories.

Inventories are more sensitive to general business fluctuations than are other assets. When demand is great, merchandise can be disposed of quickly, and large quantities of inventories appear to be appropriate. Yet, with a downward trend in the business cycle, merchandise will move slowly, stocks will pile up, and obsolescence becomes a spectre hovering over the manager's shoulder.

One essential of inventory planning and control is an accounting system of accurate records, consisting of the information required by management to make manufacturing, merchandising, and financial decisions. Such an accounting system is often referred to as a *perpetual inventory system*.

QUESTION: What is a perpetual inventory system?

ANSWER:

In a *perpetual inventory system*, information is available at any time on the quantity of each item of material or type of merchandise on hand. Many varieties of such systems are in use. Basically, they are divided into two types: detailed inventory records that constitute support for the general ledger inventory account, or detailed records that do not tie in with the general ledger and constitute an information system outside the accounting system.

In the first type of perpetual inventory system, purchases of raw materials, or inventory of a certain type, are debited directly to an inventory account. As the inventory is sold or transferred to a work-in-process account, it is credited from the inventory account. Thus, the balance in the account at any time should equal the dollar value of inventory on hand. Exhibit 6.1 shows an example of the perpetual inventory system.

In the second type of perpetual inventory system, the records are

EXHIBIT 6.1
Perpetual Inventory System

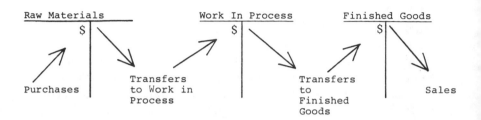

Manufacturing Concern

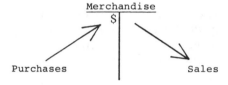

Trading Concern

similar to the first type. The basic difference is that dollar values are not maintained and debits or credits do not enter into the accounting system.

Computers have greatly facilitated the process of inventory control and planning. Due to the data processing capacity of computers, additional information can be kept and maintained in the perpetual inventory system. Some types of information suitable to such a system are: a description of the inventory item, item number, location, minimum and maximum quantities to be maintained in inventory, vendor, amount on order, amount and cost of items on hand.

Whether the perpetual inventory system is tied into the accounting system or is a separate information system, it is necessary periodically to take a physical inventory. A physical inventory is necessary at least once a year for all inventories. In order to maintain control over inventories that can be stolen easily, either by customers or employees, merchandising firms take inventories more often.

In recent years, many companies have developed inventory controls, or methods of determining inventories that also are effective in determining inventory quantities. These methods are characteristically based on statistical sampling. The reliability of these methods makes an annual physical count of each inventory item unnecessary.

Another possibility is to take physical inventories throughout the year on a rotating basis. Thus, instead of taking one complete annual physical inventory, there is a continued physical inventory throughout the year. In this way, all inventory items are counted and the detail records corrected at least once during the year.

QUESTION: How is inventory valued for accounting purposes?

ANSWER:

There are three primary methods of valuing inventory and costs of goods sold for accounting and for tax purposes — first-in, first-out (FIFO); weighted average; and last-in, first-out (LIFO). (See discussion in Chapter 2.) Exhibit 6.2 presents an example of the calculation of the ending inventory values and the cost of goods sold under the three methods. As can be noted in the exhibit, in a period of rising prices, LIFO produces a cost-of-goods-sold figure that is greater than the cost of goods sold produced by FIFO. The advantage of LIFO lies in the fact that it produces a higher cost-of-goods-sold number in a period of inflation. Since the effect of LIFO is to reduce reported net income, it follows that the tax burden also is reduced.

In certain situations, the LIFO cost flow will be representative of the physical flow of the goods into and out of the inventory. In most situations, however, LIFO will be simply an accounting and tax convention and will not be useful for control of inventory. An advantage of the LIFO method is that it matches current costs with current revenues, thus eliminating holding gains from reported profits. In other words, recent costs are matched against current revenues to provide a better measure of current disposable income. Essentially, though, LIFO has become popular for the practical reason of income tax benefits. As long as the price level of inventories increases and the inventory quantities do not decrease, an indefinite deferral of income taxes occurs. Even if the price level later decreases, a company will have been given a temporary deferral of its income taxes.

Some criticisms of LIFO are worth mentioning. First, the inventory valuation on the balance sheet is outdated and irrelevant because the oldest costs remain in the inventory. This causes several problems, especially relating to the measure of working capital of the company. The difference between identical companies — one on FIFO and one on LIFO

EXHIBIT 6.2
Example of Inventory Valuation

Assume:	Units	Unit Cost	Total
Beginning Inventory	2	$10	$20
Purchases:			
1...	1	11	11
2...	1	10	10
3...	1	12	12
4...	1	13	13
Cost of goods available for sale			$66
Total quantity available for sale	6		
Total sold during period	4		
Ending inventory units	2		

Weighted Average
Cost of goods available for sale		$66
Total units available for sale		6
Average cost		$11
Ending inventory value (2×$11)		$22
Cost of goods sold (4×$11)		$44

First-in, First-out (FIFO)
Ending inventory: 1 @ $13 = $13
1 @ 12 = 12 → $25

Cost of Goods Sold:
Cost of goods available for sale	$66	
Less: Value of Ending Inventory	25	$41

Last-in, First-out (LIFO)
Ending inventory: 2 @ $10 = $20
Cost of Goods Sold:
Cost of goods available for sale	$66	
Less: Value of Ending Inventory	20	$46

— where working capital is concerned, depends on the rate of change in the replacement cost of the inventory. Although other factors also must be considered, in general, it may be said, that the working capital under LIFO will be smaller.

Second, LIFO does not measure real income in the economic sense. In order to measure real income, as opposed to monetary income, the costs of goods sold should not consist of the most recently incurred costs, but rather of the costs that will be incurred to replace goods that have been sold. The Securities and Exchange Commission (SEC), through its Accounting Series Release No. 190, requires an estimate of this real income for approximately the 1,000 largest companies in the United States.

Third, with LIFO, involuntary liquidation is a factor. This problem arises if the base layers of old costs are liquidated. Since old costs can be matched against current revenues, bizarre results can follow. Not only can this lead to an overstatement of reported income for a given period, but also the income tax consequences could be highly detrimental.

Fourth, in an attempt to avoid the negative consequences of the third criticism, management may make poor judgments about inventory purchases. At year-end, unnecessary purchases may be made in order to restore liquidated LIFO inventory base layers.

Many companies use LIFO inventories without keeping track of base and incremental layers of specific items and units of items in inventory. This is accomplished by combining all, or most items of inventory in one pool. The dollars of inventory in this pool at the initial date of the adoption of LIFO are then considered to be the base layer of the LIFO ending inventory. (The physical inventory system is maintained on a FIFO basis.) At the end of each year, the base and incremental layers of dollars in inventory are adjusted by a price-level index, which is constructed with reference to the change in prices for the year. This is called the *dollar value LIFO* inventory method. Exhibit 6.3 presents an example of a dollar value LIFO system.

The *Internal Revenue Code* specifically allows dollar value LIFO inventory systems for tax reporting. The base-year cost of the inventory

---

EXHIBIT 6.3
Dollar Value LIFO System

Assume a company begins in year 1 and adopts dollar value LIFO.

	Year 1
FIFO Ending Inventory	$10,000
Replacement cost index (beginning and end of year)	100
LIFO Ending Inventory	$10,000

EXHIBIT 6.3
continued

Year 2

FIFO Ending Inventory		$13,000
Replacement cost index (end of year)		110

Year 1 Base: $10,000 × $\frac{110}{100}$ = $11,000

Year 2 Increment: $13,000 − $11,000 = $2,000

LIFO Ending Inventory

Year 1 Base:	$10,000	
Year 2 Increment:	2,000	$12,000

Year 3

FIFO Ending Inventory		$15,000
Replacement cost index		121

Year 1 Base: $10,000 × $\frac{121}{100}$ = $12,100

Year 2 Increment: 2,000

Year 3 Increment: $15,000 × $\frac{121}{100}$ = $14,300 (Step 1)

$15,000 − $14,300 = $700 (Step 2)

LIFO Ending Inventory

Year 1 Base:	$10,000	
Year 2 Increment:	2,000	
Year 3 Increment:	700	$12,700

Year 4

FIFO Ending Inventory		$15,000
Replacement cost index		127

Year 1 Base: $10,000 × $\frac{127}{100}$ = $12,700

Year 2 Increment: 2,000 × $\frac{127}{110}$ = 2,300

Year 3 Increment: 700 × $\frac{127}{121}$ = $\frac{735}{15735}$

LIFO Ending Inventory:

Year 1 Base: $10,000		
Year 2 Increment: $2,000		$12,000

The Year 3 Increment has been eliminated through liquidation.

---

must be established for the entire inventory in the pool at the beginning of the tax year in which the method is first adopted. This pool remains the same for all later years, unless the IRS approves a change. The *base-year cost* is the total cost of all items in the pool. The closing inventory value for the pool must be established by the double-extension method, unless the district director accepts an index method or link chain method.

QUESTION: *What is the double extension method of dollar value inventory costing?*

ANSWER:
The double extension method is a way to state the dollar value of the increase or decrease in your closing inventory, in relation to base-year cost. The base-year unit cost of a new item entering the pool is usually its price or production cost. The IRS may also accept an estimated base-year unit cost. To apply the method, first find the value of the closing inventory at the unit cost for the base year, and the value of the inventory at the unit cost for the current year. Then divide the total current cost by the total base-year cost, in order to obtain a ratio that is applied to any increase in inventory for the year. The current-year cost may be determined by using the FIFO, or by using the weighted average methods. There is an inventory increase for the year when the total dollar value of the closing inventory, in base year terms, exceeds the original base-year cost. The inventory increase is converted to current dollar value by applying the ratio.

Each year's increase must be recorded and accounted for as a separate unit, and decreases or liquidations of inventory must be absorbed first by the latest increase, and successively by the next earlier increases, until the decrease is fully absorbed. The ratio established for each year's increase also is used when that increase is liquidated. Base-year inventory is reduced only when the total of all decreases is more than the total of all increases. There is an inventory decrease when the closing inventory for a year is less than the opening inventory if both amounts are stated at base-year unit costs.

Example: XYZ Co. elected the dollar-value-life method for the coming tax year and established an inventory pool for items A, B, and C. The inventory on January 1 was: A–1000 units at a cost of $3 per unit; B–2000 units at $4; C–500 units at $2; for a total base-year cost of $14,000. The total current year cost of the December 31 closing inventory, determined from items last bought during the year, is $24,250 (FIFO basis). This cost includes: A–3,000 units at a unit cost of $6; B–1000 units at $5; C–500 units at $2.50. At the base-year unit costs (A — $5, B — $4, C — $2) the closing inventory would cost $20,000.

The closing inventory stated at dollar value life is $20.75 calculated as follows:

Closing inventory at base-year cost	$20,000
Base-year inventory cost	24,250
Increment in base-year dollars	$ 4,250

Ratio of current-year ending inventory stated in current-year prices to current-year ending inventory stated in base-year prices:

$$\$24,250 \div \$20,000 = 1.2125$$

Ending dollar value LIFO inventory:

Base-year inventory cost	$14,000
Increment restated by ratio $4,250 × 1.2125	5,153
	$19,153

Dollar-value LIFO pools for manufacturers and processors may include the entire inventory of a natural business unit. This natural unit may be an entire business or a separate division of a business. The circumstances surrounding the operation of a business determine whether it has one or more natural business units. Separate pools for substantially similar inventory items that are not part of a natural business pool can be established. Goods bought from others for wholesaling or retailing must be pooled as goods of a merchandiser.

Merchandisers' pools must be established categorically — by major lines, types, or classes of goods, according to customary business classifications. A department of a department store is an example. The IRS usually allows a natural business pool for wholesalers, retailers, jobbers, and distributors.

The use of LIFO is a tax election, for which application must be made, on Form 970, or by a statement acceptable to the IRS commissioner in the tax year the method is first to be used. Once the method is adopted, it must be continued unless the IRS requires a change to another method or authorizes a change.

The IRS will invalidate a LIFO election if during the election year a taxpayer uses FIFO, or any other valuation method, for its financial reports. However, a LIFO election remains valid if later financial reports are required to comply with income-disclosure rules set by the SEC.

Change cannot be made to dollar value LIFO from another LIFO method without IRS consent. Special adjustments are required when a change in the make up of pools is allowed or required.

In the application for the LIFO election, the taxpayer must specify the part of his inventory to which the election is to apply. If a taxpayer adopts LIFO for a specified part of his inventory then this taxpayer may continue to take the rest of his inventory, for tax purposes, on a cost or market basis, or any other basis that is properly adopted and approved. The IRS can, however, require use of the LIFO method for other items in the taxpayer's inventory if it is necessary for a clear reflection of income. The IRS also may require the use of LIFO for similar goods of another trade or business of the taxpayer.

Retail merchants often have difficulties when it comes to financial control, decision making, and the tax consequences of inventories. The conventional method is a special method of inventory measurement and valuation that has been developed to aid the retail merchant. There is also a LIFO variation on the conventional retail method.

Under the conventional retail method, goods in inventory are valued at the retail selling price, usually by count. This inventory value is then reduced to approximate cost through multiplication by an appropriate cost-to-retail ratio. A separate ratio must be determined for each department or class of goods. Exhibit 6.4 presents an example of a conventional retail method calculation of ending inventory.

EXHIBIT 6.4
Conventional Retail Inventory Method

	Cost		Retail
Beginning Inventory	$10,000		$ 20,000
Purchases	80,000		160,000
Freight-in	500		
Purchase Returns	(2,000)		(4,000)
Mark-ups			1,000
	88,500		177,000
Cost/Retail Ratio: $\frac{88,500}{177,000} = .50$			
Sales			(100,000)
Mark-downs			(1,500)
Ending Inventory	$37,750	.50	$ 75,500

Note that all costs including costs in the beginning inventory, freight-in, and purchases are added to the cost side or numerator of the ratio. The retail value of the beginning inventory and the retail value of the purchases are added to form the denominator. Also added to the denominator are additional mark-ups over the standard mark-up on costs. This mark-up has the effect of minimizing the ratio. The retail value of the ending inventory is then determined in the normal manner and the cost-to-retail ratio is applied to the ending inventory stated at retail in order to determine the ending inventory stated at cost.

In order to transform the conventional retail method into a retail LIFO method, it is necessary to understand that the beginning inventory will become the base layer of the ending inventory. Therefore, the beginning inventories are not included when calculating the cost-to-retail ratio. The cost of all purchases plus freight-in and other charges form the numerator of the ratio. The retail value of purchases plus mark-ups, less any mark-downs, form the denominator. The ratio is applied to the excess of the ending inventory stated at retail over the beginning inventory stated at retail. The result is added to the beginning inventory stated at cost, in order to derive the ending inventory stated at cost. Exhibit 6.5 presents an example of a retail LIFO inventory method.

EXHIBIT 6.5
Retail LIFO Inventory Method

	Cost	Retail
Beginning Inventory	$10,000	$ 20,000
Purchases	80,000	160,000
Freight-in	500	
Purchase Returns	(2,000)	(4,000)
Mark-ups		1,000
Mark-downs		(1,500)
	$78,500	$155,500
Cost/Retail Ratio: $\dfrac{\$\ 78,500}{\$155,500} = .5048$		
Goods Available	$88,500	$175,500
Less: Sales		100,000
Ending Inventory:		$ 75,500
Original Layer	$10,000	.50 $ 20,000
Increment	28,016	.5048
		$ 55,500
	$38,016	$ 75,500

QUESTION: *Must factory overhead be included as a part of the value of inventory in manufacturing operations?*

ANSWER:

Taxpayers involved in manufacturing operations must use the full-absorption method of inventory costing. This means that factory overhead will be included in inventory. All direct production costs must be included as inventoriable costs. Certain indirect production costs that are necessary for production must also be included, regardless of their financial reporting treatment. For example, expenditures for repair and maintenance, utilities, rent, indirect labor, supervisory wages, indirect materials, tools and equipment (if not capitalized), and quality control costs are examples of inventoriable costs. Some indirect production costs are specifically excluded from being inventoriable. Such indirect costs are expenditures for marketing, advertising, selling, distribution, interest, research and development, losses, percentage depletion in excess of cost depletion, depreciation, and amortization used for taxes, in excess of that reported in financial statements. Other indirect costs such as state and local property taxes are treated for tax purposes the same as they are in the taxpayer's financial reports. The indirect costs to be included must be allocated to goods in ending inventory by using an allocation method that fairly apportions these costs among the various items produced. For example, the depreciation, taxes, and mortgage costs on a building may be apportioned to a product on the basis of the number of square feet occupied by the particular machines used to manufacture that product, in relation to the total square feet occupied by all machinery in the building.

As another example, supervisory wages may be allocated to a product based on the number of direct labor hours it takes to manufacture one unit of the product.

A problem may develop when two separate products are developed from the same production process. The IRS regulations provide that when such a circumstance exists, a relative-sales-value approach may be used to allocate the joint costs. For example, if coal is used to produce gas, then a by-product, coke, may result. The cost of production may be allocated to the gas and also to the coke in proportion to their respective selling values.

QUESTION: *Can items be withdrawn from the business inventory for personal use?*

ANSWER:

The cost of goods withdrawn for personal use is excluded from the total amount of merchandise brought for sale, unless the proprietor pays for the withdrawn goods with personal funds. If he does not pay for the withdrawn goods, then he must adjust his account of the merchandise bought for sale. This adjustment is necessary to avoid an understatement of the net profit from the business. Without the adjustment, the cost of goods used by the taxpayer would be charged against the total sales. The adjustment may consist of crediting the purchases account with the merchandise withdrawn for personal use and charging the proprietor's drawing account with the cost of the withdrawn merchandise. A separate account of all goods withdrawn for personal or family use should be kept.

QUESTION: Is there an advantage from a tax standpoint by donating inventory to charity?

ANSWER:
In the past, there could be a tax advantage in making donations of inventory. It worked as follows. Assume that a unit of inventory could ordinarily be sold for $1. and that it has an inventory cost of 40 cents with a tax rate of 50 percent. Costs to sell plus administrative costs amount to an additional 40 cents. If sold, this would leave a taxable profit on the unit sold of 20 cents, taxes of 10 cents. Thus, giving the unit away would be a break-even proposition in comparison with selling it.

Sell		Donate	
Sale Price	$1.00	Fair Value Tax Deduction	$1.00
Inventory Cost	.40		
Selling and Administrative Cost	.40	Tax Saving @ 50%	.50
Tax	.10	Inventory Cost	.40
Net	$ .10	Net	$ .10

If the tax rate were to be above 50 percent, which is often the case when state taxes are included, or if the selling and administrative expenses were to exceed the inventory cost, then an actual benefit from donating rather than selling could be achieved. Circumstances were similar when, in the early 1960s, several corporations donated inventory to Cuba as a ransom for some political prisoners. Congress felt that this particular quirk of the tax law should be corrected. Consequently, in 1969, Congress decided to limit the deduction for charitable gifts of inventory to the inventory cost basis of the items donated. Recently, this rule has been changed so that up to one-half of the difference between the fair value of the inventory and its cost may be deducted as a charitable item.

QUESTION: *How can a person manage the acquisition of inventories in order to minimize the amount of money tied up?*

ANSWER:

Depending on the industry involved, the investment in inventories will vary. Although there can be wide variations, inventory to sales ratios are generally concentrated in the 12 to 20 percent range, and inventory to total asset ratios are concentrated in the 16 to 30 percent range. Ratios outside these ranges should be investigated.

The major determinants of investment in inventory are level of sales, length and technical nature of the production process, and durability versus perishability or style factors of the product. Inventories in the tobacco industry, for instance, are high because of the long curing process. In the machine-tool industry, inventories also are large because of the long production process. However, inventory ratios are low in mining, oil, and gas production because no raw materials are used. Also, the goods in process are small in relation to sales. In the canning of fruits and vegetables, the inventories are large because of the seasonality of the raw materials.

In respect to durability and style factors, large inventories are found in the hardware and precious metals industries because durability is great and the style factor is not significant. Inventory ratios are low in food manufacturing, such as baked goods, because of the perishability of the final product. Inventories are low in printing because the items are manufactured to order and do not require finished goods inventories.

Within limits set by the economics of a firm's industry is a potential for improvement in inventory control through the use of computers and simple mathematical techniques.

Managing assets of all kinds is basically an inventory problem. A comparable analysis applies to cash and fixed assets as applies to inventories. First, a basic stock must be on hand to balance inflows and outflows of the asset with the size of the stock, depending on the patterns of flows. Secondly, because of uncertainty, it is necessary to have *safety stocks,* which guard against costs incurred if stock falls short of demands. Thirdly, additional amounts may be required to meet future growth needs, known as *anticipation stocks.* Related to anticipation stocks is the awareness that there are optimum purchase sizes, defined as *economic order quantities.* In borrowing money, buying raw materials for production, or purchasing equipment, it has proved less expensive to buy more than the minimum to meet immediate needs. Under such circumstances, the costs involved in making orders and arranging for purchases are reduced.

Exhibit 6.6 presents a theoretical basis for determining what the optimal investment in inventory should be. Some costs rise with larger

EXHIBIT 6.6
Determination of Optimum Inventory

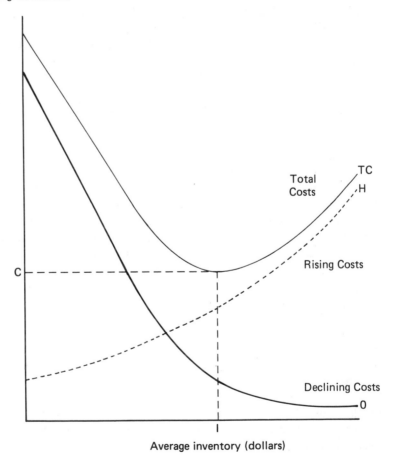

inventories. Examples include warehousing costs, interest on funds invested in inventories, insurance, and potential costs due to obsolescence. Other types of costs tend to decline with larger inventories. Examples include loss of profits due to lost sales caused by insufficient stock, costs of wasted time and interruptions in production because of insufficient inventories, and decreases in costs due to volume purchase discounts.

The costs that decline with higher inventories are indicated by curve H in Exhibit 6.6. Costs that rise with larger inventories are indicated by curve 0. Curve TC is the total of the H and 0 curves, indicating the total cost of ordering and holding inventories. At the point where the slope of the H curve is equal to the slope of the 0 curve, the TC curve is at a minimum. This point represents the optimum size of investment in inventory.

The optimum investment in inventory can be developed mathematically. The total cost of investing in inventory for a year equals the number of orders for inventory during the year, multiplied by the costs of making an order, plus the average number of units of inventory on hand during the year multiplied by the cost of holding a unit in inventory. The number of orders placed during a year will be equal to the annual purchases of inventory divided by the size of an average order. The average inventory on hand during the year will equal the average size of an order divided by two (that is, maximum units in inventory will equal the size of an order and minimum units in inventory will equal zero). Exhibit 6.7 presents an analysis of the optimal investment in inventory from a mathematical perspective. Through relatively simple algebraic manipulation, it is possible to show that the recommended average size of an inventory order (in other words, the economic order quantity) equals: the square root of twice the order cost (per order) times the annual purchases of inventory divided by the average holding cost per unit of inventory. (See Exhibit 6.7.)

EXHIBIT 6.7
Mathematical Determination of Optimum Inventory

Assume:

TC = Total cost of holding and ordering Inventory

H = Cost of holding one unit of inventory during the year

O = Cost of making one order

EXHIBIT 6.7
continued

D = Annual purchases of inventory in units

EOQ = Economic Order Quantity, or optimal size of inventory

Then:

$\dfrac{D}{EOQ}$ = Number of orders placed during the year

$\dfrac{EOQ}{2}$ = Average size of inventory during the year

$$TC = O\left(\dfrac{D}{EOQ}\right) + \dfrac{EOQ}{2}\,(H)$$

The total cost is at a minimum when the derivative of the total cost function is equal to zero.

$$\dfrac{dTc}{EOQ} = \dfrac{O \times D}{EOQ^2} + \dfrac{H}{2} = O$$

Therefore:

$$EOQ = \sqrt{\dfrac{2\,(O \times D)}{H}}$$

7

Depreciation

Depreciation, and the related topics of depletion and amortization, are important areas of accounting, taxation, and financial decision making. Since the following terms will be used frequently in this chapter, they are defined here.

In accounting terms, *depreciation* is the process of allocating against revenues the cost expiration of tangible property. Depreciation also carries the connotation of decline in value due to use or wear and tear.

Depletion is the process of allocating against revenue the cost expiration of an asset represented by a natural resource, such as an oil well.

Amortization is the process of allocating against revenue the cost expiration of intangibles represented by special rights, such as patents or leaseholds.

QUESTION: *How is depreciation determined?*

ANSWER:

To determine the amount of depreciation, depletion, or amortization to be recorded for a period, or the amount that may be deducted for tax purposes, it is essential to know first:

1. The cost of the asset
2. The estimated economic useful life of the asset
3. The estimated salvage or residual value of the asset at the end of its useful life.

Example: If you purchase a machine for $11,000 and it has a 5-year economic life and an estimated salvage value of $1,000, then by using a straight-line depreciation method you could record $2,000 depreciation expense per year and deduct this amount against revenues and other income in calculating taxable income.

$$\frac{\$11,000 - \$1,000}{5} = \$2,000$$

An important consideration, then, is the determination of the cost of an asset for depreciation, depletion, or amortization purposes.

DETERMINING THE COST OF AN ASSET

QUESTION: *How is the cost of an asset determined?*

ANSWER:

The acquisition of an asset is measured by the cash outlay made to acquire the asset; or, if other than cash is exchanged for the asset, then the fair market value of the other consideration given at the time of the transaction will be the measure of cost. In the absence of a determinable fair market value for the consideration given, the asset is recorded at its fair market value, based on list prices.

An asset is generally not considered to be acquired for accounting or tax purposes until it has been placed in the position in which it is ready to be used and is suitable for production. Thus, all reasonable and legitimate costs incurred in placing an asset in service are considered to be part of the cost.

Cash Purchase

If an asset is purchased for cash, any outlay that a prudent buyer would make for the asset, including costs of installation, should be capitalized.

The capitalizable costs include the invoice price, plus incidental costs, such as insurance during transit, freight, duties, title search, registration fees, and installation costs.

Credit Purchases

If an asset is acquired on a deferred payment basis, then the cash equivalent price of the asset, excluding interest, should be capitalized. Actual or imputed interest on the note payable or other liability should be charged to current expense when it is paid or accrued. Even if the purchase contract does not specify interest on the liability, imputed interest should be deducted in determining the cost of the asset.

Example: To illustrate the purchase of an asset on credit, assume that a machine was purchased under a contract that required equal payments of $3154.70 at the end of each of four years when the prevailing interest rate was 10 percent per annum. To record the asset at $12,618.80 ($3154.70 × 4) would include interest in the cost of the asset. The actual cost of the asset is the present value of the four payments discounted at 10 percent:

$$PV = \text{Annual Payment} \times \text{Present Value of an Annuity}[1]$$
$$= \$3154.70 \times 3.1699$$
$$= \$10,000$$

Therefore, the cost of the machine would be $10,000. Likewise, the difference between the $10,000 cost and the total of the installment payments ($12,618.80) represents interest expense that may be deducted as it is paid.

Assets Acquired by Exchange for Securities

If assets are acquired in exchange for securities, then the determination of cost may be difficult to achieve. The reason for this situation lies in the absence of readily determinable fair market value for the securities or the assets involved. In addition, the assets may have been transferred to the business in exchange for stock. This transfer of assets is often a related party transaction in which the owners of the company are contributing assets to the company. The value of cost of both the acquired asset and the associated stock or notes is difficult to determine. As a consequence, the *Internal Revenue Code* typically indicates that, where assets are transferred to a corporation or a partnership in exchange for ownership inter-

---

[1] See Chapter 5 on Receivables.

ests, the cost basis of the asset will be the same in the hands of the corporation as it was in the hands of the transferor or stockholder.

Assets Acquired in Exchange for Other Assets

If assets are acquired in exchange for other assets, then further problems arise regarding the determination of the cost of the acquired assets. Items of property, plant, and equipment are frequently acquired by trading in an old asset in full, or part payment, for another asset. In some cases, two or more assets are exchanged. In other cases, an asset is acquired by exchanging another asset plus payment or receipt of cash. Cash paid or received in an exchange transaction is often referred to as *boot*.

For tax purposes, the cost basis of an asset acquired through an exchange is equal to the cost of the asset given up plus any cash boot given.

Example: If a person acquired a truck three years ago for $9,000 that has an estimated life of six years, with no salvage value, and used straight-line depreciation, then the current *book value*, or *basis*, of the truck would be $4500.

$$\$9,000 \div 6 = \$1500$$

$$\$9000 - 3\ (\$1500) = \$4500$$

If a person traded in the old truck for a new truck and paid $3,000 cash in addition, this person would then have a new truck with a book value, or basis, for accounting and tax depreciation purposes of $7500, despite the fact that the new truck might have a list price higher or lower than that amount.

$$
\begin{array}{r}
\$4500 \\
+\ 3000 \\
\hline
\$7500 \\
\hline
\end{array}
$$

INVESTMENT TAX CREDIT

QUESTION: *Why is it important to determine cost?*

ANSWER:

It is important to determine the cost of an asset not only for depreciation purposes but also for an equally valuable reason from a tax perspective, namely, the *Investment Tax Credit.* The Investment Tax Credit was established by Congress in order to stimulate the purchase of machinery and equipment throughout the economy. It was first created in 1962, and has been modified subsequently several times. An investment credit is allowed against a person's tax liability when certain qualified business property is placed into service. The credit also may apply to progress payments made during the course of building or acquiring qualified property. The credit has no effect on regular depreciation.

QUESTION: How is the investment tax credit determined?

ANSWER:
Taxpayers can take a 10 percent credit for investments in qualified business property acquired after January 2, 1975. A corporate taxpayer may elect an 11 percent credit if an amount equal to 1 percent of the investment is contributed to an *Employee Stock Ownership Plan*. The maximum amount of credit that can be taken in any one taxable year is $50,000 plus 1/2 of the tax liability in excess of $50,000. This limitation will not affect most individuals or corporations, but for large corporations, with large investments there may have to be a deferral of the use of the credit to future tax years. The credit can be deferred up to seven years.

Example: Your tax liability before the investment tax credit is $100,000. The maximum credit allowable is $75,000 ($50,000 + 1/2 of $50,000). If you buy qualified property costing $200,000, your credit would be $20,000, and your tax liability would be $80,000. Depreciation would be calculated on the basis of $200,000.

The amount of qualified investment depends on the useful life of the property to which the credit applies. It is determined from the cost of used or new property. This is why the cost of an asset is quite important.

Example: If you trade in a machine with a book value of $4,000 and pay $1,000 cash in addition for a new machine, the cost of the new machine would be $5000 and you would be allowed an investment credit of $500 (10 percent of $5,000).

However, if the machine you acquire is used rather than new, then only the excess cost above the book value of the trade-in qualifies for the investment credit. Therefore, in the previous example, your investment credit would be reduced to $100 ($5000 − $4000 times 10 percent). The reduction in the investment credit for used property has no effect on depreciation. You still can depreciate $5,000 of cost over the life of the acquired machine.

The rule about used property applies even if you sell an asset and then later reinvest the proceeds in a used asset of a similar type.

Example: If you sell a truck, which has a book value of $3000, and then later buy a truck for $5,000, the amount of cost that qualifies for the investment credit is limited to $2,000.

QUESTION: What constitutes qualified property?

ANSWER:

The investment tax credit applies to *depreciable tangible personal property*, which means it applies to property used in your trade or business that has a physical existence and that is not inventory, supplies, or real estate. Livestock of a farmer is included, except for horses. Examples of qualified property include: office equipment, machinery in a factory, counters in a store, neon signs for advertising. Even the cost of producing a motion picture or television film has been considered to be qualified property, though it is more intangible than tangible. Some costs that are ordinarily considered to be costs of real property qualify for the investment credit if the real property is used as an integral part of a manufacturing, mining, or utility type of facility.

The investment credit also applies to real property in certain circumstances. In order to qualify, the real property must be an integral part of either a manufacturing, production, mining, or utility operation, or must constitute a research facility or a facility for bulk storage of commodities. Examples of real property qualifying for the investment credit include: blast furnaces, oil derricks, oil and gas pipelines, broadcasting towers, and railroad tracks.

QUESTION: When should you claim the investment tax credit?

ANSWER:

The credit is allowed for the year that the qualifying property is placed into service. This is the earlier of either the first year that depreciation on the asset can be taken or the year the asset becomes ready for its intended purpose.

There is a limit on the amount of investment in used property and equipment that will qualify for the investment tax credit. The limit is $100,000 for corporations and the same for individuals. However, if you are married and file a separate tax return, the limit is $50,000. For a partnership, the limitation is $100,000 for the partnership as a whole.

QUESTION: What types of property are there that do not qualify for the investment credit?

ANSWER:

No investment credit is allowed for property with a useful life of less than three years. A government agency or a tax-exempt organization cannot take an investment credit. Used property will not be qualified if, after you acquire it, it is used by the person from whom you acquired it. An example of this might be a sale and lease-back arrangement. Property used before or property repossessed will not qualify. Property that you acquire from a greater-than-50-percent-owned subsidiary, or from your parent company if you are a more-than-50-percent-owned subsidiary, would not qualify. If you sell or give personally owned property to a business that you control, the business cannot take a credit.

No credit is allowed for property that is used primarily for housing or to provide lodging, such as a hotel or motel. However, facilities related to housing or lodging may qualify, such as a restaurant in a hotel, or laundry machines in an apartment building, and also, the furniture in a hotel or motel qualifies.

Useful Life Limitations

In order to qualify for the full investment credit, the useful life of the asset must be at least seven years. If the useful life is five or six years, then only 2/3 of the cost of the asset qualifies for the credit. If the useful life is three or four years, then only 1/3 of the cost qualifies. If the useful life is less than three years, then, too, the asset does not qualify for the credit.

Example: Assume that you purchase a delivery truck, a small computer, and a lathe.

Asset	Useful Life	Cost	Percentage	Qualified Amount
Delivery truck	3	$ 9,000	33 1/3	$ 3,000
Computer	5	12,000	66 2/3	8,000
Lathe	7	15,000	100	15,000
				$26,000

Investment Credit ($26,000 x 10 percent) =$2,600

QUESTION: *What if you cannot take advantage of the full investment tax credit because of insufficient taxable income?*

ANSWER:

If the credit is not used in the period in which it is earned, it may be carried back to offset taxes paid up to three years previously, and may be carried forward up to seven years. Investment tax credits carried forward from previous years are used to reduce current taxes before credits earned in the current year.

QUESTION: *What if the asset is sold before seven years have elapsed?*

ANSWER:

(Remember, the asset must have a useful life of seven years or more in order to qualify for the full credit.) The investment credit may have to be recaptured if it is not held at least seven years. Even if the asset is destroyed, recapture of the credit will occur.

Example: If you bought a machine in 1976 that has a useful life of ten years and cost $8,000, in 1976 you could have taken an $800 credit. However, if the machine is destroyed by fire in 1978, the $800 will be added to your tax liability for 1978.

Once you have acquired a depreciable asset and have determined its cost, then the question of depreciation arises.

The Internal Revenue Code recognizes that a depreciation allowance is necessary because property gradually approaches a point at which its usefulness is exhausted. Therefore, depreciation is allowed only on property that has a definitely limited useful life. Depreciation may even be allowed on fruit trees if it can be shown that the trees have a limited life.

Intangible property can be depreciated if its use in a business is of limited duration. Examples of depreciable intangibles include licenses, franchises, patents, and copyrights. Ordinarily, depreciation of intangibles is referred to as *amortization*.

QUESTION: *What types of depreciation methods may be used?*

ANSWER:

The *Internal Revenue Code* specifies three particular methods of computing depreciation:

1. Straight line
2. Declining balance
3. Sum-of-years-digits

Other methods also may be used. You do not need to use the same method for all of your depreciable property, but once you choose a method for a particular property, you must continue using that method unless you obtain approval from the IRS to change methods. Obtaining approval to change is not usually a problem. You simply file Form 3115 during the first 180 days of the year of the change.

QUESTION: How is a useful life established?

ANSWER:
You may enter into an agreement with the IRS as to the useful life, depreciation method, and salvage value of any property. However, Internal Revenue Regulations have established classes of property that have asset depreciation ranges. If you choose a useful life within the limits of the asset depreciation range for a given asset, you will not be challenged by the IRS.

QUESTION: How is salvage value determined?

ANSWER:
Salvage value, established at the point at which property is acquired, is the amount that can be realized when the property is no longer useful to the taxpayer. It may be no more than junk value, or it may be a large portion of the original cost, depending on the length of time before the end of the asset's useful economic life, which is determined by when the taxpayer plans to dispose of it. An estimated salvage value of less than 10 percent of original cost may be disregarded in computing depreciation. However, no asset may be depreciated below a reasonable salvage value.

Salvage value must be subtracted from original cost in computing straight-line and sum-of-years-digits depreciation. It is not subtracted in computing declining balance depreciation.

Example: A machine is purchased for $10,000 that has a salvage value of $2,000 and a useful life of five years. The first year of depreciation under each of the three methods is as follows:

Straight Line: $10,000 minus $2,000 divided by 5 = $1600
Sum-of-Years-Digits: $10,000 minus $2,000 times 5/15 = $2667
Double Declining Balance: $10,000 times 40% = $4,000

QUESTION: How are the various methods of depreciation calculated?
ANSWER:

Straight Line

The formula for straight-line depreciation is: Cost minus salvage value divided by useful life in years = depreciation for each year.

Sum-of-Years-Digits

Sum-of-years-digits depreciation allocates a declining portion of the total cost to depreciation expense in each year. In the example in which a machine was purchased for $10,000 and had a salvage value of $2000 and a useful life of five years, sum-of-years-digits depreciation would be calculated as shown in Exhibit 7.1.

EXHIBIT 7.1
Sum-of-Year-Digits Calculation

Year	Factor	Cost Minus Salvage	Depreciation Expense
1	5/15	8,000	2,667
2	4/15	8,000	2,133
3	3/15	8,000	1,600
4	2/15	8,000	1,067
5	1/15	8,000	533
			Total:$ 8,000

QUESTION: How is the denominator of the sum-of years-digits fraction calculated?

ANSWER:
A useful formula for calculating the denominator of the sum-of-years-digits fraction is:

$$\frac{n\,(n+1)}{2}$$

Where n = useful life

Example:

Useful life = 10 years

$$\text{Denominator} = \frac{10 \times 11}{2} = 55$$

Declining Balance

The declining balance method applies a constant percentage to the declining book value of the asset. Using the same assumptions as above, follow the example in Exhibit 7.2, with the cost of the machine at $10,000 and a useful life of 5 years. Note that the total depreciation exceeds the original cost minus salvage value of $8,000. This would not be allowed for tax purposes. Therefore, in year four only $160 of depreciation could be taken (in order to bring the book value equal to the salvage value), and in year five no depreciation would be taken.

EXHIBIT 7.2
Double Declining Balance

Year	Percentage	Book Value	Depreciation
1	40%	$10,000	$4,000
2	40%	6,000	2,400
3	40%	3,600	1,440
4	40%	2,160	864
5	40%	1,296	518.40
		Total:	$9,222.40

QUESTION: Is there a limit on the use of declining balance depreciation?

ANSWER:
The maximum rate on declining balance depreciation is specified in Exhibit 7.3. The factor is multiplied by the straight-line rate in order to find the maximum declining balance rate.

EXHIBIT 7.3
Double Declining Balance Conversion Factors

Type of Property	Factor
New equipment	2
Used equipment	1 ½
New real estate	1 ½
Used real estate	1
Used residential rental property	1 ¼

Example: A person buys a new apartment building with a fifty-year useful life. The maximum usable percentage on declining balance depreciation is 3 percent (1½ times 1/50).

QUESTION: *Is there a limit on the use of sum-of-years-digits depreciation?*

ANSWER:
Sum-of-years-digits cannot be used for real estate, except for new residential rental buildings, such as apartment houses.

QUESTION: *How is depreciation calculated when an asset is acquired during the year?*

ANSWER:
Usually when you acquire an asset during a year, you pro rate the depreciation that you owe on the asset.

Example: On April 1, you acquire a machine for $12,000 that has a useful life of ten years. You decide to use straight-line depreciation. The depreciation expense for the year of acquisition would be $900 ($12,000/ 10) times (9/12).

If the decision is made to use sum-of-years-digits depreciation, the calculation is more complicated. In the first year, $1,636 may be taken in depreciation ($12,000 times 10/55 times 9/12). In the second year, $2,018 may be taken. ($12,000 times 10/55 times 3/12 plus $12,000 times 9/55 times 9/12).

Under the class life *Asset Depreciation Range* system, you may adopt a convention whereby any assets you acquire in the first six months of the year take a full year of depreciation, and any assets you acquire in the last six months of the year cannot be depreciated. This convention simplifies the calculations involved in computing depreciation.

QUESTION: *What is the Class Life Asset Depreciation Range System?*

ANSWER:
The Class Life Asset Depreciation Range System (Class Life ADR) was introduced by the Tax Reform Act of 1969 in order to simplify calculations with respect to depreciation. Class Life ADR is based on broad industry classes of assets as defined in *Internal Revenue Code* Section 167 (m) and *Internal Revenue Regulation* Section 1.167 (a)–11. All classes have a range of years called an *asset depreciation range*. This range runs from 20 percent lower to 20 percent above the actual estimated life of the asset.

Example: If you buy a machine with an estimated useful life of 5 years, then you have the option under Class Life ADR of choosing a useful life for depreciation purposes of either 4 (20 percent lower), 5, or 6 (20 percent higher) years.

Class Life ADR is an annual election. If ADR is elected for any year, the election covers all eligible property placed into service during that year. Eligible property is basically defined as equipment, although some real estate can qualify as well.

Exhibit 7.4 presents the classes under the ADR system as of 1977. The procedure is to categorize various assets purchased during a particular year into a given class.

Example: If you buy ten typewriters in 1978, you would categorize the typewriters into Asset Guideline *Class No. 00.11* "office furniture, fixtures and equipment." It is then possible to choose a useful life for all ten typewriters of either eight, ten, or twelve years. Under Class Life ADR, a taxpayer may use the straight-line, sum-of-years-digits, or double declining balance method for new equipment type property. In the case of used equipment, only the straight-line or 150 percent declining balance method may be used.

Example: Assume that the ten typewriters purchased in the previous example had a cost of $300 each and that you decided to use a ten-year life and straight-line depreciation. Annual depreciation expense would be $300 ($3,000/10). Double declining balance depreciation would be $600 ($3000 × 2 (1/10).

So far, the ADR system does not appear much different from regular depreciation. However, there are several differences:

1. A person can choose a useful life from a given range.
2. All assets of a given class purchased in the same year are depreciated as a group, rather than as individual assets.
3. If estimated salvage value is 10 percent or less, it can be ignored.
4. If repairs of less than a certain specified percentage of cost are made, such repairs can be expensed rather than capitalized. (Percentages are indicated in Exhibit 7.4.)
5. If an asset in a class is retired and if other assets remain in the same class, then the cost is not removed and depreciation proceeds as though the asset were not retired. If the retirement is due to a casualty loss, normal retirement rules apply.
6. Two first-year conventions apply under ADR.

QUESTION: *What are the first year conventions?*

EXHIBIT 7.4
Class Life Asset Depreciation Range

| Asset Guide-line Class | Description of Assets | Asset Depreciation Range (in Years) | | | Annual Asset Guide-line Repair Allow-ance Per-centage |
		Lower Limit	Asset Guide-line Period	Upper Limit	
SPECIFIC DEPRECIABLE ASSETS USED IN ALL BUSINESS ACTIVITIES, EXCEPT AS NOTED:					
00.11	Office furniture, fixtures, and equipment	8	10	12	2.0
00.12	Information systems (computers and peripheral equipment)	5	6	7	7.5
00.13	Data handling equipment, except computers	5	6	7	15.0
00.21	Airplanes (airframes and engines) except aircraft of air transport companies and all helicopters	5	6	7	14.0
00.22	Automobiles, taxis	2.5	3	3.5	16.5
00.23	Buses	7	9	11.0	11.5
00.241	Light general purpose trucks (less than 13,000 pounds)	3	4	5	16.5
00.242	Heavy general purpose trucks (13,000 pounds or more)	5	6	7	10.0
00.25	Railroad cars and locomotives, except those owned by railroad transportation companies	12	15	18	8.0
00.26	Tractor units used over-the-road	3	4	5	16.5
00.27	Trailers and trailer-mounted containers	5	6	7	10.0
00.28	Vessels, barges, tugs and similar water transportation equipment	14.5	18	21.5	6.0
00.3	Land improvements		20		
00.4	Industrial steam and electric generation and/or distribution systems	22.5	28	33.5	2.5

ANSWER:
Under Class Life ADR, the taxpayer may use one of two first year conventions:

1. *The half-year convention:* A half-year of depreciation is taken on all assets placed in service during the year.
2. *The modified half-year convention:* Assets placed in service during the first half of the year get a full year's depreciation. Assets placed in service during the second half of the year get no depreciation.

One of the two conventions must be elected for the whole tax year for all assets acquired during that year.

QUESTION: *How are gains and losses computed on sale or retirement of depreciable assets?*

ANSWER:
The rules regarding the computation of gains and losses on sale or retirement of depreciable assets are somewhat complicated. In general, capital gains and losses are taxed at different rates from gains and losses on the sale of other assets. Depreciable property has been determined not to be a capital asset, therefore, capital gains and losses are not allowable when depreciable property is sold. However, Congress decided in Section 1231 of the *Internal Revenue Code* to extend capital gain treatment to depreciable assets while preserving the benefits of ordinary loss treatment. Later, Congress changed its mind and added Section 1245 of the *Code*, which provides that for equipment that you sell, you have ordinary gain treatment to the extent of any depreciation taken on the equipment.
    Example: A person buys a machine in 1975 for $10,000 and decides to depreciate it on the straight-line method over ten years. By the end of 1977, $2,000 in depreciation has been taken. If it is then sold for $11,000, $2,000 of ordinary income gain and $1000 of capital gain must be recorded.
    Example: On January 1, 1969 a machine is bought for $6,000. Depreciation of $600 was claimed on it for each year and it sold for $2,000 on July 1, 1978. The adjusted basis on the date of sale was $300 ($6,000 less $5,700) which represents $600 a year depreciation between 1969 and 1978 (nine years) plus $300 for the half year in 1978. Therefore, the gain was $1,700 on the sale. Since the gain ($1,700) was less than the total depreciation after 1961 ($5,700), the entire gain must be included as ordinary income.
    On real property, gain is calculated as on personal property, if the following applies:

1. A person computes depreciation on the property using the straight-line method (or any other method resulting in depreciation not in excess of that computed by the straight-line method), and this person holds the property for more than a year
2. A loss on the sale, exchange, or involuntary conversion of property is realized, or
3. The person disposes of low-income rental property after holding it for 16 2/3 years or more. (In the case of low-income rental housing for which the special 60-month depreciation for rehabilitation expenditures was allowed, the 16 2/3 years begin when the rehabilitated property was placed in service.)

Otherwise, real property disposal by sale or exchange must be calculated by a special formula to determine what portion of the gain is to be treated as ordinary income. Considering the rather complex nature of the procedure, Exhibit 7.5, with an explanation of the procedure step by step is given. The steps are summarized as follows:

Step 1: In a sale, exchange, or inventory conversion of the property, determine the excess of the amount realized (value of the sale, exchange, or conversion) over the adjusted basis of the property (value on your books). In any other disposition of property, determine the excess of fair market value over adjusted basis.

Example: If the book value (cost minus depreciation) of a piece of equipment is $2,000 and you sell the equipment for $3,000, the excess of the amount realized ($3,000) over the adjusted basis ($2,000) would be $1,000.

Step 2: Determine the additional depreciation attributable to periods after 1975 (or the year 1976 and the following years). *Additional depreciation* is the excess of the actual depreciation a company has taken, above what the depreciation for the same period would have been had they used straight-line depreciation for the entire period the property was held. Additional depreciation calculations must be made when the taxpayer uses the double declining balance method, the sum-of-year-digits methods, the units-of-production method, or any other method of accelerated depreciation. Additional depreciation will not result from amortization of emergency facilities, amortization of pollution control facilities, or amortization of on-the-job training or child-care facilities, which are exempt from this step.

Other steps require calculation of additional depreciation for various time period; the following are examples of how to calculate additional depreciation that will also apply to steps 4 and 6.

EXHIBIT 7.5
Determining Loss or Gain on Sale of Depreciable
Assets — Steps

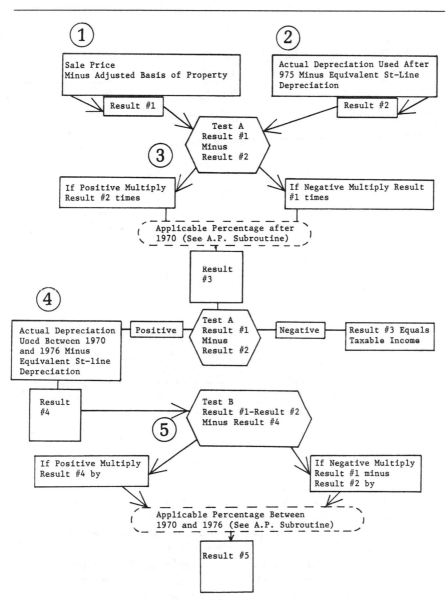

EXHIBIT 7.5
continued

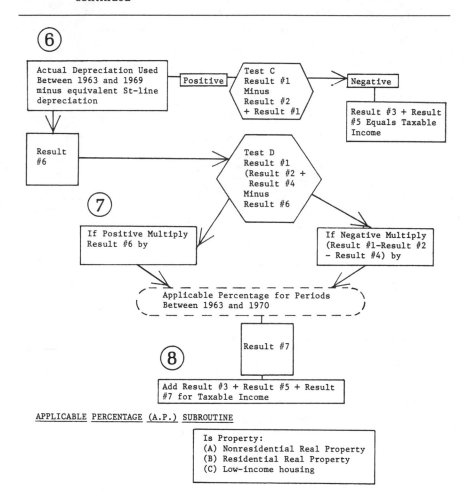

APPLICABLE PERCENTAGE (A.P.) SUBROUTINE

Is Property:
(A) Nonresidential Real Property
(B) Residential Real Property
(C) Low-income housing

If the actual depreciation for periods before January 1, 1963 is less than it was under the straight-line method the difference may be offset against the additional depreciation for period after December 31, 1963, in computing the part of the gain reported as ordinary income.

The useful life and salvage value for determining the amount that was the depreciation if the straight-line method was used generally is the same as that used under the actual depreciation method employed. If no

EXHIBIT 7.5
continued

```
For Years Before 1970

(A) 100% minus (1% x total months
    minus 20)
(B) 100% minus (1% x (total months
    minus 20)
(c) 100% minus (1% x total months
    minus 20)
```

```
For Years 1970-1975

(A) 100%
(B) 100% minus (1% x (total months
    minus 100)
(C) Non-assisted by government
    guarantee or loan 100% minus
    (1% x (total months minus 100)
    Assisted by government loan
    or guarantee 100% minus
    (1% x (total months minus 20)
```

```
For Years After 1975

(A) 100%
(B) 100%
(C) 100% minus (1% x (total months
    minus 100%)
```

useful life is used under the actual depreciation method employed (such as with units-of-production depreciation), or if no salvage value is taken into account (as with the double declining balance depreciation), then the useful life or salvage value used in the straight-line calculation is the same as if you had used straight-line depreciation from the start. The following are two examples from IRS *Publication 334* illustrating the calculation of additional depreciation:

Example 1: On January 1, 1976, Sue Parks, a calendar-year taxpayer, sells property purchased for $10,000 on January 1, 1963. Throughout the period, she computed depreciation under the declining-balance method, using a rate of 200 percent of the straight-line rate and a useful life of thirty years. Under this method, salvage value is not taken into account. If the taxpayer had computed depreciation under the straight-line method she would have used a salvage value of $1,000. The depreciation under both methods is set forth in Exhibit 7.6.

EXHIBIT 7.6
Example 1 Calculations

Year	Declining Balance	Straight Line
1963	$ 667	$ 300
1964	622	300
1965	581	300
1966	542	300
1967	506	300
1968	472	300
1969	440	300
1970	411	300
1971	384	300
1972	359	300
1973	334	300
1974	312	300
1975	291	300
Sum of depreciation deductions	$5,254	$3,600

The additional depreciation for the property is $1,654; that is, the depreciation actually deducted for the periods after December 31, 1963, ($5,254) minus the depreciation that would have resulted for such periods under the straight-line method ($3,600). Of the $1,654, $290 ($2,090 − $1,800) for 1970, 1971, 1972, 1973, 1974, and 1975 is additional depreciation after 1969, and $1,364 ($3,164 minus $1,800 for 1964–1969) is additional depreciation before 1970.

Example 2: A calendar-year taxpayer sold depreciable real property on January 1, 1976, purchased for $10,000 on January 1, 1967. For the period 1967 through 1969, the taxpayer computed depreciation deductions on the property under the declining balance method, using a rate of 200 percent of the straight-line rate and a useful life of ten years. If the taxpayer had used the straight-line method, then a salvage value of $1,000 would be used. As of January 1, 1971, the taxpayer elected to change to the straight-line method and redetermined the remaining useful life of the property to be eight years and its salvage value to be $120. The depreciation under both methods is set forth in Exhibit 7.7.

EXHIBIT 7.7
Example 2 Calculations

Year	Actual Depreciation	Straight Line
1967	$ 2,000	$ 900[1]
1968	1,600	900
1969	1,280	900
1970	625[2]	898[3]
1971	625	898
1972	625	898
1973	625	898
1974	625	898
1975	625	898
Sum of depreciation deductions	$ 8,630	$ 8,088

[1]One-tenth of $9,000 ($10,000 minus $1,000)
[2]One-eighth of $5,000 ($5,120 minus $120)
[3]One-eighth of $7,180 ($7,300 minus $120)

The additional depreciation for the property is $542; that is, the depreciation actually deducted ($8,630), minus the depreciation that would have resulted under the straight-line method ($8,088). The entire $542 is attributable to periods before 1970 since there is no additional depreciation after 1969 ($625 actual depreciation annually is less than $898 straight-line depreciation).

QUESTION: *If a leasehold improvement is sold or exchanged, how is additional depreciation calculated?*

ANSWER:
In the case of a leasehold improvement by a lessee, the lease period for determining what is to be the straight-line depreciation adjustments to calculate additional depreciation includes all renewal periods but is limited by the useful life of the improvement. This same rule applies to the cost of acquiring a lease. *Renewal period*, as defined by the IRS, means any period for which the lease may be renewed, extended, or continued under an option exercisable by the lessee. However, the inclusion of renewal periods cannot extend the lease by more than two-thirds of the period on which the actual depreciation was calculated.

QUESTION: *Rehabilitation expenditures in connection with low-income housing is allowed for a sixty-month depreciation adjustment. How is additional depreciation calculated on this type of property?*

ANSWER:

A portion of the special sixty-month depreciation adjustment is additional depreciation. If the property is held for one year or less after the expenditures are incurred, the entire special depreciation adjustment is taken into account. If the property is held for one year or less after the expenditures are incurred, the entire special depreciation adjustment is taken into account. If the property is held for more than one year after the rehabilitation expenditures are incurred, the additional depreciation is the excess of the special depreciation adjustments attributable to rehabilitation expenditures, over the adjustments that would have resulted, had the straight-line method and normal useful life and salvage been used. The following is an example from IRS *Publication 334:*

Example: On January 1, 1978, a calendar-year taxpayer sells real property, the entire basis of which is attributable to rehabilitation expenditures of $50,000 incurred in 1970. The property was placed in service on January 1, 1971, and under the special depreciation provisions for rehabilitation expenditures, was depreciated under the straight-line method using a useful life of sixty months (five years) and no salvage value. If the regular straight-line method had been used, there would be a salvage value of $5,000 with a useful life of fifteen years. Depreciation under the straight-line method would be $3,000 each year, 1/15 of $45,000 ($50,000 minus 5,000). As of January 1, 1978, the additional depreciation for the property is $29,000, computed as shown in Exhibit 7.8.

Step 3: Multiply the lesser of the result of Step 1 and Step 2 by the *applicable percentage.* (In Exhibit 7.5, result of Step 2 is subtracted from the result of Step 1 (Test A)). If the answer is positive, this calculation means that the result of Step 1 is larger than Result 2; therefore, Result 2 is the lesser amount and it is multiplied by the applicable percentage. If, on the other hand, the result of the test (Test A) shows that Result 1 is smaller than Result 2, that is, the result of the test is negative, then Result 1 is multiplied by the applicable percentage.

The applicable percentage that is used throughout the calculation varies with the type of real property involved in the sale or exchange and the time period used. Real property is divided into three groups:

Nonresidential real property, that is, property that is neither residential real property nor low-income housing

EXHIBIT 7.8
Depreciation Computation

Year	Actual depreciation	Straight line	Additional depreciation (deficit)
1971	$10,000	$ 3,000	$ 7,000
1972	10,000	3,000	7,000
1973	10,000	3,000	7,000
1974	10,000	3,000	7,000
1975	10,000	3,000	7,000
1976		3,000	(3,000)
1977		3,000	(3,000)
Total	$50,000	$21,000	$29,000

Residential real property other than low-income housing
Low-income housing, which includes:

1. Federally assisted housing projects, where the mortgage is insured under Section 221 (d) (3) or 236 of the National Housing Act, or housing financed or assisted by direct loan or tax rebate under similar provisions of state or local laws and
2. Low income rental housing on which a depreciation deduction for rehabilitation expenditures was allowed; low-income rental housing held for occupancy by families or individuals eligible to receive subsidies under Section 8 of the United States Housing Act of 1937 or similar provisions of state and local laws; and housing financed or assisted by direct loan or insured under Title V of the Housing Act of 1949.

The Applicable Percentage Subroutine diagram gives the particulars on how the various types of real property vary over certain periods of time and Exhibit 7.9 shows the applicable percentage by type of property.

Step 4: If Result 1 minus Result 2 is negative (that is, Result 2 is a larger number than Result 1), Result 3 is the taxable income. If Result 1 minus Result 2 is positive (Result 1 is the larger of the two numbers), then a person must determine the additional depreciation (see Step 2 for defini-

EXHIBIT 7.9
Applicable Percentage Depreciation Recapture

Type of property	Before 1970	Period of Time 1970 through 1975	After 1975
(A) Nonresidential real property	100% minus (1% times the total number of months minus 20 months)	100%	100%
(B) Residential real property other than low-income housing	100% minus (1% times the total number of months minus 20 months)	100% minus (1% times the total number of months minus 100 months)	100%
(C) Low income	100% minus (1% times the total numbers of months minus 20 months)	(1) federally insured: 100% minus (1% times the total number of months minus 20 mo.) (2) nonassisted: 100% minus (1% times the total number of months minus 100 mo.)	100% minus (1% times the total number of months minus 100 mo.)

tion) attributable to the periods after 1969 and before 1976. The additional depreciation minus the equivalent straight-line depreciation will give you Result 4.

Step 5: If Result 1 minus Result 2 minus Result 4 has a positive answer (Result 1 minus Result 2 is a larger number than Result 4), you multiply Result 4 by the applicable percentage between 1970 and 1976. If Result 1 minus Result 2 minus Result 4 is a negative number (Result 4 is a bigger number than Result 1 minus Result 2), multiply Result 1 minus Result 2 by the applicable percentage between 1970 and 1976.

Step 6: If Result 1 minus Result 2 plus Result 4 is a negative number (Result 2 plus Result 4 is a larger number than Result 1), then Result 3 plus Result 5 equals the taxable income. If Result 1 minus Result 2 and Result 4 is a positive number (Result 1 is a larger number than both Result 2 and Result 4), you must determine the additional depreciation attributable to periods after 1963 and before 1970, giving you Result 6.

Step 7: If Result 1 minus Result 2 minus Result 4 is a larger number than Result 6 (the answer to Test D is positive), multiply Result 6 by the applicable percentage for periods between 1963 and 1969. If Result 6 is a larger number than Result 1 minus Result 2 minus Result 4 (the answer to Test D is negative), multiply Result 1 minus Result 2 less Result 4 by the applicable percentage for periods between 1963 and 1970.

Step 8: Add Result 3 plus Result 5 plus Result 7 to get taxable income from the transaction.

Examples: Following are two examples of how taxable income is calculated on sale of assets, the first from IRS *Publication 334*, the second from the authors.

Example 1: An office building with an adjusted basis of $20,000 was sold on July 1, 1976, for $29,000. The property was purchased new on January 1, 1969 and was owned for ninety months. Additional depreciation attributable to the property is $1,500, of which $1,300 is for additional depreciation after 1969 ($200 yearly for 1970, 1971, 1972, 1973, 1974, 1975, and $100 for 1976). The applicable percentage for additional depreciation before 1970 is 30 percent (100 percent less 70 percent) and the applicable percentage for additional depreciation after 1969 is 100 percent. Gain to be recaptured as ordinary income is computed as follows:

1. Excess of amount realized ($29,000) over adjusted basis ($20,000) $9,000
2. Additional depreciation after 1969   1,300
3. Lesser of $9,000 or $1,300 times 100% $1,300
Additional steps are necessary because 1 exceeds 2:
4. Additional depreciation before 1970 $ 200

5. Lesser of $7,700 ($9,000 minus $1,300) or $200, times 30% $ 60

Gain treated as ordinary income 3 plus 5 $1,360

Example 2: Acme Mousetrap, Inc., is a calendar-year taxpayer. The company bought a warehouse (nonresidential real property) on January 1, 1963 for $120,000. It sold the warehouse on January 1, 1977 for $200,000. At that time the book value (adjusted basis) of the warehouse was $46,944. Acme used the double-declining-balance-depreciation method (with no salvage value) for a period of twenty-five yars. If it had used straight-line depreciation instead, the company would have had a salvage value of $15,000.

First, we must set up a schedule of the actual depreciation used from the date the warehouse was purchased and the equivalent depreciation had the straight-line depreciation been used. The straight-line depreciation was calculated by the following calculation:

$$\frac{\text{Cost (\$120,000) less salvage value (\$15,000)}}{\text{Years to be depreciated (25)}} = \begin{array}{l}\text{Annual straight-line}\\ \text{Depreciation}\end{array}$$

Acme Mousetraps prepared a schedule (Exhibit 7.10) to show the differences in the depreciation methods. Exhibit 7.11 shows the calculations to determine taxable income on a step-by-step, test-by-test basis.

EXHIBIT 7.10
Different Depreciation Methods for Acme Mousetraps

Year	Actual Declining Balance	Straight Line	D.B.-S.L. Difference in Methods
1963	$ 9,600	$ 4,200	
1964	5,832	4,200	
1965	8,125	4,200	
1966	7,475	4,200	
1967	6,877	4,200	
1968	6,327	4,200	
1969	5,821	4,200	
Subtotal	$43,457	$25,200	$18,257

EXHIBIT 7.10
continued

1970	5,355	4,200	
1971	4,927	4,200	
1972	4,533	4,200	
1973	4,170	4,200	
1974	3,837	4,200	
1975	3,530	4,200	
Subtotal	$26,352	$25,200	$ 1,152
1976	3,247	4,200	(953)
Sum of depreciation deductions for periods after December 31, 1963	$73,056	$54,600	$18,456

EXHIBIT 7.11
Step-by-Step Taxable Income Calculations

Step 1:	$200,000	Sales price
	− 46,944	Book value (adjusted basis)
	$153,056	Result 1
Step 2:	$ 3,247	Actual (double-declining) depreciation after 1975
	− 4,200	St.-line depreciation after 1975
	$ (933)	Result 2
Test A:	$153,056	Result 1
	− (933)	Result 2
	$153,989*	**TEST POSITIVE**
	*Note:	Subtracting a negative number is the mathematical equivalent to adding the number

EXHIBIT 7.11
continued

Step 3:	$ (933)	Result 2
	× 100%	Applicable percentage for periods after 1975
	$ (933)	Result 3

Test A:	$153,056	Result 1
	− (933)	Result 2
	$153,989	**TEST POSITIVE**

Step 4:	$ 26,352	Actual depreciation from 1970 to 1975
	− 25,200	St.-line depreciation from 1970 to 1975
	$ 1,154	Additional depreciation Result 4

Test B:	$153,056	(Result 1) minus $(933) (Result 2) = $153,989
	− 1,154	Result 4
	$152,835	**TEST POSITIVE**

Step 5:	$ 1,152	Result 4
	× 100%	Applicable percentage
	$ 1,154	Result 5

Test C:	$153,056	Result 1
	−(Result 2 ($933) + Result 4 $1,152 = $219)	
	$152,837	**TEST POSITIVE**

Step 6:	$ 43,457	Actual depreciation from 1964 to 1969
	− 25,200	St.-line depreciation from 1964 to 1969
	$ 18,257	Result 6

Test D:	($153,056 − $(933) + $1,152) Result 1 − Result 2 + Result 4	
	− 18,257	Result 6
	$146,484	**TEST POSITIVE**

Step 7:	$ 18,257	Result 6
	× (100% × (1% × 168 total mos. held − 20 mo.)	
	*applicable percentage	
	*Note:	After 10 years (120 months) the applicable percentage becomes zero ($0).

EXHIBIT 7.11
continued

Step 8:			
	$	(933)	Result 3
	+	1,152	Result 5
	+	-0-	Result 7
	$	219	Taxable Income on the sale

To summarize, the longer you hold a piece of property, then the lower the taxable income on the sale or exchange. In the IRS example of the office building, the net gain on the building was $9,000 (property held for 8 years) and the taxable income was only $1,300. In the Acme Mousetraps, Inc., example, even though Acme made a net gain of $153,056 on the sale of the property, (property held for fourteen years) the company's taxable income (not its tax, but the taxable income figure) is only $219.

8

Debt Financing

Regardless of size, every business in the United States must, from time to time, borrow money. Not only will a business borrow from a bank, but it also may borrow from commercial finance companies; state, local, and federal governments; and the public bond market. The larger the business, the more likely it is to be eligible for all of these debt sources. Conversely, the smaller the business, the more likely it is to be eligible to use only banks, government, and commercial loan sources.

The discussion in this chapter will be limited to the traditional sources of debt capital: banks, commercial financial lenders, and government (such as Small Business Administration loans). This chapter also will include details concerning financial leverage, the types of loans that are available from the different sources, the physical requirements of loan applications, and the accounting implications of debt financing.

FINANCIAL LEVERAGE

Financial leverage is customarily defined as the ratio of total debt to total assets. For instance, a firm with assets of $1 million and total debt of $500,000 has a leverage factor of 50 percent ($500,000/$1,000,000)

Perhaps the best way to understand the proper use of financial leverage is to analyze its impact on profitability under varying conditions. For instance, the example of three firms in the salvage industry Acme Salvage, Best Salvage, and Caustic Salvage, identical except for their debt percentage, can be cited. Acme Salvage has used no debt and consequently has a leverage factor of zero. Since Best Salvage has financed its firm half by debt and half by equity, it follows that they have a leverage factor of 50 percent. Caustic Salvage has a leverage factor of 75 percent. The companies' balance sheets appear in Exhibit 8.1.

EXHIBIT 8.1
Financial Leverage

Acme Salvage

		Total debt	$ -0-
		Net worth	$100
Total assets	$100	Total liab. & Worth	$100

Best Salvage

		Total debt @ 8%	$ 50
		Net worth	$ 50
Total assets	$100	Total liab. & Worth	$100

Caustic Salvage

		Total debt @ 8%	$ 75
		Net worth	$ 25
Total assets	$100	Total liab. & Worth	$100

How capitalization affects different companies' stockholder returns depends on the state of the economy in the industry. When the economy is depressed, it can be assumed that because sales and profit margins are low, the firms may earn 4 percent on assets. However, when the economy is brighter, 8 percent return is possible. Under normal conditions, these firms will earn 11 percent, under good conditions, 15 percent and a 20 percent rate of return on assets, if the industry economy is very good. Exhibit 8.2 shows how the use of financial leverage magnifies the impact on stockholders (or firm owners) who are directly related to changes in the rate of return on assets.

EXHIBIT 8.2
Economic Conditions

	Very Poor	Poor	Normal	Very Good	Good
Rate of return on total assets before interest	4%	8%	11%	15%	20%
Dollar return on total assets before interest	$4	8	11	15	20

Acme Salvage: Leverage 0

	Very Poor	Poor	Normal	Very Good	Good
Earnings in dollars	$4	8	11	15	20
Less: Int. Expense	$0	0	0	0	0
Gross income	$4	8	11	15	20
Taxes (50%)*	$2	4	5.5	7.5	10
Available to Owners	$2	4	5.5	7.5	10
Percent Return on Equity	2%	4%	5.5%	7.5%	10%

Best Salvage: Leverage 50%

	Very Poor	Poor	Normal	Very Good	Good
Earnings in dollars	$4	8	11	15	20
Less: Int. Expense	$4	4	4	4	4
Gross Income	$0	4	7	11	16
Taxes (50%)*	$0	2	3.5	5.5	8
Available to Owners	$0	2	3.5	5.5	8
Percent Return on Equity	0%	4%	7%	11%	16%

EXHIBIT 8.2
continued

Caustic Salvage: Leverage 75%

Earnings in dollars	$4	8	11	15	20
Less: Int. Expense	$6	6	6	6	6
Gross Income	$(2)	2	5	9	14
Taxes (50%)*	$(1)	1	2.5	4.5	7
Available to Owners	$(1)	1	2.5	4.5	7
Percent Return on Equity	−4%	4%	10%	18%	28%

*The tax calculation assumes tax credits for losses

As shown in the exhibits, when economic conditions go from normal to good, returns on assets for Acme (no leverage) goes up 36.4 percent. Return on equity for Best (50 percent leverage) increases 57.1 percent, and return on equity for Caustic (75 percent leverage) goes up a full 80 percent. A reverse action sets in if the economy is depressed. When the economy drops from normal to poor, Acme's return on equity declines only 27 percent; whereas Best, with a higher leverage, has a decline in return on equity of 42.9 percent. Caustic, which has the highest leverage, shows a decline in return on equity of a full 60 percent. In other words, the companies with the highest leverage (most debt as a percentage of total assets) receive the best return for owners' capital in normal or good times — but the worst return on equity in depressed economic times. The companies with the least leverage (least debt as a percentage of total assets) reap the best return in times of a depressed economy.

Using the same statistics, Exhibit 8.3 represents a graphic presentation of the interaction between rates of return on assets and net worth (equity), given the three different leverage factors. It should be noted here that the intersection of the three lines is at the point where assets are returning 8 percent, the interest cost of the debt. At this point, the return on net worth is 4 percent. The assumed 50 percent tax rate reduces the 8 percent return on total assets to a return of 4 percent on net worth regardless of the degree of leverage. When returns on assets are higher, leverage improves stockholder (or owner) returns and is considered to be favorable. When assets earn less than 8 percent, returns to owners are considered to be unfavorable. In general, whenever the return on assets

EXHIBIT 8.3
Relation Between Rates of Return on Assets and Rates of
Return on Net Worth Under Different Conditions

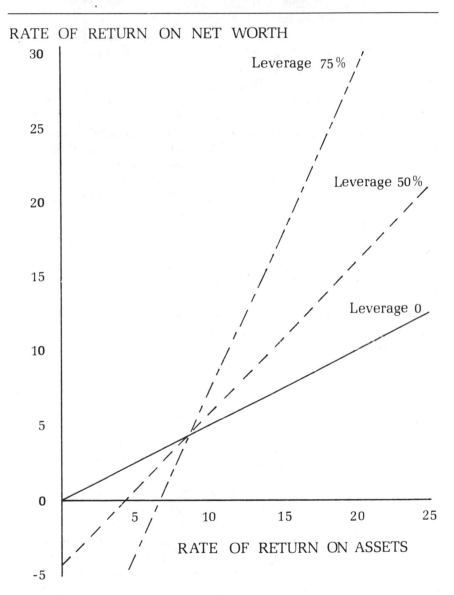

RATE OF RETURN ON NET WORTH

exceeds the cost of debt, leverage is favorable. Consequently, the higher the leverage factor is, the higher is the rate of return on owners' equity.

Expectedly, wide variations on the use of financial leverage may be observed among industries and also among the individual firms in each industry. Service industries use the most leverage, reflecting the fact that service industries generally include financial institutions that typically have high liabilities; but more importantly, many smaller firms in the service industries, as a group, are heavy users of debt. Public utility use of debt stems from a heavy fixed asset investment, coupled with extremely stable sales. Mining and manufacturing firms use relatively less debt because of their exposure to fluctuating sales.

In the manufacturing industries, wide variations in leverage are observed for individual industries. The lowest debt ratios are found in textile manufacturing due to their great competitive pressures. Low debt ratios also are found in the durable goods industries — the highest reliance on debt is found in consumer nondurable goods industries, where demand is relatively insensitive to fluctuations and general business activity.

SOURCES OF DEBT CAPITAL

Excluding public debt offerings, there are basically three sources for debt capital: banks, commercial finance companies, and government agencies.

Banks

The *advantages* of securing a bank loan are:

1. In general, with the exception of a few government and private programs, borrowing from a bank is the least expensive way to borrow.
2. Borrowing from a bank — as opposed to a government or commercial source — is usually better for your credit rating.
3. Banks have the largest loan bredth, that is, more types of loans.
4. Banks offer many business services including: credit references on customers, or potential customers of your business; financial, investment, and estate advisory services; discounting services for customers' accounts and notes payable; safe deposit boxes; night depositories.

The *disadvantages* of dealing with banks include:

1. The financially conservative nature of banks may cause difficulties; that is, bank loans are the most difficult of the loans to obtain.
2. In banks that have many branches, there is a tendency to have branch manager work at one branch for one or two years, with the result that it is difficult to develop a long-term relationship with that branch manager.
3. The technical requirements (financial spreads, projected budgets, corporate and ownership information, and other details) of presenting a loan are greater with a bank than with other sources.
4. Since banks are regulated by the federal government, and also are a profit-making organization, they must be careful that their loans do not fail. For most long-term loans, banks demand annual, semiannual, quarterly, or even monthly income statements and balance sheets for the purpose of observing business carefully. It is well to remember that they have the records of every check you have ever written.

QUESTION: *What is the best time and the worst time to approach a bank for money?*

ANSWER:
Of course, depending on your personal or company situation, anytime might be a good time or bad time, irrespective of external influences and bank policies. Moreover, a person might fall into one or the other categories of what is called the unwritten golden rule of borrowing, which says: "If you do not need money, that is the best time to get a loan."

From the point of view of the bank and the economy, here are the best times and situations under which to borrow, and the worst times and situations in which to borrow. The best environment for borrowing is:

1. When interest rates are generally low. This means two things — that the bank has more money to loan than it usually does and that the borrower will get a better deal.
2. When a bank has just opened. New banks, especially independent banks, are looking for businesses, especially deposit business. New banks will usually take more chances with a marginal business because they have to build up their loan portfolio. Sometimes the businessperson will find, however, that new banks are conservative; but if this person starts building a rela-

tionship immediately, and does not ask for a loan at the start, the bank will lend when they get better acquainted. Incidentally, in the case of a sizable business, banking with a small independent bank will perhaps mean that the new deposit is the largest. If you are their biggest depositor, they will be anxious to give good service.

3. When the economy is in an up-turn. That is, sales all over the economy are increasing, the stock market is up, and disposable consumer income is up. This condition might be reflected in lower interest rates, although not necessarily.

4. When banks in a particular area are in heavy competition, it might mean that there are too many banks in a new, developing area. To detect this competition, note if more than one bank is soliciting new business, or if banks are offering premiums for new deposits, such as, toasters, calculators, and other gifts.

5. When banks are in a generally expansionary process. During the 1960s, banks overthrew the traditional conservatism and started expanding their branch systems, including international branches, tremendously. Since there was more competition and a downgrading of traditional restraints, it follows that money was easier to get. One new aspect of banking may spark expansion — electronic banking devices, called consumer-bank communication terminals, or CBCTs. CBCTs are the electronic devices, located outside supermarkets or shopping centers, that dispense money or allow deposits without going to the bank. If the use of these devices becomes widespread, then the banks with the most deposits will also have more money to loan, at least for a while.

6. When a bank, customarily a large bank, has a special program to take high-risk loans as its moral obligation. Loans to minorities and special groups, such as Vietnam veterans, the handicapped, and displaced persons, are examples. The large banks sometimes set aside sums for these special high-risk loans. Beware, however, regardless of the bank's good intentions, if the economy is bad or if there is a high demand on loan funds. These special loans could be forced out.

The worst environment for borrowing is:

1. When interest rates are high. High rates mean that not only is there a large demand on bank funds, and in many cases, from

large, secure "Fortune 500"-type firms, but also that the bank might have reached its loan limit, as far as loan-to-deposit ratio is concerned. High interest rates do not mean that money is merely more expensive; they mean there is less of it to borrow. This was the situation in 1979.

2.   When the economy is in a recession. In recessionary times, regardless of other influences, banks tend to be more conservative in their lending. There are more chances for a business to fail in a recession. Furthermore, there is usually high demand for money in any established businesses.

3.   When a bank has reached its lending limit, or when the bank has decided to decrease its dollars outstanding to make the bank more liquid. When there is an extremely high demand for funds, the bank is tempted to loan money to secure businesses at high rates and therefore to make a better profit. There is a limit to how much money a bank can loan out — that limit is the maximum loan-to-deposit ratio. The *loan-to-deposit ratio* is simply the total loans outstanding divided by the total number of deposits. During the dark days of 1974, the banks were sometimes loaned up to 75 percent of their deposits. This situation carried potential trouble for the banks. If only 26 percent of the depositors took out their money, the bank would be in serious trouble, perhaps would go into bankruptcy. Even this 75 percent loan-to-deposit ratio might be misleading. Banks must report their loan-to-deposit ratio to the federal government once a week. Money could be borrowed from other banks for twenty-four hours to increase deposits to support the ratio. In years past, (first part of the twentieth century), the banks would seldom exceed 33 percent loan-to-deposit ratio. Consequently, it is easily seen that 75 percent is a narrow margin.

In 1975, when money became looser, loans did not necessarily follow. Although more money was available to lend out, the banks wanted to keep the money to build up their loan-to-deposit ratio and thereby make the ratio healthier.

4.   When there is very little bank competition for loans and deposits. A one-bank town is a perfect example. The best procedure to follow is to go to another town for financing.

5.   When the parent bank is in trouble or suffers severe losses. In 1973, when United California Bank had trouble with a Swiss subsidiary, for example, it was difficult to get financing from the

branches. The business section of your newspaper, the *Wall Street Journal, Business Week,* or other business publications will give indications of the bank's economic condition.

Needless to say, it is not always possible to wait for the right time to get a loan, but these "best and worst" lists will provide an assessment of the current money market.

Commercial Lenders

Commercial lenders, including commercial finance companies (factors, industrial time sales, leases), life insurance companies, foundations, and other private financial companies, usually have higher interest rates than banks, but they may make more border-line loans than banks.

Commercial lenders, in general, are more lenient with less financially strong businesses than are banks. Furthermore, commercial lenders are willing to take as security items that banks are prone to refuse, such as inventories and receivables. In short, the major advantage of commercial lenders is their flexibility.

The major disadvantage of commercial lenders lies in the fact that their interest rates are higher and sometimes much higher than banks.

Life insurance companies, pension funds, and foundations in specific cases sometimes offer money for business real estate, equipment, and working capital in larger amounts than do banks. Their interest rates are usually only slightly higher than are banks. The disadvantage of these companies is that they customarily make large loans only (in excess of $1,000,000) that require the applicant companies be financially strong, thereby eliminating most small business from consideration.

Government Loans

The largest single lender to business in the United States is the federal government—followed by state and local governments. The federal government lending program exceeds the loan programs of Bank of America, Chase Manhattan, Citi Bank, J.P. Morgan, and the rest of the ten largest banks in America. The United States government alone lends more than $1.852 trillion per year to business.

Without question, the loans with the lowest rate of interest available in this country are made by the government. Unfortunately, only a few special businesses, under very special circumstances, qualify for these loans. Most businesses, however, do qualify for government loans that have interest at a few points over prime. Although most government loans carry interest rates that are the same as or a little higher than bank rates, the government will make loans to higher-risk businesses than will the banks. For instance, a start-up business that requires $100,000 in capital but has only $35,000 would not qualify for a loan at a bank at any interest rate. The same business, however, would qualify for a Small Business Administration (SBA) loan at close to bank interest rates.

For most government loans, the equity requirements are less than those of a bank. For a start-up business, banks usually require 50 percent equity, whereas government loans require from 10 percent to 45 percent equity. A case in point is a person who wants to start a business with capital of $15,000 in cash. At the bank, he is eligible for a maximum loan of another $15,000, making a total of $30,000. If the same person applied for a government loan, then the applicant could receive $18,300 to $150,000, depending on the loan program. The advantages of starting a business with $45,000 instead of $30,000 can make a difference in the long-range success of that business.

Since the repayment period for government loans is usually longer than the repayment period for bank loans, it follows that a businessperson's monthly payment is customarily lower for a government loan than for a bank loan. For example, if a business borrows $10,000 for three years (bank average) at 10.25 percent, then the monthly payments are $323.85. If, on the other hand, the same firm borrows the same amount ($10,000) at the same interest rate (10.25 percent) for seven years instead of three years, then the monthly payments are $167.31, or $156.54 less per month than the three-year loan.

As well as these advantages of government loans, there are also some significant disadvantages. Government loans and government-guaranteed loans take from two months to two years to receive approval. The required paperwork and research for government loans is four times that of a bank loan and twice that of a commercial loan. In short, the greatest disadvantages of government loans are the time required for approval and the paperwork involved.

TYPES OF LOANS AVAILABLE FROM BANKS, COMMERCIAL, AND GOVERNMENT LENDERS

A listing of the types of loans that are available to the businessperson and a brief discussion of the kind of financing for which each is used follows.

Bank Loans

Loans that run from 30 to 90 days are called *short-term loans*. Short-term loans are customarily granted to finance inventory on which the businessperson can expect to get returns in a short period of time. New businesses seldom use short-term loans for the reason that it is difficult for a new business to realize profit during the first few months of operations. However, short-term loans are used extensively for existing businesses.

Intermediate-term loans run for more than one year, but less than five years; equipment loans fall into this category. Many businesses that request a bank loan will receive this type of loan term unless they are financing property or getting a government-guaranteed loan. If a person intends to buy an existing business and borrows money on a regular bank loan, then a loan of from three to five years' duration is probably the choice.

Long-term loans are made for five years or more. Government-guaranteed loans fall into this category, although banks will also make long-term loans on improvements and property.

Term loans are further classified as secured and unsecured loans. *Secured loans* require security; that is, the businessperson must pledge some physical property of value as security or collateral for the loan. A loan for buying equipment is a good example of a secured loan. Equipment is pledged as security that the bank can repossess in the event the borrower is unable to make the payments. *Unsecured loans* have no collateral pledged. Unsecured loans are usually granted on your good name, which is synonymous with the strength of your credit in general and in particular with that bank.

Rarely will a new businessperson, or an expanding business, obtain an unsecured loan. Even government-guaranteed loans are *partially secured* (not totally supported by collateral, but supported with collateral to a large extent).

Secured loans fall into four categories: loans secured by liquid assets (stocks, bonds, or cash); loans secured by accounts receivable; loans secured by inventory; and loans secured by fixed assets (equipment, improvements, and property).

Liquid asset loans use savings accounts, stocks, or bonds for collateral. In this kind of loan, the business deposits stock, bonds, or savings with the bank. In return, the bank loans an amount equal to (for savings) or less than (with stocks and bonds having fluctuating market value) the amount of the security. The advantage of this type of loan is that the interest rate charged is not excessive (one to two percent over what you are earning on savings or near prime in the case of stocks or bonds).

Accounts receivable secured loans, which includes both factoring and accounts receivables financing, are not available to a business just starting out. Accounts receivable financing and especially factoring tend to be expensive ways to finance a business. This type of financing is best used in a situation in which sales are growing faster than cash flow. In accounts-receivable financing (which is less costly than factoring), if the lender loans up to 80 percent of the value of the borrower's receivables (assuming all the accounts are reasonably good), then the customer pays the firm and the firm brings the endorsed check to the lender. In factoring, the lender buys the firm's accounts. When a factor buys receivables, the customer pays the factor directly and receives a statement stating that the account is owned by that factor.

Inventory loans are made to businesses that have inventory that will be tied up for a long period of time. One example of this type of business is a new car lot. It is necessary for the business to retain expensive inventory (cars) on the lot for long periods of time before they are sold. In the instance of a car lot, the company has physical possession of the inventory, but the bank owns the title. However, in the type of inventory financing used for new car lots, termed *flooring*, the borrower keeps the merchandise on the floor.

Inventory loans are not made for inventory that is: made up of many items of different prices (grocery, hardware, and most retail businesses); fast-selling items; or is work-in-process (the uncompleted goods in manufacturing). A businessperson can, however, borrow on this generally nonfinancable inventory if a business loan is received rather than an inventory loan, which includes other items such as equipment, signs, and additional property.

Fixed-asset secured loans are made for large capital items such as equipment, land and buildings, improvements, and fixtures. Fixed-asset loans are usually for the longest period of all the secured loans discussed. All fixed-asset loans are for terms of at least two years and usually exceed five years in length. Real estate loans are a good example of secured fixed-asset loans.

Government-guaranteed loans are the kind of loans that should interest most businessmen. For most beginning small businesses, the best government-guaranteed loan is the SBA guaranteed loan. This SBA loan guarantees the bank 90 percent against loss. This guarantee means that when $100,000 is borrowed from a bank with a SBA guarantee, the bank will be paid 90 percent of the loss, or $90,000, even if all of the money is lost during the first week. The SBA-guaranteed loan is for high-risk types of business, that is, for small and especially new businesses. The borrower must meet other requirements that are available from the local SBA. In most cases, however, small and new start-up businesses qualify.

Commercial Finance Companies

Types of loans available from commercial finance companies include: inventory loans; equipment and fixture loans (including commercial time financing); accounts receivable loans (including commercial time financing); and equipment leasing (leasing companies).

Inventory loans are available to accounts receivable and factoring clients. Such loans are frequently used to help the customer during periods of slow product shipments and inventory build-up or to facilitate bulk raw material purchases at advantageous prices.

Equipment loans include, two types:

1. Money loaned against presently owned equipment
2. Money loaned to finance new equipment and financed on a time sales financing basis.

On presently owned equipment, commercial finance companies will occasionally make loans. These funds are normally amortized monthly over a period of from one to five years, or even longer. The proceeds from this type of loan may require the borrower to increase working capital, discount accounts payable, or simply to purchase new equipment. Often, an equipment loan is accepted in conjunction with accounts receivable or factoring arrangements.

Industrial time sales financing is the procedure wherein a company buys equipment from an equipment supplier and the equipment supplier sells the purchase contract to a financier.

The price paid for buying installment equipment is usually high — higher, in fact, than the highest interest allowable by the state. The additional cost of financing can be higher than the maximum allowable interest rate because interest is not paid on industrial installment loans. The payment is called a *time price differential.*

The cost of buying on installment, called the time price differential, has the following rationale. A seller is presumed to have two prices: the cash price; and the time price, which assumes that the purchaser, who wants credit over a period of time, must pay an added charge to compensate the seller for his additional burden. The differential between the cash price and the time is the time price differential. This reasoning assumes that the seller is not a money lender. The price doctrine provides the legal mechanism to remove the time sale from the application of usury laws (the state laws that restrict the maximum interest chargeable on secured loans) in holding that the transaction is a credit sale and is neither a loan nor a forebearance for money.

Accounts receivable loans are the bread and butter of commercial finance companies. In fact, the commercial finance companies were originally set up to deal with these accounts. Accounts receivable loans fall into two categories: accounts receivable financing and factoring.

Accounts receivable financing at banks is nearly identical to accounts receivable financing by commercial finance companies. Accounts receivable can be pledged as collateral for loans. Characteristically, an 80 percent advance is made against eligible accounts. The assignment is handled on a nonnotification revolving basis and is self-liquidating. Interest charges are billed on the basis of actual daily cash loan balances. This monthly charge is frequently less than missed cash discounts.

Factoring is slightly different from accounts receivable financing. *Factoring* is the outright sale of trade accounts on a nonrecourse basis. Factoring enables a business to eliminate a credit and collection department as well as losses due to bad debts. A factor buys outright all accounts receivable approved by it at a nominal discount. This enables the client to concentrate on production, purchasing, and selling — the profit tools of any business.

A factor puts his legend on the bills, and the factor is paid directly by the customer. In this way, accounts receivable are assigned on a notification basis.

Categorically, there are three types of factoring: maturity factoring, advance factoring, and drop shipment factoring.

What accounts will a factor or accounts receivables lender take? What are the the considerations involved? These questions are important when deciding whether to use accounts receivable financing.

A lender's appraisal of what accounts are acceptable include two key elements:

1. Careful appraisal of the nature and value of the accounts that are the collateral for the loan
2. Estimates of the creditor pressure the borrower is under.

An accounts receivable borrower must do the following to get financing: turn over to the lender the checks from his customers in the form they are received; supply the lender with copies of invoices and the documentary evidence of shipments (usually parcel post receipts).

If the lender keeps a control ledger on the borrower for each account, then the ledger shows the amount assigned and advanced, as well as the amount remitted, and the balance.

An account of the costs and benefits of financing is well summarized in *Commercial Financing* (see Exhibit 8.4):

> The advantage to the borrower of pledging accounts is that it accelerates his cash flow. It frees his capital from the waiting period required by normal trade terms. In effect, the financier does the waiting [for the payment by the account debtors] and the borrower's capital can be more profitably re-employed for other purposes. The increased rate of turnover of the borrower's capital enhances the leverage of that capital and should produce increased profits. More specifically, the accelerated cash flow can result in any combination of tangible results such as increased volume, earning of trade discounts on purchases from suppliers, or development of ability to make more advantageous purchases by having available cash.[1]

Leasing is also a type of financing, as well as a way of financing the full amount of the needed equipment, fixtures, or buildings. Leasing is the infant of the traditional, funding methods. There is still a lot of debate, however, on its benefits for businessmen. To add to the controversy, there are no standards for leasing. A piece of equipment can be rented with or without maintenance, or with partial maintenance, or leased by the month, year, or several years. Leases can also be obtained with the option to purchase. So far, the leasing of working capital has not been tried.

Leasing is more fully discussed in Chapter 9; the following gives some of the advantages and disadvantages of leasing. Some of the advantages of leasing are:

1. Leasing offers a tax advantage. When property is owned outright, not only does it necessitate lengthy bookkeeping to calculate depreciation for tax purposes, but also the cost is recovered only slowly. If inflation proceeds at the same pace as in recent years, the tax saving becomes due to the decreasing value of the dollar, as the depreciation table stretches into the future. Despite current efforts to slow inflation, there is little reason to expect that it can be kept under control. Leasing expenses are operating expenses

[1]R. Monroe Lazere, *Commercial Financing.* New York: Roland Press Co., 1968.

EXHIBIT 8.4
Accounts Receivable Financing

Date	Accounts Assigned	Cash Advanced	Cash Collected	Equity Remitted	Collateral Balance	Loan Balance
11/1	$10,000	$8,000	—	—	$ 10,000	$ 8,000
11/2	10,000	8,000	—	—	20,000	16,000
11/3	10,000	8,000	—	—	30,000	24,000
11/4	10,000	8,000	—	—	40,000	32,000
11/5	10,000	8,000	—	—	50,000	40,000
11/6	10,000	8,000	—	—	60,000	48,000
11/7	10,000	8,000	—	—	70,000	56,000
11/8	10,000	8,000	—	—	80,000	64,000
11/9	10,000	8,000	—	—	90,000	72,000
11/10	10,000	8,000	—	—	100,000	80,000
11/11	—	—	—	—	100,000	80,000
11/12	—	—	$10,000	$2,000	90,000	72,000
11/13	—	—	10,000	2,000	80,000	64,000
11/14	—	—	10,000	2,000	70,000	56,000
11/15	—	—	10,000	2,000	60,000	48,000
11/16	—	—	10,000	2,000	50,000	40,000
11/17	—	—	10,000	2,000	40,000	32,000
11/18	—	—	10,000	2,000	30,000	24,000
11/19	—	—	10,000	2,000	20,000	16,000
11/20	—	—	10,000	2,000	10,000	8,000
11/21	—	—	—	—	10,000	8,000
11/22	—	—	—	—	10,000	8,000
11/23	—	—	—	—	10,000	8,000
11/24	10,000	8,000	—	—	20,000	16,000
11/25	10,000	8,000	—	—	30,000	24,000
11/26	10,000	8,000	—	—	40,000	32,000
11/27	—	—	—	—	40,000	32,000
11/28	—	—	—	—	40,000	32,000
11/29	—	—	—	—	40,000	32,000
11/30	—	—	—	—	40,000	32,000

Source: *Commercial Financing, R. Monroe Lazere, Roland Press Co., New York, 1968.

and do not have to be depreciated, extended, held to future years, or back-charged to previous years.

2. In the choice of a maintenance contract with the lease (a good

example is maintenance-included leases on copy machines), the maintence is done by the maintenance company.

3. When a lease expires the equipment is returned to the lessor even if it is outmoded or inefficient; no more payments are required. In short, leasing is more flexible than ownership.
4. The lessee need not worry about the obsolescence of equipment — merely stop the lease.
5. The cost of the equipment is fixed by the lease agreement, making the cost predictable for projections.
6. Money that might be tied up in expensive fixed assets can be used for other purposes.

The disadvantages of leasing include:

1. The counterargument against the tax advantages of leasing holds for which a purchaser of equipment may take depreciation and interest as tax deductible expenses. Studies of comparative tables of parallel transactions (using the same depreciation formula, cost of equipment, and interest charge) are available for reference. These conclusions indicate that leasing does not increase or decrease the total tax savings. Furthermore, as the lease term is extended the annual differential on tax savings seems to become less.
2. Down payments from leasing were at one time less costly than purchase down payments. Now, however, the prepayments on leases are only 2 to 5 percent less than the down payment required for a purchase contract.
3. The costs for purchasing or buying are about the same, but when the equipment is purchased from the leasing company at the end of the period, the costs of leasing are higher.
4. If a company loses control over maintenance, then it is at the mercy of the leasing company when the equipment needs repairs and the amount of downtime involved.

In short, leasing requires a little less down payment at the start, but is generally more expensive than standard equipment purchase. Leasing is most satisfactory if you need the flexibility of temporary use of the equipment. See further discussion of leasing in Chapter 9 under the section entitled "Cost Comparison."

Due to the growth of the industry, the accumulation of assets in life insurance companies has been rapid and substantial. It has been estimated that these companies are accumulating assets at the rate of $6 billion per year. The outflow of their funds can be statistically predicted. Hence, a part of their portfolio is available for long-term financing in the form of mortgages on industrial, commercial, and housing real estate. Loans are also made to businesses but require substantial enterprises with long earnings records and dealing in markets not subject to rapid change. The average small or medium-sized business does not qualify, however, because life insurance companies must follow certain loan policies: 1. borrower has to be a corporation; 2. there is a minimum time for the borrower to be in business; 3. the borrower should have sufficient historical and current earnings to meet a formula of established obligations, including debt repayments. A life insurance company grants two types of loans: commercial and industrial mortgage loans and unsecured loans. The costs for mortgages by insurance companies are comparable to traditional bank loans.

A prevailing type of life insurance company loans is on an unsecured basis to a business with good financial standing. Life insurance lenders are most interested in long-range financial data demonstrated by projected sales, cash flows, and others.

In addition to the sources mentioned, less known sources of capital include: credit union and pension funds and foundations.

1. Credit unions make loans. A member of a credit union can get reasonable interest loans for small amounts. Credit union services are offered only to members of credit unions; the credit union law restricts membership within any single credit union to a homogeneous group of members with like interests. Credit union laws restrict the rate of interest charge and the amount of allowable loan for a single borrower.
2. Pension funds and foundations, due to investment returns, have experienced a rapid and large accumulation of assets with a predictable outflow. Their standards of investment are also similar to those of the life insurance companies and charges are about the same for interest rates. A substantial percentage of pension funds is used for sale-leasehold arrangements. Foundations make loans in excess of $1,000,000 for periods averaging ten years. When applicants are evaluated, special emphasis is placed on company management, business background, and realistic projections.

Applying for Government Loans

Exhibit 8.5 contains data on loan-granting, government agencies, and the types of loans obtainable and may be helpful to those interested.

Guidelines for government loans differ with each loan-granting organization, but in general, the government tries to assist business in order to increase employment when it would otherwise be financially difficult for that business. The government guarantees loans to businesses in financial situations that banks and other financial institutions will not. Private and commercial lenders tend not to make risky loans in nontraditional lending categories.

Although government loans are not easily obtained, yet the government agencies tend to loan money to high-risk businesses with usually low interest rates. However, the loan requirements are generally complicated.

Applying for government loans requires time and effort to prepare the necessary documentation. The technical requirements — the proposal (business analysis, including budgets) — requires many details and technical work. If a firm decides to apply for government loans it is then advisable to consult a specialist in the field. Another alternative is to read *Business Loans: A Guide to Money Sources and How to Approach Them Successfully* by Rick Stephan Hayes, (co-author of this book), published in 1977 by CBI Publishing Company, Boston. This book covers all the procedures and requirements of government loans in detail.

LETTERS OF CREDIT

The letter of credit is a special category of loans used for importers and exporters.

Few hard and fast rules exist for letters of credit. Each one is different. This type of loan is made on the merits and circumstances of the particular case. Other than the time period involved, however, export letters of credit fall into a few basic types:

1. *Revocable credits* are credits, or more properly *advices*, issued by a bank abroad on behalf of a customer (the importer) processed through a United States bank in favor of the exporter (or beneficiary). (See Exhibit 8.6.) This advice or process may be amended or cancelled at any time, with or without notification from the exporter. Revocable credits are given merely to assist the shipper

EXHIBIT 8.5
Government Loans

The following is a list of all the government agencies that make business loans, and the types of loans they make.

Type of Loan	Purpose	Who May Apply	Where to Apply
Small Business Administration			
Business Loans	To assist small firms to finance construction, conversion, or expansion; to purchase equipment, facilities, machinery, supplies or materials; and to acquire working capital. Loans are direct or in participation with banks.	Small Businesses	Nearest SBA Field Office
Economic Opportunity Loans	To assist small firms operated by those who have marginal or submarginal incomes or those who have been denied equal opportunity (Title IV of the Economic Opportunity Act).	Low-income disadvantaged persons desiring to strengthen or establish a small business	Nearest SBA Field Office
Disaster Loans	To assist disaster victims to rebuild homes or business establishments damaged in SBA-declared disaster areas.	Individuals, business concerns, and nonprofit organizations	Nearest SBA Field Office

EXHIBIT 8.5
continued

Type of Loan	Purpose	Who May Apply	Where to Apply
Economic Injury Loans	To assist small concerns suffering economic injury resulting from: (1) a major or natural disaster declared by the President or Secretary of Agriculture; (2) Federally-aided urban renewal or highway construction programs; (3) inability to market or process a product because of disease or toxicity resulting from natural or undetermined causes; (4) US trade agreements.	Small business firms suffering such economic injury	Nearest SBA Field Office
Development Company Loans	To assist small firms by helping to establish and finance the operation of state and local small business development companies which make loans to small firms for equity capital, plant construction, conversion, or expansion.	State and local development companies	Nearest SBA Field Office

Economic Development Administration (EDA)

Business or Public Loans	To aid unemployment and underemployment areas in their economic development	States or components, nonprofit organizations, and private borrowers	Administrator, Economic Development Administration, Washington, DC 20230
Export-Import Bank of the United States (Eximbank) and Overseas Private Investment Corporation	Export-Import Bank of the United States (Ex-Im Bank): To assist in financing US foreign trade through the following programs (in all cases, advance commitments are available without charge).		
	Authorizing the Foreign Credit Insurance Association (FCIA) to issue policies covering commercial and/or political risks on short and medium-term credit extended by US exporters to their overseas customers.	Exporters or banks	Exporters' insurance agent or broker, or directly to FCIA, 250 Broadway, New York, NY 10007
	Guaranteeing payment of medium-term export paper purchased without recourse by commercial banks.	Commercial banks and Edge Act Corporations	Commercial banks apply to Eximbank (exporter applies to his bank)
	Guarantees directly to US firms covering commercial and political risks involved in the performance of services abroad and in the leasing, consignment, or exhibition of US goods in foreign markets.	Exporters	Eximbank, Washington, DC 20571

EXHIBIT 8.5
continued

Type of Loan	Purpose	Who May Apply	Where to Apply
	Direct loans to overseas buyer of US goods and services, enabling them to pay cash to the US exporters.	Overseas buyers or interested exporters	Eximbank, Washington, DC 20571
	"Discount" loans against eligible export debt obligations held by commercial banks, providing liquidity to banks financing US exports and, where necessary, more competitive interest rates.	Commercial banks; Edge Act Corporations	Eximbank, Washington, DC 20571

Overseas Private Investment Corporation (OPIC)

Private Enterprise Development	OPIC offers a variety of services to private US companies interested in establishing new businesses or expanding present facilities in less developed countries. These services include investment information and counseling; preinvestment and project development financing;	US citizens or corporations, partnerships, or associations substantially and beneficially US-owned	OPIC, Washington, DC 20527

project insurance against the risks of currency inconvertibility, expropriation, and war, revolution or insurrection; and project financing through loan guaranties and direct dollar and local currency loans.

Agricultural Business Loans Commodity Credit Corporation (Department of Agriculture)

Agricultural	To provide nonrecourse loans on commodities stored on the farm or in commercial warehouses in order to provide price support and enable farmers to carry out an orderly marketing program.	Farmers	The local county office of the Agricultural Stabilization and Conservation Service
	To expand or build farm storage facilities, or to buy drying equipment for use with stored commodities.	Farmers	The local county office of the ASCS

Farmers Home Administration (Department of Agriculture)

Operating	To family farmers for land improvement, equipment, labor, and development resources necessary to successful farming including the development of recreational and other nonfarm enterprises to be operated on the farms.	Operators of not larger than family farms	Local farmers Home Administration office

EXHIBIT 8.5
continued

Type of Loan	Purpose	Who May Apply	Where to Apply
Farm Ownership	To buy, improve, or enlarge farms and to provide essential services including buildings and land for nonfarm enterprises needed to supplement farm incomes.	Farmers and ranchers who are or will become operators of not larger than family farms	Local FHA office
Irrigation	Loans to develop irrigation systems, drain farmland, and carry out soil conservation measures.	Groups of farmers and ranchers	Local FHA office
Grazing and Forest Lands	Loans for shifts in land use to develop grazing areas and forest lands.	Groups of farmers and ranchers	Local FHA office
Rural Housing	To construct and repair needed homes and essential farm buildings, purchase previously occupied homes, or buy sites on which to build homes.	Farmers and other rural residents in open country and rural communities of not more than 5,500	Local FHA office
Rural Rental Housing	Loans to provide rental housing for the rural elderly and for younger rural residents of low and moderate income.	Individuals, profit corporations, private nonprofit corporations	Local FHA office

Housing for Labor	Loans to finance housing facilities for domestic farm labor.	Individual farmers, groups of farmers, and public or private nonprofit organizations	Local FHA office
Conditional Commitments	Assurance to builder or seller that homes to be constructed or rehabilitated will meet FHA lending requirements if built as proposed and that the agency would be willing to make loans to qualified applicants who may want to buy homes.	Individual, partnership, or corporations engaged in construction of homes	Local FHA office
Disaster	Emergency loans in designated areas where natural disasters such as floods and droughts have brought about a temporary need for credit not available from other sources.	Farmers	Local FHA office

Farm Credit Administration (An independent agency that supervises nationwide farmer-owned and controlled Farm Credit System.)

Banks for cooperatives	To provide complete loan service for farmer cooperatives.	Farmers cooperatives	Bank for cooperatives serving area
Federal Land Banks	To provide long-term mortgage credit to purchase, enlarge, or to improve farms, to refinance debts, and other purposes.	Farmers (full-time or part-time) and farming corporations	Federal land bank association serving area

EXHIBIT 8.5
continued

Type of Loan	Purpose	Who May Apply	Where to Apply
Production	To provide short- and intermediate-term credit for farm production, farm home, or farm family purposes.	Farmers (both full-time or part-time) and farming corporations	Production credit association serving area
Federal Reserve Board Guarantee			
Defense Production	To facilitate and expedite the financing of persons having contracts or engaged in operations deemed necessary for national defense.	Contractors, subcontractors, and others, doing business with Army, Navy, Air Force, Defense Supply, Agency, Interior, Agriculture, Commerce, GSA, AEC, or NASA	At a bank or other financing institutions, which in turn applies through a Federal Reserve Bank to the appropriate government department or agency for a loan guarantee
Other Loans	Other loans include, for the federal government: Veterans Administration; Maritime Administration; and Natural Resource Loans under the Department of the Interior. For the state and local governments, loans include: State of California Job Creation Law Board; and local development companies.		
Veterans Administration			
Real Estate Loans for Business	For the purchase of land or the purchase, construction, repair, alteration, or improvement of buildings to be used for the purchase of engaging	Eligible World War II, Korean Conflict, and Vietnam veterans	Nearest VA Office for approval of eligibility. Loan application is made to a bank or other private lender

Program	Purpose	Eligibility	Where to Apply
	in business or pursuing a gainful occupation.		Nearest VA Office for approval of eligibility. Loan application is made to a bank or other private lender
Farm Operation Loans	For the purchase of property other than real estate, such as supplies, equipment, machinery, etc. or for working capital required in operation of a farm.	Eligible World War II, Korean Conflict, and post-Korean veterans. Servicemen with at least two years active duty	Nearest VA Office for approval of eligibility. Loan application is made to a bank or other private lender
Business Loans	For the purchase of property other than real estate such as inventory, equipment, or machinery; or for working capital required for engaging in business or pursuing a gainful occupation.	Eligible World War II and Korean Conflict veterans	Nearest VA Office for eligibility. Loan application is made to a bank or other private lender
Housing Credit Shortage Loans	Direct Loans to provide for homes in certain designated housing credit shortage areas.	Eligible World War II, Korean Conflict, and post-Korean veterans. Servicemen with at least two years active duty	The VA office having jurisdiction over the area where the home is located

The Maritime Administration

Program	Purpose	Eligibility	Where to Apply
Shipbuilding	To insure construction loans and/or mortgages to aid in financing the construction, reconstruction, or reconditioning of vessels.	Private ship owners	Maritime Administration, Washington, DC 20235

EXHIBIT 8.5
continued

Type of Loan	Purpose	Who May Apply	Where to Apply
Natural Resource Loans, Department of Interior			
Bureau of Indian Affairs			
	To encourage industry and income producing enterprises and for the education of certain Indians needing funds for that purpose.	Indians, Eskimos, and Aleuts	The Indian Agency Superintendent or a local Indian relending organization
Geological Survey			
	To encourage domestic minerals exploration by providing financial assistance on a participating basis.	Individuals, partnerships, corporate enterprises	Field Offices and Washington, DC, Office of Minerals Exploration, Geological Survey
Bureau of Commercial Fisheries			
	To assist in strengthening the domestic fishing industry, loans are made to finance and refinance the cost of purchasing, constructing, equipping,	US citizens, as defined in Section 2 of the Shipping Act, 1916, as amended, who have the qualifications necessary to operate and maintain the	Division of Loans and Grants of a Regional Office of the Bureau of Commercial Fisheries, US Dept. of Interior

| | | vessel or gear to be used |
| maintaining, repairing, or operating new or used commercial fishing vessels or gear. | | |

Bureau of Reclamation

Loans and grants for the development of small reclamation projects, primarily for irrigation, in the seventeen western states and Hawaii.	Nonfederal entities having authority to contract with the US under federal reclamation law	Regional Offices of Bureau of Reclamation

Source: Rick Stephan Hayes *Business Loans*. CBI Publishing Company, Inc., Boston, Mass.

EXHIBIT 8.6
Advice of Authority to Pay

LETTERS OF CREDIT

SIGHT DRAFT   ### USANCE DRAFT

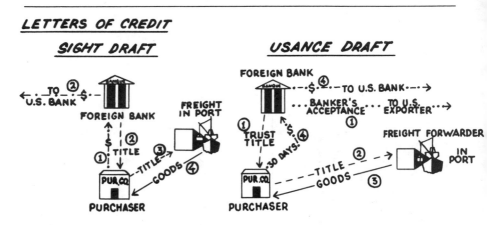

in preparing and presenting the necessary documents. It gives no
assurances that the draft and documents will be honored when
presented to the advising (exporter's) bank or the correspondent
bank.

2. *Unconfirmed irrevocable credits* (Exhibit 8.7) are letters of credit
    issued by a foreign bank on behalf of its customer in favor of the
    exporter and are advised (processed) through a United States
    bank. They contain an irrevocable obligation on the part of the
    foreign bank to honor the exporter's drafts and documents, pro-
    vided they fulfill the credit terms. This letter of credit cannot be
    cancelled or amended in any manner, without the consent of the
    exporter.

3. *Correspondent's irrevocable credit* (Exhibit 8.8) is a letter of
    credit issued by a foreign bank on behalf of its customer in favor
    of the exporter and is advised through a United States bank to
    honor the beneficiary's drafts and documents. In addition, some
    other banks add confirmation to the credit, obligating the
    domestic bank in the same manner as the foreign bank. To be
    amended or cancelled, the letter of credit must have the consent
    of the exporter and a fixed expiration date.

With *import* letters of credit (as opposed to the export letters of credit

EXHIBIT 8.7
Irrevocable Letter of Credit

CABLE ADDRESS

TRUST COMPANY
· NEW YORK, N. Y.,

CORRESPONDENT'S NO._____
_____OF_____

ADVICE OF AUTHORITY TO PAY

OUR NUMBER_____

(BENEF)

GENTLEMEN:

WE INFORM YOU THAT   (O/B)

HAVE AUTHORIZED US TO HONOR YOUR DRAFTS FOR ACCOUNT OF_____

FOR A SUM OR SUMS IN U.S. DOLLARS NOT EXCEEDING A TOTAL OF_____

ON US, AT_____ TO BE ACCOMPANIED BY:

(THIS IS A SAMPLE OF AN ADVICE OF AUTHORITY TO PAY - THIS
CONVEYS NO ENGAGEMENT ON OUR CORRESPONDENT OR ON OUR PART.)

ALL DRAFTS SO DRAWN MUST BE MARKED "DRAWN UNDER   TRUST COMPANY
ADVICE NO._____"·

DRAFTS SO DRAWN, WITH DOCUMENTS AS SPECIFIED, MUST BE PRESENTED AT OUR
OFFICE NOT LATER THAN_____·

THE AUTHORITY GIVEN TO US IS SUBJECT TO REVOCATION OR MODIFICATION AT ANY
TIME WITHOUT NOTICE TO YOU.

THIS AUTHORITY IS SUBJECT TO THE UNIFORM CUSTOMS AND PRACTICE FOR DOCUMENTARY
CREDITS (1962 REVISION), INTERNATIONAL CHAMBER OF COMMERCE BROCHURE NO. 222.

THIS ADVICE CONVEYS NO ENGAGEMENT ON OUR PART OR ON THE PART OF THE ABOVE
MENTIONED CORRESPONDENT AND IS SIMPLY FOR YOUR GUIDANCE IN PREPARING AND
PRESENTING DRAFTS AND DOCUMENTS.

VERY TRULY YOURS,

This credit/advice is subject to the Uniform Customs and Practice
for Documentary Credits (1962 Revision), International Chamber of
Commerce Brochure No. 222.

SPECIMEN

PER PRO.

EXHIBIT 8.8
Correspondent's Irrevocable Letter of Credit

CABLE ADDRESS

TRUST COMPANY
• NEW YORK, N. Y.,

IRREVOCABLE CREDIT NO.

□ Forwarded through   □ Copy sent to

Gentlemen:

We hereby authorize you to value on us,

for account of

for a sum or sums in U. S. Dollars not exceeding a total of

by your drafts at
accompanied by:

Partial shipments   permitted.
Bills of lading must be dated not later than

Drafts must be negotiated or presented to the drawee not later than

Insurance to be effected by
All negotiation charges are for your account.
All drafts must be marked "Drawn under   TRUST COMPANY Credit No.   ," and all draw-
ings negotiated under this credit must be endorsed on the reverse hereof by the party so negotiating. If any draft is
not negotiated, this credit and all documents as specified must accompany the draft.
This credit is subject to the Uniform Customs and Practice for Documentary Credits (1962 Revision), International
Chamber of Commerce Brochure No. 222.
We hereby agree with you and negotiating banks or bankers that drafts drawn under and in compliance with the
terms of this credit shall be duly honored on due presentation to the drawee.

Very truly yours,

F 3332
ABC 6-65
(10-65)

mentioned above) the same terms apply, but the United States bank issues
the letters for its customers, in this case, in favor of exporters from
overseas. The letters of credit are issued by a domestic bank for a
customer in favor of an exporter in a foreign country, usually located near

EXHIBIT 8.9
Standard Letter of Credit

TRUST COMPANY
· **NEW YORK, N. Y.,**

Correspondent's No.
Letter—Cable of
Our Number

ADVICE OF CORRESPONDENT'S
IRREVOCABLE STRAIGHT CREDIT

MAIL
TO

Gentlemen:

We are instructed by

to inform you that they have opened their irrevocable credit in your favor for account of

for a sum or sums in U. S. dollars not exceeding a total of

available by your drafts on us, at
to be accompanied by:

All drafts so drawn must be marked "Drawn under   Trust Company Advice No.   :"
This credit is subject to the Uniform Customs and Practice for Documentary Credits (1962 Revision), International Chamber of
Commerce Brochure No. 222.

The above mentioned correspondent engages with you that all drafts drawn under and in compliance with the terms of this advice
will be duly honored on delivery of documents as specified, if duly presented at this office on or before

THIS LETTER IS SOLELY AN ADVICE OF CREDIT OPENED BY THE ABOVE MENTIONED
CORRESPONDENT AND CONVEYS NO ENGAGEMENT BY US.

F 2629
ABC 7-63
(7-63)

and advised through one of the United States bank's correspondents
abroad (Exhibit 8.9).

All letters of credit are issued:

1. In favor of a definite named beneficiary
2. For a fixed and determinable amount

3. In a form clearly stating how payment is to be made and under what circumstances
4. With a definite expiration date.

Sight drafts (Exhibit 8.10) are payable in a certain time, such as 30, 60, or 90 days after presentation (sight) or even longer. Eligible time drafts may be drawn with a maturity up to 9 months.

Most letters of credit are cancelled when the total amount specified has been paid. However, they may be issued or renewed and made available again to the exporter. Letters of credit can be issued in American dollars or in any foreign currency. If they are issued in dollars, then they are made payable at the office of the correspondent United States bank; and if in foreign currency, they are payable at the correspondent bank in the country of issue. International banks maintain accounts in foreign currencies with many foreign correspondent banks. Letters of credit are ordinarily for the named exporter and cannot be transferred to a third party.

The data that the lender requires of the business varies according to the size and type of loan as well as the individual and specific requirements of a particular lender. However, the following items are generally required for most business loans:

1. Personal financial statements from the business owners.
2. Income statements (a current statement is always required, but lenders may require the last three years' financial statements also; a new business can be requested to submit to the lender a projected income statement.)
3. Accounts receivable and accounts payable aging (especially for accounts receivable and factoring loans).
4. Legal documents, such as purchase orders, incorporation or partnership agreements, customer contracts, and at times, business leases.
5. A projected budget (see Chapter 11).
6. Sometimes a lender may require one or more of the following items:
   a. Management resumes
   b. Owner's personal income tax returns
   c. Short written history of the business
   d. A market analysis
   e. Copies of special patents or licenses

EXHIBIT 8.10
Sight and Usance Drafts

ORIGINAL

CABLE ADDRESS

TRUST COMPANY
• NEW YORK, N. Y.

Cable Confirmation of Irrevocable Letter of Credit

DATE

Credit Number
of issuing bank   of advising bank

Advising Bank

Applicant

Beneficiary

Amount

Latest date for negotiation

This is a confirmation of our cable of today requesting you to advise the beneficiary

That we have opened our Irrevocable Credit in their favor having the following terms:
"We hereby authorize you to value on   Trust Company
your drafts at   marked 'Drawn under   Trust Company Credit No.
accompanied by the following documents:

Covering

| Shipment from | Partial Shipments | permitted |
| to | Transhipments | permitted |

Special conditions:

All negotiation charges are for your account.
We suggest negotiating bank forward us all documents in one mailing.

The amount of each draft negotiated, with the date of negotiation, must be endorsed on the reverse of the advice of this credit by the negotiating bank. If any draft is not negotiated the advice of this credit and all documents as specified must accompany the draft. We hereby agree with you and negotiating banks or bankers that drafts drawn under and in compliance with the terms of this credit shall be duly honored on due presentation."
TRUST COMPANY

INDICATION TO THE ADVISING BANK

NOTE — THIS CONFIRMATION IS NOT ITSELF THE CREDIT AND ALL DRAWINGS MUST BE AGAINST YOUR ADVICE OF OUR CABLE AND NOT AGAINST THIS CONFIRMATION.

SPECIMEN

Authorized Signature — Issuing Bank

F2713 E (4-70)

(vertical text, left margin) This credit is subject to the Uniform Customs and Practice for Documentary Credits (1962 Revision), International Chamber of Commerce Brochure No. 222.

    f.   Miscellaneous third-party support documents
    g.   Product shipping documents
    h.   Special lender forms (government application forms, and other documents).

When applying for a bank loan, a businessperson should bring at least the first five documents on this list. In this way time is saved.

9

Leasing

Leasing is one method of financing available to a business, although, technically, no borrowing is involved. Under the leasing arrangement, the leasing institution will own the equipment or fixture that it leases to the business firm. Originally, the concept of leasing was confined to large transactions, such as leasing railroad cars and engines to railroad companies; or special equipment leasing by companies who preferred leasing to selling (such as International Business Machines (IBM) or United States Shoe Machinery Corporation). Now a much broader scale of operation has evolved, which includes an extensive list from office machines to barges.

Instead of a lender and a borrower, in leasing arrangements there are a leasing company (lessor) and its customer (lessee). The lessor's primary requirement is to show that he is the actual owner of the equipment or fixtures to which the lessee has exclusive use. This is accomplished by the lessor affixing a nameplate or label to each piece of equipment leased, identifying it as owned by the leasing company.

The financial advantages and disadvantages of leasing were discussed in the chapter on debt financing (Chapter 8). For the value of review, however, the basic advantages of leasing are repeated here:

1.   Facilitation in purchase of needed equipment
2.   Release of funds that would otherwise be tied up in ownership of fixed assets
3.   Possible tax advantages, and
4.   Improvement of the financial statement.

These points will be discussed in detail later in this chapter.

LEASING CREDIT CRITERIA, TERMS, AND RATES

Lease financing techniques and terms will differ, depending on the lender, the kind of equipment or other fixed assets leased, the time required by the lease terms, and the prevailing interest rate. The following discussion gives the reader an idea of what is required.

Leasing Credit Requirement

The standards required by leasing and loans are nearly identical. Primarily, the leasing company is interested in the financial condition of the company and other business information. In general, however, leasing companies are less strict than lenders when the documentation of financial strength is involved. The primary concerns of a leasing company are the intrinsic value (and marketability used) of the equipment and the cash flow of the lessee.

Leasing Contract Terms

Most leasing contracts are term contracts that run from two to ten years. Longer leases involve special situations and require lessees with excellent credit ratings. Longer terms are also available to firms under special government-supported lease programs (such as the Small Business Administration Local Development Company 502 lease program). Leases running less than three years are usually for rolling stock (trucks, forklifts, and other heavy machines) and office equipment (duplicators and small computers). The greatest number of industrial leases, however, are written on five-year plus terms. When the term of the lease is discussed, it is referred to as the *basic lease term*, the initial term of the lease.

After the expiration of the specific term, the lessee usually has three options:

1. Start a new lease with a new piece of equipment
2. Purchase the equipment outright for some residual amount
3. Renew the lease with an option that usually includes reduced rent.

When a firm is leasing equipment that has a high rate of obsolescence (such as computers), the first option might be the most advantageous. Under the second option, that of purchasing the equipment at a residual rate, the lessee is given a figure that nearly totally discounts the original cost. The remaining price of the lease for which the equipment can be purchased is *residual value*. Residual values are not set by any fixed practices; but the usual residual is about 10 percent of the original cost of the equipment. Since the use of purchase options is being widely discontinued, it follows that these stipulations can remove some of the depreciation incentives available to the leasing company. For the lessee, taxes might also be a problem. If there are any tax advantages, then the exercise of a purchase option might erase the façade of a true lease with its tax deductible monthly payments.

Most renewal options are from 2 percent to 5 percent per year of the original list price of the equipment. Characteristically, options begin at 5 percent of the first year, then drop to 4 percent the second year, 3 percent the third year, and 2 percent thereafter. For example, if a piece of equipment having a value of $100,000 was leased to a company for five years, when the company decided to renew the lease, the first year of the renewal period would be perhaps only $5,000 per year. Chances are that the lease would cost the company more than $20,000 for the first five years it was leased. Thus, the first year payments on the renewal period would be at least $15,000 per year less than during the original lease period. The reason for this reduced cost during the renewal period is obvious. The leasing company has received all of its original investment back, so they can afford to keep the cost of the lease low for renewals.

Leasing Rates

Leasing rates and charges vary widely, depending on the risk involved in leasing the equipment. Generally, the more specialized the equipment or the longer the term of the lease, the higher the risk to the lessor.

The most widely used format for leasing charges is the add-on interest rate, ranging from 4 percent to 9 percent add-on. *Add-on interest* is higher than the same percentage interest on a simple basis. The add-on percentage is multiplied by the contract term in years to get the total charge. For example, a 5 percent add-on interest rate for a $100,000, four-year lease is $20,000 (4 times $5,000 (5 percent of $100,000)). The total repayment of the lease would be $120,000. This represents a simple interest rate of 9.24 percent. If the leasing companies used a simple interest rate of 5 percent on $100,000 for 4 years, the total monthly payments would only be $110,541, $9,459 less with add-on interest of 5 percent. Usually the add-on is quoted as a separate increment to the contract, otherwise the lease is set up as a certain percentage of the original equipment cost per month (2 percent of the cost of the equipment per month is roughly equivalent to a 5 percent five-year add-on interest rate.)

Leases made to companies with good ratings are written on a simple interest basis, usually ranging from 7 percent to 11 percent simple interest. On occasion, some companies may offer better rates on their interest. These arrangements are offered by leasing operations that are part of a larger company that has substantial taxable income. These companies have gone into leasing because, by owning the equipment that they lease, they have tax benefits from depreciation and (recently) investment tax credits. Because of these tax savings, the interest rate charged may be below the rates already quoted. To qualify for these special low-interest leases, the lessee must be a financially strong company, and the equipment must be new, and have a widespread general use, and cost more than $100,000.

Some businesspeople worry about not being able to purchase the leased equipment, if later they want to. Others think that they should have the option to purchase the equipment because they have already nearly paid for it in the lease payments. The leasing companies are in the business of leasing, not manufacturing, wholesaling, or retailing. As long as payments are made by the lessee, no lessor wants finally to possess the equipment. Consequently, the lessor may agree to sell the equipment after the lease has expired. Lessees often can negotiate purchases midway through a lease contract. The provision for such possibilities obviously cannot be preagreed or inserted into the lease contract as it would possibly negate the authenticity of a true lease, which serves the tax needs of both lessee and lessor.

QUESTION: *How much does a company have to deposit initially in order to get a lease?*

ANSWER:

Since new equipment is purchased at its standard price, it follows that the leasing company is making a 100 percent advance on market price. The lessor will require that the lessee put up a *lease deposit*. This lease deposit usually equals the first month's rent (lease payment) plus one additional month's rent for each year of the contract life of the lease. For example, a five-year lease might call for a total deposit equivalent to six months' rent payments. The lessor can view this as a reserve, but the lessor still has to make an advance of 90 percent of the market value of the lease equipment that the leasing company is purchasing.

Some lessors require only first and last months rent, but also require a *set-up charge* or *security deposit* in addition to the rent advances.

TYPES OF LEASES

Many different forms of leases exist, but here, the discussion will be limited to the three major types:

Sale and Leaseback

Under a *sale and leaseback* arrangement, a firm owning land, buildings, or equipment sells the property to a financial institution and simultaneously executes an agreement to lease the property back for a specified period under specific terms. If real estate (land and buildings) is involved, the financial institution is generally a life insurance company; if the property consists of equipment and machinery, the lessor could be an insurance company, a bank, or a specialized leasing company.

The seller (to become the lessee) immediately obtains the purchase price from the buyer (to become the lessor). At the same time, the seller-lessee retains the use of the property. This parallel is carried over to the lease payment schedule. Under a mortgage loan arrangement, the financial institution would receive a series of equal payments sufficient to amortize the loan and provide the lender with a specified rate of return on the investment. Under a sale and leaseback arrangement, the lease payments are set up in exactly the same manner — the payments are sufficient to return the full purchase price to the financial institution, in addition to providing it with a stated return on its investment.

A variety of situations can qualify for these types of leases. For example, a user of special metal presses designs and builds his own presses, sells them to a leasing company at cost, then leases them back. In business acquisitions, many acquiring companies have had a leasing company buy the equipment of the company being purchased. The acquiring company then leases the equipment back. Airlines commonly sell and lease back equipment to keep their cash flow at a manageable level.

Service Leases

Service or *operating leases* include both financing and maintenance services. IBM is a pioneer of the service contract lease. Computers, copiers, and rolling stock (trucks, cars, and other vehicles) are the primary types of equipment involved in service leases.

Another important characteristic of the service lease is that it is frequently not fully amortized (that is, the lease expires before the equipment is totally paid for). The lease contract is written for considerably less time than the expected life of the leased equipment. The lessor expects to recover the cost in subsequent renewal payments or on disposal of the leased equipment.

Such leases frequently contain a cancellation clause providing the lessee with the right to cancel the lease and return the equipment before the expiration of the basic lease agreement. This clause is an advantage to the lessee; it enables him to return the equipment if technological advances render it obsolete.

Financial Leases

A strict *financial lease* does not provide for maintenance services, is not subject to cancellation, and is fully amortized (that is, the lessor receives rental payments equal to the full price of the leased equipment). The standard arrangement involves the following steps:

1. The firm that will use the equipment selects the specific items it desires and negotiates the price and delivery terms with the manufacturer or distributor.
2. Next, the user firm arranges with a bank or leasing company to buy the equipment from the manufacturer or distributor, and the user firm simultaneously executes an agreement to lease the equipment from the financial institution. The terms call for full amortization of the financial institution's cost plus a return of

from 6 to 10 percent a year on the unamortized balance. The lessee is generally given an option to renew the lease at a reduced rental when the basic lease expires, but he does not have the right to cancel without completely paying off the financial institution.

Financial leases are almost exactly the same as the sale and leaseback arrangements except that the leased equipment is new and the lessor buys it from the manufacturer or distributor rather than from the user-lessee.

TAX ASPECTS OF LEASING

The possible tax advantages of the use of industrial leasing may or may not apply; each tax situation must be judged individually. No leasing institution will make sweeping claims of tax advantages, yet, unquestionably, many have realized substantial tax benefits.

Certain leases may easily qualify for tax write-offs. A case in point is the equipment required for a particular project with a known period of usage. For example, construction machinery needed for a long-range new town building project in which the entire life of the equipment will probably be spent on the project would be considered a clear case of legal tax write-offs. Defense industries will lease certain production machinery for a particular use to a specific contract (especially cost-plus contracts). This use gives the defense contractor a much better write-off than does the government-allowed depreciation. Leasing contracts that tie in closely with the normal life of the underlying equipment are more likely to qualify for tax write-offs.

To determine the applicability of tax write-offs allowed, the company that pays the lease (lessee) should determine whether the agreement for the lease is a lease or a conditional sales contract. If the agreement is a lease, then the company may deduct rental payments for the use of the equipment. If the agreement is a conditional sales contract (which means that the lessee firm has or will acquire title or equity in the equipment), then the payments on the contract will be considered payments for the purchase of the equipment.

Conditional Sales Contract

An agreement usually is considered a *conditional sales contract* (even if it is called a lease) rather than a lease if any of the following conditions are present:

1. Portions of the periodic payments are specifically applicable to an equity to be acquired by the lessee (the firm paying the contract payments).
2. Title will be acquired on payment of stated amounts of rentals that the lessee are required to make under the contract.
3. The total payment required for a relatively short period of use constitutes an excessively large portion of the total sum required to be paid to secure the transfer of the equipment.
4. The agreed rental payments materially exceed the current fair market rental value for the same equipment. This extra charge may indicate that the payments include an element other than compensation for the equipment.
5. The property may be acquired under a purchase option at a price that is below normal in relation to the value of the property at the time when the option may be exercised, as determined at the time of entering into the original agreement, or that the price is a relatively small amount when compared to the total payments the lessee is required to make.
6. Some portion of the periodic payments is specifically designed as interest or is otherwise readily recognizable as the equivalent of interest.
7. Title will be acquired on payment of an aggregate amount (the total of the rental payments plus the option price, if any) that approximates the price, plus interest and carrying charges, at which the lessee could have purchased the equipment at the time the agreement was made.

The following is an example of a lease treated as a sale:

Example: Sally Jones contracted for installation of a fire extinguishing sprinkler system in her warehouse. The system was estimated to last forty years. The contract, designated a lease, provided for use of the system for five years for an aggregate rental of $2,000, payable $400 annually. Sally was required to keep the system insured for an amount at least equal to the total rentals and was to bear the risk of loss from any cause. The liability of the lessor in the event of failure of the system or any defect therein, or for maintenance services called for in the contract, was limited to $100. Sally had the privilege of renewal for an additional 5-year period at a nominal rental of $20 a year.

This arrangement, for federal income tax purposes, constitutes a conditional sale, rather than a lease. The amounts paid as rentals, except to the extent they represent interest, insurance repairs, and maintenance charges, are capital expenditures recoverable through annual deductions for depreciation over the estimated useful life of the sprinkler system.

Leveraged Lease

Certain transactions purporting to be leases of property are commonly referred to as *leveraged leases*. Such transactions involve three parties: a lessor, a lessee, and a lender to the lessor. Usually these are net leases, wherein the lease term covers a large portion of the useful life of the leased property, and the lessee's payments to the lessor are sufficient to discharge the lessor's payments to the lender.

A person planning to be a party to a transaction that appears to be a leveraged lease may wish to consider securing an advance ruling. *Revenue Procedure 75-21, 1975-1 C.B. 715* sets forth guidelines that will be used for advance ruling purposes only in determining whether leveraged leases are, in fact, leases for federal income tax purposes. Among these guidelines are:

1. The lessor must have made a minimal, unconditional at-risk investment in the property.
2. The lessee may not have a contractual right to purchase the property from the lessor at less than fair market value when the right is exercised.
3. The lessee may not invest in the property.
4. The lessee may not lend money to the lessor for investment purposes.
5. There must be a profit motive on the part of the lessor.

Other facts and circumstances also may be present in the lease arrangement, however, that may disqualify the transaction as a valid lease even though these five guidelines have been met. See also *Revenue Procedure 75-28, 1975-1 C.B. 752* for guidelines setting forth information and representations to be furnished by a taxpayer requesting an advance ruling in this area.

Bona Fide Lease Transaction

The full amount of the annual lease payments is deductible for income tax purposes provided that the IRS agrees that a particular contract is a genuine lease and not simply an installment loan (conditional sales contract) called a lease. The lease contract should be written in a form acceptable to the IRS. The major requirements for a bona fide lease transaction from the standpoint of the IRS are:

1. The term must be less than thirty years, otherwise the lease may be regarded as a form of sale.
2. The rent must represent a reasonable return to the lessor; *reasonable* currently means a range of from 6 to 11 percent return on the investment by the lessor.
3. The renewal option must be bona fide; this requirement can best be met by giving the lessee the first option to meet an equal bona fide outside offer.
4. There shall be no purchase option, but if there is, the lessee should only be given parity with an equal outside offer.

COMPARISON OF LEASING WITH OWNERSHIP

Cost Comparison

To understand the possible advantages and disadvantages of lease financing, the cost of leasing must be compared with the cost of owning the equipment. In the average case, a firm that contemplates the acquisition of new equipment must also think about how to finance the equipment. To finance equipment there are three choices:

1. A lease agreement
2. A conditional sales contract
3. A term loan secured by a chattel mortgage on the equipment.

To judge the cost of leasing a comparison must be made to leasing of the two borrow-to-purchase alternatives mentioned. Exhibit 9.1 compares the methods. The table assumes that the firm is acquiring a piece of equipment costing $10,000 and that the firm has the choice of borrowing the $10,000 at 10 percent, to be repaid in ten annual installments of $1,627, or of leasing the machine for $1,627 per year. Under the lease agreement, the firm is paying a 10 percent implicit interest rate — the rate the lessor is earning.

EXHIBIT 9.1
Comparison Debt vs. Leasing

	Year 1	Year 2	Year 3	Year 4	Year 5	Year 6	Year 7	Year 8	Year 9	Year 10	Year 11
Loan:											
(1) Total Payment	1,627	1,627	1,627	1,627	1,627	1,627	1,627	1,627	1,627	1,632	16,275
(2) Interest Portion	1,000	937	868	792	709	617	516	405	283	148	6,275
(3) Principal Portion	627	690	759	835	918	1,710	1,111	1,222	1,344	1,484	10,000
(4) Remaining Balance	9,373	8,683	7,924	7,089	6,171	5,161	4,050	2,828	1,484	-0-	-0-
(5) Depreciation	1,000	1,000	1,000	1,000	1,000	1,000	1,000	1,000	1,000	1,000	10,000
(6) Tax Deductible Expense (2)+(5)	2,000	1,937	1,868	1,792	1,709	1,617	1,516	1,405	1,283	1,148	16,275
(7) Tax Savings 50% of (6)	1,000	969	934	896	854	809	758	702	642	574	8,138
(8) Net Cost of Ownership (1)−(7)	627	658	693	731	773	818	869	925	985	1,053	8,132
Lease:											
(9) Annual Payments	1,627	1,627	1,627	1,627	1,627	1,627	1,627	1,627	1,627	1,632	16,275
(10) Tax Savings 50% of (9)	813	813	813	813	813	814	814	814	814	816	8,137
(11) Net Cost of Leasing (9)−(10)	814	814	814	814	814	813	813	813	813	816	8,138
(12) Advantage to Owning (11)−(8)	187	156	121	83	41	(5)	(56)	(112)	(172)	(237)	-0-

Exhibit 9.1 reveals that there is really no long-range tax advantage to leasing over ownership in this example. In practice, due to the rounding of figures, a $6 advantage to owning is shown in the table. In the short run (the first years of operation using the equipment) there are tax advantages to ownership. In the long run, however, these tax advantages disappear when compared to leasing in the last years of operation; inflation or some other future-oriented deflator — (as in a discounted cash flow study), notwithstanding — savings in the first years of an operation are worth more than savings in later years. More succinctly, when we consider the time-cost of money, ownership offers advantages over leasing.

An advantage of ownership over leasing that cannot be ignored is that in ownership the equipment belongs to the firm; if the equipment has a value at the end of the depreciation period, the equipment can be sold for a cash gain.

A step-by-step, line-by-line analysis of Exhibit 9.1 follows here.

Loan

1. The total payments represented here are the interest and principal payments each year for ten years on a $10,000 equipment loan at 10 percent interest per year. The payment is increased $5 in the last year to allow for rounding errors in the previous annual payments.

2. *Interest portion* is the interest portion of each annual payment. The interest payments are considered to be expenses and are tax-deductible.

3. *Principal portion* is the amount of each annual payment that is applied to the balance owing the lender to reduce the indebtedness. This principal portion of the annual payment is not considered to be an expense and therefore is not tax-deductible.

4. *Remaining balance* is the amount still owed on the loan at the end of the year, after the annual payment is made. It can be seen that the previous year's balance is reduced by exactly the amount of the principal portion of the annual payment.

5. *Depreciation* is the allowable write-off amount for tax purposes against the equipment asset that was purchased. In this case, we used ten-year, straight-line depreciation, assuming no salvage value for the equipment. The firm is allowed to write off for tax purposes both depreciation and the interest expense of the annual payment.

6. *Tax deductible expense* is the depreciation and interest expense (line 2 plus line 5).

7. *Tax savings* represents 50 percent of the total deductible expenses. This percentage assumes that the firm is in the 50 percent income tax bracket.
8. *Net cost of ownership* represents the total annual payment (line 1) minus the tax savings (line 7). The real net cost to the firm is the money laid out each year ($1,627) less the tax savings generated by that investment and related costs.

Lease

9. Annual payments represent the payments made to the leasing company for use of the equipment. The payment in the last year was increased by $5 to allow for rounding errors.
10. Tax savings represents 50 percent of the payment (line 9) and assumes that the firm is in the 50 percent income tax bracket.
11. Net cost of leasing represents the total payment (line 9) minus the tax savings (line 10).

Advantage to Owning

12. Advantage to owning represents the difference between the net cost of leasing (line 11) and the net cost of owning (line 8). There is an advantage to ownership in the first five years, but the advantage becomes negative, that is, there is an advantage to leasing) in the last five years. Over the long run, however, there is no advantage to either ownership or leasing.

A table similar to Exhibit 9.1 but presented from the lessor's point of view, shows that leases provided higher returns than loans, under similar conditions, because under a lease the lessor can take advantage of the accelerated depreciation. Furthermore, in this situation, the lessor is permitted some profit flexibility in setting lease terms, and competition among leasing companies could reduce the costs of leasing.

QUESTION: *What would happen to the relative cost of leasing versus owning if the example in Exhibit 9.1 were modified to allow for accelerated depreciation?*

ANSWER:
Accelerated depreciation would produce a higher tax write-off, hence lower taxes, in the early years. This would reduce the net cost of owning (line 8) in the early years and raise it later on. Since the lease net cost (line 11) is unaffected, the result would be to increase the advantage to owning (line 12) in the early years and lower it in the later years.

Assumptions Commonly Made Regarding Cost of Leasing versus Owning

Exhibit 9.2 summarizes some of the variations in leasing conditions and their assumed implications on leasing costs, as opposed to ownership costs. The table in Exhibit 9.2 summarizes frequently encountered arguments about advantages and disadvantages of leasing. Each assumed implication represented in the table is subject to qualification or even error. Each assumed condition will be discussed in turn.

Use of Accelerated Depreciation

Argument often is presented that due to use of accelerated depreciation methods, owning must be less costly than leasing. This argument considers the competitive aspects of the money and capital markets. Competition could force leasing companies to pass along tax advantages such as accelerated depreciation and tax credits to the lessee in the form of reduced payments. The payment pattern for leasing can be flexible. Therefore, any advantages available to the leasing companies that own the equipment will probably be reflected in the competitive system of rates charged by leasing companies.

Implicit Interest Rates are Higher

Leasing is said to involve higher interest rates. Perhaps, but in general, if

EXHIBIT 9.2
Assumed Cost of Leasing vs. Ownership Under Various Conditions

| | Cost of leasing vs. ownership | |
Condition	Lower	Higher
Firm uses accelerated depreciation		X
Implicit interest rates are higher for leasing than for borrowing		X
Equipment has large residual values		X
Equipment experiences rapid obsolesence	X	

the lessee's integrity is weighed, then there should be little difference in the rates allowable to the firm for leasing or loans. Difficulties also arise when an attempt is made to separate the money costs of leasing from costs of other services that may be in a leasing contract. If the leasing company can perform the nonfinancial services, such as maintenance of the equipment, at lower cost than the lessee could perform them, then the effective cost of leasing may be lower than borrowing. Efficiency gained by the specialization of services may decrease operating costs to a lower total than the lessor would be charged for the total package of services offered.

Large Residual Values for Equipment

The lessor owns the property at the expiration of the lease. The value of the property at the end of the lease is the *residual value*. Superficially, it appears that where residual values are large, owning will be less expensive than leasing. However, the advantage may be subject to substantial qualification. On most leased equipment, the obsolescence factor is large and rarely will there be substantial residual values. Theoretically, if residual values appear favorable, then competition among leasing companies will force leasing rates down to compensate for the large residual values involved. However, in connection with decisions whether to lease or to own land, the obsolescence factor will be negligible, and residual values are almost guaranteed. In a period of optimism concerning land values, the tendency may be to overestimate rates of increase in land values. Consequently, the current purchase of land involves a price so high that the probable rate of return on owned land may be relatively small. Under this condition, leasing land may be a more economical alternative. On the other hand, if the probable increase in land values is not fully reflected in current prices, then it will be advantageous to own land.

Rapid Obsolescence

Another fallacy is the feeling that leasing costs will be lower because of rapid obsolescence of some kinds of equipment. If the obsolescence rate on equipment is high, leasing costs must reflect such a rate. It is possible, however, that certain types of leasing companies may be well equipped to handle the obsolescence problem. For example, IBM is a manufacturer, reconditioner, and specialist in office equipment and has its own sales organization and system of distributors. These capabilities may enable

IBM to write favorable leases for equipment. If the equipment becomes obsolete to one user, it may still be practical to another.

Leasing companies, by combining leasing with other specialized services, may reduce the costs of obsolescence and increase effective residual values. Some special companies, through integrated operations, reduce the effective cost of equipment. Moreover, some institutions that do not combine leasing and other specialist functions, such as manufacturing, reconditioning, and servicing, may, in conjunction with financing institutions, perform the overall functions as efficiently as do integrated leasing companies.

Cost of Capital Tied Up in Purchase

Even though other methods of acquiring equipment may cost less than leasing (cash purchases without financing costs least) they represent money savings on the financing of the purchase only. Loss of opportunity to make a profit on the additional capital that leasing avails may offset the savings of purchase. This is particularly true when the firm is making a good-to-excellent return on its investment. For instance, a company with an investment of $200,000 averaging annual sales of $1,000,000 with a net profit of 5 percent ($50,000) is earning 25 percent each year on its investment. If growth of this type of company merely requires the use of more capital, any money freed by leasing instead of purchasing, theoretically, could return 25 percent per annum to the company.

The money freed by leasing instead of purchasing usually represents the difference in the down payment that a firm would make if they were financing, and the rental deposits that would be required for leasing. Down payments are characteristically more than deposits; therefore, for the firm mentioned above with a 25 percent return on investment, its return would represent 25 percent of the difference between the cost of the down payment and the cost of the lease deposits.

For example, for a piece of equipment (worth $10,000) the down payment would generally be between 15 percent and 25 percent ($1,500 to $2,500). The lease deposit — since the lease will be for ten years — would be ten months' lease payments (first month plus one month for each year of the life of the contract). This amount would be $1,322 if the equipment were worth $10,000 and there were an implicit interest rate of 10 percent per annum. All other things being equal, it would cost $2,000 in down payment to purchase and $1,322 to lease. Thus, the company has $678 available in capital for reinvestment. If the capital returned 25 percent per year, then the company could make $6,314 more by leasing instead of purchasing (assuming that the initial $678 earned the interest and was reinvested, with interest each year for ten years).

ACCOUNTING IMPLICATIONS OF LEASING

The bookkeeping implications of leasing are that the total lease payment is reflected as an expense. A lease payment would be recorded as shown in Exhibit 9.3.

EXHIBIT 9.3
Bookkeeping Implications of Leasing

	General Journal		
Date	*Transaction*	*Debit*	*Credit*
1/30/77	Lease Expense	$1,600	
	Cash		$1,600
	To record monthly payment of lease on forklift due ABZ Leasing		

Balance Sheet Implications

Two possible situations may make leasing advantageous for firms seeking the maximum degree of financial leverage. First, it is agreed that firms can obtain more money for longer terms under a lease arrangement, than under a secured loan agreement, for the purchase of a specific piece of equipment. Secondly, leasing may not have a great impact on future borrowing. This point is apparent in the following balance sheet from firms X and Y. Firm X borrows $100,000 to buy equipment and firm Y leases $100,000 worth of equipment. Their balance sheets are the same before the respective purchase or lease. (See Exhibit 9.4.)

The companies decide to acquire assets (in equipment) of $100,000. Firm X decides to borrow $100,000, thus an asset and a liability are entered on its balance sheet, and its equity-to-debt ratio increases to 75

EXHIBIT 9.4
Balance Sheet Leasing Comparison

Before Equipment Secured			*After Equipment Secured*			
Firms X & Y			*Firm X*		*Firm Y*	
Total	Debt	$100	Total	Debt $200	Total	Debt 100
Assets $200	Equity	100	Assets $300	Equity 100	Assets $200	Equity $100
Totals $200		$200	Totals $300	$300	Totals $200	$200
			Figures in thousands			

percent. Firm Y leases the equipment. The lease may call for as high, or even higher, fixed charges than the loan; but the debt ratio of Firm Y remains the same as before the lease (50 percent), thus enabling Firm Y to borrow money when Firm X, because of its higher equity-to-debt ratio, could not.

Financial Accounting Standards Board Statement on Leasing (No. 13)

Financial Accounting Standards Board (FASB) *Statement No. 13* sets down the most recent requirements for leases. This opinion supersedes APB *Opinions 5, 7, 27, 31* and paragraph 15 of APB *Opinion No. 18.*

FASB *Statement No. 13* divides leases into two groups: 1. Capital leases, which are really considered purchases of assets; and 2. Operating leases, which include items that are not capital leases.

Capital leases

If at its inception a lease meets one or more of the following four criteria, the lease is classified as a *capital lease.*

1. "The lease transfers ownership of the property to the lessee by the end of the lease term.
2. "The lease contains a bargain purchase option [a provision allowing the lessee, at his option, to purchase the leased property for a price that is substantially lower than the expected fair market value of the property on the option date].

3. "The lease term is equal to 75 percent or more of the estimated economic life of the leased property. However, if the beginning of the lease term falls within the last 25 percent of the total estimated economic life of the leased property, including earlier years of use, this criterion shall not be used for purposes of classifying the lease.

4. "The present value at the beginning of the lease term of the minimum lease payments, excluding that portion of the payments representing executory costs, . . . costs paid by the lessor, equals or exceeds 90 percent of the excess of the fair market value of the leased property to the lessor. However, if the beginning of the lease term falls within the last 25 percent of the total estimated economic life of the leased property, this criterion shall not be used for purposes of classifying a lease."

If the lease is a capital lease, the lease is recorded as an asset in an amount equal to the present value of the lease payments during the term of the lease. An equal amount is recorded as a liability or lease obligation. The present value calculation would exclude such costs as insurance, maintenance, and taxes to be paid by the lessor. If this present value exceeds the fair market value of the leased property at the beginning of the lease period, the capitalized lease asset is recorded at fair market value.

The capitalized lease asset must be amortized (depreciated) as follows:

If the capital lease meets items 1 or 2 above, the asset can be amortized in a manner consistent with the lessee's normal depreciation policy for owned assets. If the lease does not meet items 1 or 2, the leased asset is amortized in the normal manner, except that the period of amortization must be the term of the lease.

During the term of the capital lease, each lease payment is allocated between a reduction in the lease obligation and interest expense in the same way repayment of a debt is handled.

Assets recorded as capital leases and the amortization of this asset must be separately identified in the lessee's balance sheet and in the footnotes to the balance sheet.

QUESTION: What is the accounting treatment of changes in the provisions of a capital lease?

ANSWER:
Any changes in the provisions of a lease, a renewal, or extension of an existing lease or a termination of the lease before the expiration of the present lease is accounted for as follows (quoting from Statement 13):

a. If the provisions of the lease are changed in a way that changes
    the amount of the remaining lease payments and the change
    either (i) *does not* give rise to a new agreement (an agreement
    which changes the lease to an operating lease or extends the lease
    term beyond the previous expiration date) or (ii) *does* give rise to
    a new agreement but such agreement is also classified as a capital
    lease, the present balances of the asset and the obligation shall be
    adjusted by an amount equal to the difference between the
    present value of the future . . . lease payments under the
    revised or new agreement and the present balance of the obliga-
    tion.

b. Except when a guarantee or penalty is rendered inopera-
    tive . . . , a renewal or an extension of an existing lease shall be
    accounted for as follows: [A capital lease is accounted for as
    described in the previous paragraph.] If the renewal or extension
    is classified as an operating lease, the existing lease shall con-
    tinue to be accounted for as a capital lease to the end of its original
    term, and the renewal or extension shall be accounted for as any
    other operating lease.

c. A termination of a capital lease shall be accounted for by remov-
    ing the asset and obligation, with gain or loss recognized for the
    difference.

QUESTION: *What disclosures are required in the financial statements
            for both capital and operating leases?*

ANSWER:

Capital leases require the following disclosures:

1. The gross amount of the capital leases by nature or function.
2. Future lease payments as of the date of the balance sheet and in
    aggregate for each of the five succeeding years. Separate deduc-
    tions representing executory costs (costs paid by lessor) and the
    amount of imputed interest necessary to reduce the lease pay-
    ments to present value must also be included.
3. The total amount of sublease rentals to be received in the future
    under noncancelable subleases.
4. Total contingent rentals (rentals dependent on some factor other
    than the passage of time) incurred in each period for which there
    is an income statement.

Operating leases require the following disclosures:

1. Future rental payments required as of the date of the balance sheet and in aggregate for each of the five succeeding fiscal years.
2. The total rentals to be received in the future under noncancelable subleases.
3. Rental expense for each period for which an income statement is presented. Separate amounts for rentals, contingent rentals, and sublease rentals should be shown.

For both capital and operating leases, the following disclosures are required:

1. The basis on which contingent rental payments are determined.
2. The existence of and terms of renewal or purchase options and escalation clauses.
3. Restrictions imposed by lease agreements, such as those concerning dividends, additional debt, and further leasing.

FASB *Statement No. 13*, issued November, 1976, also contains specific recommendations for direct financing leases, sale-and-leaseback, leveraged leases, and land and building leases. To answer other specific questions not covered in this book, the reader should consult the FASB *Statement.*

10

Pensions and Executive Compensation

Accounting, the tax and financial decision-making aspects of pensions, profit sharing, and executive compensation will be considered in this chapter. Since the high rates of taxation and inflation continue to take more and more from salary and compensation levels, it is urgent to plan for personal financial security and also for the security of employees. In 1974, Congress passed important pension legislation. Regulations interpreting this legislation have only recently become bully understood by accountants, lawyers, and other people associated in the field of compensation.

The Pension Reform Act of 1974, officially called the *Employee Retirement Income Security Act of 1974* (ERISA), was a landmark piece of legislation in the area of employee economic security. A result of approximately ten years of legislative process that began with the President's Cabinet Committee Report of 1965, this Act insures that pensions be financed and operated in such a manner that employees receive the benefits promised to them.

Employment benefit plans in the United States have an interesting legislative background. The Social Security Act of 1935 was the first major employee benefit legislation. Before this act became law, old-age survivors and disability insurance benefits were limited to governmental pension plans and a few voluntary private plans. However, growth in private plans occurred during the 1940s and was influenced significantly by the wage restrictions imposed by the government and by a highly competitive labor market. All of this new legislation resulted in companies' offering pension plans and other fringe benefits as a means of recruiting and retaining employees.

Not only did the growth of labor unions have an impact on the development of private benefit plans, but also the Taft-Hartley Act amended previous legislation in regard to the conduct of labor-management negotiations. A section of that legislation addressed the subject of union-negotiated employee benefit plans. The Act provided for the joint administration of plans by management and union representatives, annual audits of plans, and restrictions on the use of contributions to such plans. In 1949, a court decision involving Inland Steel firmly established that the terms of a pension plan are subject to mandatory collective bargaining. Unions have been active in pension plans since that time.

In 1958, Congress passed the Welfare and Pension Plans Disclosure Act, which provided for the filing of a plan description and an annual report form for employee benefit plans. In 1974, ERISA greatly expanded governmental involvement in employee benefit plans. Although ERISA does not require an employer to establish or maintain a plan, it provides for certain minimum standards for participation, vesting and funding, expanded trustee responsibility, and disclosure requirements, as well as for termination insurance, if the employer goes out of business. The Act also provides for governmental agencies to interpret and enforce the law. Most pension and profit-sharing plans have had to be amended as a result of ERISA.

Before ERISA, an employer was able to design a pension or profit-sharing plan with strict eligibility and vesting provisions. IRS rules concerning antidiscrimination and regulations concerning tax-exempt status were the main influence in these areas. Technically, vesting was not required before normal retirement age. However, antidiscrimination rulings and collective bargaining resulted in earlier vesting and other benefits. ERISA established minimum age and service requirements and minimum formulas for vesting.

The Act also established minimum funding standards for pension plans. Prior to ERISA, unfunded plans were allowed. The benefits paid under unfunded plans depended entirely on the continued existence and earnings of the employer. ERISA provides that if a pension plan is established, sufficient cash funds must be set aside each year to pay the future pensions earned during that year.

The amount of cash required to be contributed in any year to a pension plan is generally based on actuarial valuations. Prior to ERISA, there was wide flexibility in the choice of actuarial assumptions in the method used to amortize past service liabilities over future years. Employers had much flexibility in the funding of plans. The minimum cash contribution required by the IRS was the amount necessary to keep the unfunded past service liability from increasing beyond its initial level.

Example: If a pension plan were adopted in 1977 for a company that had been in business since 1972, the company had already a liability for past service of its employees. Before ERISA, however, it would have been necessary only to provide cash sufficient to pay only the interest on this past service liability. The minimum funding now required under ERISA specifies that the past-service liability must be funded over a period of years, typically, a maximum of thirty years.

ERISA also established the *Penion Benefit Guaranty Corporation,* which is to make up deficiencies, subject to certain limitations, if a pension plan terminates with insufficient assets to pay vested benefits. Furthermore, employers can be contingently liable for up to 30 percent of their net worth for any deficiency in the assets of a terminated plan.

QUESTION: What are the minimum participation requirements under ERISA?

ANSWER:

A participant is defined as an *employee* or *former employee,* or other beneficiary who is or may become eligible to receive a benefit of any type from an employee benefit plan. Customarily, an employee cannot be excluded from a plan because of age or service, if this employee is at least 25 years old and has completed at least one year of service. The one year of service requirement may be extended to three years if full and immediate vesting is provided. *One year of service* is defined as a twelve-month period in which the employee has worked at least 1,000 hours. A defined contribution retirement plan cannot exclude an employee because he is too old at the time of employment. However, a defined benefit plan can exclude employees who start employment within five years of normal retirement age.

TYPES OF PENSION PLANS

Pension plans can be classified into two categories — defined benefit plans and defined contribution plans.

Defined benefit plans provide a definitely determinable retirement benefit when an employee reaches retirement age.

Defined contribution plans, on the other hand, provide for an individual account for each participant and for benefits based solely on the amount contributed to the participant's account including any income, expenses, gains and losses, and any forfeitures from accounts of other participants that may be allocated to such participant's account.

Pension plan benefits are usually paid out in the form of a life annuity beginning at a person's normal retirement age. Other methods of paying benefits include installment payments and lump-sum distributions.

Contributions to a defined benefit plan are based on actuarial calculations designed to estimate the amount necessary to fund the payment of specified pension benefits to be paid at retirement.

Under a defined contribution plan, the rate of contribution is either fixed — usually determined as a percentage of annual salary or as a percentage of company profits — or may be determined on a discretionary basis by the management of the company. The employer's contribution, together with the employee's contribution, under a contributory plan, as well as the employee's share in the investment experience of the plan, provides eventual retirement income or other benefits. The amount accumulated by an employee at retirement will depend on such factors as length of employee service, the amount of contributions, and the investment experience of the plan. In addition, the cost of a given amount of retirement annuity will vary according to such factors as age and retirement date. It is not possible to predict with certainty the amount of income that a person will receive under a defined contribution plan since it is not a fixed amount.

Types of Defined Benefit Plans

Defined benefit pension plans can be categorized by the method of calculating retirement benefits. The four basic benefits calculation methods are:

1. A flat-amount formula that provides a stated benefit unrelated to an employee's earnings. For example: A pension of $25,000 a year.

2. A flat percentage-of-earnings formula, which provides a benefit related to the employee's earnings. For example: A pension of 50 percent of the employee's average last three years' earnings.
3. A flat amount per year of service formula that reflects an employee's service, but not earnings. For example: A pension of $1,000 for each year of service.
4. A percentage of earnings per year formula that reflects both an employee's earnings and service. For example: A pension of 3 percent of the average last three years' earnings for every year of service worked.

The fourth benefit formula, which relates benefits to both earnings and years of service, is the most common method used to compute benefits in plans for salaried employees. The flat amount or flat amount per year of service formula is often found in plans negotiated by labor unions.

Types of Defined Contribution Plans

In general, there are five basic types of defined contribution plans:

1. *Profit-sharing Plan*. Contributions under this type of plan are based on a formula related to the earnings of the business enterprise. Contributions are allocated to participants in proportion to their compensation. *For Example:* Management decides that 25 percent of the company's income before taxes will be contributed to employee pension plans. Such money is allocated to individuals in proportion to their annual compensation.
2. *Money Purchase Plan*. An employer's contributions are based on a flat percentage of compensation. For instance, ten percent of each employee's annual compensation is deposited in an account in trust for the employee.
3. *Target Benefit Plan*. The amount of an employer's contribution to each participant's account is established at a level based on an actuarial valuation, sufficient to provide a target benefit to each participant on retirement. The plan does not guarantee that the target benefit will be paid. The only obligation is to pay whatever can be provided by the amount in the participant's account, depending on actual investment results.
4. *Stock Bonus* or *Employee Stock Ownership Plan*. This type of plan is similar to a profit-sharing plan. However, it invests

primarily in the stock of the employer company. Benefits may be distributed in the form of stock.

5. *Thrift* or *Savings Plan*. This type of plan allows the participant to contribute, within specifications, an amount that is usually a percentage of pay. The employer's contribution is then related to the amount or rate of a participant's contributions.

QUESTION: *What types of modifications can there be with respect to the form of pension plan benefits?*

ANSWER:

Several types of modifications or additions to the form of pension plan benefits may be made. One type is to integrate the pension plan with Social Security benefits. In this way, only salary paid above the Social Security minimums earns pension benefits. There is a reduced cost to the employer through integration of plan benefits. Another type of benefit modification is a joint and survivor annuity provision. ERISA actually requires that if a pension plan provides for the payment of benefits in the form of an annuity, the annuity must be in the form of a joint and survivor annuity. This means that the employee's spouse will receive a life annuity of at least one half of the original amount on the employee's death. Another type of modification is a cost-of-living adjustment clause to the amount of retirement benefits. Finally, a plan may provide for various supplemental benefits in the event of death or dismemberment before retirement or in the event of early retirement.

ADMINISTERING EMPLOYEE BENEFIT PLANS

Employee benefit plans can be classified according to the form of plan administration. The basic distinction is whether the funding agency is an insurance company (*insured plan*) or whether another institution, such as a bank, trust company, or individuals, acts as the trustees of the plan (*trustee plan*).

Insured plans exist when an insurance company is responsible for paying benefits under the plan. Contributions to the plan are paid to the insurer, who then pays benefits to eligible participants based on instructions from the plan's retirement or administrative committee. Life insurance companies offer facilities for the administration of pension plans. Employers make deposits required under a plan and insurance companies will maintain required records, file necessary reports, and make disbursements to retirees.

The primary responsibility of a trustee, under a trusteed plan, is to hold title to and possession of plan assets. The trustee is responsible for the safekeeping of assets and for the management of assets. A trust agreement sets forth the duties and responsibilities of the trustee, including nondiversion of trust assets, investment powers, periodic reports, and record-keeping requirements.

QUESTION: What is vesting and what are the vesting requirements under ERISA?

ANSWER:

Vested benefits are benefits that are contingent on a participant continuing in the service of an employer. In other words, vesting means that an employee's rights to his accrued benefits are not forfeitable, even if the employee terminates employment.

The minimum vesting schedules established by ERISA are stated in terms of a percentage of a participant's accrued benefit. For defined contribution plans, a participant's accrued benefit is the balance in his plan account. In the case of a defined benefit pension plan, a participant's accrued benefit is his benefit as determined under the terms of the plans expressed in the form of an annual benefit commencing at normal retirement age.

ERISA requires that a plan meet one of the following minimum vesting rules:

1.   Ten-year service rule: 100 percent vesting after 10 years of service.
2.   Graded 5-to-15-year service rule: 25 percent vesting after 5 years of service, 5 percent additional vesting for each year of service from year 6 through 10, 10 percent additional vesting for each year of service from year 11 through year 15, so that an employee is 100 percent vested after 15 years.
3.   Rule of 45: 50 percent vesting when the sum of an employee's age and years of service total 45, if the employee has completed at least 5 years of service, and 10 percent additional vesting, for each year of service thereafter. Also, a participant under the Rule of 45 must be 50 percent vested after 10 years of service, and 60 percent by eleven years, so that an employee is at least 50 percent vested after 10 years and 100 percent vested after 15 years, regardless of age.

In addition, ERISA requires that defined benefit pension plans must meet one of the following three rules for the computation of accrued benefits to which the above-determined vesting percentages are applied:

1. *The 3 percent Rule:* For each year of service (up to 33 1/3 years) an employee must accrue at least 3 percent of the benefit that would be payable under the plan, if participation were begun at the earliest possible age and retirement begun at a normal retirement age.

2. *The 1 1/3 percent Rule:* The annual rate at which a participant can accrue benefits cannot exceed 1 1/3 times the rate for any prior year. This is a rule against backloading. For example, if an employee accrued benefits at 3 percent a year, in later periods the maximum rate at which a benefit could be accrued would be 4 percent.

3. *The Fractional Rule:* The estimated number of years left until retirement is calculated and the benefit is accrued on a straight-line basis over that number of years. For example, if it is estimated that an employee will work 25 years before retirement, then 4 percent of the benefit would be accrued each year.

QUESTION: *What are the limitations on tax-deductible contributions to a retirement plan? What are the limitations on benefits paid?*

ANSWER:
The amount of tax-deductible contribution to a benefit plan is limited and is stated as a function of a limit on the amount of benefit paid. Generally, a defined benefit pension plan that pays a specific amount to a person, cannot provide benefits to the retired employee greater than $75,000, or 100 percent of average salary for the three highest consecutive years, if that average is less than $75,000. The $75,000 maximum is adjusted upward every year for cost-of-living increases. As of January 1, 1979, the maximum stood at $98,100.

For a defined contribution plan, the maximum amount that can be added to the account of a participant in the plan is the lesser of either $25,000 or 25 percent of compensation. The $25,000 limitation is also adjusted upward every year for cost-of-living increases. As of January 1, 1979 the maximum stood at $32,700.

QUESTION: *For the defined benefit plan, how does the maximum benefit limitation actually work?*

ANSWER:

Assume that the objective is to receive the maximum benefit under a defined benefit plan and that there are twenty years until retirement, with an expected pay-out period of fifteen years after retirement. The plan earns at a rate of 5 percent per annum (see Exhibit 10.1).

EXHIBIT 10.1

Payments in
20 years

Payments out
15 years

Today

Retirement
Date

End of
Benefits

The maximum amount that can be deducted against taxable income each year is determined by finding the amount of the annual annuity payment which, when deposited in a fund bearing interest at 5 percent, will grow to an amount necessary to pay the pension benefits at retirement age.

First, the amount necessary to pay the pension benefits must be determined. The amount necessary to pay the pension benefits is equal to the present value of an annuity of 15 payments discounted at 5 percent, times the maximum annual benefit of $84,525.

$84,525 × (Present value of annuity 15 years at 5 percent)

$84,525 × 10.3797 = $877,340

Therefore, at retirement age, a fund of $877,340 would be needed to pay the maximum benefit over 15 years. In order to accumulate such a fund by retirement age, it would be necessary to deposit a certain amount each year. This amount is the maximum tax-deductible amount. It is found by taking the future value of an annuity of 20 payments accumulating interest at 5 percent and dividing it into the amount necessary to pay the pension benefits.

$877,340 ÷ (Future value of annuity of 20 payments at 5 percent)

$877,340 ÷ 33.066 = $26,534

Therefore, the maximum tax-deductible contribution each year for 20 years for this pension plan would be $26, 534.

QUESTION: What is the minimum amount that can be contributed to a pension plan each year?

ANSWER:

Prior to ERISA, employers had much flexibility in funding defined benefit plans by selecting actuarial assumptions and a policy of amortization of past service liability. ERISA now requires that employers meet certain minimum standards in funding accrued pension liabilities and in selecting actuarial assumptions.

All pension plans are required to make annual minimum contributions equal to the so-called normal cost plus amortization over thirty years of unfunded accrued liabilities. The normal cost is defined as the annual cost of future pension benefits.

Example: If a plan is adopted that will pay the maximum benefit, then the maximum tax-deductible amount and the minimum amount of cash funds that must be set aside in a given year must be determined. In general, the actuarially determined amount necessary to pay a benefit under a pension plan will be the minimum amount required to be contributed in cash to the plan. If the minimum amount required to be contributed to a plan is not contributed, a penalty tax will be assessed.

QUESTION: What are the responsibilities of employers and trustees under pension plans?

ANSWER:

ERISA defines a person as a fiduciary under a pension plan to the extent that he or she exercises discretionary authority or control over a plan or the disposition of its assets, renders investment advice to the plan for a fee, or has any discretionary authority or responsibility in administration of a plan. A fiduciary must be guided in his conduct by the prudent-man rule. This rule requires "care, skill, prudence, and diligence under the circumstances then prevailing that a prudent man, acting in a like capacity and familiar with such matters, would use in the conduct of an enterprise of a like character with like aims." (Pension Reform Act of 1974 § 404(a)(1)(B)). A fiduciary also is required to diversify the investments of a plan in order to minimize the risk of large loss.

Certain types of investments for pension plans are limited or even prohibited. Defined benefit plans cannot invest more than 10 percent of plan assets in employer securities or employer real estate. Defined contribution plans can invest more than 10 percent of their assets in employer securities, if that procedure is the explicit intention of the plan. However, a defined contribution plan still cannot invest more than 10 percent of its assets in employer real estate. The definition of *employer real estate* is a building that is owned by the pension plan and is leased to the employer.

Fiduciaries are prohibited from engaging directly or indirectly in certain transactions with a party-in-interest. A *party-in-interest* is defined as the employer, the union, if any, persons rendering service to the plan, officers and employees of the plan, and relatives of any of the foregoing. The prohibited transactions include:

1. A sale, exchange, or lease of property between the plan and a party-in-interest.
2. A loan or extension of credit between the plan and a party-in-interest.
3. The furnishing of goods, services, or facilities between the plan and a party-in-interest.
4. A transfer of plan assets to a party-in-interest or a transfer for the use or benefit of a party-in-interest.
5. An acquisition of employer securities or real estate in violation of the provisions of the Act relating to the 10 percent limitation discussed above.

QUESTION: What happens to benefits paid out of a pension plan? How are they taxed?

ANSWER:
Pension benefits can be paid in one of two ways:

1. As a lump-sum distribution
2. As an annuity

A *lump-sum distribution* is a payment of the entire balance due an employee within one taxable year. Normally, this payment would be due to death, or separation from service before normal retirement age. However, a lump-sum payment may be made any time after age 59 1/2.

Any amounts of the lump-sum distribution contributed by the employee are not taxed.

The recipient of a lump-sum distribution may elect a ten-year averaging rule. The rule works this way:

1. *Figure the taxable portion of the lump-sum distribution. Example:* Assume the lump-sum distribution is $50,000 and that $10,000 of

this was contributed by the employee. The taxable portion would be $40,000.

2. *Subtract a minimum distribution allowance from the taxable portion.* (The minimum distribution allowance is 1/2 of the first $20,000 of the taxable portion of the lump-sum distribution. If the taxable portion is more than $20,000, the minimum distribution allowance must be reduced by 20 percent of the excess.) *Example:* The taxable portion is $40,000. The minimum distribution allowance would be 1/2 of $20,000, or $10,000, except that this amount must be reduced by 20 percent of the excess above $20,000 (20 percent of $20,000) or $4,000. Therefore, the minimum distribution allowance is $6,000 ($10,000 − $4,000). The taxable portion of the lump-sum distribution is now $40,000 less $6,000, or $34,000.

3. *Compute a tax on $2,200 plus 1/10 of the figure obtained in 2. above and multiply by 10.* (Use the tax-rate table for single individuals.) *Example:* The tax is based on $2,200 + $3,400, or $5,600. The tax on this amount is $376. Multiplied by 10 equals $3,760.

4. *Multiply the tax obtained in 3. above by a ratio obtained by dividing the number of months of participation in a pension plan after January 1, 1974 by the total number of months of participation under the plan.* (This number will be added to other taxes payable.) *Example:* The recipient of the $50,000 lump-sum distribution retires on December 31, 1980 after being employed and participating in a pension plan for twenty years. The number of months from January 1, 1974 to December 31, 1980 is 84. The total months in 20 years is 240. Therefore $1,316 (84/240 times $3,760) would be the ordinary income portion of the tax on the lump-sum distribution.

5. *Multiply the taxable portion of the lump sum distribution by one minus the fraction obtained in 4. above.* (This amount is considered a long-term capital gain.) *Example:* The taxable portion of the lump-sum distribution, $40,000 is multiplied times 156/240. This amount, $26,000, is included in taxable income as a long-term capital gain (usually taxable at a maximum of 28 percent).

QUESTION: *How is an annuity taxed?*

ANSWER:

An annuity is taxed as ordinary income in the year the payment is received to the extent that the payment represents income that has not been previously taxed to the recipient.

Example: Assume the $50,000 lump-sum distribution discussed above will be paid in 10 equal installments over 10 years. Each year the recipient would get $5,000 and of this $4,000 would be taxed.

$$(\$40,000 \div \$50,000) \times \$5,000$$

OTHER RETIREMENT PLANS

QUESTION: *What happens if a person is self-employed or works for a company that does not have a pension plan?*

ANSWER:
Congress has provided that a person who is self-employed or works for a company that does not have a pension plan may create his or her own plan. For self-employed persons, a Keogh Plan is available. For persons who work for a company that does not have a pension plan, the Individual Retirement Account (IRA) is available.

The Keogh Plan

Under the *Self-Employed Individuals Tax Retirement Act* of 1962, self-employed individuals can be covered under qualified retirement plans, known as HR–10 plans or *Keogh Plans.* The qualification requirements for a Keogh Plan are similar to the requirements for a corporate retirement plan. However, the requirements for qualification are more stringent where a Keogh Plan covers an "owner-employee" (that is, an individual who derives income from an unincorporated business and who is also a proprietor or a partner who owns more than 10 percent of the capital).

ERISA increased the maximum deductible contributions a self-employed individual can make to a qualified plan to 15 percent of earned income up to $7,500 per year. In applying the $7,500 deduction limitation, the self-employed person can count only the first $100,000 of earned income. This stipulation means that the self-employed person must contribute to the plan at a rate of 7.5 percent of compensation for both himself and his employees in order to achieve the $7,500 limitation. The limitation is also applicable to shareholder employees of Subchapter S corporations (discussed in Chapter 13).

Individual Retirement Accounts

An employee who is not an active participant in any qualified pension, profit-sharing, stock-bonus, or annuity plan is entitled to set up a personal retirement plan. Annual contributions in cash up to the lesser of 15 percent of compensation or $15,000 may be made to an individual retirement account and deducted from an employee's gross income.

Earnings on IRAs are accumulated tax free and distribution may be made after age 59 1/2. IRAs cannot purchase life insurance as an investment, but annuities are permissible.

QUESTION: What other forms of executive compensation are used beyond pension plans?

ANSWER:
One form of executive compensation common in the past is a stock-option plan. Because of the Tax Reform Act of 1976, which eliminated most of the favorable aspects of stock option plans, and because of the lackluster performance of the stock market in recent years, stock-option plans have fallen into disfavor. However, some types of stock options or pseudostock options are still being used.

In general, if a company grants a stock option to an employee, then the employee recognizes income, and the company receives a deduction for the difference between the fair market value of the stock and the option price.

Example: If an employee is granted an option to purchase 100 shares of stock at $5 per share, and the stock is currently selling for $8 per share, then the employee has taxable income, and the company is entitled to a compensation-paid deduction of $300. If the stock has no market value, or if the option is highly restricted as to its exercisability, then the recognition of taxable income may be deferred until the restrictions lapse or the option is exercised.

Because of the taxable nature of stock options, many companies are considering the adoption of so-called tandem stock option and stock appreciation rights plans.

Stock Appreciation Rights

Many companies would like to give employees the economic benefits inherent in stock option arrangements. However, the Tax Reform Act of 1976 eliminated the formerly favorable tax treatment of qualified stock options. For this reason, and also to eliminate some of the risks involved in holding shares after exercise of an option, and to make it unnecessary for employees to incur debt to finance the exercise of options, many companies have supplemented their option plans with stock appreciation rights.

Stock appreciation rights are rights granted to employees to receive the excess of the market value per share of stock above a stipulated price either in cash, or in stock, or in some combination of both.

Tandem Plan

A *tandem plan* provides that a stock appreciation right and a stock option are granted simultaneously and may be exercised by the employee over a certain length of time. The exercise of the option cancels the stock appreciation right, and vice versa. This dual nature to the plan allows the employee to choose the features that best suit the employee's tax situation and anticipation with respect to future appreciation of the stock.

11

Budgeting

The essence of budgeting is the process of trying to predict future sales, costs, profits, and purchases (capital expenditures). If a company predicts costs and income by means of a budget, then it can use that budget as a management control tool to keep costs down and sales as high as possible.

Since the future performance of a company is essential to its continuance, most firms find it beneficial to try to predict the kinds of financial operations that will be the most satisfactory for future policy. The discussion of cash flow management in Chapter 4 indicated that budgets are essential to careful financial management; cash flow management also helps management determine future cash needs and if there will be extra capital to invest for a certain time. In short, the better able a firm is to predict future performance, the better chances are for good management decisions that will promote profitability and avoid company failure.

TYPES OF BUDGETS

Budgets comprise two time groups: short-term and long-term. Budgets also differ in that the funds in one may be directed toward profit and loss or cash flow purposes, while funds in the other may be fixed or flexible. There are also separate budgets for capital purchases (equipment and buildings) and for internal purposes. A description of the purposes and uses of many types of budgets follow:

1. *Short-term budgets* are any budgets—cash flow or profit and loss, internal or for capital purchases—that are of one year's duration, or less. Short-term budgets also tend to be the most accurate and the most widely used by all companies.
2. *Long-term budgets* are budgets for more than one year, but customarily run from three to ten years. A long-term budget furnishes the company with a long-term overview of what its market performance and capital needs may be. Due to the time factor, long-term budgets are less accurate than short-term, and are more prone to revision. Long-term budgets are valuable in reflecting needs for long-term borrowing or capital.
3. *Profit-and-loss budgets* indicate income as it is billed and shipped to customers and expenses as they are incurred (as in an income statement—profit-and-loss statement). The profit-and-loss budgets do not reflect all the cash movements.
4. *Cash-flow budgets* use the actual cash inflow and outflow of a company. A cash-flow budget will show income when it is received, not when it is billed, and will show expenses when they are actually paid, not when they become due. A cash-flow budget will consider the capital expenditures of the firm when they are paid and loan proceeds when they are disbursed to the firm.
5. *Fixed budgets* use sales and operating costs as fixed amounts.
6. *Variable budgets* are designated for different sales and conditions. For example, variable budgets allow for expenses to increase if sales have increased over the expected levels, or to decrease if sales are less than expected.
7. *Capital budgets* are concerned with purchases of equipment, buildings, and other capital expenditures. Capital expenditure budgets usually span a longer period of time than operating budgets (profit-and-loss budgets, cash-flow budgets, and internal budgets).
8. *Internal budgets* are used in the various departments or in the firm as operating guides.

In practice budgeting can be complex, especially in large organizations. But no company should avoid budgeting for fear of its complexities; even the simple approach is helpful. If a company has used the plans as guides and measured actual performance against them, then it has practiced budgetary control.

A *formal budget* is a presentation in financial terms of specified future expectations. Nevertheless, it is based in large part on the experience of the past.

In determining whether to use both the fixed budget and the variable budget (the operating budgets), it is particularly important for a company to understand how each cost or expense is affected by the changes in the volume of activity for each area of operations being budgeted.

Exhibit 11.1 shows the nature of the relationship of various types of cost to the changes in volume of activity.

EXHIBIT 11.1
Relationships of Various Types of Costs to Changes in Volume of Activity

---

1. A *fixed cost* (such as depreciation):

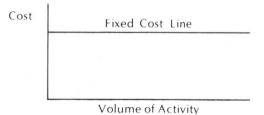

2. A *directly variable cost* (such as sales commissions):

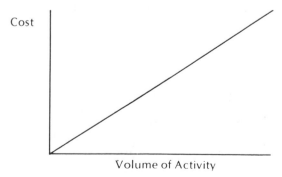

EXHIBIT 11.1
continued

3.   *A semivariable cost,* such as fringe benefits where the cost varies with the amount of direct labor expended in the given cost center.

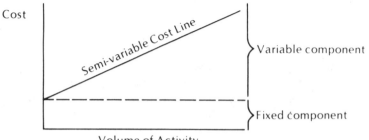

4.   *A semivariable expense,* such as indirect labor or material handling in which there is a fixed component plus a variable component. The latter rises in steps as volume increases because of the necessity of hiring another full-time worker, rather than a part-time worker for many jobs.

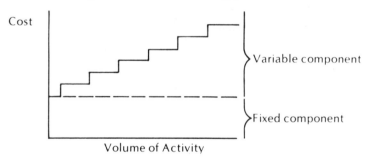

5.   *A semivariable expense,* such as repairs and maintenance, part of which may be deferred but undertaken later when financial conditions are better.

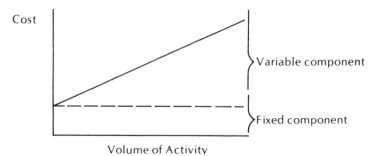

EXHIBIT 11.1
continued

---

6. *A semivariable expense*, such as small tools or minor items of equipment, charged off as expense each year instead of being capitalized in the instance where a certain portion must be purchased regardless of volume must be purchased as the volume of activity increases, even though the amount of cost per unit of activity declines while volume increases.

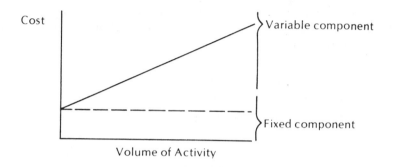

PROJECTING SALES

Planning is a continuous process, as is budgeting, particularly in the development of cost and revenue data. Based on cost, revenue data, and estimates of expected economic conditions, the first item to be budgeted is sales. The sales forecast, once adopted, establishes the expected fixed volume of activity on which the budget is based.

A projection of expected sales and other income within the budget's time period is the beginning point for most budgets. Thus, contingent factors such as operating expense, inventories, and capital needs are determined by expected sales.

There are basically two methods of projecting sales. The first method is a practical one. The managers, salespeople, and others involved in sales attempt to arrive at a reasonable approximation of the level of sales the firm can expect in the upcoming budget period. The firm's management might consult other industry-associated people, including accountants or bankers, to get an in-depth view in order to arrive at a more accurate sales figure.

The second method of projecting sales, called *regression analysis*, involves a statistical and scientific approach to the problem. It predicts future sales based on the trend of historical sales. Two commonly used types of regression analysis are:

1. simple linear regression
2. curvilinear regression

Simple Linear Regression

A simple linear regression, or *scatter diagram* forecast method is a graphic portrayal of joint relations. The table and graph in Exhibit 11.2 illustrate the use of the simple regression method and demonstrate its superiority over other forecast methods.

EXHIBIT 11.2
Relations Between Sales and Inventory

Year	Inventory	Sales
1972	$ 44,000	$100,000
1973	48,000	200,000
1974	52,000	300,000
1975	56,000	400,000
1976	60,000	500,000
1977	64,000	600,000
1978	68,000	700,000
1979	72,000	?

In Exhibit 11.2, Hero Manufacturing has the historical sales and inventory figures from 1972 to 1978. Management aims to predict sales in 1979, at which time they will have an estimate of expected inventories.

If the management of Hero Manufacturing uses the simple regression method, they will then draw a line through the points on a graph where sales and inventories meet in each year. By extending the line for another year, they can determine what sales in that year will be. The lines fitting the scattered points that show where inventory and sales meet in each year is called the *line of best fit*—the *regression line*. In general, all points will not fall exactly on the best-fit line, but all points will be relatively close to it.

Exhibit 11.3 indicates where the sales-inventory points fall and how the 1979 figure can be predicted.

In Exhibit 11.3, the expected sales for 1979 will be $100,000.

The procedure for a linear regression (scatter diagram) is as follows:

1. Forecast or project the sales of the firm based on inventory,

---

EXHIBIT 11.3
Hero Manufacturing

Regression Points for Sales and Inventory

Inventory(in thousands)

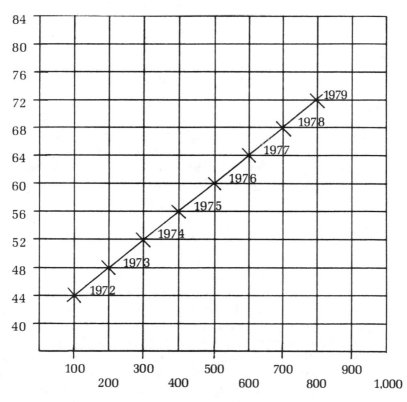

Sales (thousands of dollars)

industry sales, GNP, or other logical indicators using historical numbers.

2. Fit the regression line (line of best fit) by free hand or by numerical calculations.

3. By extending the line beyond the historical figures, a reasonable idea of expected sales can be obtained.

Other crucial figures besides sales can be predicted by this method. A person can plot several balance sheet items such as accounts payable, income tax provisions, retained earnings, cash, receivables, inventories, and fixed assets as a function of sales. Increases in sales tend to affect all of these items. People sometimes plot sales on the basis of the number of years in business only. For example, Acme Mousetrap has the following sales during specific years:

Year	Sales
1972	40,000
1973	70,000
1974	100,000
1975	105,000
1976	130,000
1977	140,000
1978	185,000

To determine expected 1979 sales for Acme Mousetrap, a simple regression based on the scatter diagram in Exhibit 11.4 is used. In the Acme Mousetrap scatter diagram example, predicted sales for 1979 are $195,000. Notice in the example that most of the sales points on the regression analysis do not fall exactly on the line, but that no one point is too far from the line.

Simple Curvilinear Regression

Linear scatter diagrams (linear regressions) are based on the assumption that the slope of the regression line is constant. This condition frequently does exist, but not always. The diagram in Exhibit 11.5 is an example of the application of curvilinear regression to forecasting financing relationships. This hypothetical relationship shows a flattening curve, a decreasing relationship between sales and inventory beyond point X, the current level of operations. In this case, the forecast of inventory requirements at sales level of 250 would be too high if the simple linear regression method were used.

EXHIBIT 11.4
Acme Mousetrap Sales

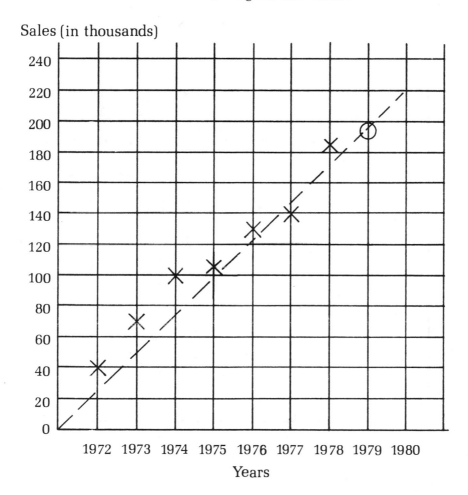

Plotted as Regression Points

Sales (in thousands)

Years

Projecting Sales for New Operations

Until this point we have assumed that the model business preparing the budget was an existing business with a history of sales and other financial data on which to base sales. When a firm is in the process of beginning a

EXHIBIT 11.5
Applying the Curvilinear Regression to Forecast
Financing Relationships

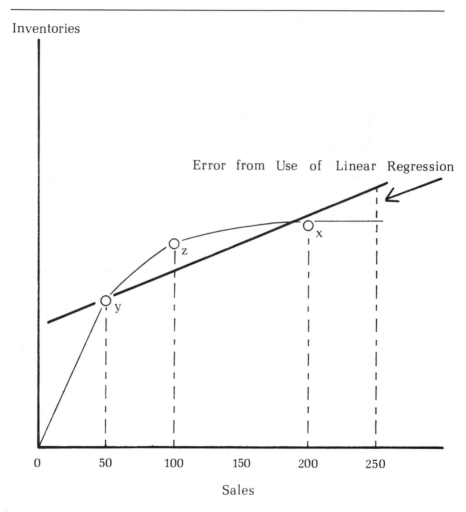

new business or when expanding an existing business into new areas, direct historical financial data do not exist. Since the managers of the new firm need to know how to proceed, and since new operations customarily need outside financing, it is probably more essential for new operations to have projected funded budgets than do existing operations.

The first step to projecting sales for a new operation is to gather market data; specifically, market data that can be related directly to sales. For example, in a ski resort project in which one of the authors assisted in initial financing and planning, all possible financial industry data were secured, especially information concerning average sales per year in certain areas and minimum and maximum sales required for operations. Also, a questionnaire was sent to existing ski resorts, requesting such financial data as gross sales, capitalization, asset and liability structure, and other pertinent details. Contact was made with the local government and commercial agencies for their information on skier visits in the area, increases in visitors and dwelling structures, proposed expansion in highways leading into the area, and the present and future state of other means of transportation (such as airplanes and trains) into the area.

One key piece of information uncovered was the number of skiers who were turned away from the existing resorts during the previous year because those resorts were operating at capacity. Another key figure was the rapid and continued increase in skier visits to the area over the previous years. Putting together these pieces of information and others, we discovered that if the new resort could handle only 60 percent of the people who were turned away the previous year at $10 per lift ticket, the resort could operate at profitable levels. Since the number of skiers were increasing rapidly and the capacities of the existing resorts were not expanding, it followed that the needed level of sales was not only possible but likely.

This is the suggested procedure for projecting sales for new operations:

1. Conduct a market study of all industry and local area sources, concentrating on statistical aspects of the market that would be related to sales.
2. Determine what proportion of the available market the new enterprise can safely service.
3. Determine the expected income per customer.
4. Multiply the expected income per customer times the number of customers that can be expected.

THE NATURE OF BUDGETING

The techniques already discussed lend themselves to short-term as well as long-term financial planning; but generally, when considering budgeting, most people think of short-term financial forecasting. Historically, budgeting was treated as a device to limit expenditures. The more modern approach is to view the budgeting process as a tool for obtaining the most productive and profitable use of the company's resources.

The budgeting process is a method to improve operations; it is a continuous effort to get the job done in the best possible way. Budgets are reviewed to compare plans and results in a process sometimes called *controlling to plan*. Establishing standards requires a realistic under-standing of the firm's activities. Arbitrary standards set without a basic understanding of the minimum costs of the operation can do more harm than good. Budgets represent planning and control devices that enable mangement to anticipate change and adapt to it. The budgeting process, in summary, improves internal coordination.

Financial Control Policies

Financial control policies include the organization and content of various types of financial control budgets. These budgets may include a budget for individual products and for every significant activity of the firm. In addition, budgets will be formulated into control operations at individual branch offices. These budgets may, in turn, be grouped and modified to control regional operations.

If a company prepares several budgets that will be combined into one company-wide budget, then management should be careful of the inter-relation between the budgets. For example, the production budget will reflect the use of materials, parts, labor, and facilities. Each of these items may require separate budgets (that is, a materials budget, a budget of labor and personnel requirements, and possibly related budgets). Increased use of the facility and machinery may require attention in the capital budget. Production will affect the marketing budget.

The results of projecting all of these cost elements are reflected in the projected income statement. The anticipated sales give rise to the various types of investments needed to produce the products. To finance these investments, a cash budget is required. The cash budget indicates the combined efforts of the budgeted operations on the firm's cash flow.

Problems of Budgeting

Four major problems are encountered when using budget systems:

1.   Budgetary programs can grow to be so complete and detailed that

they become expensive, cumbersome, and sometimes meaning-less.

2. Budgetary goals may come to supersede enterprise goals. Budgets should be considered a tool and not an end in themselves. Enterprise goals should supersede subsidiary plans, of which budgets are part.

3. Budgets may contribute to inefficiencies by continuing initial expenditures in succeeding periods without proper evaluation. Budgets that grow from precedent usually contain undesirable expenditures. The budgetary process must contain provisions for reexamination of standards of planning by which policies are translated into numerical form.

4. Evidence suggests that the use of budgets as a pressure device defeats their basic objectives. Budgets used as pressure devices can cause resentment and frustration and lead to inefficiency. One method of counteracting this effect is for management to encourage participation of workers in planning.

FIXED BUDGETS

A typical *fixed budget* shows expected revenues at assumed selling prices and volumes for the period of time being budgeted. It lists expected expenses for the same period, with allowance for inventory changes. The fixed-budget procedure also involves the preparation of separate schedules of sales, production, capital expenditures, and cash.

To identify the budget with individuals responsible for performance, the budget is broken down to a separate schedule of revenue and expense items for each cost center, department, division, or other section of a business. In small companies, the budget is often prepared by only one or by a few members of top management. Ideally, however, each individual who is to be held accountable under a budget should have a separate schedule for the organizational unit under his or her supervision and should participate in budget preparation.

Production Budgets

Given sales estimates, manufacturing company executives are then responsible for planning the necessary production to meet these sales. Since sales are typically subject to fluctuations beyond the control of the producer, it is generally necessary to build up and draw down inventories in order to reconcile smooth production and fluctuating sales.

Given production estimates by months for each product line, it is possible to estimate material and labor costs involved in producing these units. One approach is first to convert the production estimates into their values at estimated selling prices and then to apply to these estimated sales values percentages developed from experience of the relationship between material and labor costs and sales.

A more accurate approach is to apply standard material and labor costs for assumed typical units within each product line to the budgeted units to be produced. If materials must be ordered before they are needed, it is necessary to know what specific materials must be ordered, and when. The needs for major materials, especially those requiring long lead times, must be estimated. It also is a good idea to break down labor estimates on the basis of operating units involved. Assuming that the actual costs of material and labor are expected to be in line with standard costs, then the product costs would affect inventory.

To determine factory burden, the percentage relationship of factory burden to sales for periods in the past is applied to the estimated sales value of the budgeted production. Another approach to estimating factory burden is by using standard product costs. The standard product costs for factory burden used in budgeting provide figures for the amount of factory burden expected to be absorbed by goods produced.

The difference between the amount of budgeted factory input burden cost each month and the budgeted amount of burden to be absorbed by goods produced each month represent the expected amount of burden to be overabsorbed or underabsorbed. The amount of this expected variance for any given month represents the extent to which production for that month is greater than, or less than, the volume on which the standard product costs are based.

Selling Expenses

Selling expenses such as salesmen's salaries, commissions, and travel; sales office salaries and overhead; and advertising are considered selling expenses. They do not necessarily bear any short-run relationship to either production volume or sales volume. In the long-run, there is usually some relationship between selling expenses and sales achievement.

The budgeting of selling expenses usually starts with a review of the organization and expenses based on past performance together with a review of how past goals and budgets have been met. Since sales expenses do not necessarily bear any short-run relationship to sales volume, they would not be budgeted to fluctuate from month to month with budgeted sales. However, it is a good idea to consider adjustments brought on by major changes in budgeted sales over past sales.

The budgeting of selling expenses involves an analysis of the company's current strengths and weaknesses in the marketing area.

Administrative Expenses

As in the case of selling expenses, administrative expenses (other than those related to production) do not bear any short-run relationship to changes in the volume of sales or production. They generally would not fluctuate from month to month.

If the costs of the payroll department or billing department were considered administrative expenses, these components of total administrative expense might fluctuate with sales.

Procedures in budgeting of administrative expenses are generally the same as those in budgeting of selling expenses. These include the review of past expenses and accomplishments, the survey of current strengths and weaknesses, and the budgeting of organization, facilities, and expenses relative to plans tied to overall company goals.

CASH BUDGETS

Because cash flow is so vital to a firm's continued existence, cash flow cannot be left to chance; it must be planned. Toward this end, management must attempt to forecast if, when, for how long, and in what amounts either a cash surplus or cash deficit might result from operations. The initial object of preparing a short-term cash forecast is to reveal the cash and bank balances at the end of each period within the forecast (month, quarter, or year).

The cash budget determines not only the total amount of financing that will be required, but also its timing. The cash budget indicates the amount of funds that will be needed month by month or even week by week; it is one of financial management's most important tools. The ultimate object of preparing the short-term cash forecast must be to guide appropriate and timely management action toward improved control of cash flow. This control of cash is where the value of a cash forecast lies. Management action should be directed towards one or more of the following ends:

1. Planning the management of future cash inflows and outflows in
    order to project the most favorable control period (month, week,
    year) closing balances.
2. Taking steps to ensure that adequate financing is available as and
    when required to meet any anticipated cash deficit.
3. Taking steps to ensure that any anticipated cash surplus is fully
    used to the maximum possible benefit to the firm.
4. Taking appropriate control action to maintain financial stability
    in the ongoing situation as the actual cash flow position unfolds.

Format of the Forecast

The format of the cash flow budget may vary widely from company to
company because of the different expense and sales categories involved.
The format in Exhibit 11.6, however, can serve as a general design.

This format is not concerned with every detail of receipt and payment.
Rather, it is concerned with rough groupings that will highlight the more
significant items over which management has the most control. Exhibit
11.6 uses monthly period headings, but some companies may prefer to use
weekly headings. It is not desirable to have too long a control period
because the closing cash balance figure represents what it should be at the
close of the period and it may be at different levels during the control
period.

QUESTION: How frequently should a firm prepare a cash budget?

ANSWER:
The budget for a firm is frequently done on an annual basis and perhaps
updated every six months. However, the cash position is too vital to be
left for annual or even six-month consideration. Once it has started its life
in the annual budgeting routines, the cash forecast should be seen as
continuing responsibility in its own right.

Ideally, cash forecasting should be undertaken on a rolling monthly
basis. If the first forecast runs from January to December, the next will run
from February to January, the next from March to February, and so on. In
this way, the earliest warning of impending crises is given and appropriate management action can be planned, rather than reacted to. When

EXHIBIT 11.6
Forecast Format

Line No.		APL.	MAY	JUN	JUL	AUG.	SEPT.	OCT.	NOV.	DEC.	JAN.	FEB.	MAR.
	CASH RECEIPTS												
1	Collections from customers												
2	Cash sales												
	Miscellaneous:												
3	Routine, e.g. rent, interest												
4	Special, e.g. sale of assets												
5	TOTAL RECEIPTS (R)												
	CASH PAYMENTS												
6	Payments to suppliers												
7	Wages, salaries and labour-related exps.												
8	Miscellaneous routine items												
9	Rent, telephone, electricity, rates												
10	Taxes												
11	Purchase of building, plant, equipment												
12	Interest and dividend payments												
13	Repayment of borrowings												
14	Special items												
15	TOTAL PAYMENTS (P)												
17	CURRENT SURPLUS (DEFICIT): (R − P)												
18	Cash and bank balances at end of previous month												
19	CASH AND BANK BALANCES AT END OF CURRENT MONTH												

financial trouble strikes, it is often not so much the nature of the trouble itself that creates the difficulty for the firm, but the speed with which management can recognize the situation and respond to it.

Cash Forecast

In a cash forecast, (see Cash Management, Chapter 4) the most essential elements are the cash inflow receipts, cash sales, collections from customers, and the cash outflow, including all expenses except depreciation plus physical cash outlays (such as principal payment on a loan, purchases of assets, and tax).

Cash inflow is a result of the following sources:

1. Cash sales.
2. Collections from customers on accounts or notes receivable.
3. Increases in liabilities, such as a loan from the bank or an extension of credit from a supplier.
4. Sales of assets.
5. Increase in invested capital, such as the sale of stock in the company or other owner's investments.

Cash outflow is caused by the following:

1. Payment of expenses. (Depreciaton is not paid by the company and is not considered a cash expense.)
2. Payment of taxes (whether they are deductible or not).
3. Payment of the principal portion of a loan repayment installment. (The principal portion of a loan repayment is not considered to be an expense and is not tax deductible.)
4. Purchase of assets.
5. Payment of dividends or owner's draw.
6. A cash investment in treasury stock, stock of another company, purchase of a bank certificate of deposit, a bond, or any other outside investment.

Cash Inflow

The cash sales portion of cash inflow is simply the sales income received by a firm in the form of cash when the sale is made. This amount, of course, does not include sales made on account.

Perhaps one of the more difficult items to predict — and yet perhaps the most critical to the cash flow of the firm — is *collections from customers* who buy on account. The ability to collect accounts receivable can mean the difference between the survival or the collapse of a firm. When forecasting collections, a company tries to predict both the amount of sales invoiced and the length of time that will elapse before settlement. Unfortunately, neither factor lies entirely in the control of management. The *collection period* (the time required to collect the receivables) is the factor that causes the most difficulty in forecasting. Sales have already been invoiced for the first month or so of the forecast period and backlogs of orders help predict sales beyond that point. Unfortunately, uncertainties as to sales and to collection periods increase as the forecast is extended into the future.

If the firm forecasting is in an industry such as construction or other contract work, then most details of sales and collection times have been worked out in the contract. This makes prediction easier than in other industries that are on a month-to-month sales basis.

Most cases, however, will be concerned with general invoicing to customers for payment on a month-to-month basis. The anticipated collection period for these companies must be based on target credit levels that are realistic and take into account both past experience with collections and any particular mix of either sales or customers. In analyzing past performance of your firm, the analysis in Exhibit 11.7 should be helpful in isolating any pattern that might exist. If a consistent pattern does not emerge from this analysis form, it might be necessary to undertake a more detailed causal analysis. A more detailed analysis also might be required if different credit terms are allowed to different types of customers. If significant differences between classes of customer or individual customer exist, then a shift in their relative mix within any month's sales will clearly cause imbalance in future collections.

When a firm secures a loan or increases its credit line with suppliers, this increases the cash flow and is considered cash inflow. Loans and expansion of credit can be fairly well planned.

Sales of assets are one cash inflow source that is under complete control by management and can be planned months in advance. Increases in invested capital usually have to be forecast well in advance. This increase includes sales of stock or other owner investment in the company. Of course, increases in invested capital can be controlled easily by management if there is a long enough lead period.

EXHIBIT 11.7
Analysis of Cash Movements

Month	Sales invoiced $	Averages sales/day $	Collections outstanding at month end $	Average no. days sales outstanding Days	Percentage of sales collected within:			
					1 month %	2 months %	3 months %	Over 3 mths. %
April								
May								
June								
July								
August								
September								
October								
November								
December								
January								
February								
March								

Analysis of cash movements - collections from customers

Cash Outflow

Payment of expenses is an ongoing cash outflow for a firm, one that is generally considered to be consistent from year to year. Some expenses such as leases and rentals are easily predicted because they are under contract and have a specific amount payable over a certain period of time. Payment of interest is also easily predicted. Expenses such as salaries, supplies, telephone, utilities, and lesser items, do fluctuate from time to time, but they do not fluctuate widely and therefore are fairly easy to predict. In forecasting expenses, historical experience is a good indicator of future costs. Remember, depreciation is not a cash expense and therefore should not be considered in cash-flow projections.

Tax payments are a considerable factor when compiling the cash forecast. Tax payments are required not only for federal, state, and sometimes local income tax, but also for personal property tax, payroll tax, property tax, sales tax, and others. Timing is usually crucial with taxes because they are due on a specific day, after which penalties are charged that increase the costs. Taxes, which are usually very predictable as to time and amount, should definitely have a place in the cash-flow forecast. Careful planning is usually required to meet these demands.

Payment of the principal portion of a debt should not be overlooked. Although it is included in the periodic payment, along with interest of the debt, some forecasters ignore it as a payment that must come out of net profit after taxes. Since, like interest, principal is paid in periodic payments, it is easy to predict for cash forecast purposes.

Purchase of assets is usually planned in advance and is one of the easiest of cash outflows to predict.

Payment of dividends or owners' draw can vary according to the availability of funds. Generally, dividends or draw are determined more by need and stockholder relations than by availability of cash. These payments should not be ignored when preparing a cash forecast.

Cash investments are under the control of management and should be considered especially when the cash flow forecast indicates temporary or short-run cash surpluses.

Management Decisions

On completion, the forecast may reveal a cash position at some time in the future that may be unacceptable to management. Exhibit 11.8 is a graphic representation of the movement of cash balances to demonstrate this

EXHIBIT 11.8
Cash Movement Over Time

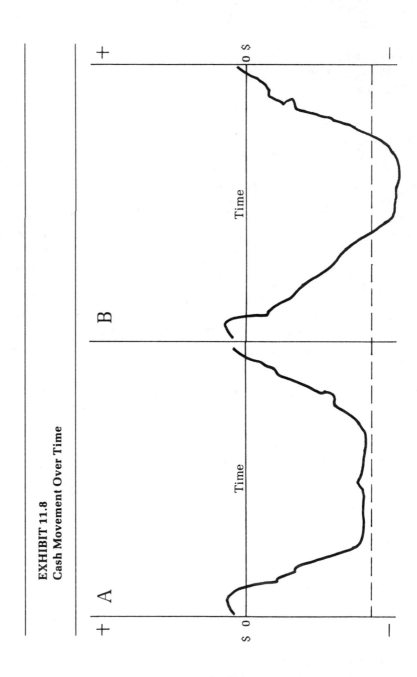

point. If the broken line represents the maximum cash deficit permitted by existing bank facilities, then situation A is acceptable but situation B is unacceptable. To avoid the unacceptable situation, management must reconsider some of the decisions that were built into the cash forecast. Management may decide to accelerate certain receipts or to delay certain payments in order to restructure the forecast. Decisions planned are more likely to be rational and logical than is the alternative of last-minute panic measures taken in the face of a rapidly deteriorating situation.

VARIABLE OR FLEXIBLE BUDGETS

The principal weakness of the fixed budget is that when the volume of activity of operations for a period turns out to be different than forecasted, expense control and measurement of performance are difficult. Under these circumstances, the budgeted amounts are no longer appropriate for these expenses, which should vary in some degree with changes in volume of operations activity.

Under a variable or flexible budget, managers in charge of particular cost centers are provided with a table of allowances. With these, the managers can determine what expense should be at a given level of operations. The managers know what their spending allowances are in advance of actual operations.

The variable budget is particularly useful in the control of variable burden in manufacturing companies. It is inappropriate, however, in the control of selling and administrative expenses, where costs are not readily responsive or cannot be quickly adjusted to changes in the volume of operations. That is, although the flexible budget can be more effective than a fixed budget in the control of certain expenses, it does not replace the need for a fixed budget for other expenses and for general company control. Whereas all companies need a fixed budget, the usefulness of a variable budget depends on the circumstances in each particular case.

The essence of the variable budget system is to introduce flexibility into budgets by recognizing that certain types of expenditures will vary at different levels of output. Thus, a firm might have an alternative level of outlay budgeted for different volumes of operation — high, low, or medium. It is commonly prepared in the form of a schedule or table of allowances (as in Exhibit 11.9) that lists level of operations and number of people required.

Note that the table in Exhibit 11.9 shows the allowance for a given expense at a certain volume of predicted sales.

EXHIBIT 11.9
Budget Allowances

% of total volume	Employees allowed	Weekly payroll in $
60	31	$ 5,580
70	36	6,480
80	41	7,380
90	46	8,280
100	51	9,180
110	56	10,080

A variable budget may also be developed as a series of formulas — one for each type of expense involved in the operating unit being budgeted. The formula shows an amount expected to be the fixed component of a given type of expense plus a factor for the variable component to be applied to the fixed case. For example, the fixed expense may be $2,000 per month for warehouse rent plus 1 percent of all sales over $500,000. If sales were $500,000, the rent allowed would be $2,000. If sales were $600,000, the rent allowance would be the base of $2,000 plus 1 percent of $100,000 ($600,000 minus $500,000), or $3,000. At $700,000 in sales, the rent allowance would be $4,000 ($2,000 + (0.01 × $200,000)), and so on.

Expenses also could be expressed as a percentage of the labor cost; an amount per person or machine hour; an amount per unit of product produced; and so on.

Volume of Activity

The variable referred to in a variable budget is the volume of activity. Thus, selecting an appropriate measure of that activity is important. The measure of the volume of activity could be direct labor hours; units, pound, or tons of material handled; or sales volume. A variety of different measures may be chosen; but to simplify the procedures, a single important measure of activity is usually selected for any one department or cost center.

Expenses such as indirect labor, heat, light, power, and supplies occur while workers and machines are in operation and largely in an amount proportional to hours expended. What or how much is produced in these hours is another matter. The variable budget is particularly useful for assisting in the control of spending relative to input measures of activity.

When variable burden allowances are based on an output measure of activity (such as the amount of product produced), the control responsibility is not clear-cut, since spending efficiency and operating efficiency are merged. Standard costs, rather than the variable budget, should be used in costing the efficiency of operations (Chapter 2).

People who use an output measure of activity for determining variable budget spending allowances do so because they believe that spending control should be tightened when operating performance is below standard. An output measure of activity also would have a looser standard for a spending when operating performance is above standard.

QUESTION: Should a firm restrict the variable budget to variable and semivariable expenses or should it also include fixed costs?

ANSWER:
In many companies, the variable budget is restricted to directly variable and semivariable expenses. Fixed costs such as depreciation, real estate taxes, and insurance, as well as the costs of many service departments, are omitted. The primary arguments commonly given for not including these costs in the variable budget are that the department being budgeted has no control over them. Furthermore, such costs are so large in comparison with the variable burden that if they were included in the budget, the manager would be discouraged from attempting to control variable costs that are a smaller part of the whole.

However, fixed costs are very important from a total company standpoint, and these costs are becoming increasingly more important with the heavy costs involved in increased automation. The only way to recoup these higher costs is to get orders for goods to be made by the facilities for which the costs were incurred.

CAPITAL BUDGETS

Capital budgeting is the process of planning expenditures the returns of which are expected to extend beyond one year. Some examples of capital outlays are expenditures for buildings, land, equipment, and permanent additions to working capital (especially inventories) associated with plant expansion. Since advertising campaigns have an impact beyond one year they, too, come within the classical definition of capital budgeting expenditures.

Capital budgeting requires a commitment to the future. For example, the purchase of a piece of equipment with an economic life of eight years requires a long period of waiting before the final results of the action can be known. Management must commit funds for this period and, thus, become a hostage of future events.

Asset expansion is generally related to expected future sales. A decision to buy or to construct a fixed asset that is going to last five years involves an implicit five-year forecast. Therefore, failure to forecast accurately will result in either overinvestment or underinvestment in fixed assets.

The wrong forecast of asset needs can result in serious consequences for a firm. If the firm invests too much in assets, it will incur heavy expenses. If, on the other hand, the firm does not invest enough in fixed assets, two serious consequences may occur. First, the equipment the company has may not be sufficiently modern to enable it to produce competitively. Second, if it has inadequate capacity, the firm may lose a portion of its share of the market to competitors. To regain lost customers usually requires heavy selling expenses, or price reductions, or both.

Good capital budgeting will also improve the timing of asset acquisitions and the quality of assets purchased. Until firms see that total sales are going to exceed capacity, no capital goods are ordered. This situation may occur simultaneously for many firms. When the heavy orders come in, the producers of capital goods go from a situation of idle capacity to one in which it is difficult to meet all new orders. Consequently, large backlogs of orders accumulate. Since the production of capital goods involves long lead times, some firms may have to wait a year or more before orders are filled. This situation has obvious implications for purchasing and plant managers.

Asset expansion typically involves substantial expenditures. When a company is going to spend a considerable amount of money, it must make the proper plans. A company completing a major capital expenditure program may need to arrange its financing several years in advance to be sure of having the funds for the expansion.

Capital Budgeting and Economic Theory

Capital budgeting is basically an application of a classic proposition from the economic theory of the firm; that is, a firm should operate at a point at which its marginal revenue is just equal to its marginal cost. In capital budgeting, marginal revenue is taken to be the percentage rate of return on investments, and the marginal cost is the firm's cost of capital.

A simplified version of this concept is shown in the two graphs in Exhibits 11.10 and 11.11. In the first graph (Exhibit 11.10) the horizontal axis measures the dollars of investment during a year and the vertical axis shows both the percentage cost of capital and the rate of return on projects. The projects are denoted by the boxes. Project A calls for an outlay of $20,000 (horizontal axis) and has a rate of return on investment of 26 percent (vertical axis). Project B has a rate of return on investment of 24 percent for a $30,000 investment. Project C costs $60,000 for a 21 percent return on investment, and so on. Project G represents an investment with a fixed return, such as government bonds that can have any amount of investment.

EXHIBIT 11.10
Capital Budgeting Decision Process

1) INVESTMENT PROJECT

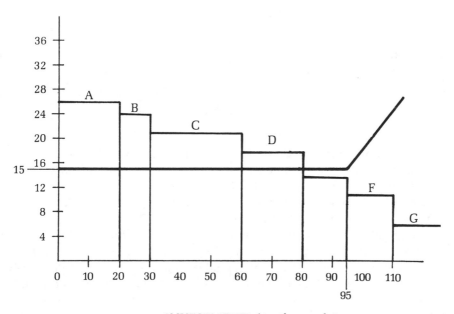

INVESTMENT (in thousands)

EXHIBIT 11.11
Capital Budgeting Decision Process (2) Investment
Opportunity Schedule

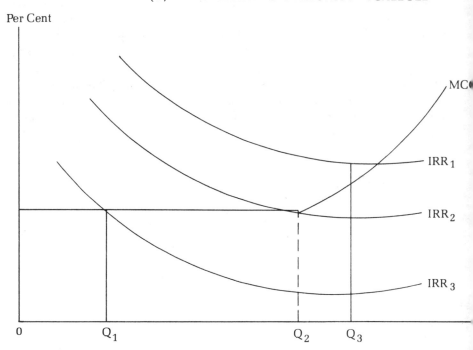

(2)   INVESTMENT   OPPORTUNITY   SCHEDULE

INVESTMENT   (in   thousands)

The second graph (Exhibit 11.11) illustrates how the concept is generalized to show smooth investment opportunity schedules (IRR). The investment opportunity schedules measure the rate of return on each project. The initials IRR stand for *internal rate of return*, which is what the rate of return on a particular project is called. The curve MCC shows the marginal cost of capital that is the cost of each additional dollar that must be acquired (borrowed, usually) to make capital expenditures. The graph shows the marginal cost of capital constant at 15 percent until the firm has raised $95,000, at which point the cost of capital turns sharply up. In other words, for this firm to maximize its profit, it should only invest in projects A through D.

The internal rate of return (IRR), or investment opportunity schedule, curves show different investment possibilities. IRR_1 has the best rate of return; IRR_3 has the worst. These three curves could represent three different companies or one company at three different times. As long as the IRR curve cuts the MCC curve to the left of Q_2 (the point at which the cost of capital goes up), the marginal cost of capital is constant. The part of the IRR curve on the right of Q_2 shows that part of the investment package will require capital at a higher cost.

Practical Application of Capital Budgeting

In a real situation, the capital budgeting process is much more complex than the preceding example suggests. A continuing stream of good investment opportunities results from hard thinking, outlays for research and development, and very careful planning. The sales and costs associated with particular projects must be estimated, usually for several years into the future.

Aside from the actual generation of ideas, the first step in the capital budgeting process is to assemble the data on all the proposed projects so that they might be appraised. Projects dealing with asset acquisition can be grouped according to the following categories:

1. Replacements
2. Expansion: additional capacity in existing product lines
3. Expansion: new product lines
4. Miscellaneous

In general, the easiest decisions to make are replacement decisions. Assets wear out and become obsolete and must be replaced to continue production. The company has a very good idea of the cost savings attendant to replacing an old asset, as well as a good idea of the consequences of nonreplacement. The outcomes of most replacement decisions can be predicted with a high degree of confidence. A high degree of uncertainty is involved in expansion, but a company may examine past production and sales experience to reduce the level of uncertainty. Expansion by adding additional capacity in existing product lines is the least risky of the expansion decisions, since the company can study past growth and estimate future growth in that product. Sometimes the decision to expand present facilities could be considered a replacement decision when it involves replacing present equipment or facilities with newer, faster, or more efficient equipment or facilities. The decision to expand into a new product area has the greatest risk of all the previous categories. This kind of expansion should be done only with a thorough survey of the market and distribution channels for the new product. Most new product decisions also require considerable research and development.

The miscellaneous category is a catch-all that includes intangibles, pollution control devices, plans for overseas expansion or mergers, and costs to improve morale (such as an employee swimming pool).

Other practical aspects of capital budgeting are the administrative details. Approvals typically are required at the top management level for other than replacement decisions. The board of directors of a company usually has to approve all the major, nonreplacement, capital expenditures.

The planning horizon for capital budgeting programs varies with the nature of the industry. In the utilities industry, where forecasts can be made with a high degree of reliability for ten to twenty years, the capital spending program tends to be planned for a correspondingly long period. Another example of a long planning period is in industries such as aerospace, where products (the space shuttle) require long development periods.

In the entire capital budgeting procedure, the most important factor is a reliable estimate of the cost savings and revenue increases that will be achieved from the proposed outlay of capital. Data on the cost savings and possible increased sales should be as detailed and as reasonable as possible. Consideration also should be given to how the new expenditures will affect present operations. For instance, a blood-diagnostic machine that can do one complete series of tests every thirty seconds may be valuable for a large hospital with thousands of patients but would be a waste of money for a small medical office with fewer than fifty patients. Even when this machine is installed in the large hospital, it will probably not affect the dollar amount of sales. It may cut costs, but the cost-benefit relationship may not be direct.

Determining Cash Flows from Capital Investment

Cash flows attributable to a particular investment can be thought of in terms of comparative income statements. The case of Acme Mousetraps, Inc., can be used to illustrate this procedure.

Acme Mousetraps, Inc., is a profitable manufacturing firm, a division of Eveningstar Technology Systems specializing in solid state mousetraps.

The company purchased a metal mulching machine five years ago for $15,000. The machine has an expected life of fifteen years and is depreciated on a straight-line basis with zero salvage value. It now has a book value of $10,000. The division manager wants to buy a machine for $20,000, which should expand sales from $20,000 to $22,000 over its ten-year life. It is expected that the machine will cut material costs from $14,000 to $10,000. The old machine has a market value of $2,000, taxes are 50 percent, and the firm's cost of capital is 14 percent. Should Acme buy the machine?

The decision calls for three steps:

1. Estimating the actual cash outlay required for the new piece of equipment
2. Determining the present value (a financial discounting by a certain interest rate) of the proposed cash flows
3. Determining if the internal rate of return on investment (IRR) exceeds the cost of capital and if the net present value is positive.

1. Estimated Cash Outlay

Acme must pay $20,000 for the new metal-mulcher machine, but the company's quarterly tax bill will be reduced by $4,000. This tax reduction is brought about by the loss on the sale of the old machine ($10,000 book value minus $2,000 market value that it can be sold for (a $8,000 loss) times 50 percent tax bracket = $4,000). Suppose that Acme had taxable income of $100,000 without the purchase of the new machine and the consequent write-off of the old machine. With a 50 percent tax bracket, Acme would have to pay the IRS $50,000 for its tax bill. However, if it buys the new machine and sells the old, it has an operating loss of $8,000, which is the $10,000 book value of the old machine minus the $2,000 market value. The loss would be considered an operating loss, not a capital loss, because it is the depreciation charges (an operating cost) that were too low during the old machine's five-year life. With this $8,000 additional cost, taxable income is reduced from $100,000 to $92,000, and the tax bill from $50,000 to $46,000. Consequently, Acme's cash outflow for taxes is $4,000 less because it purchased the new machine. An additional cash inflow from the sale of the old machine at $2,000 also is realized. The result is that the purchase of the new machine involves a new cash outlay of $14,000, which is the cost for capital budgeting purposes.

Invoice price of a new metal mulcher $20,000

Less:	Tax savings	(4,000)
	Market value of old metal mulcher	(2,000)
NET CASH OUTFLOW		**$14,000**

2. Present Value of Benefits

The first column in Exhibit 11.12 shows Acme's estimated income statement as it would be without the new machine; the second column shows the statement as it will look if the new investment is made. The difference between the old cash flows or $3,500 ($7,000 if machine is purchased minus $3,500 if the machine is not purchased) is the incremental cash flow produced by the new machine.

EXHIBIT 11.12
Comparative Income Statement for Considering Cash Flows

	Without New Investment	With New Investment
Sales	$ 20,000	$ 22,000
Raw Material Cost	(14,000)	(10,000)
Depreciation (D)	(1,000)	(2,000)
Taxable Income	5,000	10,000
Income Taxes	(2,500)	5,000
Profit after Tax (P)	$ 2,500	$ 5,000
Cash Flow (D+P)	$ 3,500	$ 7,000

The interest factor for a ten-year 14 percent annuity is 5.216 (obtained from an annuity table). When we multiply this factor by $3,500, the result is $18,256, which is the present value of the future cash flow. The present value is what it would cost today to get cash flows of $3,500 per year at a return of a specific percent (14 percent in the example) per year. For instance, in order to get $3,500 per year for the next 10 years, it would be necessary to invest $18,256 at 14 percent per year compounded annually. So the value today (present value) of the future cash flows of $3,500 per year for 10 years is $18,256. In this case, the present value of the future cash flows that Acme can receive if they install the new machine is more than the net purchase price of $14,000.

3. Net Present Value

Subtracting the $14,000 cost figure from $18,256 gives the investment a net present value of $4,256. Since the net present value is positive, the machine should be purchased.

When an investment tax credit is allowed, the outlay cost of investment in new machinery and equipment is reduced by the amount of tax credit, which would further improve the return on investment performance of the equipment investment. In other words, if the asset has a cost of $10,000 and a depreciable life of at least eight years, the outlay cost will be reduced by a certain percent (say 10 percent) tax credit on $1,000. In this way, the net present value will be raised over what it would otherwise be.

Cash Workpapers for Replacement Decisions

Exhibit 11.13 shows a workpaper used by Acme Mousetraps for making the replacement decision in the previous example. The top part of the workpaper sets forth the cash outflows at the time the investment is made. All the cash outflows occur immediately, so no discounting is required — the present value factor is 1.0. The $8,000 loss on the old machine gives rise to a $4,000 tax reduction. The $2,000 salvage value of the old machine is a reduction in cash outflows necessary to acquire the new machine.

In the lower section of the workpaper, revenues increase by $6,000 per year (a sales increase of $2,000 plus a cost reduction of $4,000). However, this amount is taxable at 50 percent; therefore, the after-tax benefits reduce the benefits from $6,000 to $3,000 per year. This $3,000 is received each year for ten years; therefore, it is an annuity. The present value of the annuity discounted at the 14 percent cost of capital is $15,648.

The depreciation on the new machine also causes cash inflows (because depreciation is a noncash expense) of $2,000 before taxes and $1,000 after taxes. This amount can be represented as a ten-year annuity with a present value of $5,216. The depreciation that the company was receiving on the old machine is subtracted from the new machine depreciation. Had the replacement not been made, the company would have the benefit of

EXHIBIT 11.13
Calculations for Replacement Decisions

	Amount Before Tax	Amount After Tax	Year Event Occurs	Present Value Factor at 14 Percent	Present Value
Outflows at Time Investment is Made					
New Equipment Cost	$20,000	$20,000	–0	1.00	$20,000
Salvage Value Old Equip.	(2,000)	(2,000)	–0	1.00	(2,000)
Tax Loss on Sale	(8,000)	(4,000)	–0	1.00	(4,000)
TOTAL OUTFLOWS (present value of costs)					$14,000
Inflows (Annual Returns)					
Sales & Cost Benefits*	$ 6,000	$ 3,000	1–10	5.216	$15,648
Depreciation on New Equip.	2,000	1,000	1–10	5.216	5,216
Depreciation on Old Equip.†	(1,000)	(500)	1–10	5.216	(2,608)
Salvage Value on New Equip.‡	—	—	—	—	—
TOTAL INFLOWS					$18,256

*$2,000 sales increase + $4,000 cost savings = $6,000 benefit

†If the replacement was not made Acme would have $1,000 per year depreciation, therefore the $1,000 must be subtracted.

‡The new equipment is estimated to have no salvage value.

the $1,000 depreciation for every year for the next ten years. With the replacement, this depreciation is immediately taken as an operating loss and shown as the tax loss on the sale in the top section.

12

Computers and Accounting

The day of universal computerized accounting systems is fast approaching. Small computers (micro- and minicomputers) are now available, complete with all the peripheral devices and accounting *software*, for under $10,000. By 1985, comparable systems should be available for about half that price. The computers that are available today for under $10,000 are more powerful than computers in the late 50s that cost more than $1 million. This means that the tremendous speed, file control, and convenience of computers are now affordable to even small businesses with less than $100,000 in sales.

One major use of a computer to any business is accounting. Although the same rules are used in accounting with a computer that are used in accounting manually, there is a quantitative difference in speed and complexity between the two. Using a manual system, records may be kept by different people in different departments, but with a computer all records are kept in one place.

WHAT IS A COMPUTER?

Knowing what the components of the computer system are and under-
standing the jargon used by computer people are important when discuss-
ing the accounting aspects of computers.

A computer is not just a single enormous device. In fact, a computer
consists of several distinct sections that can vary greatly in complexity.
Their speed varies, as do also the size of their memories, the number and
speed of their input/output devices, the types of tasks that they are best
suited to perform, and the number of peripheral devices and programs
(software) that are available with them. A total computer is more than
just an electronic brain. The brain must have a memory to store information, channels over which information can be transferred to and from the
outside world, and input/output devices that prepare data or record
results. A computer without these features is like a person who can think
but cannot remember and has no senses to provide information and no
muscles for the brain to direct.

A computer consists of three basic sections: the control section (central
processing unit, or CPU), the memory section, and the input/output section (see Exhibit 12.1). The *control section* (CPU) processes the data. It
gets the instructions from memory, decodes and executes them, performs

---

EXHIBIT 12.1
Basic Computer Design

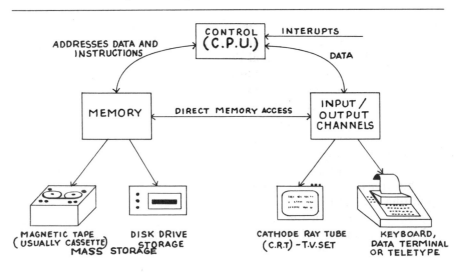

arithmetic and logical functions, transfers data to and from the memory and the input/output devices, and provides timing and control signals. The *memory section* contains storage for instructions and data. The *input/ output section* handles the communication between the computer (CPU) and the outside world.

The *memory section* may use tapes, disk drives, or integrated circuits to store information. The CPU has some memory in it; but if you need more memory than can be provided in the CPU, which is almost always the case, you need to have *peripheral* devices such as disk drives or tapes to store the information. Information or sometimes whole programs or languages are stored on a disk or magnetic tape to be accessed by the computer when the information is needed. The computer may also store information on these devices to be used when it is performing a program.

The central processing unit (CPU) has memory over and above the peripheral devices. These memories have *wired-in* memory space required for arithmetical calculations and controlling functions and language that is needed all the time and should not have to depend on external memory. The memory that is part of the CPU is a semiconductor memory; that is, memory that is built into the hardware. This memory has both data and instructions stored on a permanent or semipermanent basis.

The memory section of the CPU contains other devices besides memory itself. The address decoder uses addresses to select particular memory locations. Other circuitry can provide control signals for the memories, can allow the memory section and control section to communicate properly, and can ensure that the memory section retains its contents. Special integrated circuits are used to preserve the contents of memories. Other integrated circuits are decoders, buffers, and latches. Therefore, the memory section of all computers, even the small ones, contains several circuit boards, each with a few thousand words of memory and some supporting circuitry.

When people talk about computers, they sometimes describe them as having 8 K, 16 K, 32 K, of memory. K stands for 1,000. By a 32 K of memory it is meant that the central process has room for 32,000 *bytes* (each byte equals eight bits) of information. A bit is an on or off state at one memory cell location. The order in which a series of memory cells are on or off relates a piece of information. So a *bit* is the basic unit of information in a computer.

Since the CPU must handle more than one bit at a time to store a complex message, bits are usually grouped into a fixed length. The smallest grouping of bits is a *byte,* which is eight bits long. The best-known grouping of bits, and the basic length that a CPU can understand, is called a *word.* Computer word lengths vary from eight bits (a microcomputer) to sixty-four bit words (the biggest computer now made). Therefore, the best indicator of the size of a computer is how many bits in size its average *word length* is.

Word length is one measure of the power of a computer. A computer with a longer word length can do more work than one with a shorter word length, even if both computers operate at the same speed. A word length determines the amount of work done during each cycle. Large computers have long words. An IBM 360 has 32-bit words, a Univac 1110 has 36-bit words, and a Control Data 660 has 64-bit words. Minicomputers have shorter words — 12 bits (Digital PDP - 8) or 16 bits (Digital PDP - 11 or Data General Nova). Microcomputers usually have 8-bit words. The biggest computers with 32-plus bit words do more work in each cycle (can "crunch" more numbers), but this does not mean that they are more efficient for business purposes.

The input/output section of a computer is an interface between the computer and the outside world. The computer is a digital electronic device that has its own internal clock and uses certain specified voltage levels to indicate bit states (on or off). The input/output section must convert the input data from the outside world to a form the computer can understand and convert the output data sent by the computer to a form the outside world can understand. This conversion may be a very complex task. Often the CPU will perform part of the conversion; some large computers have separate processors that handle input/output.

Connected to the input/output section is the peripheral equipment — the *keyboard* (typewriter or teletype) and the *cathode ray* tube (CRT), which is a television screen. These peripheral input/output devices are for inputting information into the computer and for getting out information from the computer. These devices are hooked into the CPUs input/output boards, which interpret the information for the CPU as discussed in the last paragraph.

The input/output section of the computer (CPU) considers many characteristics of the transmitted signals from the peripherals and to the peripherals in order to convert the signals into their proper input or output form. The input/output section of the CPU must consider several characteristics of the signals including signal level (voltage level), signal type (type of electric current), signal duration, timing, and signal format.

Computer Cost and Size

Most of us have heard of the IBM 370 and other big computer systems that cost thousands of dollars per month to rent (few businesses, even rich ones, can afford to purchase one). But few people are aware of the new smaller computers (microcomputers) that are coming down in price. It is now possible to buy the central processing unit (CPU) of a computer in kit form for only a few hundred dollars.

The little *microcomputers* (not much bigger than a bread box) can perform almost all the number functions (accounting, calculating, storage) that a small business needs.

A microcomputer, complete with all the memory and input/output devices (keyboard and display) and software (instructions), can be rented for $300 per month from Administrative Systems, Inc., Denver, Colorado. Compare that cost to the $2,000 or more per month for the IBM and Control Data Systems that are more sophisticated but basically perform the same functions. One basic difference between large and small systems is the *language* they can use. Large systems can use COBOL and other sophisticated languages, whereas the small systems generally use BASIC, or FORTRAN languages. For most businesses, this language difference does not matter.

Businesses across the country are also realizing that it usually is less costly to have several smaller computers (like the micros we discussed) in each department than to have one large computer with a series of terminals. This trend will undoubtedly continue to accelerate.

Small computers are not number-crunchers like the large computers. That is, small computers cannot do complicated mathematical calculations or mathematical models like the big computers with any reasonable speed. But many firms do not need such capability. The functions of business, mostly sorting, printing out reports and statements, simple mathematical calculations, and storage of information can be very easily performed by the microcomputers. Moreover, if a business needs additional storage capacity or additional terminals, they can be added on as needed, thereby making the cost even more favorable.

Language and Software

Software is the program instructions that a computer needs to tell it the steps to go through in computing, finding files, filling files with information, printing out results, giving instructions to the operator for data input, and similar functions. The term *software* is generally used to describe the set of programs, written by the programmer, that causes the computer *hardware* (the CPU and input/output devices) to come to life, that is, to function. The three basic software categories are:

1. Translation programs
2. Operating system programs
3. User processing programs

Translation programs are programs in machine language used by the computer systems to translate higher-level languages into machine language. These translation programs are generally supplied by the hardware manufacturer. When a computer is programmed to do something in FORTRAN, BASIC, or other high-level languages, the translation programs interpret these languages into *machine language*, a number language that the computer can understand.

Operating system programs are also usually supplied by the computer manufacturer. They are used to regulate and supervise the sequence of activities going on at any time in the system. These programs minimize operator intervention in the actual operation of the computer and ensure a smooth, fast, and efficient transition among the varied tasks performed by the system. Other operating system programs aid the programmer in his or her own work. Functions performed by some of the more important operating system programs include:

1. Load programs into memory from mass storage (tape or disc).
2. Print messages for the operator and the programmer regarding the status of the program.
3. Perform job accounting by keeping track of who uses the computer and for how long.
4. Handle requests for input/output from executing programs.
5. Handle the collection of data from telecommunication lines (in a time-sharing system).
6. Schedule the slice of time to be allocated to each user's program in a time-sharing system.
7. Perform some routine processing of data, such as sorting and copying the contents of one data set onto a specified device.
8. Maintain the store of programs on the mass storage device, such as adding programs to the store, and deleting those no longer needed.
9. Attempt to recover from or correct errors that may occur in any segment of the computing system.
10. Interpret the job set-up and job control instructions specified by the programmer.

User processing programs, sometimes called applications programs, are programs written by individual users to solve particular problems. They may be written in a generalized fashion and modified as needed to fit the requirements of a particular system, or they may be constructed to satisfy specific needs. For example, a company may construct its own credit and collection program, billing program, or other programs.

Software for a system is usually stored on a mass storage device such as a magnetic disk (floppy disk), tape, or paper punched by a paper reader.

Language for a computer is of two basic types: machine language and high-level language.

A program can be executed by the computer only when it is stored in the computer's memory and is in machine language code. *Machine language* is the only language the computer can understand. It is a language in which arithmetic and logical operations are represented by machine-recognizable numeric codes and in which memory locations containing data and program instructions are represented by numeric addresses. Machine language programs are very detailed and difficult to write.

Each memory location has an *address*. Suppose we wanted to add the data contained in memory locations 054 and 834 and store the result in location 600. The machine instruction in machine language for this might be "4305483600." The first two numbers (43) are the operation code that is used by the control unit to determine what action (add or subtract) is to be performed on the data to be used. The data to be added occurs in memory locations 054 and 834 and the answer will be stored in 600.

43	054 834	600
Operation code	Memory address of first and second operation	Address result is to be stored in

Higher-level languages were developed to allow the user to formulate a problem in a more convenient and efficient manner. These languages are problem oriented rather than machine oriented. Higher-level languages must ultimately be translated into machine language before they can be executed by the computer. Special programs called language translators or *compilers* have been developed to provide this translation service. Some commonly used higher-level languages that are now in use are:

FORTRAN	(FORmula TRANslation)
BASIC	(Beginner's All-purpose Symbolic Instruction Code)
COBOL	(COmmon Business Oriented Language)
ALGOL	(ALGOrithmic Language)

PL/1	(Programming Language 1)
RPG	(Report Program Generator)
SNOBOL	(String Manipulation Language)

Other languages include GPSS (General Purpose Simulation System), SLIP (Symbolic List Processing), PLAN (Programming Language Nineteen-hundred), and more than 500 others more. The most popular languages for business are FORTRAN, BASIC, COBOL, and PL/1.

FORTRAN is a universal high-level, machine-independent language that is generally better suited to mathematical and scientific problems than to business applications, although a lot of business software is written in FORTRAN. Business problems that are once-only annual jobs are probably best suited to FORTRAN because it is more efficient than most other languages. For the problem of getting cost by multiplying price times quantity, the statement in FORTRAN would look like this:

$$C = P * Q$$

BASIC was developed to meet the need for a simple, easily learned language having most of the facilities of COBOL, FORTRAN, and ALGOL. In particular, BASIC caters to noncomputer people, such as students and businesspersons. However, since BASIC is a language that almost all micro- and minicomputers has available (sometimes it is the only language that is available), many small businesses are using it as their programming language. BASIC has become a working language for time-sharing systems and also a training medium for general programming. BASIC and extended BASIC offered by many manufacturers for their particular machine are becoming more important for small applications and are expected to grow in use over the next few years. A BASIC statement to find cost by multiplying price times quantity looks very similar to a FORTRAN statement.

$$LET\ C = P * Q$$

COBOL is also a high-level, machine-independent (it will run on any computer equipped with a COBOL compiler) language. As the acronym Common Business Oriented Language suggests, COBOL was devised to be used as a business language. As a matter of fact, in 1959 the United States Department of Defense specified that this language be available on any computer that it purchased. In spite of all the extensive planning and compiler-writing behind COBOL, it is still a language for professional programmers rather than the man-in-the-street. It is basically a language for big computers (main-frame). Most small computers such as micro- or minicomputers do not use COBOL because of the tremendous memory required and its inefficiency. COBOL statements are written as English words selected from a restricted range together with data names. A COBOL statement to get cost by multiplying price times quantity would be:

MULTIPLY PRICE BY QUANTITY-A GIVING COST-A

COBOL is by far the most universal language, but because of the difficulty in its use and its inefficiency its future is obscure.

PL/1 not only embodies most of the important elements of COBOL, FORTRAN, and ALGOL, but also extends even further by including additional facilities not found in these languages. Although this comprehensiveness has many advantages and might appear to be the solution to all problems, PL/1 has not yet become the universal language that it was originally intended to be. It is, however, used extensively by the users of IBM computers since IBM developed the language.

ACCOUNTING COMPUTER PROGRAMS AND DOCUMENTATION

Computer Program Layout

Accounting computer programs generally follow the design shown in the diagrams (Exhibits 12.2 through 12.9). This is a flow-chart diagram represented in symbolic figures that will be explained shortly, but are generally self-explanatory.

Each of the functional routines, sales accounting, payroll, and other accounts, produce posting data to update the ledger. These data are written by the functional routines on a storage media during the individual processing runs. The storage produced can be used to update the ledger progressively throughout the month, or if the volume is small, at the end of the month. This is shown in Exhibit 12.2.

The routines (Routine 1 through Routine 7) are for the various areas of the accounting system; Routine 1 is for payroll and manpower/machine utilization analysis. Routine 2 is for sales accounting and sales analysis. Each routine is shown by a separate graph flowchart and each will be explained in turn.

EXHIBIT 12.2
Main Routines and Interconnections

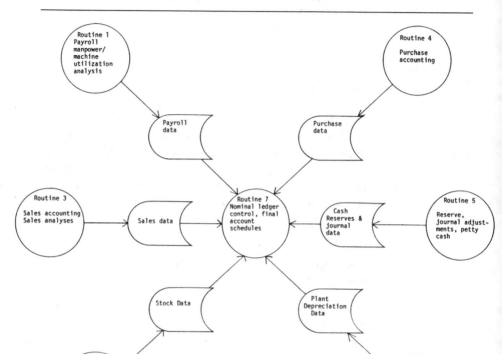

Routine 1 (see Exhibit 12.3), payroll analysis, maintains the usual payroll details but also adjusts for holiday pay, year-end earnings, and tax statements. During holiday periods, records are held in suspense and no action is taken until the payroll week is reached. The data for this routine is updated weekly on the storage media and includes wages paid (by type and location) and maintenance services charged.

Routine 2, the sales accounting, credit control, and sales analysis routine (see Exhibit 12.4) keeps customer files on an open item basis and the system relates the cash received to the correct invoice. When the cash item does not exactly match the invoiced account, it shows the amount that has been paid on account. Each settled transaction is printed monthly

EXHIBIT 12.3
Payroll Analysis Flow Chart

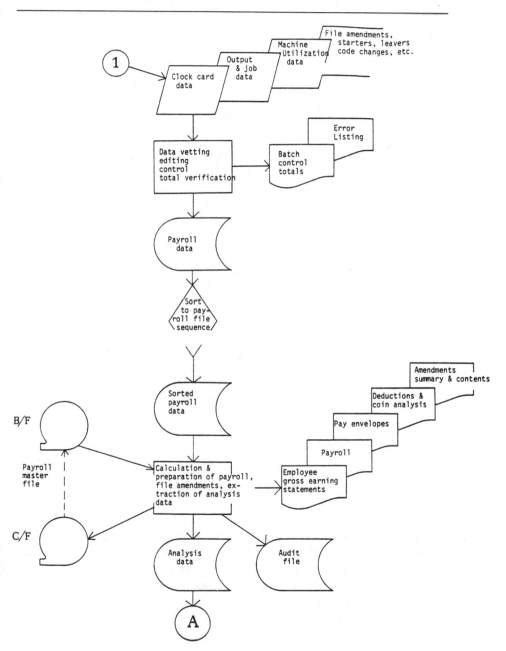

EXHIBIT 12.3
continued

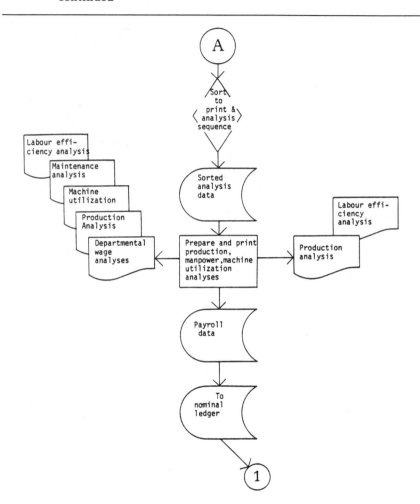

on the audit list. The aged receivables list is the main credit control report and is obtained by sorting the customer file by age of outstanding items. Sales data are analyzed by product, factory, and division and are prepared for eventual inclusion in the ledger routines.

Routine 3, the stock and purchase order control routine, (see Exhibit 12.5) contains a record for each purchase order. Orders are controlled by

EXHIBIT 12.4
Sales, Credit, Analysis Flow Chart

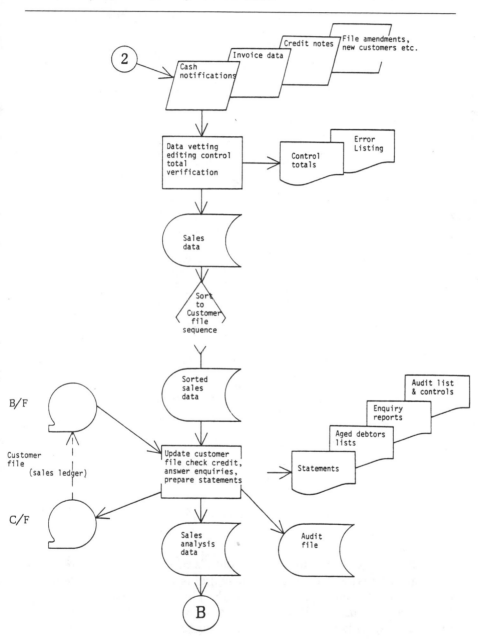

EXHIBIT 12.4
continued

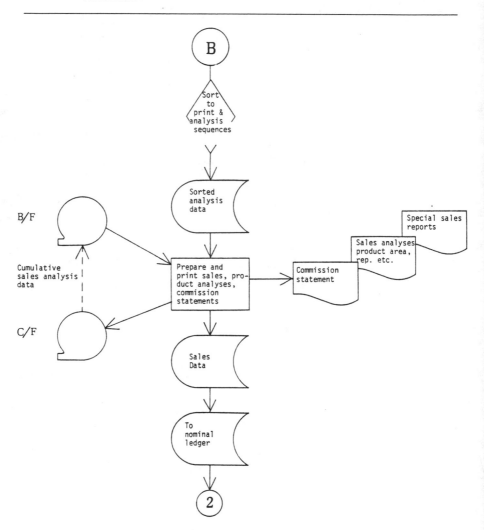

the due delivery week number, and details of orders overdue are listed until the order is satisfied. A stock file contains a record for each item held in stores, and the computer maintains the physical balances and controls the free stock position. From calculated reorder levels, the stock level exception report is produced as well as suggested economic order quan-

EXHIBIT 12.5
Stock and Purchase Order Control Flow Chart

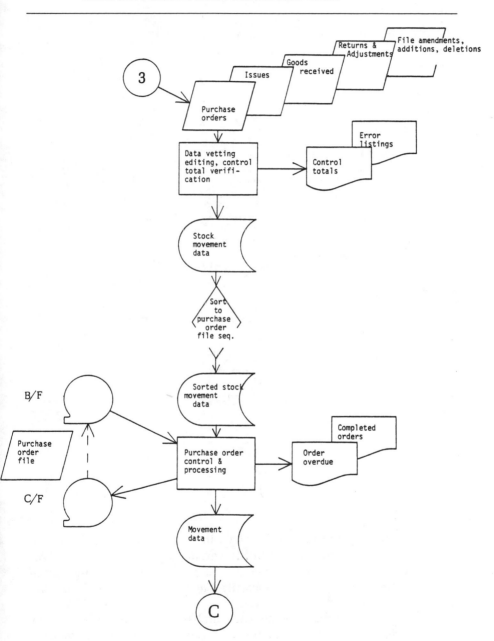

EXHIBIT 12.5
continued

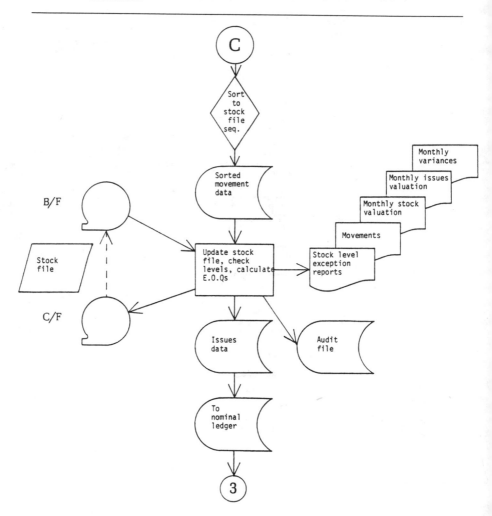

tities for action by the purchasing department. A stock ledger is maintained at standard prices and monthly variances between the standards and actual invoice value are prepared. This procedure is done by matching data from Routine 4 to the stock file. Each month, stock balances are totaled and transferred to Routine 7.

Routine 4, the purchase ledger and purchase accounting routine (see Exhibit 12.6), maintains a standard purchase ledger producing itemized remittance advices and credit slips. Payments can be delayed or speeded

EXHIBIT 12.6
Purchase Ledger and Accounting Flow Chart

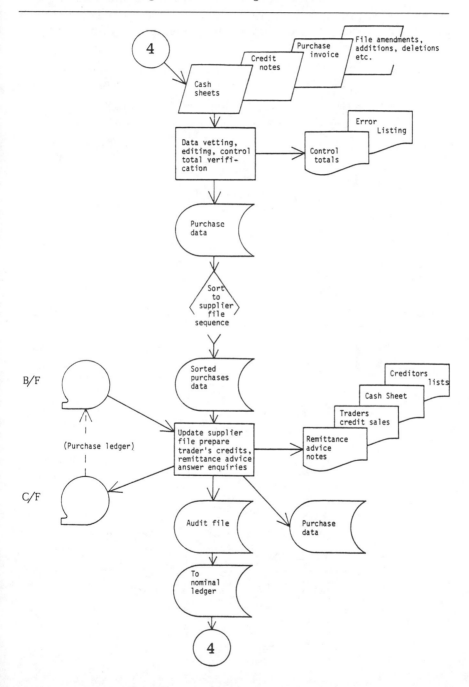

up as required by insertion of the appropriate inputs. The information is sent to Routine 7.

Routine 5, the cash reserves and journal adjustments routines, (see Exhibit 12.7) deals with the consolidation of the incidental reserves and adjustments before they are entered in the ledger routine (Routine 7).

EXHIBIT 12.7
Cash Reserves and Journal Adjustments Flow Chart

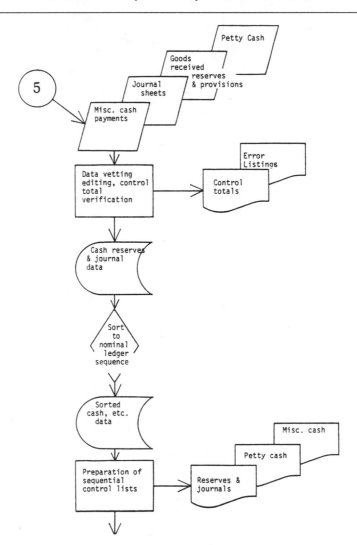

EXHIBIT 12.7
continued

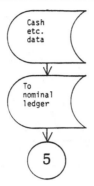

Routine 6, the asset register and depreciation records routine (see Exhibit 12.8), is controlled by asset number, account code, and cost center code. Reports can be produced at any of these levels. Depreciation is calculated monthly and sent to the ledger account, Routine 7. Control data on planned maintenance schedules is prepared and comparisons made between planned maintenance and actual maintenance carried out.

Routine 7, the nominal ledger and budgetary control account, (see Exhibit 12.9) has three main sections — balance sheet, expenditures, and revenue items. When data from the six supporting routines are consolidated, the nominal ledger becomes self-balancing. After the updating of the ledger, the account balances are grouped according to their schedule line numbers for inclusion in monthly reports. The budget file contains the budgeted expenses for each expenditure type for each cost center. The expenditure budget is stored in the form of a fixed portion and a variable portion. The budget is compared with the actual expenditures.

Documentation

All computer programs used for accounting functions (or any other functions) customarily has documentation. Documentation of the program generally includes:

1. A listing of the program code (the instructions that it follows in the language programmed).
2. English statements in the program itself, which explain what the
 · program is doing at the time (called *remark* statements).

EXHIBIT 12.8
Maintenance of Asset Register and Depreciation Records
Flow Chart

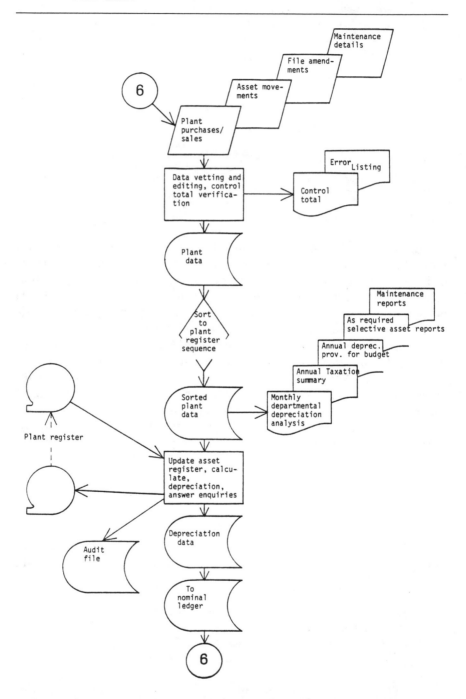

EXHIBIT 12.9
Ledger and Budgetary Flow Chart

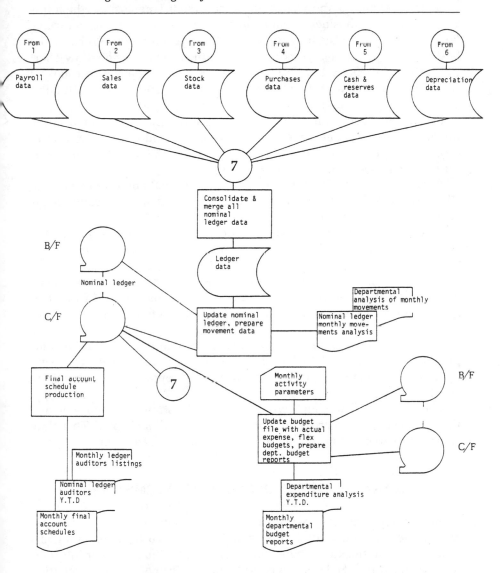

3. A written book showing how to operate the program and how the program was designed (called *Operators Manual* or *System Manual*).

4. Flow charts, such as those cited, that show in graphic form how the program operates.

The remark statements in the program and the written documentation do not take any special knowledge to understand. To read the program code itself requires a knowledge of the particular language in which it is written but most businesspersons do not necessarily need to know the language in order to see how the accounting system works. Probably the best illustration of the workings of the programs are the flow-chart illustrations (Exhibits 12.2 through 12.9). A businessperson can look at these for an overview of the system. This is shown with the chart (Exhibit 12.2) that preceded this section.

Each symbol used in the flow chart has a special, and for the most part, universal meaning. The boxes, diamonds, ovals, and circles are used to describe a particular process or peripheral device. Exhibit 12.10 illustrates the commonly used symbols and their meaning.

A variety of flow charts are constructed for a data processing system. The flow charts differ primarily in their level of detail and comprehensiveness in relation to the total system.

At lower levels, flow charts can be put into three categories: the systems flow chart, routine flow chart, and the program flow chart.

The flow chart (see Exhibit 12.11) is a *systems flow chart* that shows the interlinking of the routines comprising the total system. The chart indicates the flow of both internal and external data to the firm. The system flow chart is an outline on which further detailed flow charts are based.

The second flow chart (Exhibit 12.12) is related more closely to computer methodology than is the systems flow chart and shows processing runs, files, and input/output within a routine. It represents a *routine flow chart*.

The *program flow chart* was previously illustrated as Routines one through seven in the program layout section of this chapter. This flow chart is prepared by the programmer who designed the system.

MANAGEMENT INFORMATION SYSTEMS (MIS)

Most companies do not have separate accounting, financial, or management system reports. Rather, they are all integrated together in a comprehensive, interlocking whole generally called a management information system (MIS). H. D. Clifton and T. Lucey, in their book *Accounting and Computer Systems*, offer this definition of an MIS[1]:

It is an information system making use of available resources to provide

---

[1]H.D. Clifton and T. Lucey, *Accounting and Computer Systems*. London: Business Books Ltd., 1973. p. 6.

EXHIBIT 12.10
Commonly Used Flow Chart Symbols

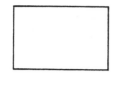

PROCESS/ANNOTATION: A rectangular-
shaped symbol is used for processing
instructions.

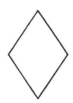

DECISION/SORTING: A diamond-shaped
symbol is used to denote decisions,
or in some cases, sorting runs
(because sorting involves decisions).
A common means of expressing a
decision is in terms of a question
that can be answered yes or no.
The decision diamond would then have
two arrows going from it, one for
yes and one for no.

TERMINATE/START: The oval-shaped
symbol is generally shown at the
beginning of a program and when it
ends. The computer instruction
START may be in the symbol to start,
and the word END or STOP will be
inside the symbol at the end of the
run.

INPUT/OUTPUT: A symbol shaped like
a parallelogram is used for input and
output instructions. For an input
operation, the instruction INPUT or
READ followed by a list of variables
is used. For output operations, the
instruction WRITE or PRINT is used.

CONNECTOR: When it is inconvenient
to draw flow lines to connect one
area of the flow chart to another,
connectors are often used. Connectors
identify a block by a label or
indicate transfer to another labeled
block. A numeric or alphabetical
label is usually placed in the circle.

CRT DISPLAY: The television display at the terminal

EXHIBIT 12.10
continued

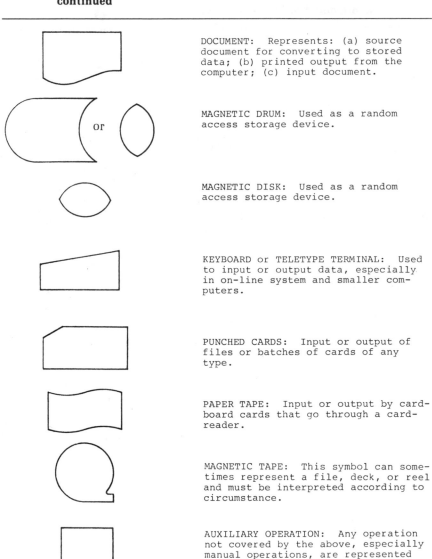

DOCUMENT: Represents: (a) source document for converting to stored data; (b) printed output from the computer; (c) input document.

MAGNETIC DRUM: Used as a random access storage device.

MAGNETIC DISK: Used as a random access storage device.

KEYBOARD or TELETYPE TERMINAL: Used to input or output data, especially in on-line system and smaller computers.

PUNCHED CARDS: Input or output of files or batches of cards of any type.

PAPER TAPE: Input or output by cardboard cards that go through a cardreader.

MAGNETIC TAPE: This symbol can sometimes represent a file, deck, or reel and must be interpreted according to circumstance.

AUXILIARY OPERATION: Any operation not covered by the above, especially manual operations, are represented by the square.

**EXHIBIT 12.11
Systems Flow Chart**

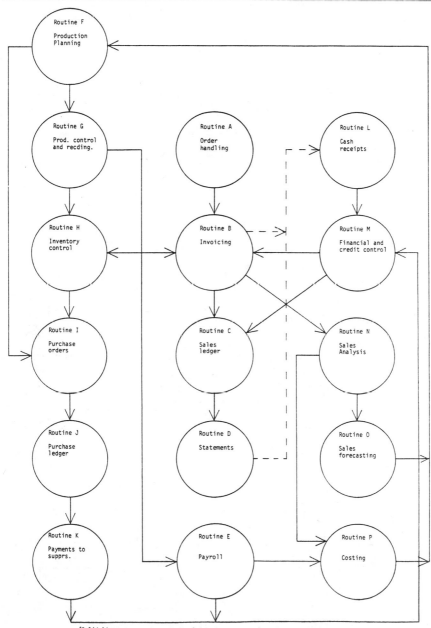

(Solid lines represent movement of data between routines, broken lines represent data movement via outside agencies)

EXHIBIT 12.12
Flow Chart of Routine N

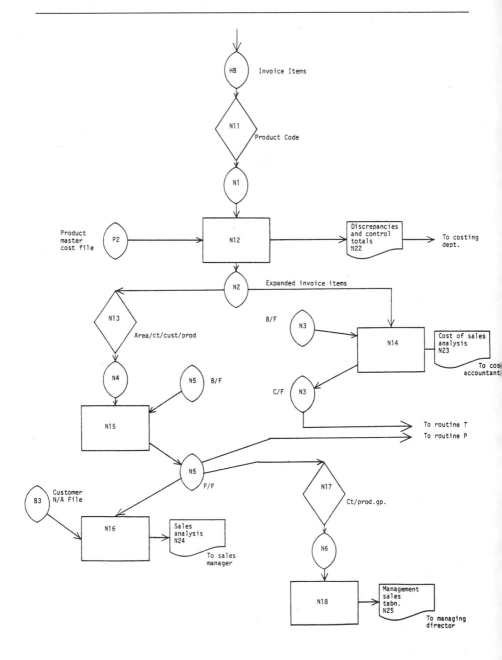

managers at all levels in all functions with information from all relevant sources necessary to enable them to make timely and effective decisions for planning, directing, and controlling the activities for which they are responsible.

Any system incurs costs only; that is, it has no intrinsic value of its own. The value of any MIS can come only from the users of that system and not from the producers of the information. The users — management — can only cause value to be attributed to the MIS as a result of actions following decisions taken using the information provided.

The value of any MIS can come only from actions that :

1. Increase profits
2. Reduce costs
3. Use resources more effectively
4. Increase sales

Information reaches management from the computer base by a series of reports. These reports are of three types:

1. Reports relating passive background information. These reports are produced at lengthy intervals, usually after the transactions involved have taken place. This type of report includes asset records and depreciation schedules.
2. Reports that provide control information to influence and guide current and short-term tactical and operating decisions. Examples are cost variance reports, credit information, and working capital summaries.
3. Reports that provide statistical data for forecasting firm planning and long-term strategic decisions. Examples include budget models and investment appraisals.

Exhibit 12.13 illustrates the different areas of a management information system and to whom they relate.

The graph in Exhibit 12.14, follows the broad pattern of operational, tactical, and strategic divisions described in Exhibit 12.13. The system depicted has at its heart the main-stream activities of production planning, inventory management, and production control. Since the accounting part of the system is shown as secondary, it follows that the firm gains benefits in these main-stream activities.

Using the same divisions of the MIS — strategic, tactical, and operational — we can see how management affects the MIS through control or feedback loops with the system. This is illustrated in Exhibit 12.14. The

EXHIBIT 12.13
Areas of a Management Information System

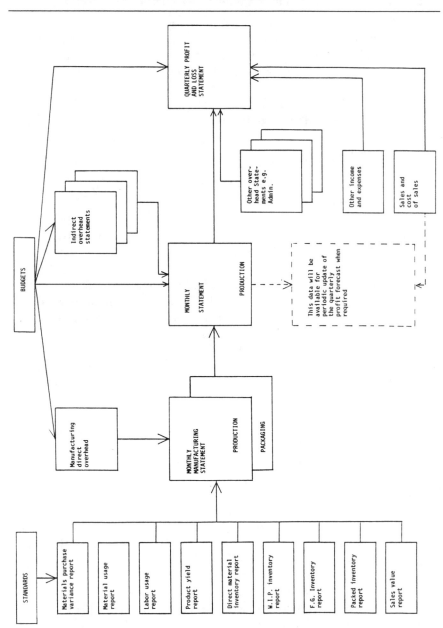

EXHIBIT 12.14
Information Flows

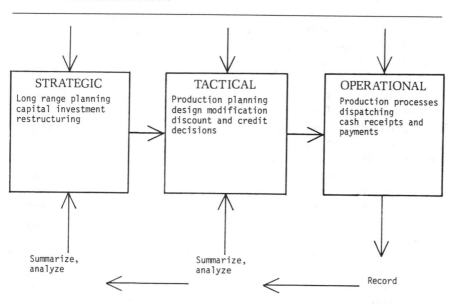

various loops depicted have differing time considerations. Generally, the time scale between decision and result, or instructions and result, diminishes as one proceeds from the strategic to the operating levels. The period of accountability may vary from the time at which there is a change in a market position, until the foreperson receives instructions to change the work schedules.

CONTROL IN DATA PROCESSING SYSTEMS

All businesspersons are likely now, or in the future, to be faced with audit and control problems associated with data processing systems. "Computers don't make mistakes, but people do" is an expression often heard in computer circles. Computers transfer, calculate, and manipulate data with unprecedented accuracy; yet errors do occur. Errors made in computer systems are usually honest mistakes caused by the input operator's making some clerical mistake, but outright fraud also has occurred in the short history of widespread computer use.

Computer Fraud

The responsibility of the auditor and accountant for financial fraud is a matter of controversy. However, recent fines imposed on auditors, especially in the United States, leave no doubt that an external auditor can be held at least partly responsible for missing a fraud, as the recent history of the Equity Funding Case clearly showed.

A computer fraud can be perpetrated by feeding a fraudulent input document to the sytem or by altering either the computer program or computer storage. For these methods to be successful, the perpetrator must penetrate the control system. The control system of the computer designed to prevent accidental error will, to a great extent, act as a deterrent to fraud.

According to studies by C. Nottingham,[2] only 35 percent of all computer frauds are committed in business corporations whereas 31 percent of such frauds are committed within banks. Half of the computer frauds committed against banks were committed by Electronic Data Processing (EDP) department employees; the remaining 50 percent were done by penetrating the computer system in some way. In corporations, 66 percent of the computer frauds were committed by EDP employees. The EDP empoyees committed 11 percent of their frauds by program manipulation, 33 percent by input media, and 56 percent by actual system penetration.

The low percentage of program manipulation frauds may be partially explained by the use in programs of the high-level languages that are not easily understood by the average person and partially by the individual idiosyncrasies of the programmer. Since there are many ways to approach a solution to a programming problem, it follows that nearly everyone will approach it differently. Many times, programmers who understand the language will not understand the logic or the programs. However, a fraud involving program manipulation is most difficult and requires a degree of sophistication that may be difficult to detect.

Non-EDP employees account for 31 percent of computer crimes. They commit 38 percent of these crimes by introducing false input and 62 percent by penetrating the computer system.

Only one computer fraud has been reported by a nonemployee — the case of Jerry Neal Schneider. Schneider visited Pacific Telephone Company under the pretext of being a writer doing an article on equipment ordering systems. After gaining information on the company computer, he posed as a customer to get information about input format, equipment

---

[2]C. Nottingham, *Survey of Computer-Related Fraud.* Unpublished doctoral dissertation, University of Bradford, 1974.

codes, and delivery sites. He then formed his own company and broke into Pacific Telephone's equipment ordering program and obtained more than $1 million in equipment before he was caught. Mr. Schneider now has his own computer fraud consulting company, which is a strictly legitimate venture.

Some other noteworthy computer frauds were:

1. A programmer working for an American bank increased his own overdraft limit from $2,000 to $200,000.
2. The unauthorized sale of spare computer time and computer print-outs containing valuable information to outsiders and competitors.
3. A pirating of system specifications, flow charts, and program details by data processing personnel and the subsequent sale of these materials to competitors.
4. Employees developing programs on a company's computers and then leaving the company, taking with them all the information on the program.

It would be unrealistic to think that a completely tamper-proof system can be devised. Given sufficient time, intelligent, determined persons can beat any system. The best thing for a company to do, then, is to ensure that a series of interlocking checks and controls over personnel, systems, and machines are maintained to make fraud difficult.

Control Procedures

The aims of the data processing manager generally coincide with those of the businessman. The data processing manager tries to insure that:

1. All data that are required to be processed are in fact processed.
2. All data processed are identified correctly.
3. Incorrect items of data are identified and dealt with either clerically or within the computer according to prescribed rules.
4. Correct data are not changed before, during, or after computer processing.
5. The data processing system is working in an efficient manner.

To carry out these functions, it is necessary to consider, in detail, the controls and security checks that must be incorporated into a comprehensive system in order to safeguard the organization. All system controls must be systematic, well documented, and supported by management. One of the greatest emphases of an auditor in relation to EDP systems is to check the existence, operation, and effectiveness of the system's controls rather than checking detailed individual entry and item vouching.

QUESTION: Why are control procedures important to EDP systems?

ANSWER:
Controls for EDP systems are important for the following reasons:

1. The general complexity and size of EDP systems.
2. The partial or complete breakdown of the normal personal, functional, and departmental divisions of responsibility.
3. The loss of traditional audit trails, owing to the integration of clerical procedures, into linked routines of computer programs where there may be little or no immediate printed output.
4. The problems associated with the invisibility of processing and recording on tapes, disks, or drums.
5. The often massive increase in paper flow from and to one department of the organization, whereas previously paper work traveled in smaller batches to many more destinations.
6. The loss of personal scrutiny inherent in many clerical systems.
7. The general unfamiliarity of non-data processing personnel with the system.

Many controls are necessary to maintain accountability. These controls may be divided into three groups: organizational controls, development controls, and procedural and operating controls. *Organizational controls* are general administrative controls over the organization, division of duties, and responsibilities in the EDP department. *Development controls* are general controls to ensure that all new systems being designed adhere to standards of documentation and procedure. *Procedural and operating controls* include clerical controls and computer checks embodied in individual programs.

Organizational Controls

In the traditional manual system, where work and documents are passed from person to person, department to department, or function to function, divisions of responsibility are largely automatic. With the EDP systems, however, all the work is carried out in the data processing department and the traditional department-to-department divisions of responsibility may be inapplicable. For this reason, it is necessary to replace the usual departmental or functional divisions of responsibility by divisions within the data processing department itself. This procedure is necessary for the same reasons that auditors have for many years insisted on adequate divisions of responsibility; that is, if no one person handles a job from beginning to end then fraud is not possible without collusion.

Typical segregation of duties in a medium-sized installation is shown on the diagram in Exhibit 12.15.

The Control Section, as the name suggests, is the heart of the control procedure. This section acts as a buffer between the computer room and the external departments being serviced.

Specific areas of responsibility within the control section are:

1. Receipt of source documents containing original transaction data (batch control slips).
2. Checking input documents against their batch control slips and rechecking against the tabulated batch totals of the cards.
3. Specification of file and program requirements to the tape/disk librarian or programmer in charge.
4. Checking output documents (invoices, pay slips, and others), keeping a document record, and maintaining a timing schedule on input/output times for all jobs (computer runs).
5. Receipt and control of all amendments to standing file data. File amendments could involve minor changes such as new vendor address, or they could be changes in discount terms, credit limits, or prices. Copies of these changes are usually sent to the internal auditing department. Different types of changes may require different authority from management. For example, the signature of a supervisor of personnel may be required for an address change, whereas the signature of a sales manager might be required when a change in discount terms to a customer is made.

This division of duties is called *stewardship controls.* Other stewardship controls suggested are that control section staff should not have other data processing duties. Only control section staff should be allowed to alter input data or to make adjustments to batch control totals. No one in the data processing staff should have access to any clerically maintained records external to the EDP department. Careful control of amendment procedure, that is, alterations of existing files, is necessary. Master file changes should be initiated from within the data processing department in exceptional cases only.

EXHIBIT 12.15
Organizational Controls

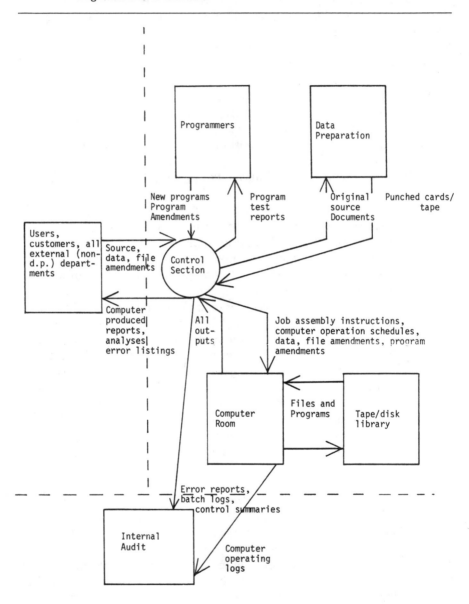

The Computer Room houses the computer itself along with the various input-output machines (CRTs, mass storage devices, and keyboards). A computer operation usually does the same job at about the same time every day or week. This cyclical schedule makes it easier to do spot checks on the operation.

Control aspects of the computer room are common sense, straightforward rules. Controls suggested are those to:

1. Ensure that all jobs have adequate and detailed operating instructions in a standard format. Any divergence from standard procedures that is required should be noted in the logbook (discussed shortly).
2. Log the basic details of jobs run.
3. Allow only authorized personnel in the computer room.
4. When possible, have two operators on duty.

Two logbooks that are kept in the computer room are the input console operator's logbook and the console typewriter logbook.

The *input console operator's logbook* is used to keep a record of the performance of the computer. The operator lists such things as jobs processed, time required, errors resulting, and subsequent action, breakdown times, interruptions, and other details.

The console typewriter is not hooked up to all computers. When it is used, it is hooked up to the computer console in such a way that any manipulation of the switches on the console and all data manually entered from the console are automatically typed up on the console typewriter. Any errors occurring during the run are also printed out. Obviously, the console typewriter is useful for control and as a back-up to the input console operator's log.

File and Program Library Control. The large number of files that most companies have and their importance requires that the company have either a competent tape/disk librarian or at least a designated operator. Some suggested controls for the *program and file library* include:

1. Standing procedures should be established for the reconstruction of files in the event of accidental destruction.
2. Adequate fire and flood precautions should be taken and all files should have duplicates stored in separate locations.
3. The overall aims of controls should be to ensure that the correct

files are used with the appropriate programs and that the files are retained until they are superseded by an updated file.

System Development Controls ensure that the often lengthy and complex task of designing and implementing a computer system proceeds according to plan and is comprehensively documented. Controls must also assure that no vital steps have been omitted, that appropriate procedural controls and safeguards have to be specified, and that an amendment procedure is available for documenting system changes.

Procedural and Operating Controls

A procedural control plan should be developed to decide whether an input will be dealt with by the computer program or manually. *Procedural controls* are clerical, operating, and programming controls, all of which are specified precisely when the system is being developed. Total information flow requires that procedural controls fall into six categories:

1. Input controls — clerical and computer
2. Main process and file controls — clerical and computer
3. Output controls — clerical and computer

1. Input Controls. Clerical input controls begin in the department handling the source data. The controls vary in detail between applications and whether the data are standing data, or whether the data relate to normal day-to-day operations.

Because of the invisibility and automatic processing of computer-held input files, it is important to counteract errors as soon as possible in order to reduce the risk of destroying files. For this reason, the editing program is first program run in any series. The input data are subjected to scrutiny by the editing program. Typical of editing programs are format checks, transaction code checks, sequence checks, feasibility checks, and checks of batch totals.

Format checks ensure that each field of the input data contains the appropriate type of information — alphabetic or numeric. Transaction code checks ensure that each input data item has valid transaction codes when compared to the required data fields. If data should be in sequence, the sequence is checked to see if there are any gaps in the series. Feasibility checks compare input data against maximum and/or minimum values expected for that data item. For example, office supplies would be less than $50,000 for most small companies, but more than $200. Previously prepared batch totals are compared to present batch numbers to see if there is any irregularity.

2. *Main Processing and File Controls.* If processing has proceeded according to plan with no errors, little clerical intervention is required. Clerical controls are used for processing and file controls only when errors are found. When an error occurs, enough information should be printed to allow a full clerical investigation. The purpose of the clerical work is to find the error and re-input the data correctly. The print-out of errors that is preferable is one in which the errors contain consecutive numbers.

Some internal computer checks cannot be made in the input/editing process. Controls are necessary to check the functioning of the program. This checking is usually done by maintaining various control accounts of two types: internal accounts used to ensure correct transmission from one processing run to another; and external accounts that are always printed out to verify clerically prepared totals.

3. *Output Controls.* The purpose of clerical controls are to make sure that the appropriate user receives the correct output. The computer cannot help distribute the printed output, but some computer controls can help. Limited checks test whether computer-calculated values fall within certain predetermined limits. Outputs other than the main production output of the system should contain the reasons for the output. Output should contain appropriate page numbers, captions, and dates.

AUDITING THE COMPUTER SYSTEM

The accepted principles of audit have not changed with the introduction of the computer. The aims of the audit are:

1. To verify the accuracy of all matters that may affect the accounts of the organization.
2. To verify the soundness of all procedures and internal checks, particularly with regard to the prevention of fraud.
3. To discover and detect fraud.
4. To verify that persons taking actions or making decisions have the appropriate authority.

The main job of the auditor in the computer-based systems is to ascertain that the organizational controls, checks, procedures, and documentation described in the final section of this chapter have been implemented and are maintained.

An audit is usually conducted in two parts. First, the auditor examines the accounting system and decides if the system is effective in containing errors. Second, the auditor selects a sample of the items processed by the system and ascertains whether these items are correct. Sample size depends on quality of the control system. The first part of the auditing process requires that the auditor examine the organization chart, work rules, and system flow charts. The second part requires that the auditor run a series of carefully prepared dummy jobs through the computer and then examine the results.

Part One — Organization and Control

The auditor should examine the organization chart and data flow chart of the system early in the audit. He or she should examine the stewardship controls discussed previously. He or she must find out how access to the computer room and tape library are gained. The control procedures on input and output of data, record and program alteration procedures, the error correction procedures, and the computer logbooks should be examined by the auditor.

The following information should be available from the organization:

1. A list of the coded instructions for the computer programs.
2. A detailed flow chart of the computer programs and subroutines.
3. A flow diagram of paperwork.
4. A list of the machine language code for the program.

Although it is not absolutely necessary that an auditor be throroughly familiar with the high-level language code in which the programs are written, it is important that he or she have this information available in case fraud is expected and also to compare it to the machine language code. Code should be checked against flow diagrams, however, to see if there is a good correspondence. It is also a good idea for the auditor to ask the EDP program to run the same program in the machine language code and in the higher-level code to see if the output corresponds.

The paperwork flow chart gives the auditor an overview of the procedures so that the control points may be located. The program flow chart is helpful both for comparison to the actual instruction code and for going through the chart with the programmer to help the auditor understand the system.

Part Two — Running the Programs

The best way to test a computer program is to run a carefully prepared set of transactions made up through the computer.

The auditor would prepare a set of dummy transactions (sometimes called *test pack*) that tests a wide range of rules built into the program, including error and control procedures. Care must be taken not to invalidate the control totals. The auditor would be present when the run is made and a check made to see that any error or exception procedures are properly triggered and corrected. The outputs are then audited against the expected precalculated results.

The primary limitation of this *simulation* or test-pack approach to testing the programs is that it is difficult to design a truly comprehensive sample job that includes a sufficient cross section of maximum values, exceptions, and errors. One advantage of the sample job is that once written, it only requires minor modifications over the years when used again.

Besides testing the system with a program, the auditor can use the computer to assist with the audit. One good way to use the computer is in statistical sampling. Auditors usually check a sample of the items rather than every item and then make a judgment based on the sample.

Another technique of using the computer to check the accounts is the *file search programs*. These are programs written so that the contents of a file can be examined. The programs are of a general nature and require that the auditor specify what particular aspects of the file he or she wishes to examine. Once the file is specified, it is scanned by the interrogation program and appropriate listings are made. For example, if the auditor specifies files containing personal accounts, the auditor might further specify the following perimeters:

1.   All accounts with an adjustment exceding $100.
2.   All accounts which have had credit posted exceding $50.
3.   A random sampling of one account in 250.

Computer manufacturers usually have file search or file interrogation programs. Many software firms who cater to CPA firms also have sample file search programs.

13

Forms of Business Organization

This chapter discusses the standard forms of business organization prevalent in the United States — sole proprietorships, partnerships, and corporations. It also considers the hybrid forms, such as trusts, joint ventures, Subchapter S corporations, and limited partnerships.

SOLE PROPRIETORSHIP

A sole proprietorship is the basic form of business organization. In a sole proprietorship, owner and business are indistinguishable for legal, accounting, and tax purposes. Personal assets and business assets are in effect commingled, and business income and nonbusiness income are reported to the IRS on the same tax form, Form 1040. Business income is segregated on Schedule C of Form 1040 (see Exhibit 13.1). A sole proprie-

EXHIBIT 13.1
Profit or (Loss) From Business or Profession

SCHEDULE C (Form 1040) Department of the Treasury Internal Revenue Service	**Profit or (Loss) From Business or Profession** (Sole Proprietorship) Partnerships, Joint Ventures, etc., Must File Form 1065. ▶ Attach to Form 1040. ▶ See Instructions for Schedule C (Form 1040).	19**78**

Name of proprietor Jane Doe	Social security number of proprietor 123 : 45 : 6789

A Main business activity (see Instructions) ▶ *Retail Sales* ; product ▶ *Clothing*

B Business name ▶ *Jane Boutique*

C Employer identification number ▶ *33-3601263*

D Business address (number and street) ▶ *50 East 21 Street*

   City, State and ZIP code ▶ *New York, New York 10023*

E Accounting method: (1) ☒ Cash   (2) ☐ Accrual   (3) ☐ Other (specify) ▶

F Method(s) used to value closing inventory:
   (1) ☐ Cost   (2) ☒ Lower of cost or market   (3) ☐ Other (if other, attach explanation)

	Yes	No
G Was there any major change in determining quantities, costs, or valuations between opening and closing inventory? . . If "Yes," attach explanation.		X
H Does this business activity involve oil or gas, movies or video tapes, or leasing personal (section 1245) property to others? (See page 25 of the Instructions.)		X
I Did you deduct expenses for an office in your home?		X

Part I   Income

1 **a** Gross receipts or sales	1a	170,000
b Returns and allowances	1b	4,000
c Balance (subtract line 1b from line 1a)	1c	166,000
2 Cost of goods sold and/or operations (Schedule C–1, line 8)	2	98,000
3 Gross profit (subtract line 2 from line 1c)	3	68,000
4 Other income (attach schedule)	4	
5 **Total income** (add lines 3 and 4) . . . . ▶	5	68,000

Part II   Deductions

6 Advertising	1,000		28 Telephone		1,000
7 Amortization			29 Travel and entertainment . . .		
8 Bad debts from sales or services .			30 Utilities		4,000
9 Bank charges			31 **a** Wages . . .	20,000	
10 Car and truck expenses			**b** New Jobs Credit .		
11 Commissions			**c** Subtract line 31b from 31a .		20,000
12 Depletion			32 Other expenses (specify):		
13 Depreciation (explain in Schedule			**a** *Miscellaneous*		1,500
C–2)	5,000		**b**		
14 Dues and publications			**c**		
15 Employee benefit programs . . .			**d**		
16 Freight (not included on Schedule			**e**		
C–1)	200		**f**		
17 Insurance	1,000		**g**		
18 Interest on business indebtedness .	3,000		**h**		
19 Laundry and cleaning			**i**		
20 Legal and professional services .	500		**j**		
21 Office supplies			**k**		
22 Pension and profit-sharing plans .			**l**		
23 Postage			**m**		
24 Rent on business property . . .	3,600		**n**		
25 Repairs	200		**o**		
26 Supplies (not included on Sched-			**p**		
ule C–1)	300		**q**		
27 Taxes	2,000		**r**		

33 **Total deductions** (add amounts in columns for lines 6 through 32r) . . . . ▶	33	40,300
34 **Net profit or (loss)** (subtract line 33 from line 5). Enter here and on Form 1040, line 13. ALSO enter on Schedule SE (Form 1040), line 5a. (For "at risk" provisions, see page 25 of Instructions.) . . . . ▶	34	37,700

263–056–2

EXHIBIT 13.1
continued

Schedule C (Form 1040) 1978   Page **2**

SCHEDULE C–1.—Cost of Goods Sold and/or Operations (See Schedule C Instructions for Part I, Line 2)

1 Inventory at beginning of year (if different from last year's closing inventory, attach explanation) .	**1**	20,000
2 a Purchases **2a** 100,000		
b Cost of items withdrawn for personal use . . . . . . **2b** —		
c Balance (subtract line 2b from line 2a)	**2c**	100,000
3 Cost of labor (do not include salary paid to yourself)	**3**	
4 Materials and supplies	**4**	
5 Other costs (attach schedule)	**5**	
6 Add lines 1, 2c, and 3 through 5	**6**	120,000
7 Inventory at end of year	**7**	22,000
8 **Cost of goods sold and/or operations** (subtract line 7 from line 6). Enter here and on Part I, line 2 . ▶	**8**	98,000

SCHEDULE C–2.—Depreciation (See Schedule C Instructions for line 13)
If you need more space, please use Form 4562.

Description of property (a)	Date acquired (b)	Cost or other basis (c)	Depreciation allowed or allowable in prior years (d)	Method of computing depreciation (e)	Life or rate (f)	Depreciation for this year (g)
1 Total additional first-year depreciation (do not include in items below) ▶						
2 Other depreciation:						
Buildings						
Furniture and fixtures . . .	1/1/78	50,000		Straight line	10	5,000
Transportation equipment . .						
Machinery and other equipment .						
Other (Specify)						
3 Totals		50,000			**3**	5,000
4 Depreciation claimed in Schedule C–1					**4**	
5 **Balance** (subtract line 4 from line 3). Enter here and on Part II, line 13 . . . . ▶					**5**	5,000

SCHEDULE C–3.—Expense Account Information (See Schedule C Instructions for Schedule C–3)

Enter information for yourself and your five highest paid employees. In determining the five highest paid employees, add expense account allowances to the salaries and wages. However, you don't have to provide the information for any employee for whom the combined amount is less than $25,000, or for yourself if your expense account allowance plus line 34, page 1, is less than $25,000.

Name (a)	Expense account (b)	Salaries and Wages (c)
Owner		
1		
2		
3		
4		
5		

Did you claim a deduction for expenses connected with:	Yes	No
A Entertainment facility (boat, resort, ranch, etc.)?		✕
B Living accommodations (except employees on business)?		✕
C Employees' families at conventions or meetings?		✕
If "Yes," were any of these conventions or meetings outside the U.S. or its possessions? (See page 26 of Instructions) .		
D Vacations for employees or their families not reported on Form W–2?		✕

tor does, however, need a license to do business in the particular locality in which the business is located.

Assuming that your sole proprietorship is a bona fide business at which you are attempting to make a living, there are certain tax advantages to this business category.

First, legitimate business expenses are deductible. These expenses include depreciation on property used in the business; necessary operating expenses, such as heat, light, power, telephone; reasonable travel and entertainment; and certain other allowable expenses. If the business is conducted from your home, the portion of your home that is devoted to business will be considered property used in the business. Salaries and wages paid to business employees are deductible expenses. Furthermore, legitimate pension, profit-sharing, and hospital and accident insurance deductions may be available. There are, however, miscellaneous taxes such as the self-employment Social Security tax and the quarterly estimated tax payment, that must be made to the federal government. These payments are made on Schedule SE of Form 1040 and Form 1040-ES, respectively.

PARTNERSHIP

A *partnership* may be two or more sole proprietors who have agreed to pool their assets and operate a business jointly. No formal agreement between the partners is necessary in order for a partnership to exist legally or for tax purposes. However, most states have partnership laws, and written partnership agreements should be drawn up by a lawyer conforming with the laws of a particular business. For federal income tax purposes, a partnership includes not only a partnership as it is known by common law, but also a syndicate, group, pool, joint venture, or other unincorporated organization that conducts any business and that is not defined as a trust, an estate, or a corporation.

A partnership as such is not taxable. Only the members are taxed in their individual capacities on their individual shares of the partnership taxable income, whether distributed to them or not.

Example: A partnership is composed of two partners sharing profits equally. In the current year, the taxable income of the business is $30,000. None of it is distributed to the partners. The partnership tax return will report the $30,000 and show shares of $15,000 to each partner. Each partner will report his or her share of the partnership taxable income on his or her own tax return, even though the income has not been distributed to each partner.

The character of the income earned by a partnership is not altered when the income passes to the partners. For example, if a partnership sells a building and realizes a long-term capital gain on the transaction, the long-term capital gain is passed through to the partners rather than being reflected as part of the partnership income. The types of income, losses, and expense that are passed to partners include: ordinary income and loss, additional first-year depreciation, dividends, interest, short-term captital gains, long-term capital gains, and contributions.

LIMITED PARTNERSHIP

A *limited partnership* is a special type of partnership authorized under many state laws. A limited partnership must have at least one general partner who has unlimited liability for the debts of the partnership and who is responsible for managing the business. The limited partners are only liable to the extent of their partnership interests and they must not participate in any way in managing the business. The advantage of a limited partnership is that it may employ leverage to earn a higher rate of return on the limited partner's invested capital than would otherwise be the case, without increasing the risk of the limited partner.

Example: A contractor becomes the general partner in a limited partnership. He agrees to acquire land, construct a building, and sell the building when it is completed. He arranges for five investors to contribute $10,000 each to the project in exchange for limited partnership interests. On the basis of the construction plans and the $50,000 equity, the contractor-general partner is able to arrange a bank loan for $200,000. The loan will be secured by a purchase money mortgage and a performance bond. Considerable leverage would be used, and most of the money contributed by the limited partners, and even money that was borrowed, would be treated as a tax deductible expense in the year of the formation of the partnership.

Congress felt that the proliferation of tax shelters was not appropriate, and so in the Tax Reform Act of 1976, tax shelters were curtailed. In essence, the rule said that amount of losses that could be claimed from certain investment activities could not exceed the total amount that the taxpayer had at risk in the partnership. Under the *at risk* rule, loss deductions are limited to the amount of cash contributed to the partnership by the partner. The limited partners have no liability beyond their initial investment. When the building is sold, the limited partners will share in the profits.

The leverage aspect of limited partnerships is the reason that most tax shelters are constructed as limited partnerships.

TAX SHELTER

In the past, a tax shelter was created when a limited partnership was formed and the limited partners contributed a certain sum to the partnership. The funds were used to drill for oil, breed or fatten cattle, lease equipment, build or own real estate, and similar ventures. The at risk rules apply to:

1. Farming, other than timber
2. Oil and gas operations
3. Equipment leasing
4. Holding, producing, or distributing motion picture films and video tapes.

Note that real estate is still a potential type of investment for a tax shelter limited partnership; even in real estate, however, the rules have been changed. One method of increasing the tax-deductible expenses in a real estate limited partnership was to write off interest *points*, interest, and taxes during the construction period of a real estate project. The new rules state that points, interest, and taxes during construction must be capitalized and amortized over a ten-year period. This rule applies to all individuals and partnerships as well as to Subchapter S corporations.

SUBCHAPTER S CORPORATIONS

In the eyes of the law, a corporation is a person; it can sue, be sued, and also pay taxes. Since the individuals who own the corporation also pay taxes on any dividends they receive from the corporation, there is in effect double taxation.

Many people argue that this double taxation should be eliminated. To a certain extent the double taxation has been eliminated by the creation of

Small Business Corporations, also referred to as tax option corporations or Subchapter S corporations.

A *Subchapter S corporation* has elected, by unanimous consent of its shareholders, not to pay any corporate tax on its income, but instead to have the shareholders pay taxes on it, even though it is not distributed. Shareholders of a Subchapter S corporation are also entitled to deduct, on their individual returns, their share of any net operating loss sustained by the corporation.

Unlike a partnership, a Subchapter S corporation is not a conduit. That is, individual items of income and deduction are not passed through to the shareholders to retain the same character in the hands of those shareholders as they had in the hands of the corporation. Instead, taxable income is computed at the corporate level in much the same way as it is computed for any other corporation. The shareholders are then taxed directly on this taxable income, whether or not the corporation makes any distributions to them. There is one exception to this no-conduit rule. The Subchapter S corporation's net capital gain is passed to shareholders and is treated by them as long-term capital gain on their individual returns.

Only a domestic corporation that is not a member of an affiliated group can elect Subchapter S status. A qualifying Subchapter S corporation may not have more than one class of stock and more than ten shareholders. The shareholders must all be individuals, or estates of deceased individuals, who were shareholders. Beginning in 1977, if a Subchapter S corporation has qualified for five consecutive years, the number of shareholders may be increased to fifteen.

The tax aspects of a Subchapter S corporation are somewhat complex. A certified public accountant, or an attorney, should be consulted if Subchapter S status is considered an appropriate form of business organization for a particular enterprise.

FORMING A CORPORATION

Most businesses not designed strictly for investment purposes eventually decide to incorporate. The reasons for this include: limits on personal liability of owner-managers, financing and growth flexibility, and transferability of interest.

The first decision faced by persons who would like to incorporate a business is where to incorporate. A corporation depends on legal statutes of a particular state for its permission to exist and for the procedure by which it will come into existence. Some state corporation laws are more attractive to incorporators than others. States such as Delaware have attracted incorporations far out of proportion to the number of corporations actually doing business there. This has occurred because Delaware has had, for many years, a corporation law that offers incorporators certain privileges, advantages, and facilities for incorporation that could not be obtained elsewhere.

Recently, however, differences in corporation laws among the major commercial states have been reduced. Incorporation now is often preferred in the state in which the major share of the business will be done, unless business will be done throughout the country and internationally.

Although the procedure of incorporation varies in detail from state to state, the pattern is much the same everywhere. Certain steps should be taken before the incorporators draw up a charter. Included among these steps are: the discovery of a business opportunity, the investigation of a business opportunity, developing financial and promotional arrangements, arranging for property and material supply, solicitation of preincorporation stock subscriptions, and reservation of a corporate name.

A Corporate Charter

Corporate charters are required to have certain clauses and permitted to have others. Usually the first clause of a corporate charter is the corporate name. The name cannot conflict with any other name used in that state. Personal names of incorporators should not be used because there is a potential of losing the right to use your own name for business purposes.

A second clause contains the business purpose. This clause sets forth the purposes, objectives, or general nature of the business. Many states permit a purpose clause to state that the corporation is formed for any lawful purpose.

A third clause of the corporate charter outlines the capital structure. Most corporation laws require a statement of the proposed corporation's capital structure, including the authorized number of shares, the rights, preferences, privileges, and restrictions on the various classes and series of shares whether the shares have a par value, and the voting rights of the shares.

Other provisions appearing in the charter pertain to the location of the principal office, the number of directors, the names and addresses of the original directors, duration of the corporation, existence of preemptive rights, powers of directors, a statement that the corporation may become a partner in a partnership, and other provisions.

Corporate By-laws

The *by-laws* of a corporation deal with the internal management rules of the corporation. The laws must be consistent with the charter of the corporation. By-laws usually deal with matters such as the duties and compensation of corporate officers, the qualifications for membership on the board of directors, executive and other director committees, the date and place of annual shareholders meetings, and provisions for audits.

Financing a Corporation

The financing of a corporation is accomplished primarily through two means: debt and equity. Debt financing is discussed in Chapter 8 under Debt Financing. Equity financing of a corporation is obtained through issuance of common stock or preferred stock.

Rights of Common Stockholders

The rights of holders of common stock in a business corporation are established by the laws of the state in which the corporation is chartered and by the terms of the charters. The terms of charters are relatively uniform on many matters, some of which have been described.

In addition, corporate charters usually address the following two rights of common stockholders.

Collective Rights

Certain collective rights are usually given to the holders of common stock. Some of the more important rights allow stockholders to amend the charter; to adopt or amend by-laws; to elect directors; to authorize sale of major assets; to enter into mergers; to change the amount of authorized common stock; and to issue preferred stock, debentures, bonds, and other securities.

Specific Rights

Holders of common stock also have specific rights, as do individual owners. They have the right to vote. They may sell their ownership shares. They have the right to inspect the corporate books.

One of the principal features of the large modern American corporation is the segregation of ownership and management. Initially, all corporations begin with management and ownership interests being the same or closely related. As the corporation grows, however, more varied sources of financing are required and professional management is needed. These growing needs lead to the segregation of management and ownership. From a legal perspective, the management of a corporation derives its authority from the ownership interests of the corporation. In order to maintain and exercise this authority, a device known as the proxy has developed.

For each share of common stock owned, a stockholder has the right to cast one vote at the annual meeting of stockholders. Provision is usually made for a temporary transfer of this right to vote by the proxy. A *proxy* is defined as a transfer of the right to vote. The transfer is limited in its duration, usually for a specific occasion, such as the annual stockholder's meeting.

The Securities and Exchange Commission (SEC) supervises the use of proxies and issues frequent rules concerning proxies. If the proxy rules were left in the hands of management solely, there is the possibility that the incumbent management would be self-perpetuated. On the other hand, if it were easy for minority groups of stockholders and opposition stockholder factions to remove incumbent management, then small groups of stockholders could gain control of the corporation for their own personal ends. In order to balance these diverse interests, a method of stockholders voting for directors has evolved and is required by law in many states. The method is called cumulative voting.

Cumulative Voting

Cumulative voting permits multiple votes for a single director by one share of stock.

Example: Assume 6 directors are to be elected. The owner of 100 shares can cast 100 votes for each of the 6 openings. In total, he or she has 600 votes. When cumulative voting is allowed, the stockholder may accumulate votes and cast 600 votes for one director, instead of 100 each for 6 directors. Cumulative voting is designed to enable a minority stockholder group to gain representation on the Board of Directors while at the same time preserving the power of the majority.

QUESTION: What are the advantages of using common stock as a
            source of financing for a corporation?

ANSWER:

There are four principal advantages of using common stock as a source of financing for a corporation:

1. Common stock does not entail fixed payments. If the company generates the earnings, it can then pay common-stock dividends. In contrast to bond interest, however, there is no legal obligation to pay dividends.
2. Common stock carries no fixed maturity date.
3. Since common stock provides a cushion against losses for creditors, the sale of common stock increases the credit worthiness of the firm.
4. Common stock may at times be sold more easily than debt. This possibility is true because common stock may have a higher expected return and because, in a period of inflation, the return will increase, whereas the return on debt remains constant.

QUESTION: *What are the disadvantages of using common stock as a source of financing for a corporation?*

ANSWER:

Some disadvantages of using common stock as a source of financing for a corporation include:

1. The sale of common stock extends voting rights or control to the additional stockholders. For this reason, additional equity financing is often avoided by small and new firms. The owner-managers may be unwilling to share control of their companies with outsiders.
2. Common stock gives more owners the right to share in income. The use of debt may enable the company to employ funds at a fixed low cost, whereas common stock gives equal rights to new stockholders to share in the net profits of the company.
3. The costs of underwriting and distributing common stock are usually higher than for underwriting and distributing preferred stock or debt. Underwriting costs for selling common stock are higher because the costs of investigating an equity security investment are greater than for a comparable debt security. Also, common stocks are more risky, which means that equity holdings must be diversified. This means that a given dollar amount of

new stock must be sold to a greater number of purchasers than the
same amount of debt.
4. Common-stock dividends are not deductible for tax purposes, but
    bond interest is.

Preferred Stock

Preferred stock has claims or rights ahead of common stock, but behind
those of debt securities. The preference may be a prior claim on earnings;
it may take the form of a prior claim on assets in the event of liquidation;
or it may take a preferential position with regard to both earnings and
assets. The hybrid nature of preferred stock becomes apparent when one
tries to classify it in relation to debt securities and common stocks. The
priority feature and the typically fixed dividend indicate that preferred
stock is similar to debt. Payments to preferred stockholders are limited in
amount, so that common stockholders receive the advantages or disadvantages of leverage. However, if the preferred dividends are not earned,
the company can forego paying them without threat of bankruptcy. In this
way, preferred stock is similar to common stock.

The possible characteristics, rights, and obligations of securities vary
widely. As economic conditions change, new types of securities are
invented. The possibilities are many, limited only by the imagination and
ingenuity of the managers formulating the terms of the security issues. It
is not surprising, then, that preferred stock can be found in a variety of
forms. Some of the more common features of preferred stock include:

Preference in assets and earning
Par or liquidation value (dividends as a percentage of par)
Cumulative dividends (that is, all dividends in arrears must be paid)
Convertibility into common stock
Participation in earnings
Call provision

QUESTION: What are the advantages and disadvantages of preferred
            stock?

ANSWER:
An important advantage of preferred stock, from the viewpoint of the
issuer, is that, in contrast to bonds, the obligation to make fixed payments
is avoided. Also, a firm wishing to expand because its earning power is
high may obtain higher earnings for the original owners by selling pre-

ferred stock with a limited return, rather than by selling common stock. By selling preferred stock, a company avoids the provision of equal participation in earnings that the sale of additional common stock would require. Preferred stock also permits a company to avoid sharing control through participation in voting. In contrast to bonds, preferred stock issuance enables the company to leave mortgageable assets unencumbered. The lack of maturity date or sinking fund provision typically makes preferred stock a more flexible financing source than bonds.

The disadvantages of preferred stock include the fact that this stock usually must be sold at a higher yield than bonds. Furthermore, preferred stock dividends are not deductible for tax purposes, which increases their cost relative to bonds even more. Utilities companies, such as telephone, gas and electric providers, issue most of all preferred stocks. For these companies, taxes are an allowable cost for rate-making purposes; that is, higher taxes may be passed on to customers in the form of higher prices. Tax deductibility of preferred dividends is therefore not an issue.

TRANSFORMING THE STRUCTURE OF A BUSINESS

One of the few remaining ways to become a well-to-do person in the United States is to found a business enterprise that becomes successful. For instance, if the company is taken into the public market in a stock offering, you may retain a healthy share of the stock yourself, and then see the stock rise significantly in price in the public market. This procedure has inherent risks in the long run, but also may win large gains.

Some lawyers, accountants, and investment bankers specialize in taking new companies into the public markets. Their goal is to be part of the "long-shot" when it comes through. The tax implications of moving away from proprietorship and partnership towards a corporation are such that generally accepted accounting principles (such as concepts of accrual, depreciation, inventory) are more frequently used in corporations. The business manager in a corporate setting must be more aware of the accounting options, and the company's accountant must be more aware of generally accepted standards of accounting and auditing, not merely taxes.

When the corporation decides to go into a public issue of stock, it may want to do many things from an accounting standpoint. For example, in a private company, saving taxes may be paramount; whereas in a public company, saving taxes is important, but reported earnings may be equally important. Therefore, a company moving from private to public status may want to reassess its depreciation and amortization policy along with other accounting treatments, such as bad-debt allowances, warranty reserves, and inventory valuation.

Going public may mean that a company will be audited for the first time by a CPA. Many local CPAs are highly competent at tax returns, tax planning, and preparing financial reports from client records, yet are only rarely engaged to perform certified audits. It is generally not possible for a CPA who is closely allied as an advisor to a business and preparer of financial statements to perform a certified audit. Going public often means that a new CPA firm must be found. This procedure is costly and can be somewhat traumatic. The benefit lies in obtaining a thorough review of your business from an objective standpoint and a general assurance that your financial statements are prepared in conformity with Generally Accepted Accounting Principles. Such conformity, plus an unqualified opinion from a respected CPA firm, will enhance the marketability of the stock of your company. This means more money if your stock is sold successfully.

QUESTION: What procedure is followed when a company decides to sell its stock to the public?

ANSWER:

A public issue of stock requires several outside consulting persons — notably an accountant and a lawyer with previous prior experience in public securities offerings, and a securities underwriter or investment banker. Each of these persons has a specific function in the issuing of public securities. The accountant must prepare a certified audit opinion on completion of the audit of the business. The lawyer will customarily prepare the written parts of any forms and documents that must be filed with the securities or franchise board of the state of incorporation or with the Securities and Exchange Commission (SEC). Typically, no documents will be required if the total funds raised are less than $100,000. If the total funds raised are between $100,000 and $1,500,000, then you may be able to avoid filing many of these documents by complying with Regulation A of the Securities Act of 1933, which specifies an exemption for small offerings. If the total funds raised are more than $1,500,000, it may be necessary to go through a complete registration statement procedure. The registration statement will be filed with and reviewed by the SEC in Washington or a regional field office. Upon completion of the review, the registration is said to go effective and your stock may be legally sold in the public markets. At this point, the underwriter's job in the issuance and sale is to judge the movement of the market and then estimate the best time to begin selling the stock in the public market. As a fee, the underwriter usually receives a certain percentage of the total amount raised, or alternatively, will purchase the new stock at a price that is estimated to be below the market price when the stock is sold publicly. In the latter case, the risk of stock price decline is often on the under-writer, which is the reason for the name *underwriter.*

Most companies that are initially required to file registration state-ments in conjunction with sales of stock must file additional annual, quarterly, and other update reports and also must revise their registration statements, prospectuses, and proxy materials from time to time. These procedures add cost in terms of the time involved for management, for accountant's and lawyer's fees, and for probable printing costs. Such costs should be considered when initially planning a public issue of stock or other securities.

14

Foreign Operations

This chapter focuses on the accounting, financial decision-making, and tax aspects of foreign operations.

The expansion of American business activity since World War II has included a significant increase in international operations. For many companies, these operations comprise import and export activities, with suppliers or customers located in other countries. Increasingly, however, involvement in foreign operations takes the form of investment in foreign firms or establishment of foreign branches or subsidiaries, either to carry on productive operations, or to serve as sales outlets, or both.

Many large business enterprises with foreign investments are so extensive and diverse that they could be characterized as multinational. However, each enterprise must select one country within which its parent corporation has legal recognition. In addition, the necessity of accumulating financial information about the enterprise as a whole means that a single currency be identified as the unit of account by which financial information will be aggregated. The basic financial records of each segment of the enterprise are generally kept in terms of the currency of the particular country in which that segment is located.

Example: The accounts of *General Motors'* subsidiaries in Germany will be kept in *Deutsche Marks.* Thus, a major problem of accounting for foreign operations involves translating financial data into a common currency unit.

Another problem of foreign operations is that transactions conducted between parties that are located in different countries generally require the purchase of currency of another country.

Example: If wine is imported from France, at some point the dollars used to pay for the wine must be converted into French francs. This is done either by the importer or by the French supplier when he decides to spend the dollars. This required purchase of a foreign currency interjects another variable into the determination of the profit of a business. The fluctuations in the value of a foreign currency may result in gains or losses to the business firm that engages in foreign operations.

The first major problem of accounting for foreign operations is the translation of account balances from foreign currency into monetary equivalents, expressed in a domestic currency. For example, you may want to translate financial statements of your branch or subsidiary located in Mexico from Mexican pesos into American dollars.

The primary objective of the translation process is to obtain valuations, in domestic terms, that are consistent with domestic accounting principles. For example, if an account balance refers to property, plant, and equipment, generally accepted accounting principles require that the account reflect the original cost less depreciation. Therefore, the procedures for currency translation should preserve the concept of original cost. Obviously, if the foreign currency financial statements were prepared using accounting practices different from those that are generally accepted in the United States, then translation procedures will not remedy the situation. In such cases, the foreign currency financial statements must be adjusted to conform to United States accounting principles and then be translated into American dollars.

METHODS FOR TRANSLATING FOREIGN
CURRENCY FINANCIAL STATEMENTS

A number of different methods of translating the assets and liabilities of a foreign currency balance sheet have developed in accounting practices. At one time, the current-noncurrent method was widely used. In this method, all current assets and current liabilities were translated at the current rate of exchange. For example, cash and accounts receivable would be translated at the year-end rate of exchange of the foreign currency for dollars. If it takes twelve pesos to make one dollar, and if the Mexican balance sheet has 12,000 pesos of receivables, then this would translate to $1,000 of receivables.

In *Statement of Financial Accounting Standards No. 8*, the Financial Accounting Standards Board (FASB) required the use of the *monetary-nonmonetary* method of translating foreign currency financial statements for all public companies. Using this method, all monetary assets and liabilities, such as cash and accounts payable, are translated at the current year-end rate, and nonmonetary assets are translated at historical rates prevailing when the asset was purchased.

The primary difference between the current-noncurrent and monetary-nonmonetary methods are that under the monetary-nonmonetary method inventory is translated at a historical rate, rather than a current rate, and long-term debt is translated at a current rate, rather than at a historical rate. (See Exhibit 14.1 for an example of translating a balance sheet.)

Generally only one method has been used in the translation of foreign currency income statements. The method is to translate all revenue and expense accounts, except for depreciation and cost of goods sold, at the average exchange rate prevailing for the year. Depreciation expense would be translated at the rate prevailing at the date of purchase of the asset being depreciated. Cost of Goods Sold consists of the Beginning Inventory plus Purchases less the Ending Inventory. The Purchases are translated at an average rate, but the Beginning Inventory and Ending Inventory are translated at the prevailing rate on the date such inventory was purchased. (See Exhibit 14.2 for an example of translating an income statement.) Obviously, it is possible to have a profit in a foreign currency, but end with a loss when the income statement is translated.

Customarily, if a foreign currency declines in value with respect to the dollar, the income in dollars will be lower than the related income in the foreign currency, primarily due to the depreciation effect. However, the effect of this income statement may be superseded by a balance-sheet effect, known as the translation gain or loss.

The translation gain or loss is generated by the translation of balance-sheet accounts. Specifically, if a company has more liabilities than monetary assets (that is, cash and receivables) and if the foreign currency declines in value against the dollar, then a gain will be realized. This gain results because fewer dollars are needed to pay off the liabilities. The balance-sheet effect can supersede the income-statement effect because

EXHIBIT 14.1
Mexican Subsidiary Balance Sheet, 12/31/78

	Pesos	Exchange Rate	Dollars
Assets			
Current Assets			
Cash	24,000	.05	1,200
Receivables	100,000	.05	5,000
Inventory	48,000	.06625	3,180
	172,000		9,380
Property Plant and			
Equipment	240,000	.0825	19,800
Less: Accumulated			
Depreciation	(120,000)	.0825	(9,900)
	120,000		9,900
TOTAL ASSETS	292,000		19,280
Liabilities			
Current Liabilities	72,000	.05	3,600
Long-Term Debt	100,000	.05	5,000
Total Liabilities	172,000		8,600
Stockholders Equity			
Capital Stock	48,000	.0825	3,960
Retained Earnings	72,000	Plug	6,720
	120,000		10,680
Total Liabilities and			
Stockholders Equity	292,000		19,280

the translation gain on the balance sheet off-sets the translation loss on the income statement.

If the foreign currency is gaining in value against the dollar, as has been the case recently with the Deutsche Mark, the Swiss franc, and the Japanese yen, then there will usually be a translation gain on the income statement and a translation loss on the balance sheet.

Statement of Financial Accounting Standards No. 8 requires that the translation gain or loss from the balance sheet be combined into one

EXHIBIT 14.2
Mexican Subsidiary Income Statement
Year Ended 12/31/78

	Pesos	Exchange Rate	Dollars
Sales	150,000	.06625	9937.50
Cost of Goods Sold			
Beginning Inventory	40,000	.0825	3300
Add: Purchases	120,000	.06625	7950
Less: Ending Inven.	(48,000)	.06625	(3180)
	112,000		8070
Gross Profit	38,000		1867.50
Operating Expenses			
Depreciation	12,000	.0825	990
Salaries and Other	20,000	.06625	1325
Operating Profit (loss)	6,000		(447.50)
Translation Gain			1722.50
Net Income	6,000		1275.00

As may be seen, the operating profit of 6,000 pesos is reduced to a loss of 447.50 dollars when translated. This is principally due to depreciation charges. However, to the operating loss there must be added a translation gain of $1,722.50, which is the change in retained earnings from 12/31/77 to 12/31/78 plus the operating loss. The translation gain is due to the net monetary liability position.

figure and called *foreign currency translation gain or loss*. This gain or loss is included in net income for the period.

In the past, translation gains or losses could be deferred, or in other words, not included in net income for the year. The FASB felt that this deferral was misleading, so they now require that translation gains or losses be included in net income. The fact that translation of gains and losses must be included in net income means that the net income of companies with extensive foreign operations will be more volatile than it was in the past, when the effects of foreign currency fluctuation could be disguised by deferring the translation gain or loss. There has been considerable criticism directed against FASB 8. As a consequence, in February 1979 the FASB decided to make modifications to the Statement. Possible modifications include greater disclosure or returning to deferral.

In this current period when the dollar is declining in value vis-a-vis other major currencies, it becomes especially important to have disclosure of the adverse impact of the dollar decline on the net earnings of companies with extensive foreign operations.

Managers of corporations with extensive foreign operations attempt to hedge against these fluctuations in an environment where exchange rates are fluctuating daily.

A Hedge

To explain a *hedge*, consider an exporter who sells live eels to a customer in Japan. The seller agrees to deliver a container of live eels to Tokyo in thirty days for 1 million yen. Since the yen has been appreciating in value against the dollar, it follows that some people may feel that the yen is basically overvalued and could drop at any time. Therefore, in order to lock in profit, the seller enters into a contract to sell 1 million yen in thirty days at the exchange rate of dollars-for-yen of today. This transaction means that if the yen drops in value, the seller is protected against the loss. However, if the yen appreciates in value the seller loses the gain he or she would have had on that appreciation.

Sophisticated commodity and currency traders often can protect themselves from movements in both directions by transactions called straddles. Basically, a straddle exists when a seller has both an option to buy and an option to sell at the same time; thus, a loss on one option will be off-set by a gain in the other option.

Hedges of foreign currency transactions, as with all hedges of commodities, have been deemed to be transactions on which a gain or a loss will be considered to be ordinary income, rather than capital gain income. This means that gains are taxed at a higher rate, but that the benefits of losses are greater than if they were considered to be capital losses.

The area of foreign currency transactions can become quite complicated, as exemplified by hedges and straddles. Even more complicated are techniques such as parallel loans and foreign currency swaps. These techniques are beyond the scope of this book, but may be of interest to people who are significantly involved in foreign trade.

TAXATION OF FOREIGN INCOME

Many countries do not tax a person or a corporation on earnings from a source outside of the country. The United States attempts to tax earnings of persons and corporations, from whatever source derived, including all foreign source income. The taxation of foreign source income is considerably more difficult and complex than domestic taxation. This situation is due to the fact that reporting standards on foreign-source income are not always complete or adequate. Furthermore, the fairness of taxing expatriate Americans is open to question, as is the additional problem of taxation of foreign source income by the country or jurisdiction in which it was earned, and the manner in which such taxes will impact United States taxes. Finally, the question of how earnings of foreign subsidiaries of domestic companies will be taxed must be considered.

Taxing the Foreign Source Income of Individuals

All United States citizens, whether residing at home or abroad, are subject to United States income taxes on their worldwide income. They are required to file an income tax return even if part or all of their income earned abroad will not be taxed. United States citizens performing personal services (that is, working for a living) abroad may qualify for the *earned income exclusion*, which means that up to $15,000 of their earned income ($20,000 for employees of certain qualified United States charitable organizations) will not be taxed by the United States.

In order to qualify for the earned-income exclusion, a United States citizen must meet one of the following tests:

1. He or she must be a bona fide resident of a foreign country for an uninterrupted period that includes an entire taxable year, or
2. He or she must be physically present in a foreign country for at least 510 days during an 18-month period.

A qualified taxpayer may elect to use the earned income exclusion. Once this election is made, it continues in effect and cannot be revoked without permission from the IRS. The earned income exclusion election is not always the best alternative for the reason that if a person paid foreign income taxes, such taxes can be used as a credit against United States taxes, up to a certain limit. However, if this person elects the earned income exclusion, then any foreign taxes paid cannot be credited against domestic taxes.

In general, it is advantageous to elect the earned income exclusion if a person is paying, and will continue to pay, foreign income taxes at a rate that is higher than the United States rate.

Foreign Tax Credit

A United States taxpayer who has paid income taxes to a foreign country may elect to credit the amount of the foreign income taxes against his United States tax liability. This applies to corporations as well. The taxpayer elects on his annual tax return whether to treat foreign income taxes as a deduction or a credit. In most cases, it will be to the taxpayer's advantage to elect the foreign tax credit, because the credit is a direct reduction of the United States tax liability, as opposed to a deduction that reduces taxable income. No credit is allowed for taxes paid to a foreign country that pertain to income excluded from United States taxable income under the earned income exclusion provision.

The amount of the credit that may be taken is limited. In essence, the limitation is equal to the United States tax rate. Thus, if a person is paying taxes to a foreign government on foreign source income at a rate equal to the United States rate, he or she will be able to credit the taxes paid to the foreign government against the United States taxes. On the other hand, if a person paid foreign taxes at a rate greater than the United States tax rate, he or she would not get a credit for the extra taxes. This prevents the taxpayer from taking the credit for the higher taxes and applying it to reduce taxes paid on domestic source income. If the foreign tax rate is less than the United Sates tax rate, then this person will be able to use all of the foreign taxes paid as a credit against United States taxes, but most likely, the difference will be paid to the United States government.

Taxing Corporations on their Foreign Source Income

Because a corporation is a United States taxpayer, it must pay income tax on its income from whatever source derived, including foreign source income. However, if a corporation operates a business overseas, it may be either in the form of a branch or as a wholly owned subsidiary. If it operates as a branch, then the income from the branch must be included in United States taxable income. If it operates as a subsidiary, then the income of the subsidiary is generally not taxed until it is remitted as a dividend or as some other form of distribution. For legal and other reasons, most companies with international operations operate in foreign countries in the legal form of wholly owned subsidiaries. For many years, the ability not to pay United States taxes on the income of wholly owned foreign subsidiaries provided a tax-shelter device. Some attractive aspects of this tax shelter have been eliminated by Subpart F of the *Internal Revenue Code*. However, there are still ramifications about which you should be aware.

The internationalism of United States businesses is a relatively recent phenomenon. After World War II and throughout the 1950s, 1960s, and 1970s, major United States corporations greatly expanded their overseas operations. As a result of this expansion, many companies realized that tax advantages could be gained through ownership and operation of foreign corporations chartered in countries with lower tax rates than those imported by United States law.

Example: A corporation might be incorporated in a country that did not impose a low rate of tax, such as the Bahamas. Licenses, franchises, intangible rights, or stock of other corporations could then be transferred to such a corporation, thereby producing royalties, dividends, rents, or fees that were not subject to United States tax as long as they were not returned as dividends to United States owners. Another option was to establish an offshore trading company that would buy goods at cost from its United States parent and sell the goods overseas. The trading therefore was not subject to United States tax.

The United States Treasury Department became concerned about the loss from United States taxation by these tax haven-type loopholes. This concern resulted in the portion of the *Code* known as Subpart F, which was enacted as part of the Revenue Act of 1962. The legislative history of the 1962 Act discusses the rationale of Subpart F as follows *(U.S. Code Congressional and Administrative News 1962, 3381)*:

> Under the law prior to 1962 foreign corporations, even though they may be American controlled, were not subject to U.S. tax on foreign source income. As a result U.S. tax is not imposed on the foreign earnings of American controlled corporations until dividends paid by the foreign corporations are received by their American parent corporations or their American shareholders. The tax at that time is imposed on the American shareholder with respect to the dividend income received, and if this shareholder is a corporation it is eligible for a foreign tax credit with respect to the taxes paid by the foreign subsidiary. In the case of foreign subsidiaries, therefore, this means that foreign income taxes are paid currently, to the extent of the applicable foreign income tax, and not until distributions are made will an additional U.S. tax be imposed. This latter tax effect has been referred to as *tax deferral*.
>
> President Kennedy questioned the desirability of providing tax deferral with respect to earnings of U.S. controlled companies, except in the case of investments in less developed countries. In this respect, he emphasized removing tax deferral in cases of what have been called *tax havens*.

The proposals of President Kennedy and the Treasury to the Congress concerning tax revision in the international arena suggested that the earnings and profits of a controlled foreign corporation, available for distribution to United States shareholders, should be included in the United States income of the shareholder, whether or not it is distributed. International corporations generally opposed this concept since it would have placed them at a disadvantage with respect to foreign competitors, particularly in countries with lower tax rates than the United States. Subpart F, as ultimately enacted, was a compromise between complete taxation, at United States rates, of all foreign income, of United States shareholders, and the opposite extreme of complete escape from United States tax of income of foreign subsidiaries.

The provisions of Subpart F apply only to controlled foreign corporations. A *Controlled Foreign Corporation* (CFC) is defined as a foreign corporation of which more than 50 percent of the total combined voting power of all stock classes entitled to vote is owned by United States shareholders. To be considered a United States shareholder, a person or a corporation must own 10 percent or more of the stock of the CFC. Joint ventures with foreign companies and investments, in widely owned foreign business, are not considered as controlled foreign corporations.

Not all income of a CFC is taxed to United States shareholders. Only Subpart F income is taxed. The definition of what constitutes Subpart F income has been broadened since 1962. Initially, Subpart F income was defined to include primarily passive type income, such as rents, dividends, interest, and royalties, and income that was attributed to a certain foreign country. It was considered Subpart F income only because a sale was made to a subsidiary located in that country, at cost, and then the subsidiary immediately sold the item at profit, to a customer in another country, who was the real intended purchaser of the item. Subpart F income also included income from insuring property located in the United States. Through tax reform acts in 1975, 1976, and 1977, Subpart F income has been defined to include such things as income from shipping or air transportation, as well as income from services such as commissions, consulting fees, design fees, and other fees. Exhibit 14.3 provides an outline of how Subpart F works.

Note that Subpart F is designed to combat tax avoidance schemes, at least in theory. If a person has a legitimate business purpose for arranging foreign operations in a particular way, he or she may be able to argue that the income of a controlled foreign subsidiary should not be included in United States taxable income under Subpart F.

Again, the provisions of the *Code* in this area are complex. A CPA who

EXHIBIT 14.3
Subpart F

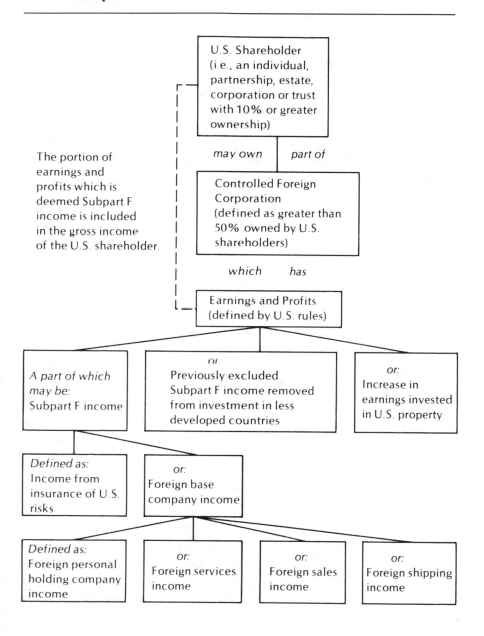

U.S. Shareholder
(i.e., an individual,
partnership, estate,
corporation or trust
with 10% or greater
ownership)

may own   *part of*

Controlled Foreign
Corporation
(defined as greater than
50% owned by U.S.
shareholders)

which   has

The portion of
earnings and
profits which is
deemed Subpart F
income is included
in the gross income
of the U.S. shareholder.

Earnings and Profits
(defined by U.S. rules)

*A part of which
may be:*
Subpart F income

or
Previously excluded
Subpart F income removed
from investment in less
developed countries

or:
Increase in
earnings invested
in U.S. property

Defined as:
Income from
insurance of U.S.
risks

or:
Foreign base
company income

Defined as:
Foreign personal
holding company
income

or:
Foreign services
income

or:
Foreign sales
income

or:
Foreign shipping
income

is experienced in the taxation of foreign source income should be consulted.

Note in Exhibit 14.3 that one type of income included in Subpart F
income is Foreign Personal Holding Company Income.

Foreign Personal Holding Company

A *Foreign Personal Holding Company* is the same as a domestic Personal
Holding Company, except that the tax on undistributed Foreign Personal
Holding Company income is not applied. Since income of a Foreign
Personal Holding Company is included in the United States taxable
income of the United States stockholder, it follows that the income cannot
be considered to be undistributed.

Personal Holding Company

A *Personal Holding Company* is a corporation that derives 60 percent or
more of its income from dividends, interest, royalties, annuities, rents, or
contracts for personal services, and that is more than 50 percent owned by
five or fewer people. As long as the income of a Personal Holding Company is distributed to its shareholders, there is no extra tax; however, on
undistributed income there is a tax of 70 percent.

QUESTION: *How can a company engaged principally in export activities reduce its tax burden?*

ANSWER:
A corporation engaged in manufacturing a product sold in foreign
markets may want to consider using a separate corporation to handle its
foreign sales operation. In addition to setting up a foreign subsidiary, the
manufacturer may want to consider setting up a *Domestic International
Sales Corporation* (DISC). The DISC provisions were added to the *Code* in
1971 in order to improve the ability of United States businesses to com-
pete in foreign markets.

A DISC, much like a Subchapter S corporation, is not subject to tax on
any of its income. Rather, the shareholders of the DISC are subject to the
tax in accordance with certain rules. Essentially, the shareholders of a
DISC are taxed on one-half of the DISC's taxable income and on all of any
interest received from certain loans. The untaxed portion of DISC profits

is taxed when it is distributed to shareholders. The DISC is therefore a tax deferral device and does not eliminate taxes completely.

The tax-deferred income retained by a DISC may be used for business expansion, for purchase of obligations of the Export-Import Bank, and for extending producer's loans to provide suppliers with funds for financing facilities, inventories, and facilities used in export production. Producer's loans must be evidenced by a note that bears interest and that has a maturity date not exceeding five years.

A DISC is typically organized as a wholly owned subsidiary of a United States Corporation. Within ninety days after the beginning of its tax year, the DISC must elect to take advantage of tax deferral. The DISC can have only one class of stock. It must have equity capital of at least $2,500. A DISC must have 95 percent of its assets in the form of qualified export assets, and 95 percent of its gross receipts must be from export sales or other export-related receipts.

Qualified export assets include inventory and property held for sale or lease in foreign markets, assets used in connection with export sales (such as storage, handling, and other aspects), accounts receivable from export sales, producer's loans, as discussed previously, and certain Export-Import Bank obligations. Other export-related receipts include receipts from leasing of exported property, services rendered in relationship to exported property, and gains on the sale of qualified export assets of the types discussed above.

Another advantage of a DISC relates to how taxable revenues and tax-deductible expenses are allocated between a domestic parent and a foreign subsidiary or group of foreign subsidiaries. Under the regulations promulgated under Section 861 of the *Code*, the IRS has the right to review allocations between parent and subsidiary and to adjust such allocations, if it appears that they were made for tax avoidance purposes. Under the DISC statute, more liberal regulations have resulted in an ability to shift income to a DISC without risking IRS challenge. This shift is primarily accomplished through more liberal intercompany pricing rules.

Many United States corporations that manufacture products sold both in this country and abroad will find it profitable, from a tax perspective, to create a DISC to handle their export operations, even though the same operations conducted through a foreign subsidiary might have saved little or no taxes.

However, there are two potential problems with DISC operations. The first concerns the continuing eligibility requirements for tax deferral. It should be noted that a DISC must have 95 percent of its assets in qualified export assets. This stipulation means that there must be continual reinvestment in export assets; otherwise, the DISC status is jeopardized. The second problem concerns the fact that President Carter may want to eliminate the DISC provisions from the tax law. In light of these potential problems, careful thought should be given to deciding to create a DISC subsidiary.

Another type of export stimulation device that has been enacted into law relates to Latin America and Canada. The device is called a Western Hemisphere Trade Corporation (WHTC). A *Western Hemisphere Trade Corporation* is a United States corporation, all of whose business is done in North, Central, or South America or the Caribbean, with 95 percent or more of its gross income from foreign sources. Furthermore, 90 percent or more of its gross income is from the active conduct of a trade or business (that is, as opposed passively to collecting rents, interest, or dividends).

A WHTC is allowed a special deduction against its taxable income. The deduction is computed as a fraction of taxable income. The numerator of the fraction is 5 percent and the denominator is 48 percent. Therefore, 10.42 percent ($.05 \div .48$) of the taxable income of a WHTC may be deducted. The WHTC provisions may be eliminated from the *Code* in the near future. Therefore, an accountant or attorney should be consulted about these provisions.

QUESTION: *How do tax treaties with foreign countries affect the taxation of foreign source income?*

ANSWER:

Tax treaties with foreign countries may supersede any provisions of the *Code*. The right to modify tax law through international treaties has been used widely by the United States government. As applicable to residents of certain foreign countries, tax treaties concluded with those countries modify the provisions of the *Code* as to what is includable in taxable income, what deductions and personal exemptions are allowable, and what tax rate applies to the taxpayers. In any foreign tax matter, it should be ascertained whether the United States has a tax treaty with the country involved. If such a treaty exists, its provisions should be checked carefully to determine their impact.

Appendix

STATEMENTS BY THE FINANCIAL ACCOUNTING STANDARDS BOARD

Although the Appendix will not endeavor to discuss the opinions of the APB and the FASB, they will be mentioned and discussed as they related to the chapters in this book.

The following is a list, in order, of FASB statements and interpretations issued through the end of 1978.

FASB Statements

FASB No. 1   Disclosure of Foreign Currency Translation Information (December 1973)

This standard has been superseded by FASB No. 8, entitled Accounting for the Translation of Foreign Currency Transactions and Foreign Currency Financial Statements.

FASB No. 2   Accounting for Research and Development Costs (October 1974)
1. Establishes standards for accounting for research and development costs.
2. Covers activities and elements of cost identified as R & D and specifies financial statements disclosures.
3. All R & D costs are to be charged to expense when incurred.
4. Statement is to be applied retroactively by prior per-period adjustment.

FASB No. 3   Reporting Accounting Change in Interim Statements (December 1974; Amends APB #28)
1. Each interim period should be viewed as an integral part of an annual period.
2. The results of each interim period generally should be based on the principles and practices used in the latest annual statements.
    a. Companies may use the gross profit method for inventory valuation with appropriate disclosure.
    b. If LIFO inventories have been liquidated at the interim date but are expected to be replaced by year-end, the cost of goods sold should not give effect to the interim liquidation.
    c. Gains and losses arising in an interim period should not be deferred unless they would be deferred at year-end.
    d. Each interim period should bear its fair share of anticipated annual amounts of costs and expenses subject to year-end adjustment.
    e. The effective tax rate for the year should be estimated and applied each interim period.
3. Extraordinary items, gains and losses on disposal of a business segment, and unusual or infrequently occurring items should be included in interim income when they occur (Do Not Pro Rate) and be disclosed separately.

4. Whenever possible, accounting changes should be made during the first interim period of the year. Otherwise, accounting changes should be accounted for in the period in which the change is made. If a cumulative effect type of change is made in other than the first interim period, no cumulative effect of the change shall be included in net income of the period of change. Instead pre-change interim periods shall be restated and the cumulative effect of the change on retained earnings at the beginning of the year shall be included in restated net income of the first interim period of the year of change.

5. Footnote disclosure in annual financial statements is required of some publicly traded companies that make a fourth quarter accounting change but do not issue a separate fourth quarter report or disclose quarterly effects of the change in their annual reports.

FASB No. 4   Reporting Gains or Losses from Extinguishment of Debt (March 1973; Amends APB #30)

1. All material gains or losses from extinguishment of debt (early or at maturity) should be reported as extraordinary items, net of related income tax effect, without regard to the criteria specified in APB Opinion No. 30.

2. FASB No. 4 does not apply to cash purchases of debt made to satisfy current and future sinking fund requirements.

FASB No. 5   Accounting for Contingencies (March 1975)

1. An estimated loss from a loss contingency shall be charged to income only if both of the following conditions are met:

    a. Information available prior to the issuance of the financial statements indicates that an asset probably has been impaired or a liability has been incurred at the date of the financial statements and

    b. The amount of the loss can be reasonably estimated

2. Loss contingencies that do not meet these two conditions require adequate disclosure.

3. Self insurance losses and catastrophe reserves are not considered to meet the two conditions and should be charged against income at the time of the event which caused the loss.

4. Contingencies expected to result in gains are not credited to income since such gains should not be recognized prior to realization.

5. A change in accounting principle resulting from compliance with FASB No. 5 will be reported in accordance with APB opinion No. 20. The cumulative effect of the change in retained earnings at the beginning of the year in which the change is made is to be included in the net income of the year of change.

FASB No. 6 Classification of Short-Term Obligations Expected to be Refinanced (May 1975)

1. Certain short-term obligations are to be excluded from current liabilities if the enterprise intends to refinánce the obligations on a long term basis and the ability to consummate refinancing is demonstrated by:

    a. A post-balance-sheet issuance of a long-term obligation or equity securities or

    b. A financing agreement is entered into before the balance sheet is issued and

        (1) The agreement does not expire within one year of the balance sheet date and is not cancellable by the lender.

        (2) No violation exists in any provision in the financing agreement.

        (3) The lender is financially capable.

2. The agreement must be adequately disclosed.

FASB No. 7 Accounting and Reporting By Development Stage Enterprises (June 1975)

1. A development stage company is defined as one that devotes substantially all of its efforts to establishing a new business and either has not begun its planned principal operations or has started such operations but has not had significant revenue from them.

2. No special accounting is applicable to development

stage companies, subsidiaries, divisions, and other units. A company should be identified as being in the development stage and its cumulative development stage costs from inception should be disclosed.

3. Statements for periods prior to the effective date should be restated with necessary adjustment accounted for as a prior period adjustment.

FASB No. 8 Accounting for the Translation of Foreign Currency Transactions and Foreign Currency Financial Statements (October 1975)

1. Foreign Financial Statements first must be corrected to reflect U.S. generally accepted accounting principles.

2. Foreign Currency Transactions should be translated as follows:

   a. Cash, Accounts Receivable, and Accounts Payable should be translated at the current rate at the balance sheet date.

   b. All other amounts should be translated at the rate in effect at the transaction data (the historical rate) except unperformed forward exchange contracts which should be translated at the current rate.

3. Financial Statements prepared in a foreign currency should be translated as follows:

   a. Cash, Accounts Receivable, and Accounts Payable should be translated at the current rate.

   b. Other Assets and Liabilities should be translated as follows.

      (1) Historical rates should be used for accounts carried at historical cost.

      (2) Current rates should be used for accounts carried at current prices or future prices.

      (3) Deferred taxes may be translated at the current rate in certain instances.

   c. Revenue and expenses should be translated at rates approximating rates in effect had the individual transactions been translated at the date incurred (average rate) except that revenue and expense items related to balance sheet accounts should be translated at historical rates, for example, depreciation.

4. Gains and Losses from foreign exchange translations should be included in current income except gains or losses from certain forward exchange contracts should be deferred.

5. The aggregate exchange gain or loss included in determining net income must be disclosed. Financial statements may not be adjusted for a rate change that occurs after the date of the financial statement.

6. Financial statements before the effective date (1–1–76) should be restated if practicable. If restatement for all prior periods is not practicable, then the cumulative effect on the retained earnings at the beginning of the earliest period restated should be included in determining the net income of that period per APB opinion No. 20.

FASB No. 9 Accounting for Income Taxes-Oil-Gas Producing Companies (October 1975; Amends APB Opinions #11 & 23)

1. The tax reduction act of 1975 substantially reduced or eliminated percentage depletion as a federal income tax deduction for certain oil and gas companies as of January 1, 1975. Accordingly, income tax allocation is now required for timing differences arising from intangible drilling and development costs and other costs that enter into the determination of taxable income in periods different than for financial reporting.

2. Oil and gas companies allocating income taxes for the first time starting Jan. 1, 1975 must use the prospective net method which requires allocation of the net change in timing differences in the period.

FASB No. 10 Extension of "Grandfather" Provisions for Business Combinations (October 1975; amends APB Opinion No. 16)

1. This standard eliminates the five-year limitation in the Grandfather provisions originally included in APB #16.

FASB No. 11 Accounting for Contingencies-Transition Method (December 1975; Amends FASB No. 5)

1. Specifies that FASB No. 5 should be applied retroactively to earlier periods if presented.
2. If restatement for all prior periods is impracticable, the cumulative effect on the retained earnings at the beginning of the earliest period restated should be included in determining the net income of that earliest period as required by APB Opinion No. 20.

FASB No. 12   Accounting for Certain Marketable Securities (Dec. 1975)
1. Marketable equity securities shall be reported at the lower of aggregate cost of market value, determined at the balance sheet date.
2. The excess of aggregate cost over market value is to be accounted for as a valuation reserve.
3. All marketable equity securities classified as current assets are to be treated as a single portfolio for a consolidated entity. All such securities classified as noncurrent shall be treated as a separate portfolio for the consolidated entity.
4. On unclassified balance sheets, marketable equity securities are to be classified as noncurrent assets.
5. If there is a change in the classification of marketable equity securities, the lower of cost or market at the date of change is to be used as the cost basis and any difference should be treated as a realized loss.
6. All realized gains and losses and all changes in the valuation for a marketable equity securities portfolio included in the current assets are to be included in the determination of net income of the period in which they occur.
7. Accumulated changes in the valuation allowance for a portfolio included in noncurrent assets or in an unclassified balance sheet shall be included in the equity section of the balance sheet.
8. The following disclosures are required: Aggregate cost and market value, gross unrealized gains and gross unrealized losses, and net realized gain or loss included in the determination of net income.

FASB No. 13   Accounting for Leases (November 1976, Supersedes APB Opinions No. 5, 7, 27, and 31)
1. Requires certain leases to be recorded as an asset and

a liability in the balance sheet as though a purchase of the asset were made.

2. Leases that meet any one of the following four criteria must be capitalized.
   a. The lease transfers title to the lessee by the end of the lease term.
   b. The lease has a bargain purchase option.
   c. The lease term is for 75% or more of the useful life of the property.
   d. The discounted present value of the minimum lease payments is 90% or more of the fair market value of the property at the inception of the lease.

FASB No. 14   Financial Reporting for Segments of a Business Enterprise (December 1976)

1. Requires a breakdown of sales and operating income by product line segments and by geographic segments if the company operates in international markets.
2. The application of FASB No. 14 was suspended for nonpublic companies by FASB No. 21.
3. The application of FASB No. 14 was eliminated for interim reporting periods of less than a year by FASB No. 18.

FASB No. 15   Accounting by Debtors and Creditors for Troubled Debt Restructurings (June 1977)

1. Requires that when receivables from a third party, or other property or equity is transferred to a creditor in a troubled debt restructuring that a gain or loss on the transaction should be recorded in accordance with the provisions of APB Opinion No. 26.
2. If the terms of the loan agreement are only modified no gain or loss is recorded.

FASB No. 16   Prior Period Adjustments (June 1977)

1. Eliminates adjustments of the financial statements of prior periods, except for corrections of errors.

FASB No. 17   Accounting for Leases — Initial Direct Costs (November 1977, Amends FASB No. 13)

1. Modifies the definition of the costs associated with negotiating and consummating a leasing transaction.

FASB No. 18   Financial Reporting for Segments of a Business Enterprise — Interim Financial Statements (November 1977, Amends FASB No. 14)
1. Eliminates the requirement of product line and geographic segment reporting for interim financial statements.

FASB No. 19   Financial Accounting and Reporting by Oil and Gas Companies (December 1977)
1. Requires the use of the successful efforts method of accounting for oil and gas exploration costs.
2. Increases the required disclosure of oil and gas reserves.

FASB No. 20   Accounting for Forward Exchange Contracts (December 1977, Amends FASB No. 8)
1. Allows the hedging of an identifiable foreign currency commitment on an after tax basis.

FASB No. 21   Suspension of the Reporting of Earnings Per Share and Segment Information by Non-Public Enterprises (April 1978, Amends APB Opinion No. 15 and FASB No. 14)
1. Suspends the application of APB opinion No. 15 and FASB No. 14 for nonpublic companies.

FASB No. 22   Changes in the Provisions of Lease Agreements Resulting from Refundings of Tax Exempt Debt (June 1978, Amends FASB No. 13)
1. Requires changes in lease agreements resulting from refundings of tax-exempt debt to be treated in accordance with APB Opinion No. 26 "Early Extinguishments of Debt."

FASB No. 23   Inception of the Lease (August 1978, Amends FASB No. 13)
1. Changes the definition of inception of the lease contained in FASB No. 13.

FASB No. 24   Reporting Segment Information in Financial Statements That Are Presented in Another Enterprise's Financial Report (December 1978, Amends FASB No. 14)
1. Suspends the requirements of FASB No. 14 for certain financial reports.

FASB Interpretations

FASB Interpretation No. 1   Accounting Changes Related to the Cost of Inventory (APB Opinion # 20)
1. A change in composition of the elements of costs included in inventory is an accounting change which must be made in accordance with APB Opinion No. 20.
2. The change must be justified as being preferable in terms of constituting an improvement in financial reporting and not on the basis of the income tax effect alone.

FASB Interpretation No. 2   Imputing Interest on Debt Arrangements Made under the Federal Bankruptcy Act (APB No. 21)
1. When a note is issued by a debtor in a reorganization arrangement, it is considered to be a note issued for property and is treated as a new note if the original terms are modified.
2. Interest on new notes should be imputed if the note does not specify a reasonable interest rate.

FASB Interpretation No. 3   Accounting for the Cost of Pension Funds Subject to the Employee Retirement Income Security Act of 1974 (APB Opinion No. 8)
1. No change is required in the minimum and maximum limits for the annual provision for pension costs as set forth in APB Opinion No. 8.
2. The FASB expressed the opinion that ERISA did not create a legal obligation for unfunded pension costs that warrants recognition as a liability unless a plan is terminated.

FASB Interpretation No. 4   Applicability of FASB No. 2 to Business Combinations Accounted for by the Purchase Method (FASB No. 2)
1. The fair value of research and development of an acquired company must be determined and identified as a specific part of the purchase price.
2. The identified research and development costs that are to be used by the acquiring company for research and development purposes must be written off in computing income.
3. Those identified R & D costs not to be used by the acquiring company or have alternative future use, may remain capitalized and be amortized over an appropriate period.
4. Adequate disclosure is required as to the amount of research and development costs acquired through a business combination accounted for as a purchase.

FASB Interpretation No. 5   Applicability of FASB No. 2 to Development Stage Enterprises (February 1975)
1. When a company in the development stage issues financial statements purporting to be in accordance with generally accepted accounting principles, research and development costs must be expensed in accordance with FASB No. 2.
2. When consolidated financial statements based on generally accepted accounting principles are issued by an enterprise, research and development costs, including those of a development stage division or subsidiary, must be expensed in accordance with FASB No. 2

FASB Interpretation No. 6   Applicability of FASB No. 2 in Computer Software (February 1975)

1. Costs incurred to purchase or lease computer software must be treated as research and development costs to be expensed as incurred if the software is to be used in research and development activities of the acquiring company.

2. Costs incurred to develop software must be treated as research and development costs to be expensed as incurred, if the software is used for developing or significantly improving a product or process that is intended to be sold, leased, or otherwise marketed.

FASB Interpretation No. 7   Applying FASB No. 7 in Financial Statements of Established Operating Enterprises (October 1975)

1. Generally the effect of a development stage subsidiary's change in accounting principle to conform its accounting to the requirements of FASB No. 7 would be reflected in the consolidated statements.

FASB Interpretation No. 8   Classification of a Short-Term Obligation Repaid Prior to Being Replaced by a Long Term Security (FASB No. 6 January 1976)

1. If a short-term obligation is repaid after the balance sheet date and subsequently a long-term obligation or equity securities are issued whose proceeds are used to replenish current assets before the balance sheet is issued, the short-term obligation should not be excluded from current liabilities at the balance sheet date.

FASB Interpretation No. 9   Applying APB Opinion No. 16 and 17

When a Savings and Loan Association or a Similar Institution is Acquired in a Business Combination Accounted for under the Purchase Method (February 1976)

1. When a savings and loan association is acquired in a business combination accounted for by the purchase method, the separate valuation method specified in APB Opinion #16 (Para #87 & 88) for valuing individual assets and liabilities must be used.

2. The net spread method of accounting for the assets and liabilities of a savings and loan association acquired in a business combination using the purchase method is not acceptable under APB Opinion #16 because it ignores the fair value of individual assets and liabilities.

3. The amount paid for separately identified intangible assets shall be recorded as the cost of the intangibles and be amortized over their estimated life as specified in APB Opinion No. 17.

4. If goodwill includes certain intangible factors whose benefits decline over the expected life, then the goodwill may be amortized on other than a straight-line basis.

FASB Interpretation No. 10   Application of FASB Statement No. 12 to Personal Financial Statements (September 1976)

1. Requires the application of FASB No. 12 to personal financial statements.

FASB Interpretation No. 11   Change in Market Value After the Balance Sheet Date (September 1976)

1. Indicates that declines or increases in value of marketable securities after

the balance sheet date may be considered when deciding whether a decline at the balance sheet date is other than temporary.

FASB Interpretation No. 12   Accounting for Previously Established Allowance Accounts (September 1976)
1. Allowances to reduce current marketable securities to market value should be eliminated by a credit to income.

FASB Interpretation No. 13   Consolidation of a Parent and Subsidiaries Having Different Balance Sheet Dates (September 1976)
1. The application of FASB Statement No. 12 to the financial statements of a consolidated subsidiary that has a balance sheet date different from that of its parent shall be as of the balance sheet date of the subsidiary.

FASB Interpretation No. 14   Reasonable Estimation of the Amount of a Loss (September 1976)
1. Requires the accrual of a loss if the amount of the loss can be estimated within a probable range.

FASB Interpretation No. 15   Translation of Unamortized Policy Acquisition Costs by a Stock Life Insurance Company (September 1976)
1. Indicates that unamortized policy acquisition costs of stock life insurance companies which are foreign subsidiaries shall be translated at historical rates under FASB No. 8.

FASB Interpretation No. 16   Clarification of the Accounting for Marketable Equity Securities that Become Nonmarketable (February 1977)
1. Clarifies the definition of nonmarketable securities in FASB No. 12.

FASB Interpretation No. 17   Applying the Lower of Cost or Market Rule in Translated Financial Statements (February 1977)
1. Specifies how the lower of cost or market rule should be integrated with the translation of inventory accounts of foreign subsidiaries.

FASB Interpretation No. 18   Accounting for Income Taxes in Interim Periods (March 1977)
1. Provides a lengthy discussion and examples of the accounting for income tax expense in interim financial statements.

FASB Interpretation No. 19   Lessee Guarantee of the Residual Value of Leased Property (October 1977)
1. Provides that the maximum amount of guaranteed residual value that is included in minimum lease payments under the provisions of FASB No. 13 shall be the amount specified in the lease and not the actual expected residual value.

FASB Interpretation No. 20   Reporting Accounting Changes under AICPA Statements of Position (November 1977)
1. Allows the AICPA to specify how a change in accounting method may be made to conform to an AICPA Statement of Position.

FASB Interpretation No. 21   Accounting for Leases in a Business Combination (April 1978)
1. Specifies how leases of an acquired company are to be accounted for in accordance with the provisions of APB Opinion No. 16 and FASB No. 13.

FASB Interpretation No. 22   Application of Indefinite Reversal Criteria
                              to Timing Differences (April 1978)
                              1.   Restricts the application of the
                                   indefinite reversal criteria to four
                                   specific instances.
                              2.   The indefinite reversal criteria apply
                                   to suspension of the accrual of de-
                                   ferred taxes in situations where tim-
                                   ing differences probably will not
                                   reverse.

FASB Interpretation No. 23   Leases of Certain Property Owned by a
                              Governmental Unit or Authority (August
                              1978)
                              1.   Allows certain leases to be treated as
                                   operating if the lessor is a govern-
                                   mental unit.

FASB Interpretation No. 24   Leases Involving Only Part of a Building
                              (September 1978)
                              1.   Requires lessees to estimate the fair
                                   value of part of a building which is
                                   leased.

FASB Interpretation No. 25   Accounting for Unused Investment Tax
                              Credits (September 1978)
                              1.   Discusses the proper accounting for
                                   unused investment tax credits.

FASB Interpretation No. 26   Accounting for Purchase of a Leased
                              Asset by the Lessee during the Term of
                              the Lease (September 1978)
                              1.   Discusses accounting for purchase of
                                   leased asset by lessee during the term
                                   of the lease.

FASB Interpretation No. 27   Accounting for Loss on a Sublease
                              (November 1978)
                              1.   Allows the calculation of a loss on a
                                   sublease.
                              2.   Discusses the loss on a sublease
                                   effected as a disposal of a segment.

FASB Interpretation No. 28   Accounting for Stock Appreciation Rights
                              and Other Variable Stock Option or
                              Award Plans (December 1978)

Bibliography

AICPA, *Professional Standards - Volume 3 Accounting - Current Text;* New York, AICPA, 1977.

Baker, C.R. "Foreign Depreciation — How it is Computed," *The International Tax Journal,* Feb., 1976

———— "A New Look at Subpart F, " *Taxes,* September, 1976.

———— "A Discussion of Drawbacks to Full Cost Accounting in the Petroleum Industry, " *Oil and Gas Tax Quarterly,* March, 1977.

Brock, Horace R, Charles E. Palmer, and Fred Archer. *Accounting: Basic Principles,* McGraw Hill, New York, 1974.

Defliese, P.L., K.P. Johnson, and R.K. Macleod. *Montgomery's Auditing* (9th ed.), Ronald Press, New York, 1975.

Diener, Royce. *How To Finance a Growing Business,* Frederick Fell Publishers, New York, 1974.

Griffen, C.H., T.H. Williams, and K.D. Larson, *Advanced Accounting* (4th ed.), Richard J. Irwin, Inc., Homewood, Ill. 1977.

Hartley, W.C.F. *Cash: Planning, Forecasting, and Control*, Business Books Ltd., London, 1976.

Hawkins, D.F. *Corporate Financial Reporting: Text and Cases*, Richard D. Irwin, Inc., Homewood Ill., 1977.

Hayes, Rick Stephan. *Business Loans: A Guide to Money Sources and How to Approach Them Successfully*, CBI, Boston, 1977.

Internal Revenue Service, *Recordkeeping for a Small Business*, Publication 583, Department of Treasury, Washington, D.C. 1973.

————— *Tax Guide for Small Business*, 1978 Edition, Publication 334, Department of Treasury, Washington, D.C., 1978

Nickerson, Clarence B. *Accounting Handbook for Non-Accountants*, CBI, Boston, 1975.

Parkinson, C. Northcote. *Parkinson's Law and Other Studies in Administration*, Houghton Mifflin, New York, 1957.

Ragan, Robert C. *Financial Recordkeeping for Small Stores*, Small Business Management Series No. 32, SBA, Washington, D.C., 1966.

Shillinglaw, G. *Managerial Cost Accounting* (4th ed.), Richard D. Irwin, Homewood, Ill., 1977.

Sommerfeld, R.H. *Federal Taxes and Management Decisions*, Richard D. Irwin, Inc., Homewood, Ill., 1977.

Welsch, G.A., C.T. Zlatkovich, and J.A. White. *Intermediate Accounting* (4th ed.), Richard D. Irwin, Homewood, Ill., 1976.

Weston, Fred, and Eugene F. Bringham. *Managerial Finance*, New York, Holt, Rinehart and Winston, 1969.

Index